Critical Reading and Writing for Advanced ESL Students

SHARON SCULL

Glendale Community College

REGENTS/PRENTICE HALL
Englewood Cliffs, New Jersey 07632

Library of Congress Cataloging-in-Publication Data

SCULL, SHARON D.
    Critical reading and writing for advanced ESL students.

    Includes index.
    1. College readers.   2. English language—Rhetoric.
3. English language—Textbooks for foreign speakers.
I. Title.
PE1417.S368 1987   808′.0427   86-21284
ISBN 0-13-194010-4

Editorial/production supervision: Patricia V. Amoroso
Interior design: Barbara Alexander
Cover illustration: John Drechsler
Cover design: Lundgren Graphics, Ltd.
Manufacturing buyer: Carol Bystrom

To John Scull

 © 1987 by Prentice-Hall, Inc.
A Simon & Schuster Company
Englewood Cliffs, New Jersey 07632

Printed in the United States of America

10 9 8

ISBN 0-13-194010-4

Prentice-Hall International (UK) Limited, *London*
Prentice-Hall of Australia Pty. Limited, *Sydney*
Prentice-Hall Canada Inc., *Toronto*
Prentice-Hall Hispanoamericana, S.A., *Mexico*
Prentice-Hall of India Private Limited, *New Delhi*
Prentice-Hall of Japan, Inc., *Tokyo*
Simon & Schuster Asia Pte. Ltd., *Singapore*
Editora Prentice-Hall do Brasil, Ltda., *Rio de Janeiro*

Contents

Preface

Critical Reading and Writing for Advanced ESL Students encourages students to develop critical thinking skills through the media of reading, writing, and discussion. The text introduces various rhetorical modes and methods of expository writing that students will have to master to succeed in freshman composition courses or in the contemporary communications-oriented business world.

Because many foreign educational systems stress memorization and rote learning, students are usually able to recount the contents of readings and relate personal experiences with considerable skill. Many advanced students also have a good understanding of grammar rules although some have difficulty applying them to writing in context. However, most nonnative students are relatively untrained in critical, expository writing and find that they cannot compete with native students in regular college or university courses or that they cannot produce the quality of written communications required by their employers. A major goal of this text is to help students approach expository writing assignments with confidence in their abilities to analyze material that they read, synthesize their findings, and propose new ideas.

The text, which is meant to be a companion to learning, analyzes problems and techniques with the students by offering information about the processes of critical thinking in many different ways. The reading process is streamlined by inclusion of glossaries based primarily on definitions from *Webster's New World Dictionary of the American Language,* 2nd ed. Students are encouraged to read quickly for content and meaning because they don't have to stop frequently to consult their own dictionaries for definitions or translations. The discussion process is stimulated by comprehension questions that follow the order of the readings and by topics for critical analysis, discussion, and writing that encourage original thought. Many of the glossaries and topics include historical background or supplementary explanations of customs or culture that promote deeper understanding of the readings. The writing process involves students in brainstorming and other prewriting activities, restricting topics, creating thesis statements, developing supporting information, and formulating evaluative conclusions. Writing topics require that students use different rhetorical techniques, and topics are worded as they would be on essay examinations, requiring comparison and contrast, argument, analysis, evaluation, examination, and discussion. The research process includes an article, written by a librarian especially for international students, explaining how to use the library. An informal research project and a formal research paper are included, plagiarism is explained, and the latest Modern

Language Association documentation techniques are presented and illustrated. The editing and revision process is gradually developed in the text by
analysis of sample readings and related student writing. The final chapter
(which includes suggestions for revision, explanations of the most common
errors that instructors identify on student essays, and a workshop that deeply
involves both students and instructor) is designed to be used in conjunction
with any writing assignment in the preceding nine chapters. Drafts of student
essays are presented, along with recreations of student-instructor conferences
that discuss revision of organization or content and correction of grammar,
punctuation, and spelling errors.

The readings cover a broad range of subjects and include essays, articles,
short stories, and poetry. Regardless of genre, all readings are intended to
provoke critical thought, discussion, and writing and to encourage students to
recognize that their college experience is enriched by their ability to recognize
and analyze interdisciplinary relationships.

I want to thank my advanced ESL and freshman composition students for
their direct and indirect contributions to this text; the many professional writers for so generously allowing their work to be reprinted; Renée Copeland
(Pasadena City College), Debra Matthews (English Language Institute, University of Akron), and all the reviewers for their constructive ideas; Jo Ray
McCuen (Glendale College) for her sound advice; Susan Vizuette (Glendale
College) for her sensible suggestions; Lisa Brummel (Prentice-Hall) for her
enthusiasm; Marshall Nunn and the library staff of Glendale College for their
research assistance; and most of all, John Scull for his invaluable help in every
aspect of the project.

SHARON SCULL

1

Learning About College Writing

UNDERSTANDING THE REQUIREMENTS

This book is designed to help you prepare for American college English. Therefore, reading and writing requirements will be different from those of previous courses you have taken. You will be asked to take a critical approach; that is, to analyze, evaluate, examine, and question everything you read and to take positions, give proof, and make judgments in everything you write.

As you read, concentrate equally on meaning and comprehension. Each selection has a glossary that covers new vocabulary, idiomatic usage, and special expressions. First, read through the selection without stopping to look up words in your dictionary. Second, answer the comprehension questions. Third, read the material again, look up any unfamiliar words that affect meaning, write notes in the margins of your book identifying major points or defining special words, and check your answers to the questions. Finally, think carefully about the topics for critical analysis, discussion, and writing.

When you discuss the reading selections in class, jot down the most difficult, interesting, or important points. Remember that related information is often introduced by the instructor or other students. Ask questions if you don't understand what you have read or what someone (including the instructor) says.

When you write, explain meanings and ideas that are suggested as well as stated in the readings. Few assignments will be based solely on your personal experiences, although you may sometimes include them if they are related to the topic and help to clarify part of the composition. Over and over again, you will have to answer the question, *"Why?"* Why is the author's idea a good one? Why does a character behave a certain way? Why is one position on a subject better than another? Why do you doubt the truth of a particular statement? Choose one or more concepts in a reading selection to write about, and don't worry about memorizing anything you read. Your instructor will want you to write in your own words.

EXPLORING THE SUBJECT

Once an essay is assigned, some exploring is necessary. If the topic is general, allowing many possibilities, you will have to *restrict* or *limit* it to *focus* on a subject. A good way to do this is by brainstorming—collecting all your ideas (rarely in complete sentences since most people think in fragments), quickly jotting them down, evaluating their importance and relationship to the topic, and choosing the subject that you can best write about. Let's brainstorm together about the following topic:

Write an essay about your visit to a national park in the United States. Restrict the topic and focus on one particular aspect of your experience.

First let's write down the names of all the parks we have visited, how long we stayed, and what we did at each one: *Yellowstone* **(Wyoming)—1 day. Drove around park. Kept car windows closed—dangerous bears. Saw Old Faithful geyser.** *Everglades* **(Florida)—1 hour. Boat ride through outskirts of park. No guide.** *Yosemite* **(California)—5 days. Some hiking. Snowbound 3 days—early fall storm. Saw El Capitan.** *Grand Canyon* **(Arizona)—7 days. Hiked daily. Saw film about park. Lectures. Guided nature walks. Shot 8 rolls of film. Exciting mule trip.**

Our obvious choice is the Grand Canyon because we stayed longer and did more there than at any other park. So, let's briefly summarize everything we can remember about that visit:

Physical Properties of the Park. The Grand Canyon (made up of hundreds of smaller canyons) is 217 miles long, four to eighteen miles wide at the top, and a mile deep. Its sides show two billion years of geologic history, layer upon layer of rock in many different colors which regularly change with the light. Indian rock paintings and artifacts, believed to be more than 800 years old, are found around the canyon.

Animal and Plant Life. Wild African burros, introduced by prospectors a hundred years ago, have multiplied to the point that they have become destructive pests. Tame mule deer are also numerous. The large, white-tailed Kaibab squirrel, which inhabits a small forested area on the North Rim, is an endangered species. Many kinds of plants grow in the canyon, from mountain wildflowers on the North Rim to tropical orchids in some of the side canyons of the South Rim.

Activities for Visitors.   The Bright Angel Trail mule trip, one terrifying mile almost straight down to the Colorado River, is popular. Wilderness trails require use permits, and some are so dangerous that even seasoned athletes often collapse on them. The observation points at the rim of the canyon afford such spectacular views of the canyon's depth that sometimes tourists are afraid to look down.

We realize that trying to focus on the trip as a whole is not a good idea. Even though our summary covers three subjects, it doesn't say enough about any of them. Instead, we have to expand a single detail from one of the three groups of facts. We can apply composition principles of closeup photography to writing: A good photographer knows that the camera lens must be focused on a limited subject, or the resulting photograph will be too general, such as a picture of your house that also includes the yard, the street, the sky, and the neighbors' houses and yards on either side. Instead of taking one wide-angle exposure that tries to show a little of everything at the Grand Canyon, the photographer frames limited subjects for individual shots: an especially pretty section of the canyon wall at sunset; a single figure in an unusual Indian rock painting; a rare glimpse of the Kaibab squirrel, its fluffy tail fluttering behind it like a white flag; a visitor gasping with astonishment at the canyon's depth. Each photograph says everything possible about the subject, and so must our essay.

Although we have learned a lot about the canyon, its plants, and its animals from sightseeing, we won't be able to add much more information about them without consulting other reference works. Therefore, let's select as our topic one activity that was especially memorable and about which we can supply many details, our terrifying burro ride six thousand feet down to the Colorado River.

Now, we have to consider the purpose of our essay. Are we writing to inform or entertain our readers? We will probably do both. Those who haven't visited the Grand Canyon will enjoy reading about our risky adventure, and those who have will relive the moment with us. What main point shall we make? Was our experience the most exciting (embarrassing, frightening, amusing, or upsetting) of this trip? Why? What happened? What was important about it? Did we learn some kind of lesson? Have our lives changed because of it? Perhaps we conquered a fear of heights or of large animals. Maybe we suddenly noticed the fragile ecology of the park when we saw the damage done to the trails by the mules' hooves. Possibly we realized, as we bumped down the sheer face of the canyon, that our lives depended on the sure-footedness of animals over which we had almost no control, rather than on our own actions.

Here are some other possible topics. Which one in each pair is more limited?

1. The beauty of the Grand Canyon
    Grand Canyon sunset
2. Wild animals of the Grand Canyon
    Deadly rattlesnake bite on the Grand Canyon trail
3. Sightseeing at the Grand Canyon
    Over the edge of the Grand Canyon in a helicopter
4. The Colorado River of the Grand Canyon
    River rafting through the Grand Canyon

We can see that the second topic of each set is more specific and promises the reader a colorful narrative. In set one, the author's description of the natural glow of the sunset, the animals silhouetted against its last rosy rays, and the descent of darkness over the land holds the reader's interest more readily than a catalog of every single beautiful sight at the Grand Canyon. In set two, a hiker writes about a snake bite suffered on one of the Canyon trails. The hiker tells of fear when the snake coiled, the attempt to dodge the snake's fangs, the pain of the bite, the terror of impending death, and finally, the unexpected rescue. This vividly detailed account is preferable to an inventory of the various animals found at the park. In the third set, the helicopter ride into the chasm is downright thrilling! The chopper is flying at an altitude of 100 feet. Suddenly, it is over the canyon's edge—6000 feet above the ground—and the passengers' stomachs seem to fall right into their shoes. They experience the depth of the canyon much more dramatically than they would if it were shown to them by a guide on a walking tour. In the fourth set, the white water rafting trip through the 2000-to-6000-foot deep, 200-mile-long canyon provides plenty of tense moments and close calls: nearly drowning when the boat upset in some especially nasty rapids, getting caught on a submerged rock, and unexpectedly shooting (going over) a waterfall. How can a general description of the 200 miles of Colorado River flowing through the Grand Canyon possibly be as much fun to read?

A good essay, then, like a good photograph, must have a focal point. A specific topic provides a sharper image than a general subject, and supporting details produce a word picture that is the equivalent of a great closeup.

WRITING THE ESSAY

After you have explored the subject, gathered interesting material, and narrowed the topic, you are ready to begin writing. An essay has three main parts:

thesis and introduction, development (body), and conclusion. A short essay usually contains a minimum of three paragraphs. Remember that a paragraph also has a topic or thesis sentence, development, and conclusion, but is much shorter than an essay. Often, an individual paragraph can be expanded into an essay by using the sentences in the body as topic sentences for separate paragraphs of development which include and discuss additional details and examples.

Thesis and Introduction

The thesis is to the essay what focusing the camera is to the photograph. A good thesis states the subject, usually in a single sentence that occurs in the first or introductory paragraph. The thesis can be:

1. a *position* that you take on some controversial subject; for example:

   Household pets are beneficial to health.

   Wives should manage family finances.

   Both men and women should perform compulsory military service.

   Husbands should make major decisions that affect their families.

2. a *judgment* that you have made after carefully considering all aspects of a particular problem; for example:

   Taxes cannot be reduced if citizens expect to have adequate police and fire protection.

   Objective tests do not measure a student's ability as well as essay examinations do.

3. a *summary* of the content of the paper; for example:

   Aunt Martha is the most beautiful and talented woman in the world.

   No one would believe the strange behavior of my eccentric Uncle Ned.

   My first date was absolutely the worst experience of my life.

   A visit to the dentist can bring both happiness and pain.

The introduction acquaints readers with your subject by identifying the author and the reading selection you are examining and by *briefly* summarizing it in two or three sentences, just as you would limit the amount of background information when introducing two of your friends. Let the reader discover more as your essay unfolds, just as your friends learn more about each other as they become better acquainted. The most effective introduction makes readers curious about and interested in what will follow.

Development

Developing the thesis is as necessary to a well-written essay as developing the film is to the finished photograph. If you include appropriate facts, examples, and illustrations in the second and subsequent paragraphs of the paper, your position on the subject gradually becomes clear, just as the photographic image does in the chemical solution.

How do you know which details to choose?

1. Be sure supporting examples are related to the focal point of your essay. If you are writing an essay about the geological characteristics of the Grand Canyon, don't include information about the hotel accommodations, the cost of meals, the endangered species living in the Canyon, or the Bright Angel Trail mule trip.

2. Make sure you can write at least one or two sentences in your own words about the importance of the example. Be especially careful to avoid listing examples without explaining or discussing them. Listing is fine for brainstorming, but it is unsuitable in an expository essay.

How can you work these details into your own writing?

1. Use a short quotation as a part of one of your sentences:

   According to this textbook, "developing the thesis is as necessary to a well-written essay as developing the film is to the finished photograph," but to many students photography is much easier than writing. When you take a picture, you just focus on a subject, click the shutter, and send the film off to the laboratory where the prints are made for you. When you write an essay, though, you not only choose the subject but also do the developing. You have to create the thesis; select examples and decide how to use them; worry about vocabulary, spelling, and sentence structure; and arrive at some interesting conclusion.

2. Begin a paragraph with the example itself; then discuss it, answering the question, "Why?"

   The Kaibab squirrel, which inhabits a small, diminishing forested area on the North Rim of the Grand Canyon, is one of many endangered species in the United States. Most of these creatures are having difficulty surviving because civilization has moved into their habitats or because the conditions that they require to live have changed drastically.

3. Begin with the discussion and follow it with the specific example:

   Many specialized species find it difficult to survive today because civilization has moved into their habitats or because the conditions that they require to survive are drastically altered. One species that is in danger of becoming extinct is the Kaibab squirrel, which inhabits a small, diminishing forested area on the North Rim of the Grand Canyon.

Conclusion

The concluding paragraph of your short paper is as satisfying to the reader as an elegant dessert at the end of a fine meal is to the diner. Avoid simply restating the thesis using the same or similar words (which is a little like offering a diner another serving of vegetables for dessert); instead, explain the value of the proof you have given in support of your thesis. What judgment can you make about what you have written? An essay about an endangered species like the Kaibab squirrel might conclude with a statement that some animals are destined to become extinct because they are so specialized. A conclusion with a different point of view might suggest ways that man can save creatures from extinction.

Read the following essay. Identify the thesis, determine whether the development is supported with examples, and evaluate the conclusion.

Mom, You Never Told Me . . .

Jeffrey L. Aran

Mom and Dad, I've decided I really do appreciate you. When you left for your extended vacation in the Orient last month, you put me in charge of the house. The result: I now know the agony you've had to put up with from us kids.

For the first three weeks, things ran smoothly. **Per your instruction**, I watered the grass every day, before 10 a.m. or after 4 p.m., and I soaked the indoor plants once a week. Also, Mom, I walked the dog four times a day just because you said it was very important that she be out that many times—I disagreed, as you'll recall, but nonetheless I walked her. Yes, I was a good boy. But when Kari, your darling daughter got home from summer camp, I had to become a part-time parent. That's when the trouble all started.

First, she made a shopping list. Now, as you know, Kari is a **vegetarian** and everything she wanted to eat, well, I didn't. But, of course, little sister must always win out. So I went to the market and when I got home with what I

By permission of the author. This first appeared in the *Los Angeles Times*.

thought were excellent buys and good, healthy, comparison-priced groceries, I was met with: "What kind of yogurt is this?" *and* "Why couldn't you have bought some real ice cream?"

"Well!" and "Humph!" I replied. After all, I told her, I'm the one who went to the market.

Such **indignation**! *Such* **manipulation**! If this is parenting, I thought, thank goodness you're coming home soon.

Then Sis invited a friend to stay overnight—which I really didn't mind. What I did mind was that the half-gallon of lemonade I made the previous day disappeared in 24 hours and the half-gallon of artificial mint chip ice cream—which Kari had **roundly** criticized as so **unorganic**—was also consumed. All of it.

Now I have some idea, Mom and Dad, of how you must react when, having made thousands of gallons of frozen orange juice, you yourself feel a **craving** for orange juice, run to the refrigerator, pull open the door, full of desire for that tall, refreshing glass—only to find an empty **Tupperware** bottle with dried pulp stuck to the sides and bottom. Did I ever drink the last drop? *Naw*, it couldn't have *been me.*

Soon Kari enlivened my week even more. One morning I gave the kitchen floor a close look and decided it could use a good **mopping.** For the first time in my life, I poured cleanser into a bucket, dipped in the mop and put it to the kitchen floor. Mom, you never told me how strong that ammonia is. Phew!— but it got the floor sparkling clean and off to work I went.

When I got home, what did I discover? You guessed it. Not a dirty floor— a sticky one. How could that be? Ammonia and water never got sticky before. A little **prodding** from me finally got the facts out. Having spilled the sugar intended for her Wheat Chex, Kari mopped up the mess with warm water. Well, Mom, you know how it is, water and sugar make a pretty **gooey** combination.

Oh yes, we've had a slight **catastrophe**. You probably haven't heard about this over in the Orient, but Southern California got some rain not long ago from tropical depression **Doreen**. Perhaps you knew we had a little hole in the roof—I certainly didn't know or I'd have taken action. Anyway, don't be surprised to find that the ceiling in the master bedroom now lies on the floor.

The insurance man said it would cost $15,000 or so to fix, but not to worry.

I'm glad you're coming home, because I can't take all this much longer. What with raising a family, teaching proper morals, emptying dishwashers and walking dogs, I just don't see how you find any time for yourselves.

So to you, Mom and Dad, and to any other parents who may feel somewhat neglected, unappreciated, and undercredited, I offer these words as full payment for past debts in the hope I can somehow make up for all ungrateful sons: Thank you for everything you've done. It took me 20 years to say it, but I appreciate you—really I do, I promise.

Glossary

catastrophe *(noun)* disaster

craving *(noun)* intense desire

Doreen *(noun)* tropical storms are assigned male or female first names

gooey *(adjective; slang)* sticky

indignation *(noun)* anger caused by some injustice or improper behavior

manipulation *(noun)* artful skill of influencing or managing a person or situation

mopping *(verb)* washing the floor by rubbing or wiping it with a wet, soapy mop (a sponge or a bundle of coarse yarn fastened to a long handle)

naw *(slang)* no

per your instruction *(colloquialism)* according to your instruction

prodding *(verb)* poking, jabbing

roundly *(adverb)* vigorously, severely; thoroughly; completely

Tupperware *(noun)* brand name for a special kind of plastic containers

unorganic *(adjective)* usually meaning foods subjected to chemicals during growing or processing. Organic foods are grown using only animal wastes or vegetable composts for fertilizer.

vegetarian *(noun)* person who eats no meat

Notice the logical order of the essay. In his thesis, Aran acknowledges the inconveniences his parents have suffered because of their children's behavior. The development begins with small, unimportant events, building slowly to the grand disaster of the $15,000 hole in the ceiling of the master bedroom. Each example is given in chronological order, but each is a part of some lively discussion or anecdote. In the penultimate (next to last) paragraph, Aran summarizes all the problems he faced during his parents' absence, and in the final paragraph, he concludes that parents deserve more appreciation from their children.

THE WRITER'S RESPONSIBILITY TO FULFILL THE READER'S EXPECTATIONS

Critical writing demands that you:

1. *Take a stand or a position on the subject near the beginning of the essay.* Obviously, your thesis will be based on your feelings about the reading; however, you will have to give proof to convince readers of your views. Avoid

concentrating on whether you like or don't like the selection. Focus on accuracy of information, use of examples, author's attitude, and relationships between reading selections. Be sure to identify the author and title of the material you are discussing.

2. *Write in your own words*. Nothing should be copied from the text unless it is properly identified and quoted; otherwise, the material is plagiarized. *Plagiarism* is taking the written ideas of another person and using them in your paper as if they were your own, a form of cheating just as serious as copying a friend's paper and turning it in to the instructor as your original work. Since published material is protected by copyright laws, you may only use small portions of it in your writing and only under special circumstances. You must enclose phrases or sentences that you copy exactly in quotation marks. Identify the page number where the material was printed in your book (do the same when you paraphrase an author's ideas). Use quoted material to *support* your ideas, not to fill space. Keep quotations short—not more than two handwritten lines each—in essays that you write in class. Limit use of the text when you are writing in order to practice expressing your ideas in your own words.

3. *Avoid retelling*. Don't write a summary of the reading selection. Instead, discuss the significance or meaning of all or parts of it.

4. *Make examples work for you*. Choose specifics that lend force to your statements; ask yourself, "Is this the strongest proof I can use to support my point?" Aran does this with examples of Kari's indignation, manipulation, and lack of consideration. Prove your thesis by combining analysis of portions of the text with your original ideas.

5. *Limit inclusion of personal experiences*. Use events from your life only if they can enhance your discussion of the topic. Don't stray from your thesis. Even if an entire essay is based on something that happened in your life, the topic should deal with a single aspect of that experience, as in Aran's article. Notice that he doesn't include information about his job, his friends, or his other activities. He concentrates only on his "parenting."

6. *End with a conclusion*. Don't worry about a fancy finish; just don't leave the reader wondering. When you are writing an essay in class, it takes the same amount of time to write, "Sorry, I didn't have time for a conclusion," as it does to compose just a one-sentence judgment or opinion to complete your paper. Of course, you should strive to write a concluding paragraph if you possibly can.

7. *Compose your own title*. But wait to do it until you have finished the entire essay. That way, you will have more ideas and be better able to relate the title to important points in your paper. Don't use the author's title as if it were your own.

8. *Strive for correctness and legibility.* Ask for help if you have questions about grammar, spelling, or punctuation. Always read your finished essay all the way through before you turn it in. Try to identify and correct all errors. If you habitually make the same grammatical mistakes, such as omission of articles or prepositions, be especially alert for these as you proofread. (Your instructor may refer you to chapter 10 to correct persistent problems with grammar, style, and punctuation.) Always write in blue or black ink. If you use erasable ink, be sure to completely remove the old material before you write in the new; otherwise, line out mistakes and make corrections neatly above them.

Now let's write an essay together about Jeffrey Aran's article. Our thesis should answer the following question: **What lesson does Aran learn from his experiences?** Our development should present and explain at least two specific examples. Our conclusion should make judgments about some questions: Why is Aran's lesson important? Is he changed in any way by his experiences? Will his relationship with his parents be different in the future? How does he feel about his past behavior now?

Underline the thesis and the major examples in our essay:

The Joys of Parenting

Jeffrey Aran's article, "Mom, You Never Told Me . . ." describes his transformation from child to parent when he writes about assuming responsibility for his younger sister while his parents are away on vacation. Aran learns a valuable lesson from his experience: Children often fail to appreciate and are inconsiderate of their parents until the children become parents themselves.

Aran really begins to understand what his mother contributes to the running of the household when he has to do the marketing, and he is rather proud of himself when he comes home with "excellent buys and good, healthy, comparison-priced groceries." Unfortunately, he has to contend with a fussy eater, his vegetarian sister, Kari, who doesn't like anything he purchases. He feels frustrated and angry because of her attitude and complains, "If this is parenting, . . . thank goodness you're coming home soon." But his frustrations multiply when he opens the refrigerator the next morning and finds that Kari and her overnight guest have consumed everything he bought the day before even though Kari complained that the food was "unorganic." He is not so upset, however, that he cannot see both humor and justice in the situation. Now he knows how his parents used to feel when they wanted a glass of orange juice and repeatedly found only an "empty Tupperware bottle with dried pulp stuck to the sides and bottom" in the refrigerator because he had consumed it all.

The author also has to do the housework in his mother's absence, and this gives him another chance to see how unthinking and careless young people can be. He says that "for the first time in my life, I poured cleanser into a bucket, dipped in the mop and put it to the kitchen floor." With that first dreadful whiff of ammonia, he learns the unpleasantness of another household task that his mother performs regularly. It is not surprising that Aran is annoyed when he comes home from work and finds that his sister has not properly cleaned up some sugar that she spilled on the floor, so it is already sticky. Again, he admits parallels between himself and Kari when he says, "Well, Mom, you know how it is, water and sugar make a pretty gooey combination."

At the end of the essay, Aran thanks his parents for all they have done for him and apologizes for having been an ungrateful son. However, he would never have realized how irresponsible and thoughtless a teenager he had been if he had not substituted as a parent for his younger sister. Kari commits all the same "crimes" that Aran knows so well, but this time he is the victim, not the perpetrator. Clearly, Aran's experiences prove the old saying, "experience is the best teacher."

Notice the quoted material in "The Joys of Parenting." In some cases, short quotes are complete sentences. In other instances, one of Aran's phrases is quoted and added to a sentence in the essay. The final quote is a well-known maxim. Quotes may be inserted anywhere that they make sense, but they should be used sparingly. Again, quoted material is *always* set off by quotation marks; it is *never* just copied and included as part of your own writing.

Remember our earlier discussion of plagiarism? Here is an example of it: A student who was unsure of the way to develop "The Joys of Parenting" might have written paragraph 2 like this (the exact wording from Aran's essay is in **boldface** type):

Aran really begins to understand what his mother contributes to the running of the household when he has to do the marketing. **Now, as you know, Kari is a vegetarian and everything she wanted to eat, well,** he **didn't. But** Aran **went to the market and when** he **got home with what** he **thought were excellent buys and good, healthy, comparison-priced groceries,** Kari criticized the food even though she ate it all. Now Aran knows how his parents **must react when, having made thousands of gallons of frozen orange juice,** they **feel a craving for orange juice, run to the refrigerator, pull open the door, full of desire for that tall, refreshing glass—only to find an empty Tupperware bottle with dried pulp stuck to the sides and bottom.**

Even though the student changed the pronouns from the first person, most of the paragraph is copied *exactly* as Aran wrote it and is not acceptable as original composition.

In summary, the essay is analogous to the human body. A body with too little or too much fat or muscle is unattractive and uninteresting, but a body that has proportional fat and properly developed muscle for its bone structure and height is beautiful, even fascinating. Examples should be carefully selected and interestingly discussed to prove the point being made. They should invite the reader to think about their meaning.

WRITING TO COMMUNICATE

Since the purpose of writing is communication, ask yourself these questions before you begin. What is the purpose of the essay and who is the audience (reader)? In college, of course, the reader is an instructor, and the purpose is usually to fulfill some assignment and to earn the highest possible grade. In fact, many courses besides English require that students write essays. According to an international student studying engineering at the University of California, Berkeley, "The (engineering) professor doesn't want students just to take out their calculators and work the problem mathematically because they forget it in a few weeks. Instead, students have to write essays that show they understand the problem and explain how to solve it. Then they remember the information for years. So tell your students that even for engineering courses they have to write clearly." But good writing is demanded in most businesses and professions, too, and when you finish college you may be required to write proposals for funding, arguments for or against a method of business operation or a new project, justifications for major equipment expenditures, reports to stockholders, technical evaluations, letters, etc. In business, the "grade" for a particularly well-written assignment may be a promotion to a higher position or a substantial increase in salary, so it is important to be able to present the necessary information to complement your purpose.

Is the essay an argument? Then use serious examples that include facts, figures, and data calculated to prove the point and convince the reader. Is the essay a narration of an interesting experience or an explanation of some process like painting the kitchen or learning to ride a horse? Here the purpose may be very different. You may want to touch the reader's emotions by relating anecdotes that describe the funny or frustrating moments of that experience. Is the essay an explanation of a difficult concept? Then an analogy, similar to that comparing writing with photography, might be useful.

The following selections have very different purposes, but all communicate effectively. As you read them, determine the audience, the thesis, and the kinds of supporting information used. Finally, decide whether the conclusion makes some kind of judgment based on the evidence given.

The Land of the Lock

Bob Greene

Bob Greene is a feature writer whose column is published in many newspapers throughout the United States. His articles explore particular aspects of contemporary life—news events, political issues, and social problems.

   Years ago in America, it was customary for families to leave their doors unlocked, day and night. In this essay, Greene regrets that people can no longer trust each other and have to resort to elaborate security systems to protect themselves and their valuables. Although the author is writing his opinion, he uses many examples to reinforce his ideas and to prove his thesis.

   In the house where I grew up, it was our custom to leave the front door on the latch at night. I don't know if that was a local term or if it is universal; "on the latch" meant the door was closed but not locked. None of us carried keys; the last one in for the evening would close up, and that was it.

   Those days are over. In rural areas as well as in cities, doors do not stay unlocked, even for part of an evening.

   Suburbs and country areas are, in many ways, even more vulnerable than **well-patroled urban streets**. Statistics show the crime rate rising more dramatically in those **allegedly tranquil** areas than in cities. At any rate, the **era** of leaving the front door on the latch is over.

   It has been replaced by **dead-bolt locks**, security chains, electronic alarm systems and **trip wires** hooked up to a police station or private guard firm. Many suburban families have sliding glass doors on their patios, with steel bars elegantly built in so no one can pry the doors open.

   It is not uncommon, in the most pleasant of homes, to see pasted on the windows decals announcing that **the premises are under surveillance** by this security force or that guard company.

   The lock is the new symbol of America. Indeed, a recent public-service advertisement by a large insurance company featured not **actuarial charts** but a picture of a child's bicycle with the now-usual **padlock** attached to it.

   The ad pointed out that, yes, it is the insurance companies that pay for stolen goods, but who is going to pay for what the new **atmosphere** of distrust and fear is doing to our way of life? Who is going to make the **psychic payment** for the **transformation** of America from the Land of the Free to the Land of the Lock?

Reprinted by permission: Tribune Company Syndicate, Inc.

For that is what has happened. We have become so used to defending ourselves against the new atmosphere of American life, so used to putting up **barriers**, that we have not had time to think about what it may mean.

For some reason we are satisfied when we think we are well-protected; it does not occur to us to ask ourselves: Why has this happened? Why are we having to **barricade** ourselves against our neighbors and fellow citizens, and when, exactly, did this start to take over our lives?

And it has taken over. If you work for a medium- to large-size company, **chances are that** you don't just wander in and out of work. You probably carry some kind of **access card**, electronic or otherwise, that allows you in and out of your place of work. Maybe the security guard at the front desk knows your face and will wave you in most days, but the fact remains that the business you work for feels threatened enough to keep outsiders away **via** these "keys."

It wasn't always like this. Even a **decade** ago, most private businesses had a policy of free access. It simply didn't occur to managers that the proper thing to do was to distrust people.

Look at the airports. Parents used to take children out to departure gates to watch planes land and take off. That's all gone. Airports are no longer a place of education and fun; they are the most **sophisticated** of **security encampments**.

With electronic X-ray equipment, we seem finally to have figured out a way to hold the terrorists, real and imagined, at bay; it was such a relief to solve this problem that we did not think much about what such a state of affairs says about the quality of our lives. We now pass through these **electronic friskers** without so much as a sideways glance; the machines, and what they stand for, have won.

Our neighborhoods are bathed in **high-intensity light**; we do not want to afford ourselves even so much a luxury as a shadow.

Businessmen, in increasing numbers, are purchasing new machines that hook up to the telephone and analyze a caller's voice. The machines are supposed to tell the businessman, with a small margin of error, whether his friend or client is telling lies.

All this is being done in the name of "security"; that is what we tell ourselves. We are fearful, and so we devise ways to lock the fear out, and that, we decide, is what security means.

But no; with all this "security," we are perhaps the most insecure nation in the history of civilized man. What better word to describe the way in which we have been forced to live? What better **indictment** of all that we have become in this new and puzzling time?

We trust no one. Suburban housewives wear **rape whistles** on their station wagon key chains. We have become so smart about self-protection that, in the end, **we have all outsmarted ourselves**. We may have locked the evils out, but in so doing we have locked ourselves in.

That may be the **legacy** we remember best when we look back on this age: In dealing with the unseen horrors among us, we became prisoners of ourselves. All of us prisoners, in this time of our troubles.

Glossary

access card *(special term)* card that allows a person admission to a controlled area. Some access cards have magnetic strips on the back. They are inserted in a special magnetic card reader to determine whether the holder is authorized for admission. Other access cards use photographs for identification.

actuarial charts *(insurance term)* mathematical tables that identify insurance risks and the premiums (payments) required to cover them

allegedly tranquil *(common usage)* supposedly calm or quiet

atmosphere *(noun)* social environment

barricade *(verb)* obstruct; put up physical defenses

barriers *(noun)* obstacles used for defense

chances are that *(idiom)* probably; in all probability

dead-bolt locks *(noun)* keyed locks with steel bolts that extend one to two inches into the door frame

decade *(noun)* ten-year period

electronic friskers *(slang)* electronic instruments that search people to try to detect weapons

era *(noun)* earlier period of time that is noteworthy for special developments or events that occurred; for example, an era of scientific discovery

high-intensity light *(noun)* very strong light

indictment *(noun)* accusation

legacy *(noun)* property or money given by a last will and testament

padlock *(noun)* removable lock that can be fastened to a chain or a metal clasp. Padlocks are commonly used to safeguard bicycles.

psychic payment *(special term)* psychological or emotional price

rape whistles *(noun)* whistles (something like those used in sports) capable of producing very loud, shrill noises intended to scare off attackers

security encampments *(special usage)* security equipment located in special areas in airports like camps of soldiers on the battlefield

sophisticated *(adjective)* changed from natural and simple to artificial; highly advanced technologically

the premises are under surveillance *(police term)* the property is being watched

transformation *(noun)*   change

trip wires *(technical term)*   hidden wires that "trip" or activate an electronic alarm. Sometimes the wires are installed under carpets and are set off by foot pressure.

via *(preposition)*   by way of

we have all outsmarted ourselves *(idiom)*   We have been so smart that it may hurt rather than help us.

well-patroled urban streets *(common usage)*   city streets that are carefully watched by policemen to protect citizens against crime

Comprehension Questions

1. Explain the term "on the latch."
2. Are the suburbs less likely to suffer crime than the cities?
3. What kinds of safeguards do people use in addition to regular keyed locks?
4. Insurance companies pay for loss of personal property, so why should people worry so much about theft?
5. What is the "psychic payment" Greene mentions?
6. Greene says people are satisfied when they feel well-protected, but security has become too important in our daily lives. Give four specific examples of precautions people take to "lock the fear out."
7. What is the legacy we will remember best when we look back on this age?

Topics for Critical Analysis, Discussion, and Writing

1. Advances in technology have made it possible to develop very clever and sophisticated security devices. Although a person is physically safe, what is his or her psychological state? What happens to people when trust is lost? How do they behave?

2. According to Greene, how has the nature of society changed since he was a youth? What does he think is the major cause of the change? Is there any way to reverse the situation?

3. Greene is writing about the quality of life in metropolitan areas of the United States. Is he taking this situation (the need for locks on the doors) too seriously? Is the concern for personal safety and security of property as great in other countries as in the United States? Why or why not? Give specific instances to prove your answers.

4. Define the word *trust* as it applies to Greene's article. Then give and discuss examples of trust or the lack of it in specific situations that you know

about, either in your country or in the United States. What conclusions can you reach about trust in contemporary society?

5. What is the main idea, or *theme,* of Greene's article?

Why Couples Really Fight

Norman Lobsenz

In some cultures, couples never show anger toward each other. They do not communicate to straighten out their differences; instead, they subordinate their personal problems to social tradition. In the United States, however, the situation is quite different. Husbands and wives often disagree openly. Although divorce is common, many social forces are dedicated to helping couples solve their problems before such a final action becomes necessary. Partners are urged to talk over their problems honestly with each other. Because wives who work outside the home often share financial burdens that were once solely their husbands' responsibilities, many husbands share some of the household duties in return. But even when married couples take on extra tasks willingly, they sometimes feel angry and cheated, and when they fight, they hide the real reasons for their disagreements. In developing his article, Lobsenz uses examples to clarify the problems faced by couples today. Watch for the rhetorical question that signals the beginning of the conclusion in which Lobsenz suggests possible solutions.

If you asked any couple to give the reason behind their marital **spats**, they'd probably be able to do so easily—and with one word or phrase. Couples often think their problems **stem from** a single specific cause—such as money troubles, interference from inlaws, sexual incompatibility, differences bringing up the children.

But most marriage counselors today believe that, except in rare instances, the specific complaint named by **squabbling** partners is merely a **symptom** of a deeper **conflict** between them. Unfortunately, that conflict may be difficult to recognize, and this makes some fights **tough** to resolve. "Unless a couple understand what they are really fighting about," says Los Angeles therapist Dr. Hendrie Weisinger, "and deal with the underlying cause, their arguments will continue."

Here are what a consensus of family counselors consider to be some of the "hidden" causes of marital fighting.

By permission of the author. Reprinted from *Family Weekly,* copyright 1980, 1515 Broadway, New York, New York 10036.

The need to feel in control of the relationship: "I don't understand it," said Phyllis K., "Ted and I have been married five years and he has never questioned how I spend household money. Now if I'm a few dollars over our **budget,** he gets **furious** and accuses me of being wasteful. And he changed every charge account to his name so he can examine all the bills. It seems we fight over money all the time!"

In counseling sessions this couple took part in, it was revealed that Phyllis had not worked outside the home since her marriage, and Ted handled all the family finances. A few months earlier, however, Phyllis' uncle had died and left her $2,500. She opened her own checking account and used the inheritance from time to time to buy small luxuries for herself and for the family.

"It had always been important to Ted to feel that he was totally in charge of the couple's finances," the counselor says. "But once Phyllis had money of her own that she could spend as she pleased, the situation changed. Ted was no longer in control. The anxiety this caused him found its **outlet** in the **fights he picked** with Phyllis. And checking the bills was Ted's way of trying to convince himself was still the boss."

Arguments over sex are also usually rooted in the battle for control. Many **spouses** use sex to try to establish dominance over each other, often without realizing what they are doing.

Differences in family backgrounds: "I'm a superb cook, but my husband argues about the meals I serve him," one woman says. "I enjoy making special sauces and unusual dishes, but he says there's never anything he can eat. He wants me to make **meatloaf** and potato soup. I'm *sick* of hearing about his mother's potato soup!"

In this instance, the husband grew up in a family where simple, hearty food was a symbol of loving warmth, and "fancy" dishes were for guests or strangers.

Today, as more and more men and women marry across the social, cultural and religious boundaries within which they grew up, conflicts over their different attitudes are bound to occur.

Concentrating on the negative in marriage: A good deal of marital fighting stems from the fact that many people focus attention on the problems in their relationship and neglect the positive factors that brought them together in the first place. One **therapist** helps couples with this kind of problem by forcing them to talk about the qualities they admire in each other, the pleasures they share, the goals they mutually set out to reach. "**You can almost see the antagonism draining away,**" the therapist says. "Partners tend to **take each other's virtues for granted** and **pounce** upon the flaws."

One couple, **embroiled** in constant squabbling, were asked to list all the things they liked and valued about each other. "Until then," the husband said, "I didn't realize how many there were or how important they are to me."

Normal crises you encounter in the course of marriage: Some areas of conflict are to be expected at certain stages in the marital "life cycle." "A marriage in its first year experiences certain normal **stresses** as the young couple learn to adjust to each other's **temperaments**," says counselor Weisinger. "Other tensions arise when a first child is born. An older couple may find themselves arguing more frequently after the husband's retirement."

The marital life cycle is **booby-trapped** with a whole series of similar events: a promotion to a demanding job, a serious illness, a period of unemployment, a move to a new community. Ordinarily, in and of themselves, each of these events is loaded with the potential for change. They can and do **trigger clashes**, but a couple may not recognize the cause.

The inability to accept today's changing sex roles for husband and wife: Take, for instance, the middle-aged man who constantly accuses his wife—who recently returned to work as a nurse—of neglecting their children. "I'm proud of her," he says. "It's fine that she's working. But she ought to be home when the kids need her."

Another man encouraged his wife to take a job that involved a good deal of travel. "But when I'm out of town for even one night, **he has a fit**," the woman says. "Every time I have to go away he accuses me of not caring about him. And I really get angry when he calls my hotel several times a night to make sure I'm in my room!"

"The fact is that many men have **ambivalent feelings** about **liberated wives**," a counselor remarks. "A husband may be proud of his wife, but he may also feel resentful, neglected or threatened. Because he can't *admit* these feelings, he lets them out indirectly by picking things to fight about."

How can couples **cope with** these hidden causes of marital fighting? Here are some suggestions:

Don't fall into the trap of trying to "win" an argument. In virtually every instance, one spouse's "victory" eventually turns into a loss for both partners because it reduces a marriage to an endless struggle for power.

Learn to communicate ideas and feelings more clearly. One marriage-enrichment program teaches the art of "dialoging." A husband-wife conversation is aimed at clarifying the facts and emotions involved in a troubling argument. The purpose of dialoging is to help a couple share and accept each other's attitudes.

Resist the popular notion that it is always healthy to vent your hostile feelings in order to "clear the emotional air." According to family sociologist Murray Straus, an expert on violence in the family, "**letting it all hang out**" usually serves only to increase both persons' anger and to **aggravate** the problem that caused it. Moreover, it seldom helps a couple **come to grips intelligently with the basic reason for their quarrel**.

Instead of trying to change what's different about your spouse, try to respect and learn from those differences.

Be alert to the underlying causes of arguments. Seek to learn the hidden motives for **irritation**, **frustration**, anger. One counselor suggests using **the image of a "mental safety catch" on one's emotional trigger**. "When a fight starts is the time to pause and ask yourself, why am I furious? What is really at issue here? You have a right to feel and express anger, of course. But unless you try to find out the *why* of it, the arguments will probably repeat themselves without any progress toward solving the problem."

Glossary

aggravate *(verb)* worsen

ambivalent feelings *(common usage)* mixed emotions; some good and some bad feelings

booby-trapped *(verb, common usage)* full of seemingly innocent events that actually trick or trap others and catch them off guard so that they do foolish things

budget *(noun)* plan for controlling expenses so that they do not exceed income

come to grips intelligently with the basic reason for their quarrel *(common usage)* understand the cause of their argument by using logic and reason

conflict *(noun)* fight; battle; struggle

cope with *(verb)* contend with; handle emotionally

embroiled *(verb)* mixed up in; involved in

fights he picked *(idiom)* fights he started

frustration *(noun)* feeling of defeat that results from being blocked or thwarted when trying to reach an objective

furious *(adjective)* intensely angry

he has a fit *(idiom)* he becomes angry

irritation *(noun)* annoyance; impatience

"letting it all hang out" *(slang)* saying everything you feel; not holding anything back

liberated wives *(special term)* wives who are freed from the traditional role of the homemaker. A liberated wife is one whose position is equal, rather than subordinate, to her husband's; for example, if she works at a job outside the home, her husband shares the household duties.

meatloaf *(noun)* inexpensive, but tasty, meat dish in which ground beef and other ingredients are mixed together and formed into a rectangular loaf that is baked and served sliced

outlet *(noun)* means of expression

pounce *(verb)* attack and seize (as a cat pounces on a mouse)

spats *(noun)*   little unimportant quarrels (small fights) or disputes

spouses *(noun)*   members (husband and wife) of a married couple

squabbling *(verb)*   noisy, petty quarreling or arguing

stem from *(verb)*   originate

stresses *(noun)*   strains; pressures; difficulties

symptom *(noun)*   sign; indication

take each other's virtues for granted *(idiom)*   automatically expect and accept, and therefore not appreciate, the good points about the other person. Most people do not like to be taken for granted.

temperaments *(noun)*   dispositions; natures

the image of a "mental safety catch" on one's emotional trigger *(figurative expression)*   the imaginary picture of anger as a gun. The safety catch on the trigger of the gun is carefully controlled so that it won't go off accidentally. People are advised to think of the consequences before allowing themselves to become explosively angry.

therapist *(noun)*   specialist (usually a psychologist or psychiatrist) who treats people that have emotional or marital problems

tough *(adjective)*   difficult

trigger clashes *(common usage)*   start arguments

"You can almost see the antagonism draining away" *(special usage)*   the anger visibly diminishes or lessens

Comprehension Questions

1. Is it easy to determine the true cause of arguments between marriage partners?
2. What are the areas of disagreement that married couples think are causing all their problems? Choose the best answer(s).
   a. lack of money
   b. arguments over the way the children should behave
   c. disagreements about sex
   d. interfering fathers- or mothers-in-law
   e. all of the above
   f. none of the above
3. Family counselors agree that some or all of the preceding problems
   a. are the real causes of marital fighting.

b. are symptoms of much more serious problems.

c. are common in all marriages everywhere.

4. Identify the five major examples used in the article to explain the hidden reasons couples fight.

5. What is really wrong when couples fight over money or sex?

6. When a husband wants his wife to cook the kinds of foods his mother does, what do counselors identify as the deeper problem?

7. What happens when couples concentrate on the negative aspects of marriage?

8. What are some of the normal crises that occur in marriage?

9. What kinds of problems result from changes in the traditional roles of husbands and wives?

10. Briefly list the counselors' suggestions for avoiding marital conflict.

Topics for Critical Analysis, Discussion, and Writing

1. What happens in your country when two people from different backgrounds marry? Do the parents interfere? Does one person feel inferior to the other? How is the marriage affected? Do husbands and wives from different backgrounds in your country behave similarly to couples with the same problem in the United States?

2. Is one person usually dominant in marriage in your country? What determines dominance? What is its effect on the marital relationship?

3. Arguments between husbands and wives don't always lead to divorce. Many couples remain married even though they fight frequently. What is the function of fighting in their marriages? Why do they stay together?

4. Often neither husband nor wife can adjust to new demands when their marriage roles change. Some husbands resent wives trying to assume additional authority; some wives resent husbands expecting the home life to continue as comfortably as if the wives weren't working outside. How should couples handle a situation like this?

5. Using examples from your knowledge or experience, discuss at least two of the problems caused by normal crises encountered in almost every marriage, and explain how these problems were solved.

6. Lobsenz reports that counselors agree on several methods to solve the problem of marital fighting. Would these solutions work in your country? Why or why not?

From

The Little Prince

Antoine de Saint Exupéry

The Little Prince is a deceptively simple story about a small boy's search for friendship and understanding. The little prince is the only inhabitant of his tiny planet (actually an asteroid), which has only enough room for him and his three miniature volcanoes, his baobab tree, and his rose. It is his relationship with the rose that causes him to leave his home. The rose is the most beautiful of his possessions. As a result, she is very spoiled and demands special care—screens must be put around her to protect her from drafts, insects must be driven away from her, and water must be applied at precise intervals. Her pride, conceit, and vanity eventually anger and sadden the little prince, and one day he decides to set out on a journey to search for a more satisfying, reciprocal relationship.

On his travels, though, everyone he meets is too absorbed in his own special interests to pay much attention to the little prince. He asks countless questions about life, but never receives a satisfactory answer—until he meets the fox. Observe that in the beginning of this selection, the little prince asks the fox "What does that mean—'tame'?" three times before the fox finally replies. The child has learned to keep asking until he receives a reply. But unlike all the people who were too busy to give the little prince guidance, the fox does answer and his response is the beginning of the boy's understanding of the responsibility of friendship and the essence of self-worth.

Watch for the extended examples the fox uses to explain the word "tame" and to communicate the importance of "rites" in taming an animal.

But it happened that after walking for a long time through sand, and rocks, and snow, the little prince at last came upon a road. And all roads lead to the **abodes** of men.

"Good morning," he said.

He was standing before a garden, all a-bloom with roses.

"Good morning," said the roses.

The little prince gazed at them. They all looked like his flower.

"Who are you?" he demanded, **thunderstruck**.

"We are roses," the roses said.

And he was overcome with sadness. His flower had told him that she was the only one of her kind in all the universe. And here were five thousand of them, all alike, in one single garden!

"She would be very much annoyed," he said to himself, "if she should see that . . . . She would cough most dreadfully, and she would pretend that she was dying, to avoid being laughed at. And I should be obliged to pretend that I was nursing her back to life—for if I did not do that, to **humble myself** also, she would really allow herself to die. . ."

Then he went on with his **reflections**: "I thought that I was rich, with a flower that was unique in all the world; and all I had was a common rose. A common rose, and three **volcanoes** that come up to my knees—and one of them perhaps **extinct** forever . . . .That doesn't make me a very great prince. . ."

And he lay down in the grass and cried.

It was then that the fox appeared.

"Good morning," said the fox.

"Good morning," the little prince responded politely, although when he turned around he saw nothing.

"I am right here," the voice said, "under the apple tree."

"Who are you?" asked the little prince, and added, "You are very pretty to look at."

"I am a fox," the fox said.

"Come and play with me," proposed the little prince. "I am so unhappy."

"I cannot play with you," the fox said. "I am not tamed."

"Ah! Please excuse me," said the little prince.

But, after some thought, he added:

"What does that mean—'tame'?"

"You do not live here," said the fox. "What is it that you are looking for?"

"I am looking for men," said the little prince. "What does that mean—'tame'?"

"Men," said the fox. "They have guns, and they hunt. It is very disturbing. They also raise chickens. These are their only interests. Are you looking for chickens?"

"No," said the little prince. "I am looking for friends. What does that mean—'tame'?"

"It is an act too often neglected," said the fox. "It means to establish ties."

"'To establish ties'?"

"Just that," said the fox. "To me, you are still nothing more than a little boy who is just like a hundred thousand other little boys. And I have no need of you. And you, on your part, have no need of me. To you, I am nothing more than a fox like a hundred thousand other foxes. But if you tame me, then we shall need each other. To me, you will be unique in all the world. To you, I shall be unique in all the world . . . ."

"I am beginning to understand," said the little prince. "There is a flower . . . I think that she has tamed me. . . ."

"It is possible," said the fox. "On the Earth one sees all sorts of things."

"Oh, but this is not on the Earth!" said the little prince.

The fox seemed **perplexed**, and very curious.

"On another planet?"

"Yes."

"Are there hunters on that planet?"

"No."

"Ah, that is interesting! Are there chickens?"

"No."

"Nothing is perfect," sighed the fox.

But he came back to his idea.

"My life is very **monotonous**," he said. "I hunt chickens; men hunt me. All the chickens are just alike, and all the men are just alike. And, in consequence, I am a little bored. But if you tame me, it will be as if the sun came to shine on my life. I shall know the sound of a step that will be different from all the others. Other steps send me hurrying back underneath the ground. Yours will call me, like music, out of my **burrow**. And then look: you see the grain-fields **down yonder**? I do not eat bread. Wheat is of no use to me. The wheat fields have nothing to say to me. And that is sad. But you have hair that is the color of gold. Think how wonderful that will be when you have tamed me! The grain, which is also golden, will bring me back the thought of you. And I shall love to listen to the wind in the wheat. . . ."

The fox gazed at the little prince, for a long time.

"Please—tame me!" he said.

"I want to, very much," the little prince replied. "But I have not much time. I have friends to discover, and a great many things to understand."

"One only understands the things that one tames," said the fox. "Men have no more time to understand anything. They buy things all ready made at the shops. But there is no shop anywhere where one can buy friendship, and so men have no friends any more. If you want a friend, tame me. . . ."

"What must I do, to tame you?" asked the little prince.

"You must be very patient," replied the fox. "First you will sit down at a little distance from me—like that—in the grass. I shall look at you out of the corner of my eye, and you will say nothing. Words are the source of misunderstandings. But you will sit a little closer to me, every day. . . ."

The next day the little prince came back.

"It would have been better to come back at the same hour," said the fox. "If, for example, you come at four o'clock in the afternoon, then at three o'clock I shall begin to be happy. I shall feel happier and happier as the hour advances. At four o'clock, I shall already be worrying and jumping about. I shall show you how happy I am! But if you come at just any time, I shall never know at what hour my heart is to be ready to greet you. . . . One must observe the proper **rites**. . . ."

"What is a rite?" asked the little prince.

"Those also are actions too often neglected," said the fox. "They are what make one day different from other days, one hour from other hours. There is a rite, for example, among my hunters. Every Thursday they dance with the village girls. So Thursday is a wonderful day for me! I can take a walk as far as the vineyards. But if the hunters danced at just any time, every day would be like every other day, and I should never have any vacation at all."

So the little prince tamed the fox. And when the hour of his departure drew near—

"Ah," said the fox, "I shall cry."

"It is your own fault," said the little prince. "I never wished you any sort of harm; but you wanted me to tame you. . . ."

"Yes, that is so," said the fox.

"But now you are going to cry!" said the little prince.

"Yes, that is so," said the fox.

"Then it has done you no good at all!"

"It has done me good," said the fox, "because of the color of the wheat fields." And then he added:

"Go and look again at the roses. You will understand now that yours is unique in all the world. Then come back to say goodbye to me, and I will make you a present of a secret."

The little prince went away, to look again at the roses.

"You are not at all like my rose," he said. "As yet you are nothing. No one has tamed you, and you have tamed no one. You are like my fox when I first knew him. He was only a fox like a hundred thousand other foxes. But I have made him my friend, and now he is unique in all the world."

And the roses were very much embarrassed.

"You are beautiful, but you are empty," he went on. "One could not die for you. To be sure, an ordinary passerby would think that my rose looked just like you—the rose that belongs to me. But in herself alone she is more important than all the hundreds of you other roses: because it is she that I have watered; because it is she that I have put under the **glass globe**; because it is she that I have sheltered behind the screen; because it is for her that I have killed the **caterpillars** (except the two or three that we saved to become butterflies); because it is she that I have listened to, when she **grumbled**, or **boasted**, or even sometimes when she said nothing. Because she is *my* rose."

And he went back to meet the fox.

"Goodbye," he said.

"Goodbye," said the fox. "And now here is my secret, a very simple secret: It is only with the heart that one can see rightly; what is **essential** is invisible to the eye."

"What is essential is invisible to the eye," the little prince repeated, so that he would be sure to remember.

"It is the time you have wasted for your rose that makes your rose so important."

"It is the time I have wasted for my rose—" said the little prince, so that he would be sure to remember.

"Men have forgotten this truth," said the fox. "But you must not forget it. You become responsible, forever, for what you have tamed. You are responsible for your rose. . . ."

"I am responsible for my rose," the little prince repeated, so that he would be sure to remember.

Glossary

abodes *(noun)* dwelling places; homes

boasted *(verb)* exaggerated; bragged

burrow *(noun)* hole in the ground made by a small animal and used for shelter

caterpillars *(noun)* worm-like larvae (immature form) of butterflies or moths

down yonder *(colloquial expression)* over there (in the distance)

essential *(adjective)* vital; important

extinct *(adjective)* extinguished; dead

glass globe *(noun)* spherical glass cover

grumbled *(verb)* complained

humble myself *(common usage)* lower or debase myself

monotonous *(adjective)* having little or no variation; therefore, tedious or boring

perplexed *(adjective)* confused; puzzled

rites *(noun)* ceremonies; rituals

reflections *(noun)* deliberations; contemplations; thoughts

thunderstruck *(adjective)* confounded; astounded; amazed

volcanoes *(noun)* vents or holes in the earth's crust through which molten rock is expelled

Comprehension Questions

1. Why is the little prince surprised and sad to find a garden filled with roses? How would his rose have reacted if she had seen the garden?

2. After he reflects on the value of his possessions, what does the little prince decide about himself? What is he doing when the fox appears?

3. Why does the little prince want the fox to play with him?

4. The fox asks the little prince if he is looking for chickens. What does the boy respond?

5. How does the fox define "tame"?

6. What does the fox want to know when he learns the little prince is from another planet? How does the fox react to the boy's answer?

7. Describe the fox's life. What is his routine?

8. Why does the fox want to be tamed? How will his life be affected? What will symbolize the relationship between the fox and the boy?

9. Why does the boy at first refuse to tame the fox? Why is this a mistake, in view of his explanation of what he is searching for? How does the fox convince the little prince?

10. What procedures does the fox recommend the little prince use to tame him? What is a rite? How does the fox explain the word?

11. How does the fox feel when the boy's departure draws near? How is this different from his attitude when they first met?

12. Explain the fox's statement that being tamed has done him good "because of the color of the wheat fields."

13. What does the little prince discover when he goes back to visit the roses in the garden?

14. What is the fox's secret?

15. What is the "truth" that men have forgotten?

Topics for Critical Analysis, Discussion, and Writing

1. Why did Saint Exupéry choose an animal to teach the little prince important values? Explain the fox's secret, "It is only with the heart that one can see rightly; what is essential is invisible to the eye."

2. Examine the fox's idea that "you become responsible, forever, for what you have tamed." How does this relate to family, social, business, or international relationships? What is the difference between "responsible for" and "responsible to"?

3. What is important about the way the fox teaches the little prince? Why doesn't the fox just tell the boy the secret and explain to him about responsibility? How would you teach a child to accept responsibility?

4. Write an essay about the value that you feel is the most important in

life. You might choose a value like honesty, integrity, courage, or modesty. Your thesis should explain why you hold this value dear. In your development, give examples showing this value being used in daily life. Conclude by explaining how this value has affected your behavior.

5. The fox chooses to be tamed. What is the importance of choice in our lives, and how does choice relate to responsibility? Give examples to support your statements.

Truman's Initiatives Still Affect Us

Robert J. Donovan

Robert J. Donovan is the author of Tumultuous Years: The Presidency of Harry S. Truman 1949–1953.

The author asks several questions in the first paragraph, but he does not expect the reader to answer them. These are rhetorical questions *used to arouse interest and to introduce the subject. Donovan's thesis, the first sentence in paragraph 2, is a general statement responding to all the questions asked in the first paragraph; specifics follow. If you use rhetorical questions, be sure to supply the answers. Also, avoid using them in the concluding paragraph of an essay.*

Donovan uses examples very cleverly in his article. Details closely follow one another in paragraphs 5, 6, and 7, but they are not just listed. Each fact is reported in a sentence that explains its importance. In paragraph 8, Donovan begins a long discussion of the whole body of evidence he has presented, and he carefully explains the relationship of each fact to his thesis.

What was the critical, underlying, formative condition of the **Truman Administration**? What, 10 years after his death, was important about Harry S. Truman? What did his Administration contribute to the future course of the United States? What made it possible for him to achieve the major **initiatives** that he undertook—initiatives that still affect our role in the world today?

The condition that made the Truman Administration a turning point in American history was the remarkable, broad, **bipartisan consensus** on foreign policy that emerged in the United States at the end of World War II. It favored a dominant U.S. role in the postwar world. It favored international moral, political and military leadership by America. It favored support of capitalist interests throughout the world—and preventing Soviet expansion.

It has been said that Truman was ineffective because he could not get his **Fair Deal** domestic reforms through Congress. However, many of the reforms had been legislated under Franklin D. Roosevelt, and, especially by his election victory in 1948, Truman was able to preserve those reforms against heavy Republican **assault**.

The more important fact is that, in nearly eight years of historic activity in foreign affairs, Truman never lost a single major piece of foreign-policy legislation in Congress, even while Republicans were in control in the 80th Congress of 1947–48.

The steps taken under Truman, with the support of the great consensus, are familiar. In **stark** contrast to the Senate rejection of U.S. membership in the League of Nations after World War I, the United States joined the United Nations in 1945. Following that, Truman extended a $3.75-billion loan **to stave off** economic collapse in Great Britain. Then came the **Truman Doctrine**—in effect, making "**containment**" the basis of U.S. policy. And, in the face of the Soviet blockade of Berlin, he preserved the American position in Germany with an **airlift.**

Thereafter, the Administration **fostered** the formation of an independent West German government and its alliance with the victorious Western powers. Then came the **landmark initiatives** of the Marshall Plan and the North Atlantic Treaty (the latter ending our historic resistance to permanent alliances outside the Western Hemisphere). Together, the purposes of the Marshall Plan and NATO were **to put Western Europe back on its feet after the ravages of war** while providing **a military shield** against possible attack from the East.

With almost **unanimous** support in favor of drawing the line against further communist **encroachment**, Truman committed U.S. forces to the war in Korea. Without a **murmur of disapproval** from Congress or the public, he also made the first **commitment** by the United States aimed at preventing a communist takeover of Vietnam. And he concluded an **enlightened, non-punitive treaty** with Japan, thereby bringing our World War II enemies into a constructive, friendly relationship with the United States.

What made the record possible was the prevailing consensus—the bipartisan foreign policy. It was not originated by Truman, nor was it imposed on him. In a small way, he had been part of it as a senator, for, although he came from a region that was heavily **isolationist between the wars**, he believed in **Woodrow Wilson's League of Nations policy**. When Truman entered the Senate in 1935, in time for the debates on neutrality and aid for the allies, he favored Roosevelt's resistance to the **Axis powers**. Had that not been so, Truman never would have been nominated for vice president. As a senator, he favored Roosevelt's war aims after Pearl Harbor, and **prominent** among those aims was the founding of the United Nations, America included.

Thus, Truman came naturally to the consensus that he was to lead after the war. In light of the **League of Nations fight** and Roosevelt's bitter struggles with the isolationists, the consensus that emerged in favor of a dominant U.S. role in the world after 1945 was a remarkable development.

There was, of course, the deep fear aroused in this country by Hitler, and later by Stalin. There was the "lesson of Munich," the conviction that isolationism and **appeasement** lead only to war. And there was Roosevelt's skill in winning ultimate acceptance of his war aims. Support for **unconditional surrender** probably helped build the consensus. There was also the **veritable earthquake in the GOP** in 1940 that **routed** the isolationists and produced the **nomination** of the internationalist-minded Wendell L. Willkie, the strong **press** support for the ideal of collective security and the fateful switch from isolationism to internationalism by Sen. Arthur H. Vandenberg (R–Mich.), who was to become the chairman of the Senate Foreign Relations Committee at a **crucial** time after the war.

There was the powerful influence of men like Gen. George C. Marshall and Dean Acheson, and Gen. Dwight D. Eisenhower and John Foster Dulles, who negotiated the Japanese peace treaty for Truman. The consensus brought together not only Republicans and Democrats, but civilians and military leaders, too.

Indeed, the Truman period was often filled with **raging controversy**. But, unlike the **prevailing** differences on domestic questions, Truman, in matters of foreign policy, found himself **aligned** with powerful groups in the banks, in the large law firms, in the universities, in the press, in organized labor, in Congress and in the civilian and military bureaucracies. It was this consensus that made his historic foreign policy possible—and that, to me at least, is the fundamental fact about the Truman presidency.

Glossary

airlift *(noun)* Airplanes "lifted" or carried food and supplies into West Berlin, which is separated from the rest of West Germany, when the Russians refused to let trucks or trains pass across the borders.

aligned *(verb)* in agreement with

a military shield *(term)* protected by armed forces. Western Europe is still safe-guarded by American and European troops.

appeasement *(noun)* policy of giving in to the demands of a threatening or hostile country to avoid war. Many historians believe that British Prime Minister Neville Chamberlain's policy of keeping the peace by giving in to Hitler's demands led to World War II.

assault *(noun)* attack

Axis powers *(war term)* countries that joined together against the United States and its allies in World War II: Germany, Fascist Italy, and Japan

bipartisan consensus *(political term)* Both major parties (Republican and Democratic) of the government agree unanimously (100 percent) on some issue.

commitment *(noun)* pledge; assurance; promise

"containment" *(noun, foreign policy term)* policy preventing further spread of Soviet power after World War II

crucial *(adjective)* decisive; critical; of supreme importance

encroachment *(noun)* act of trespassing or advancing beyond agreed limits. Often countries that want more territory take (or encroach upon) neighboring lands without permission, but without going to war.

enlightened, non-punitive treaty *(special term)* Commonly, a peace treaty punishes a country that loses a war by making it pay for the losses of the winner. Sometimes the victor takes over all or part of a conquered country. The treaty with the Japanese was designed to aid Japan's postwar recovery.

Fair Deal *(political term)* In 1948, Harry S. Truman campaigned for the presidency by promising a "fair deal for all," a broad program of social reforms. The Fair Deal was a continuation of Franklin D. Roosevelt's New Deal, which featured sweeping economic changes that benefited the average citizen.

fostered *(verb)* promoted; stimulated; encouraged; helped develop

initiatives *(noun)* introduction of new legislative matters

isolationist between the wars *(historical term)* Between World Wars I and II, the United States did not become widely involved in foreign affairs. Many people felt that social welfare, labor, racial discrimination, and economic problems in our own country should be solved first.

landmark initiative *(historical term)* piece of legislation that is a high point or turning point of a period or a historical period

League of Nations fight *(historical term)* the controversy in the Senate and among the general public over whether the United States should become a member of the League

murmur of disapproval *(idiom)* complaint made in a very low, indistinct voice

nomination *(noun)* the naming of a person to run for political office

press *(noun)* a collective term used for writers employed by newspapers, magazines, and journals

prevailing *(adjective)* widely existing

prominent *(adjective)* noticeable; important

raging controversy *(idiom)* violent or angry disagreement

routed *(verb)* completely defeated

stark *(adjective)* sharp; severe

to put Western Europe back on its feet after the ravages of war *(idiomatic expression)* to help Western Europe recover economically and physically from the destruction of World War II

to stave off *(idiom)* to hold off or put off. The $3.75 billion loan helped Britain avoid economic collapse.

Truman Administration *(political term)* Each President appoints cabinet members (executive officials) to help him govern during his term of office. The President, with the advice of his cabinet, sets policy for both internal and external affairs. The four-year term of office of each President is called his administration.

Truman Doctrine *(historical term)* specified that Turkey and Greece should be given money and other aid to help them resist communist takeover. In general, the Doctrine stated that the United States should assume the responsibility for helping any democratic country maintain its freedom.

unanimous *(adjective)* complete; 100 percent

unconditional surrender *(war term)* Truman insisted on absolute, complete surrender whereby the Japanese gave up all rights.

veritable earthquake in the G.O.P. *(figurative term)* This figure of speech refers to a great change in policies of the Republican Party (Grand Old Party).

Woodrow Wilson's League of Nations policy *(historical term)* After World War I, Wilson supported U.S. membership in an organization similar to the United Nations and tried to win Senate approval. The Senate was still heavily isolationist, and the United States never joined the League.

Comprehension Questions

1. What was the subject of the bipartisan consensus that made the Truman Administration a turning point in American history?
2. What were the three major points of U.S. foreign policy adopted by the Truman Administration after World War II?
3. Why was it unimportant that Truman could not get his domestic reform program, a "fair deal for everyone," passed by the Congress?
4. What was significant about Truman's foreign policy legislation?
5. List several of the steps taken under Truman that were supported by "the great consensus."
6. How did Truman feel about: (a) Woodrow Wilson's League of Nations

Policy? (b) Roosevelt's resistance to the Axis powers and his war aims after Pearl Harbor? (c) the founding of the United Nations?

7. What was the "lesson of Munich"?

8. What changes occurred in the United States in 1940 that affected the country's position on world affairs?

9. What civilian and military leaders had powerful influence on Truman?

10. What does the author conclude is the fundamental factor in the Truman presidency?

Topics for Critical Analysis, Discussion, and Writing

1. Donovan writes, "It has been said that Truman was ineffective because he could not get his Fair Deal domestic reforms through Congress." Yet, when you examine paragraphs 5, 6, and 7 of Donovan's essay, Truman's accomplishments in foreign policy were clearly enormous. Choose three of the examples given in the stated paragraphs and use them to support the following thesis:

Although President Truman was ineffective in domestic affairs, his foreign policies were the most important of any President's in the twentieth century.

2. Examine Truman's attitude toward Soviet expansion. Discuss specifics from the article to support your ideas.

3. Truman at first declined to run for Vice President in 1944 because he preferred to remain in the Senate. However, President Roosevelt (who was running for his fourth term of office) convinced Truman to accept the nomination. As Vice President, Truman was not included by Mr. Roosevelt in affairs of state, so when the latter died in 1945, Truman knew almost nothing about the great responsibilities and decisions required of the President. He had to learn on the job. How would you evaluate Truman's performance as a United States President? Illustrate your position with facts and details from Donovan's article.

4. Truman kept a sign on his desk that read, "The Buck Stops Here," meaning the final responsibility for any decision lay with the President. This sign was a criticism of people who always tried "to pass the buck" (the blame for their actions) to someone else. Based on the article and supplementary material in the text, do you believe President Truman acted responsibly during his term of office? Why or why not? Use examples from the article to support your position.

2

Classification: Everything in Its Proper Place

CATEGORIZING TO BRING ORDER TO DAILY LIFE

You keep the lawn mower in the garage, the sugar in the kitchen, your suits in the closet, and the toothpaste in the bathroom. Each of these items is a member of a larger group. For example, the lawn mower is one of many garden tools that you probably can't wait to use every weekend. Sugar is one of several foods that you always keep on hand for cooking. Other kinds of clothing—coats, jackets, blouses, shirts, or dresses—probably hang beside your suits in the closet. Toothpaste is only one of the personal hygiene products in your bathroom; others are soap, shampoo, and deodorant. Classification is so automatic that sometimes we forget we weren't born with the ability to sort things into smaller groups or to place individual items in their proper categories. However, all of us had to learn these principles in order to meet the demands and expectations of our families, in particular, and society, in general. We have learned that life is chaotic if things are not kept in their proper places.

But classification doesn't stop there. Businesses use it extensively. Records are kept alphabetically, numerically, or chronologically so that files and documents can be located easily. Work is assigned according to departments or divisions, such as research, manufacturing, or sales. Workers are grouped by training, ability, or experience. A hospital, for instance, might have its staff divided into three areas of responsibility: medical (doctors, nurses, and X-ray and laboratory personnel), administrative (business and office employees), and support (kitchen, laundry, and maintenance workers). Look in any telephone directory, a good example of alphabetical classification, and you will find many departments listed under city, state, and federal governments.

36

Telephone companies also publish a reverse directory, which lists the numbers in numerical order and follows each with the name of the subscriber.

Even recreation is categorized to appeal to individual tastes. Active persons play tennis, golf, handball, volleyball, baseball, or basketball. Those who prefer passive entertainment attend movies, plays, concerts, or ballets. For many people, it's not what they do, but where they go that is important. Nature lovers go to the mountains or the beach. Amusement park addicts visit theme parks featuring computerized and mechanized rides and activities. Animal lovers go to zoos, to wild animal parks, marine preserves, or even their local animal shelters to adopt pets. Even those who just stay home and read books have choices between fiction and nonfiction.

RESTRICTING A SUBJECT TO FOCUS ON A TOPIC

After a category is broken down into smaller and smaller groups and finally individual units by classification, a single unit may be further broken into parts so that one or more of them may be analyzed separately. This is called *division*. Classification and division are shown in Figure 2-1.

We began restricting by eliminating all but theater entertainment from our major category. Then we selected four major types of events that occur in theaters. Of the four, we narrowed our interest to one, plays, and listed two major kinds, comedy and tragedy. Under tragedy, we noted two well-known

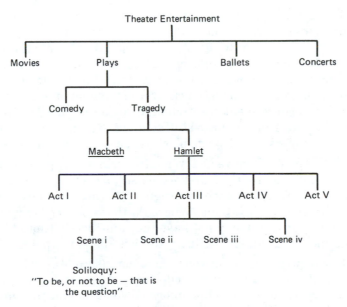

Figure 2-1

plays by Shakespeare, *Macbeth* and *Hamlet.* Of these two single units, we chose to analyze *Hamlet,* which we divided into acts. Next we chose Act III, and divided it into scenes. We then limited our scope to Scene i, and finally focused on Hamlet's famous soliloquy.

Use the technique illustrated in Figure 2-1 to categorize the following occupations (key words are printed in **boldface**): **jockey; physician; opera singer; banker; tennis star; dentist; dancer; stockbroker.** What do these types of work have in common? All are professional, have high earning potential, and are open to either sex. But how are they different? You probably noticed at once that the opera singer and the dancer are **entertainers,** and even though the jockey and the tennis player are **sports figures,** they still "perform" before fans and enthusiasts at horse races and tennis matches. What these four occupations have in common is that they require skill or talent to attract large numbers of the **public** who pay to watch the work being performed. The other four professions require different skills and talents, and all are based on **private** relationships with the patient or client. Physicians and dentists are **health care professionals** who seldom perform medical and dental procedures publicly. **Financial experts** who handle business related to banking and the stock market generally keep these transactions confidential. Whether they work in or out of the public eye, people in any of these eight occupations have an opportunity to make a lot of money.

Here are some problems that your class might try to solve by using classification:

1. Suppose you have just wrecked your car and have to buy another quickly. What car will you buy if you are (a) a student who runs a delivery service, (b) a real estate agent, (c) a popular young television star, or (d) a parent with four small children? Categorize various makes of automobiles according to appearance, proposed use, initial cost, and economy of operation. The student can use a van, truck, station wagon, or sedan for deliveries. But does a real estate agent want clients to ride in the back of an open pickup truck? Does a parent want to stuff four children into a tiny sports car? Does a television star want to drive to black-tie parties in a beat-up, second-hand van?

2. Suppose you have just won a free trip to any place in the world. Where will you go if you are (a) an archaeologist, (b) a skier, (c) an artist, (d) a marine biologist, or (e) an automobile designer? An archaeologist will be looking for ruins of earlier civilizations. Where do these occur? Why will a skier and a marine biologist probably not have the same destinations? Will an artist and an automobile designer be likely to visit the same place? Why or why not?

3. Suppose you are in your sophomore (second) year of college. You have taken all the necessary general education courses to meet graduation requirements. Your counselor has just informed you that you now have to decide on an academic major. Will your decision be based on (a) the current job market, (b)

the wishes of your parents, (c) the subjects that most interest you, or (d) the subjects in which you earned the highest grades? Won't your decision be somewhat affected by your or your family's financial situation? What if the subjects that most interest you offer no training for a career? What if the subjects in which you earned the highest grades were incredibly boring? What if your father and mother expect you to join the family business?

MOVING FROM GENERAL TO SPECIFIC

Most people think in short, disconnected fragments about a wide variety of other things while they are focusing on a main subject. For example, even though you believe you are paying close attention to the class discussion of a reading selection, if you actually write down everything that runs through your mind during a five-minute period, you may have a string of ideas (and notice that you don't always think in complete sentences) like this: *Is that answer to question 4 right? What time is it? Hungry. What did that student in the front row say? Starting to rain. Forgot my umbrella. Have to review one page in chemistry book before test next period. Good answer to question 5. Wish I had said that! Need something to eat. Shoes are killing me! Should have raised my hand to answer question 6. Have to get an apple before that test. Only two minutes of class left. Look at that rain! Copy the homework assignment off the board.*

Luckily, people can't read your mind and won't have to sort out your varied thoughts. However, people can and will read your essays, so the final draft of your paper must be carefully structured. You have already solved problems by using classification and division, often working from general to specific. Paragraph and essay development frequently follow this same pattern, with theoretical, abstract, or broad statements reinforced by discussion of clear, concrete examples. In Chapter 1, when we prepared to write about a national park we had visited, we automatically used classification during our prewriting activities to help us restrict the topic to one park, the Grand Canyon, and division to focus on one experience, the Bright Angel mule trip, which could be expanded with a discussion of supporting examples, facts, and illustrations.

Here is a paragraph that contains everything but a concluding sentence. All the other sentences are out of order. List the numbers of the sentences in the correct order beginning with the most general and concluding with the most specific. Then write the last sentence.

(1) My favorite restaurant is Suzanne's. (2) I love to eat out. (3) Everything at Suzanne's is delicious, but my favorite part of the meal is dessert. (4) Suzanne's specializes in elegant food. (5) The Blackout Cake is chocolate with fudge frosting and is served with whipped cream. (6) I always order the Blackout Cake.

1. _____
2. _____
3. _____
4. _____
5. _____
6. _____
7. _____
   _____

The answers are as follows: 1. (2); 2. (1); 3. (4); 4. (3); 5. (6); 6. (5).

LOGICAL ORDERING OF INFORMATION

Logical order results when you arrange information according to some system that can be easily understood by others. Be careful to group items of the same importance together; for example, don't include specific subgroups of Christianity, such as Catholicism and Protestantism, in a group of major religions that includes Buddhism, Islam, Judaism, Confucianism, and Hinduism. Use Christianity instead. In addition, be sure that you group only items of the same class together. Throw out those that don't belong. Using the principles you have learned, identify the incorrect member in each of the following groups and explain your choice:

1. automobile, truck, bus, motorcycle, bicycle, moped
2. football, baseball, soccer, swimming, tennis, volleyball

If you agree that the bicycle should be eliminated from group 1 because all the other vehicles have motors, and if you decide that swimming is the only sport that doesn't require a ball of some kind, you understand the concept.

You should also follow some consistent pattern for ordering your information in an essay. Work from largest to smallest, youngest to oldest, beginning to end, first to last, inexpensive to expensive, or most to least (exciting, interesting, successful, handsome, beautiful, affordable, or practical). Call attention to important details by enumerating (numbering or naming) them. Discuss three equally important people alphabetically to avoid seeming to favor one over the others. Analyze several very different friends, all of whom you like a great deal, by beginning with the one you have known the longest.

PREPARING A TOPIC OUTLINE

Finally, classification and division are the basics of outlining, which is essential in planning an in-class essay examination or the final draft of any other essay. If you have plenty of time, unstructured writing is a form of brainstorming that can help you shape ideas before you outline. You may even write several different practice versions of an essay while you are exploring a topic. When you are confident enough to tackle the final draft, select from your notes or drafts (or from memory if you are writing a timed essay examination) only the material that clearly relates to the topic and supports the thesis. Then prepare a *five-minute topic outline*. It can make the difference between a paper that is well-organized and developed and one that is unfocused and vague.

The topic outline is to the essay what the skeleton is to the body: bare bones providing structural definition. Except for the thesis, complete sentences are unnecessary. The idea is to prepare it *quickly,* especially if you are writing in class. Topic outlines follow this format:

Thesis:　(This complete sentence will be included in the first paragraph of your essay.)

　I. (major point)
　　A. (minor point)
　　B. (minor point)
　II. (major point)
　　A. (minor point)
　　B. (minor point)
　III. Conclusion: (may be a sentence fragment)

Outlines, like mathematical equations, must be balanced. If you have a I., you *must* have a II. If you have an A., you *must* have a B. Otherwise, combine the major point and the single minor point. You *can* have an outline that includes minor points under only one of the major points, but it is better to develop ideas equally. You may include as many major points as you wish although the model shows only two. You may also show only major points, if you have more than two, and omit minor points. Do not include numerals and letters from the outline in your essay (after all, you don't tack the architectural plans and drawings on the front door of your newly completed house, do you?).

Let's use the following procedure to plan an essay about a famous American movie star of the past, Marilyn Monroe:

1. List all the facts.
2. Identify a few basic categories under which to group them.
3. Choose one category.
4. Select one or more units to divide for detailed analysis.

First, we jot down everything we can remember about Miss Monroe: *movie star; posed for calendar pictures; blonde hair; needed constant attention*

as an adult; shapely figure; fair actress; married three times; beautiful; person-
ally insecure; sex symbol; committed suicide; unhappy childhood; drawn to
prominent men.

Second, we group these details under a few basic categories:

Appearance	Behavior/Personality	Career
blonde hair	needed constant attention	movie star
shapely figure	married three times	calendar pictures
beautiful	personally insecure	fair actress
	committed suicide	sex symbol
	unhappy childhood	
	drawn to prominent men	

Third, we try to imagine the kind of essay the facts in each column would support. Which category would be the most interesting to develop and discuss? The first, *Appearance,* contains too few facts to write more than a brief, general description. The third, *Career,* includes information about the kind of work Miss Monroe did before entering the film industry, about her acting ability, and about her public image. A paper on this subject could be expanded satisfactorily. The second, *Behavior/Personality,* presents a wealth of data about Miss Monroe that might explain her actions, and is probably the best choice.

Fourth, we select specific units we want to discuss. If only the facts about her unhappy childhood, her need for constant attention as an adult, her insecurity, and her suicide are examined, they are sufficient to show that she had emotional problems. Each fact can become a topic sentence for an expanded paragraph of discussion.

Now, *you* write the thesis and conclusion for our topic outline:

Thesis:

  I. Unhappy childhood
  II. Constant need for attention as an adult
  III. Personal insecurity
  IV. Committed suicide
  V. Conclusion

To summarize, classification and division allow the logical arrangement of anything according to some systematic method. Classification is also a technique used for writing expository prose in which ideas or facts must be ordered specially to prove a point. Before you begin to write the final draft of any essay, you must plan.

READINGS

What Your Body Language Says About You

Gerald Astor

When you talk to other people, do you always mean exactly what you say? Experts say no. Your face and body betray your words with expressions and gestures that you may produce quite unconsciously. For instance, an acquaintance may stand too close to you or place a hand on your arm while telling you a funny story. Even though you are laughing and enjoying the story, you may automatically move away from the other person because the closeness makes you feel uncomfortable. Your acquaintance may be confused, even angered, by your apparently mixed positive/negative response and abruptly walk away, leaving you wondering what happened.

In his article, Gerald Astor categorizes the various forms of nonverbal communication and explains their meanings. He uses the structure of the essay, instead of subtitles, to identify the body parts and their communicative functions. Each category is introduced by a topic sentence at the beginning of a paragraph.

"Your lips say, 'No, no, no,' but your eyes say, 'Yes, yes, yes'" is a line from an old popular song. It may sound somewhat **phony**, but the author was hinting at that kind of nonverbal communication known as body language. It can reflect a person's views more accurately than any words coming from his or her mouth.

Body language covers the infinite range of facial and body movements, including the **myriad** ways to smile, to walk, to manipulate your eyes, to move your hands and arms. We draw messages from body language, whether it's the "no" that a shake of the head conveys, the "I'm not interested" that a turning away of the head can suggest, or the "**Hey, I'm bad**" statement Richard Pryor and Gene Wilder expected their swaggers to make in *Stir Crazy*. Sometimes, the messages are conveyed through deliberate, conscious gestures; other times, our bodies talk without our even knowing. But conscious or not, our body language helps us **portray** a wide range of feelings, including boredom, amusement, impatience, fatigue, concentration, interest, puzzlement, and embarrassment.

Some of our body-language expressions are common idioms. To most people, for example, the thumb and forefinger forming a circle means "Everything's okay." A fist with the thumb pointing up is "Good luck" or "All systems go." Desmond Morris, a behavioral scientist and the author of *The Naked Ape* (McGraw-Hill), was among those who studied the interpretations of twenty specific gestures by people in Europe, North Africa, and the Middle East. He found similarities in understanding despite the geographic and cultural differences. (The most universally recognized signal was the thumb at the tip of the nose with the fingers spread!)

Body language becomes more complicated when we try to translate the movements, postures, and facial expressions that a person has little or no control over—the actions that spring from the dark well within us, our unconscious. These bits of body language are often **subtle**, may contradict our words, and frequently involve a series of actions.

The eyes are one of the most revealing instruments of body language. Keith, seventeen, from Montclair, New Jersey, learned the hard way about one message the eyes can convey. "I had a teacher who graded heavily on classroom discussion," Keith says. "He seemed to have a **weird** ability to know just when I didn't have the answers. I couldn't figure out how he could be so sharp. Then it dawned on me. Whenever I didn't know the answer, I would avoid looking at him. When I did know what to say, I always stared straight back at him. From that moment on, I taught myself to look him in the eye, whether I knew the work or not. That trick has saved me a lot of grief."

Many people, including some policemen, believe eye contact is a good test of honesty. If someone can't **look you dead in the eye**, then he or she is not playing straight, they insist. After many experiments, however, a number of experts have concluded that good liars can fake eye contact. (If you still believe that a chap **staring straight into your baby blues** will never lie to you, then someday, I'd like to interest you in a share of the Grand Canyon.)

Eye contact, though not a sure sign of honesty, is a clear way to show interest in another person. When a person looks at you and continues to do so, you know his attention is focused on you. When he turns his head away, his mind is probably elsewhere: you are no longer "**numero uno**." But there are exceptions. A shy person may have trouble making and maintaining eye contact, no matter how interested he is in the other person. And certain nationalities, such as the British and the Germans, are much less oriented to **eyeball-to-eyeball encounters** than, say, the French and the Arabs.

When the eyes act **in concert** with other parts of the face, communication becomes increasingly **explicit**. In a study in which psychologists A. Thayer and W. Schiff showed a series of facial diagrams to a panel of people, there was very strong agreement on the messages (the results of their study were published in the *American Journal of Psychology* in 1969). Pleasure widens the eyes and is usually accompanied by a smile. Thus, poker players who are dealt a good hand must learn to control their body language and develop a "**poker face**." The "drop dead" or "if looks could kill" expression is produced by wrinkling the eyebrows, narrowing the eyes, and turning down the corners of the mouth. Surprise sends the eyebrows skyward and widens the gaze. Despair **hoods** the eyes, makes the mouth droop, and often causes the entire body to slump.

Like the eyes, the smile is remarkably varied. The genuinely happy smile flashes both upper and lower teeth and is accompanied by open eyes and relaxed brows. In the **sheepish** smile—you've spilled your soda pop and that nice fellow offers his help—the corners the mouth are turned up, the eyebrows lifted. The **fiendish** smile consists of a wide grin and a **scrunching** of the eyebrows.

Hand movements are another area where there is common understanding of the action. Shake your fist, and everyone realizes that you're angry. Rub your palms together, and you're probably anticipating something good. Rub your palms and the backs of your hands, and you're probably just cold. Point, and you are signaling a direction. Point a finger at someone, and you're making an accusation.

Sometimes a person brings a hand up to his mouth while talking. That gesture could be an effort to stop others from hearing or an unconscious admission of doubt or that there's something being concealed. A hand at the throat may indicate some uncertainty about the words being spoken.

Politicians frequently use hand movements to hold the attention of an audience. Former President Gerald Ford, regarded as a **less than spellbinding orator**, was once counseled by advisers to add a number of gestures to punctuate a speech. He did so—but apparently unsuccessfully. A poll of those who listened revealed that one third agreed with Ford, one third disagreed, and one third were so distracted by his **gesticulations** that they didn't know what he had said. Artificial movements are the bad grammar of body language and confuse listeners (which is why some politicians and actors rely on experts to coach them in effective nonverbal communication).

One of the most clearly recognized expressions of body language is the handshake. (It is believed that originally a handshake was a way of showing a person that one came unarmed.) We draw information from the quality of the squeeze. A **flabby** grip suggests weakness or a lack of interest. Too much pressure signals a desire to dominate.

The position of the entire body is also important when interpreting nonverbal communication. "When I meet someone sitting with his legs or ankles crossed tightly and his arms folded over his chest, I feel that he's closed off from me and uninterested," says sixteen-year-old Julie, a Brooklyn high school senior. She has correctly interpreted a posture that translators of body language classify as "closed." If an individual feels relaxed, giving, and receptive, he's usually in an "open position": His arms are unclasped, and his legs apart.

Closed positions tend to discourage intruders. And as Marianne La

France and Clara Mayo, the authors of *Moving Bodies* (Wadsworth) note, anyone in this **posture** is also far less likely to be convincing in a discussion; listeners may feel he's not revealing as much as he should. It's important, though, to keep in mind that whether or not a person assumes a closed or open position may have a lot to do with upbringing. Women, for example, because of the female tradition of wearing skirts, have customarily been taught to assume a "ladylike" position and keep their legs together (though that may be changing with the growing acceptance of women wearing pants).

Of course, there are other communicative postures besides the closed and open positions. For example, resting the chin upon the hand—the posture of Rodin's sculpture "The Thinker"—is an accepted sign of **cogitation**. But, says Ellen, an eighteen-year-old from New York, "When a person rests his cheek on his hand, it can mean, 'I'm uninterested.'"

Posture—indeed, all of body language—is wrapped up in a person's self-image. People uncomfortable with their bodies may adopt a round-shouldered slouch and wear baggy clothes. People who are content with their self-image are more likely to stand straight and wear form-fitting apparel.

Body language can also serve as a kind of dialogue between two people. For example, if two people sit on a couch with their arms and legs in similar positions, it usually means they're in agreement. A man and a woman on the same couch who have adopted widely different ways of sitting and who are not looking at one another are probably out of touch with each other. A male and female sitting on a couch, facing each other, are announcing closeness. If one leans forward, that one is trying to get even closer. If the other is not interested in more involvement, he or she may lean back.

But once again, cultural differences play a role. Wendy, a high school junior from Scarsdale whose parents are Korean and who spent her first years of life in Korea, says, "I don't like showing signs of closeness in public. I feel uncomfortable greeting people at a party with a hug or kiss. I wasn't brought up that way." Those unaware of the cultural differences might mistakenly read her body language as a sign of **aloofness** or coldness.

Other mistakes are common when trying to translate body language. Says Kathy, a seventeen-year-old from New York, "When someone just spreads himself out, I can't tell whether he's terribly relaxed or just a **slob**." When an adolescent slouches in front of an adult, it may be a rebellious statement (parents are always demanding that one stand up straight), or it may be that the person is very much at ease.

But although you can never fully understand another's body language— or fully control your own—you can be aware that nonverbal **cues** are as important to communication as words. Increase your knowledge of body language, and you'll be a little less confused in a world of many different messages.

Glossary

aloofness *(noun)* distance; disinterest. An aloof person is reserved and cool with others and may be difficult to get to know.

cogitation *(noun)* deep thought

cues *(noun)* suggestions; hints

explicit *(adjective)* clear; definite; plain. Anyone can understand exactly what the speaker really means.

eyeball-to-eyeball encounters *(slang)* occasions when people have eye contact

fiendish *(adjective)* wicked; cruel; devilish

flabby *(adjective)* limp; soft; lacking firmness

gesticulations *(noun)* gestures with the hands and arms

"Hey, I'm bad" *(slang)* "I'm excellent"; "I'm wonderful." This expression means exactly the opposite of what it says. "Hey!" is an exclamation used to express mild anger (perhaps someone crowds in front of you in line), as a greeting ("Hey! How are you?"), or as an attention getter to preface some other remark.

hoods *(verb)* covers; hides. If a person has no hope, his or her eyes show no emotion or expression.

in concert *(adverbial phrase)* together

less than spellbinding orator *(descriptive expression)* dull or boring speaker. A spellbinder is so eloquent in word and gesture that the audience seems fascinated or enchanted, as if by magic.

look you dead in the eye *(slang)* look straight into your eyes

myriad *(adjective)* countless; innumerable; greatly varied

"numero uno" *(Spanish)* number one

phony *(adjective)* fake; not genuine; insincere

poker face *(colloquialism)* expressionless face. Emotions are completely hidden.

portray *(verb)* make a picture of; show; describe; represent

posture *(noun)* standing or sitting position of the body

scrunching *(verb)* pulling down or together

sheepish *(adjective)* embarrassed; awkwardly shy

slob *(colloquial noun)* sloppy, messy, or coarse person

staring straight into your baby blues *(slang)* staring into your eyes (which may or may not be a light shade of blue)

subtle *(adjective)*   indirect; not obvious; not easily detected

weird *(adjective)*   strange; odd; fantastic; bizarre

Comprehension Questions

1. What is body language?
2. Identify some facial and bodily movements that are found in body language. Explain what each means.
3. When does body language contradict spoken words?
4. What lesson did Keith learn about messages the eyes can convey? What trick did he develop?
5. Is it true that a person who won't look you in the eye is dishonest?
6. What do you know about a person who continues to look at you?
7. What is a poker face?
8. How can a person's eyes smile?
9. Identify three kinds of smiles that the author describes.
10. What do hand movements tell an observer about a person?
11. Why are artificial hand movements "the bad grammar of body language"?
12. What was the original significance of the handshake? What is its importance now?
13. Give several examples of the way body position and posture communicate attitude.
14. How can body language serve as a dialog between two people?
15. What problems in interpreting body language arise from cultural differences? What other misunderstandings occur?

Topics for Critical Analysis, Discussion, and Writing

1. Write an essay in which you classify and discuss at least three examples of body language commonly used in your country. Be sure to explain what each gesture means and ways that it can be interpreted by others. Your paper should have a clear thesis, and you should reach some conclusion.

2. Explain two or more misunderstandings that you have had in the United States because of differences in the meaning of body language here and in your country. How did you resolve the problems you experienced? What did you learn?

3. The author states that "good liars can fake eye contact." How important is it in our society to be a good liar? Here are some situations for you to evaluate:

(a) Your co-worker is nice, but terribly unattractive. She goes to a large department store and has a "complete makeover"—new hairdo, makeup, and clothes. It doesn't help. However, when she comes to the office the next day, you can see that she feels absolutely beautiful. She asks, "How do you like my new look?" How do you respond in words and actions?

(b) You have placed an advertisement in the newspaper to sell your car. You really need the money because you have already bought a new one. You know that although the brakes still work acceptably, they will soon need repair. What do you say and do when a prospective buyer says, "What is the condition of the brakes? I don't want to buy a car with poor brakes."

4. How can we become conscious of the kinds of body language we use? Can we succeed in relating these facial expressions, bodily gestures, or special positions to our verbal communication?

5. How can body language help or harm you in a romantic relationship?

6. Examine the author's use of classification in the article.

The Problems of the Cities

Robert F. Kennedy

The difficulties that Senator Kennedy identifies, in these excerpts from his statement before a Senate subcommittee examining the federal role in urban affairs, are found in some of the major cities in the United States but are certainly not unique to this country. Many populous cities around the world are experiencing severe environmental, economic, community, and racial problems that are destroying the quality of life of the inhabitants.

In the United States, a major challenge to city government is the rapid decay of some of the buildings, either because of the type of construction or because of abuse. Before World War II, many buildings (especially in the West) were made of wood, which is subject to damage by insects, fungus growths, and fires. In addition, many structures are desperately overcrowded, and they sim-

United States. Cong. Senate. Committee on Government Operations. *Federal Role in Urban Affairs: Hearings Before the Subcommittee on Executive Reorganization.* 89th Congress, 2nd session, 2 vols. Washington: GPO, 1966.

ply wear out. In some cities, it is routine practice for demolition companies to inspect large buildings during construction so that they know where the major structural supports are located when they have to tear down the building years later. Finally, cities in the United States are always in the process of redevelopment, and the federal government makes funds available to help cities rebuild areas that have become dangerous liabilities. Private investors also become involved in both commercial and residential projects. An example of private redevelopment is the exclusive Georgetown area of Washington, D.C. It was once a filthy slum of row houses. Now only the historic shells of the original buildings remain. All the interiors are new or rebuilt.

Other problems that Kennedy discusses are also as relevant today as they were in 1966. Environmental pollution still plagues us. Unemployment continues to be a major concern. Public transportation in many large cities is still inadequate. Although the Civil Rights Movement of the 1960s did much to lessen racial discrimination, minorities are only beginning to be accepted into major corporate management structures, an important step toward economic equality. Our sense of community has been further eroded by the loss of trust so well described in Bob Greene's article "The Land of the Lock" in chapter 1.

As you read the selection, notice how neatly Kennedy makes classification work for him to order the material so that it is easy to follow. The evidence builds overwhelmingly to justify his moving conclusion.

To say that the city is a central problem of American life is simply to know that increasingly the cities are American life; just as **urban** living is becoming the condition of man across the world. Everywhere men and women crowd into cities in search of employment, a decent living, the company of their fellows, and the excitement and stimulation of urban life.

Within a very few years, 80 percent of all Americans will live in cities—the great majority of them in concentrations like those which stretch from Boston to Washington, and outward from Chicago and Los Angeles and San Francisco and St. Louis. The cities are the nerve system of economic life for the entire Nation, and for much of the world.

And each of our cities is now the seat of nearly all the problems of American life: poverty and race hatred, **stunted** education and saddened lives, and the other ills of the new urban Nation—congestion and filth, danger and purposelessness—which afflict all but the very rich and the very lucky. . . .

. . . The city is not just housing and stores. It is not just education and employment, parks and theaters, banks and shops. It is a place where men should be able to live in **dignity** and security and **harmony**, where the great achievements of modern civilization and the ageless pleasures afforded by natural beauty should be available to all.

If this is what we want—and this is what we must want if men are to be free for that **"pursuit of happiness"** which was the earliest promise of the American Nation—we will need more than poverty programs, housing programs, and employment programs, although we will need all of these. We will need an outpouring of imagination, **ingenuity,** discipline, and hard work unmatched since the first adventurers set out to conquer the wilderness. For the problem is the largest we have ever known. And we confront an urban wilderness more **formidable** and resistant and in some ways more frightening than the wilderness faced by the pilgrims or the pioneers. . . .

One great problem is sheer growth—growth which crowds people into slums, thrusts suburbs out over the countryside, burdens to the breaking point all our old ways of thought and action—our systems of transport and water supply and education, and our means of raising money to finance these **vital** services.

A second is destruction of the physical environment, **stripping** people of contact with sun and fresh air, clean rivers, grass and trees—condemning them to a life among stone and concrete, **neon lights** and an endless flow of automobiles. This happens not only in the central city, but in the very suburbs where people once fled to find nature. "There is no police so effective," said **Emerson**, "as a good hill and a wide pasture . . . where the boys . . . can dispose of their **superfluous** strength and spirits." We cannot restore the pastures; but we must provide a chance to enjoy nature, a chance for recreation, for pleasure and for some restoration of that essential dimension of human existence which flows only from man's contact with the natural world around him.

A third is the increasing difficulty of transportation—adding concealed, unpaid hours to the workweek; removing men from the social and cultural **amenities** that are the heart of the city; sending destructive swarms of automobiles across the city, leaving behind them a band of concrete and a poisoned atmosphere. And sometimes—as in **Watts**—our surrender to the automobile has so crippled public transport that thousands literally cannot afford to go to work elsewhere in the city.

A fourth destructive force is the concentrated poverty and racial tension of the urban **ghetto**—a problem so **vast** that the **barest** recital of its **symptoms** is profoundly shocking:

> **Segregation** is becoming the governing rule: Washington is only the most prominent example of a city which has become overwhelmingly Negro as whites move to the suburbs; many other cities are moving along the same road—for example, Chicago, which, if present trends continue, will be over 50 percent Negro by 1975. The ghettoes of Harlem and Southside and Watts are cities in themselves, areas of as much as 350,000 people.
>
> Poverty and unemployment are **endemic**: from one-third to one-half of the families in these areas live in poverty; in some, male unemployment may be as high as 40 percent; unemployment of Negro youths nationally is over 25 percent.
>
> Welfare and dependency are **pervasive**: one-fourth of the children

in these ghettoes, as in Harlem, may receive Federal Aid to Dependent Children; in New York City, ADC alone costs over $20 million a month; in our five largest cities, the ADC bill is over $500 million a year.

Housing is overcrowded, unhealthy, and **dilapidated**: the last housing **census** found 43 percent of urban Negro housing to be substandard; in these ghettoes, over 10,000 children may be injured or infected by rat bites every year.

Education is segregated, unequal, and inadequate: the high school dropout rate averages nearly 70 percent; there are academic high schools in which less than 3 percent of the entering students will graduate with an academic diploma.

Health is poor and care inadequate: infant **mortality** in the ghettoes is more than twice the rate outside; **mental retardation** among Negroes caused by inadequate prenatal care is more than seven times the white rate; one-half of all babies born in Manhattan last year will have had no **prenatal care** at all; deaths from diseases like tuberculosis, influenza, and pneumonia are two to three times as common as elsewhere.

Fifth is both cause and consequence of all the rest. It is the destruction of the sense, and often the fact, of community, of human dialog, the thousand invisible strands of common experience and purpose, affection and respect which tie men to their fellows. Community is expressed in such words as neighborhood, civic pride, friendship. It provides the life-sustaining force of human warmth and security, a sense of one's own human significance in the accepted association and companionship of others. . . .

. . . Community demands a place where people can see and know each other, where children can play and adults work together and join in the pleasures and responsibilities of the place where they live. The whole history of the human race, until today, has been the history of community. Yet, this is disappearing, and disappearing at a time when its sustaining strength is badly needed. For other values which once gave strength for the daily battle of life are also being eroded.

The widening gap between the experience of the generations in a rapidly changing world has weakened the ties of family; children grow up in a world of experience and culture their parents never knew.

The world beyond the neighborhood has become more impersonal and abstract. Industry and great cities, conflicts between nations and the conquests of science move **relentlessly** forward, seemingly beyond the reach of individual control or even understanding. . . .

But of all our problems, the most immediate and pressing, the one which threatens to **paralyze** our very capacity to act, to **obliterate** our vision of the future, is the plight of the Negro of the center city. For this **plight**—and the riots which are its product and symptom—threaten to divide Americans for generations to come; to add to the ever-present difficulties of race and class the bitter **legacy** of violence and destruction and fear. . . .

It is therefore of the utmost importance that these hearings go beyond the temporary measures thus far adopted to deal with riots—beyond the first hoses and the **billy clubs**; and beyond even sprinklers on fire hydrants and new swimming pools as well. These hearings must start us along the road toward solutions to the underlying conditions which afflict our cities, so that they may become the places of fulfillment and ease, comfort and joy, the communities they were meant to be.

Glossary

amenities *(noun)*   agreeable features or circumstances

barest *(adjective)*   plainest; least developed

billy clubs *(noun)*   short clubs (sometimes called night sticks) carried by policemen

census *(noun)*   official, periodic count of population, age, sex, race, economic conditions, etc.

dignity *(noun)*   self-respect; proper pride

dilapidated *(adjective)*   broken down; in a terrible state of disrepair

Emerson *(noun)*   Ralph Waldo Emerson (1803–82), American essayist and poet

endemic *(adjective)*   native to the population

formidable *(adjective)*   causing fear or dread

ghetto *(noun; ghettoes, pl.)*   section of a city in which many members of a national or racial group live together

harmony *(noun)*   peace and friendship; agreement in ideas, interests, and feelings

ingenuity *(noun)*   cleverness; originality

legacy *(noun)*   anything (regardless of value) handed down from an ancestor

mental retardation *(noun)*   intellectual slowness; lowered intelligence

mortality *(noun)*   death

neon lights *(noun)*   lighted signs made of tubes shaped to form designs or letters. Although neon gas produces only the red color (mercury vapor produces blue and green), all signs of this type are called "neon."

obliterate *(verb)*   blot out; erase

paralyze *(verb)*   render helpless; cause powerlessness

pervasive *(noun)*   prevalent throughout a particular group

plight *(noun)* condition; predicament; difficulty

prenatal care *(medical term)* medical care of the mother and fetus during the mother's pregnancy

"pursuit of happiness" *(historical term)* search for happiness. The Declaration of Independence (July 4, 1776) states: "We hold these truths to be self-evident, that all men are created equal, that they are endowed by their Creator with certain inalienable Rights, that among these are Life, Liberty, and the Pursuit of Happiness."

relentlessly *(adverb)* persistently; without pausing or slowing

segregation *(noun)* division or separation into groups according to race

stripping *(verb)* depriving

stunted *(adjective)* shortened; checked; slowed

superfluous *(adjective)* excess; surplus

symptoms *(noun)* signs

urban *(adjective)* characteristic of the city (as opposed to the country)

vast *(adjective)* widespread; great

vital *(adjective)* necessary for life

Watts *(noun)* section of Los Angeles that is heavily populated by black people

Comprehension Questions

1. How does Kennedy define a city, if it is not just houses, stores, schools, businesses, parks, and theaters?

2. What is the significance of the term "pursuit of happiness"?

3. What will we need besides poverty, housing, and unemployment programs to attain the kind of society we want?

4. What kinds of problems are caused by sheer growth?

5. Identify several ways that cities are destroying the physical environment.

6. What kinds of transportation problems are found in the cities?

7. List the six major difficulties faced by those who live in the urban ghetto.

8. Explain Kennedy's term "the sense of community."

9. Of all the cities' problems, which is the most immediate and pressing? Why?

10. In his final paragraph, how does Kennedy suggest the nation proceed to correct all the problems he has identified?

Topics for Critical Analysis, Discussion, and Writing

1. Choose one of the major problems identified by Kennedy that you feel is severe today in any city in the world. State your thesis, then give substantial evidence (facts, figures, details) to show the seriousness of the problem. Finally, offer your solution.

2. Kennedy offers fact after fact and detail after detail to support his statements, but his speech is not boring. What elements are included to provide interest?

3. Kennedy was born into a wealthy family, but from childhood he was taught that it was his duty and responsibility to help the poor and underprivileged. Do you think this speech reflects his upbringing? Why or why not?

4. What do you think are the three most important social problems today (in the United States or your own country)? Write down all the facts you can find about each problem; then organize a short paper by classifying your information for the most effective presentation. Use Kennedy's essay as a model. Notice his inclusion of adjectives to strengthen his evidence. Be sure that you begin with a clear thesis and end with a conclusion that gives possible solutions.

5. Write about the importance of one or more of the following human values: dignity and a sense of self-worth, a sense of community, respect and responsibility for others, a sense of security, friendship, or civic pride. What causes people to have and respect these values? What happens to individuals and communities when people lose them?

At the Mercy of Mankind: A Lament for the Whales

George F. Will

George F. Will is a columnist who writes on domestic and international affairs. In this article, he uses classification to point out two compelling reasons for stopping whaling. First, whales are on the endangered species list, which means that they have nearly disappeared from the oceans. Second, since products that formerly required whale oil can all be made with other materials now, and since there is little demand for whale meat, Will and many conservationists believe that no more of the mammals should be killed.

Whales have inhabited the seas for millions of years. Their brains are many times larger than ours. Some scientists believe that as the brain size increases, the ability to think and reason also is increased, although no exact data have been produced to show exactly how whales think. Researchers are very interested in the way these huge mammals respond to human contact. Anyone who has ever watched a killer whale in an aquarium show can not envision the creature killing anything. These performers seem to have a natural instinct for showmanship; they love affection and applause. Attempts have been made to teach dolphins (also members of the cetacean order of mammals) to speak or otherwise communicate interactively with humans, but so far the dolphins that are able to reproduce simple sounds of human speech are not able to relate them to meaning. Still scientists keep trying, hoping to learn some of their secrets before these mammals disappear from the seas.

Whales, which have quite enough problems, have now got caught in the angry waters of U.S.–Japan relations. But the persons protesting on the whales' behalf during last week's visit by Japan's prime minister have a grand cause.

The campaign to save the whales is a rare and refreshing example of intelligence in the service of something other than self-interest. That is one reason why it has progressed tremendously. Last summer, the member nations of the International Whaling Commission, responding primarily to appeals to **conscience** from groups like Greenpeace and the Animal Welfare Institute, voted 25–7 for a five-year **moratorium** on commercial whaling, beginning in late 1985. (**Subsistence whaling** by Eskimos and other natives around the Arctic Sea would continue.) But the three nations that kill 90% of the whales—the Soviet Union, Norway and Japan—may not **comply**.

Cheap substitutes now exist for all whale products, and no nation's whaling industry could exist **unsubsidized**. Japan kills the most whales and buys almost all the oil and meat from other nations' whaling. Japan's compliance with the moratorium probably would end commercial whaling. Whale meat provides less than 1% of Japan's protein. Japan's whaling industry has shrunk from five **fleets** to one, but several thousand jobs are involved.

The International Whaling Commission is **toothless**, but U.S. law is not. Nations in defiance of the commission's rulings can be denied fishing rights within the U.S. 200-mile zone, and imports of their fish can be stopped. The value to Japan of the fishing and imports is at least 10 times the value of Japan's whaling industry. Congress favors **sanctions** if commercial whaling continues in 1986.

Japan's policy may seem another instance of that nation's **bloody-mindedness**, and of **Oriental** concern with **saving face**. But the disapproval of Western nations, and especially the United States, strikes Japan as **Occidental hypocrisy**. In the 1830s and 1840s American whalers depleted stocks in the seas around Japan. When **Commodore Perry's** fleet arrived in Japan in 1853, he was seeking supply stations for American whalers. Japan notes that Americans became **fastidious** about whaling only when whale products were no longer needed for lamp oil and margarine.

But such **point-scoring** misses the point—two points, in fact. The campaign against whaling has two **distinguishable motives**, **conservation** and **humanitarianism**.

More than 300,000 whales have been killed in the decade since the United Nations called for a moratorium. Every species of whale except the small Minke is endangered. It may be too late to save the magnificent blue whale. (They can exceed 100 feet in length; a baby can gain 200 pounds a day.) Whaling commission **quotas** have been cut from around 50,000 in the early 1970s to 12,365 in 1983. Whaling is a dying industry; the question is whether it will be **extinct** before some species are.

Humanitarian concerns include, but go beyond, the refusal of Japan and others to abandon "cold" **harpoons** which, lacking explosives, cause a prolonged death agony. Japan opposes explosive harpoons because they damage some of the meat.

It probably is virtually impossible to kill humanely a creature that large. But even if the problem of pain could be solved, this problem would remain: There is something **unseemly,** something **subversive** of our own dignity, about killing such **splendid** creatures.

Whether whales, with their complex brains, really are, as some scientists say, "our **neurological** relations" is less important than this: Whales have individual personalities, complex social behavior, and remarkable memories and capacities for communication.

As I sit with pen poised over paper, I am struck by the oddness of cataloging reasons for abandoning the killing—the cruel and utterly unnecessary killing—of such mysterious creatures, about which we have so much to learn. It is possible, and not exactly wrong, to give practical reasons why saving the whales would be useful. But there are times, and this is one, for rising above utilitarianism.

It is important to say that life is enhanced **aesthetically** by the knowledge that these sociable creatures are swimming—and singing—on the surface of the sea, and in the sunless depths below.

Furthermore, mankind has **dominion** over the Earth, but **mankind's unsteady, serpentine path toward finer sentiments** can be measured, in part, by **evolving** standards of what constitutes civilized dominion over lower animals.

Surely it involves a **conviction**, more **intuitive** than reasoned, that Creation, and we as the responsible portion of it, are diminished by **wanton** behavior toward creatures that so stunningly exemplify the mysteriousness of the natural.

Glossary

aesthetically *(adverb)* according to the principles of aesthetics, which are based on a love of beauty

bloody-mindedness *(noun)* fierce and evil disposition; barbaric nature

Commodore Perry *(noun)* Matthew Calbraith Perry (1794–1858), the United States naval officer who persuaded Japan to open trade with American merchant ships in 1854

comply *(verb)* obey

conscience *(noun)* knowledge of right and wrong

conservation *(noun)* preservation or protection from loss, decay, or injury

conviction *(noun)* firm belief

distinguishable motives *(common usage)* motives that may be easily perceived or separated from all others

dominion *(noun)* the power or right of controlling; authority

evolving *(adjective)* gradually developing

extinct *(adjective)* extinguished; at an end

fastidious *(adjective)* very critical; oversensitive

fleets *(noun)* a number of ships that act together under a single command

harpoons *(noun)* spears, with lines attached to them, that are used to strike and kill whales. The original harpoons, like javelins, were thrown by seamen who then tied the line to the ship so the whale could not escape. New harpoons have an explosive charge that kills the whale faster.

humanitarianism *(noun)* the belief in promoting the welfare of humanity by showing kindness, mercy, and sympathy to all creatures

hypocrisy *(noun)* pretense of having beliefs or principles that one does not really have

intuitive *(adjective)* known or learned without the conscious use of reasoning; almost instinctively perceived or understood

mankind's unsteady, serpentine path toward finer sentiments *(figurative expression)* mankind's unsure, crooked path toward high ideals and principles

moratorium *(noun)* authorized delay or stopping of a specific activity

neurological *(adjective; medical term)* relating to the nervous system of the body

Occidental *(adjective)* Western peoples and culture (as opposed to Oriental, describing peoples of the East)

point-scoring *(special term)* identifying the faults of the opposition

quotas *(noun)* assigned shares allowed to various nations

saving face *(idiom)* avoiding embarrassment and, thereby, loss of respect

splendid *(adjective)* grand; superb; magnificent

subsistence whaling *(special term)* Eskimos and other small groups that depend on whale meat to keep from starving would be allowed to continue hunting and killing whales for food. These peoples use all parts of the whale; nothing is wasted.

subversive *(adjective)* destructive; ruinous

toothless *(adjective; figurative expression)* powerless to impose penalties

unseemly *(adjective)* improper

unsubsidized *(adjective)* not financially supported by the government

wanton *(adjective)* deliberately malicious; unjustifiably cruel

Comprehension Questions

1. Why does Will think the campaign to save the whales has progressed so well?

2. How long is the moratorium on commercial whaling supposed to last? Who set it? Did all countries agree to it?

3. What is subsistence whaling? What provisions are made for it in the moratorium?

4. Why do some nations subsidize their whaling industries?

5. What would end commercial whaling?

6. What are the powers of the International Whaling Commission? What can individual nations do to force other countries to comply with the moratorium?

7. What is the nature of the disagreement on whaling between the United States and Japan?

8. The author categorizes "two distinguishable motives" for ending whaling. What are they, and what facts and figures are used as supporting evidence?

9. Does Will think it is important that whales are "our neurological relations"? Why or why not?

10. Will says he is "struck by the oddness of cataloging reasons for abandoning the killing." What does he mean?

11. Does Will think humans always understand their motives? How do attitudes evolve? What is "civilized dominion"? How does human treatment of lower animals reflect on humanity itself?

Topics for Critical Analysis, Discussion, and Writing

1. "There is no free lunch," an old saying in the United States, means that people should not expect to get something for nothing. However, we have been getting many things free throughout the history of humanity. We take as many fish as we want from the ocean, as many minerals as we can find from the earth, all the water we can use from the streams, and all the air we can breathe from the atmosphere. What we give back is not very pleasant. We bury our garbage in the ground and pipe our sewage out to sea. We fill the air with fumes and smoke from factories and automobiles. Many scientists believe that we are poisoning our environment to such an extent that humans may one day be added to the list of endangered species. Do you believe we humans can change our ways? How does the fate of the whale relate to our own destiny? Will saving the whale make any difference?

2. Choose another student in the classroom to work with you on the following project: You are both foreign service diplomats. One of you represents the United States, and the other Japan. You must negotiate differences between your two countries on the issue of whaling. Discuss the problem as thoroughly as you can. Then each of you should write a short paper in which you use classification to present your position. After you have finished, exchange papers and discuss their content.

3. How can you explain "humanitarianism" as Will uses it in relation to the whale and the whaling industry?

4. Write an essay in which you defend or attack the whaling industry.

A Word to Presidential Aspirants:
The Rose Garden Has Its Thorns

William Fitzgibbon

Classification is commonly used by newspaper and magazine writers to draw attention to their material and make it easy to read. Often sections are emphasized or highlighted by using enumeration, as William Fitzgibbon has done in his article.

   The thorns that Fitzgibbon writes about are really the disadvantages (and they are countless) of being President of the United States. Even so, many politicians aspire to the presidency because it is the highest office in the nation, it affirms their personal popularity, and it is evidence of the public's approval of their party's stand on current issues. Some candidates are so eager to be elected that they announce their intention to run for the office up to two years in advance of the election. Perhaps Fitzgibbon's article should be required reading for anyone who wants the job.

It is said that becoming President of the United States is the dream of every patriotic American youngster. Perhaps so. Certainly it is the **cherished** dream of many of the nation's more ambitious politicians. All those who seek the presidency know that in order to win an election, sacrifices must be made, debts **incurred**, other dreams **deferred**.

And yet the **testimony** of many of the men who have **sought** and won that highest of offices tends to characterize the job as being more of a burden than a blessing. If there are any among you who hope one day to reside in the White House, perhaps after reading the following comments from former presidents, your ambition will have been **tempered**, your dreams **chastened**.

George Washington: "My movements to the chair of government will be accompanied by feelings not unlike those of a **culprit** who is going to the place of his execution."

John Adams: "Had I been chosen President again, I am certain I could not have lived another year."

Thomas Jefferson: "To me (the presidency) brings nothing but increasing **drudgery** and daily loss of friends."

"Five weeks more will relieve me from a drudgery to which I am no longer equal."

John Quincy Adams: "I can scarcely conceive a more **harassing**, **wearying**, teasing condition of existence (than occupying the presidency). It literally **renders** life **burdensome**. What retirement will be I cannot realize, but have formed no favorable **anticipation**. It cannot be worse than this **perpetual** motion and **crazing** cares. The weight grows heavier from day to day."

"The four most miserable years of my life were my four years in the presidency."

Andrew Jackson: "I can with truth say mine is a situation of **dignified** slavery."

James K. Polk: "In truth, though I occupy a very high position, I am the hardest working man in this country."

"No President who performs his duty faithfully and conscientiously can have any leisure."

Zachary Taylor: "The appointing power vested in the President imposes delicate and **onerous** duties."

James Buchanan: "When I parted from President Lincoln, on introducing him to the Executive Mansion, according to custom, I said to him: 'If you are as happy, my dear sir, on entering this house as I am in leaving it and returning home, you are the happiest man in this country!' I was then thinking of the comforts and **tranquility** of home, as contrasted with the troubles, **perplexities** and difficulties inseparable from the presidential office."

Abraham Lincoln: "From my boyhood up, my ambition was to be President. I am President of one part of this divided country at least, but look at me! I wish I had never been born! It is a **white elephant** on my hands, and hard to manage. With a fire in my front and rear, having to contend with the jealousies of the military commanders and not getting that cordial cooperation and support from Congress which could reasonably be expected; with an active and **formidable** enemy in the field threatening the very lifeblood of the government, my position is anything but a bed of roses."

"I hope that I may never have another four years of such anxiety, **tribulation** and abuse."

Rutherford B. Hayes: "The strain is hard to bear. It grows harder as time passes."

"Human nature cannot stand this too long."

"Nobody ever left the presidency with less regret, less disappointment, fewer **heartburnings** or more general content with the results of his term (in his own heart, I mean) than I do."

"I am glad to be a freedman."

James A. Garfield: "My God! What is there in this place that a man should ever want to get in it?"

Grover Cleveland: "The office of President has not, to me personally, a single **allurement**."

"I believe I shall buy or rent a house near here where I can go and be away from this cursed constant **grind**."

"I do not want the office. It involves a responsibility beyond human strength to a man who brings conscience to the discharge of his duties."

Benjamin Harrison: "It is a rare piece of good fortune during the early months of an administration if the President gets one wholly uninterrupted hour at his desk each day. His time is so broken into bits that he is often driven to late night work, when preparing a message or other paper requiring unbroken attention."

William McKinley: "I have had enough of it (the presidency). Heaven knows! I have had all the honor there is in the place, and have responsibilities enough to kill any man."

William Howard Taft: "One trouble is no sooner over in this office than another arises."

"I'll be damned if I am not getting tired of this. It seems to be the profession of a President simply to hear other people talk."

"I'm glad to be going—this is the loneliest place in the world."

Woodrow Wilson: "The office of President requires the constitution of an athlete, the patience of a mother, the endurance of an early Christian."

"The amount of work a President is supposed to do is preposterous."

"I never dreamed such loneliness and **desolation** of heart possible. . . . The very **magnitude** and **fatefulness** of the task I am every day to face dominates me."

Warren G. Harding: "God, what a job!"

"I knew this job would be too much for me."

Calvin Coolidge: "The duties of the presidency are extremely heavy."

Herbert C. Hoover: "Many years ago I concluded that a few **hair shirts** were part of the mental wardrobe of every man. The President differs only from other men in that he has a more extensive wardrobe."

Franklin D. Roosevelt: "In Washington, as you know, the working day of a President in these days averages 15 hours. Even when I go to Hyde Park or to Warm Springs, the White House office, the callers, and the telephones all follow me."

Harry S. Truman: "To be President of the United States is to be lonely, very lonely, at times of great decisions."

"There is no exaltation in the office of the President—sorrow is the proper word."

"Within the first few months I discovered that being a President is like riding a tiger. A man has to keep on riding or be swallowed."

Dwight D. Eisenhower: "I would say that the presidency is probably the most **taxing** job, as far as tiring of the mind and spirit."

"The old saying is true, 'A President never escapes from his office.'"

John F. Kennedy: "When I ran for the presidency, I knew that this country faced serious challenges, but I could not realize—nor could any man realize who does not bear the burdens of this office—how heavy and constant would be those burdens."

Lyndon B. Johnson: ". . . Then at 8 A.M. when I am trying to read a report from a general, all the tourists are going by right under your bed. And when you are trying to take a nap, Ladybird is in the next room with 80 ladies talking about the daffodils on Pennsylvania Avenue."

Glossary

allurement *(noun)* fascination; charm; temptation; enticement

anticipation *(noun)* expectation

burdensome *(adjective)* heavy; hard to bear

chastened *(verb)* corrected; subdued; refined

cherished *(adjective)* held very dear or valuable

crazing *(adjective; not common usage)* crushing; extremely heavy

culprit *(noun)* guilty person

deferred *(verb)* postponed or delayed

desolation *(noun)* destruction or expulsion of inhabitants; devastation; lonely grief; misery. "Desolation of heart" refers to Mr. Wilson's loneliness and depression after the death of his wife in 1914. He had been very dependent upon her companionship.

dignified *(adjective)* honorable; noble

drudgery *(noun)* hard or unpleasant work

fatefulness *(noun)* having significant consequences

formidable *(adjective)* strong and fearsome; to be dreaded

grind *(noun)* laborious work. (Sometimes a person who works very hard and never has any recreation is called a *grind*.)

hair shirts *(noun)* shirts made of harsh hair that is worn next to the skin. Religious persons used to wear hair shirts to inflict punishment on themselves for committing sins. Today the term symbolizes self-punishment. Mr. Hoover means that the president punishes himself and suffers more than the average man.

harassing *(adjective)* troubling; disturbing; tormenting

heartburnings *(noun; not common usage)* causes for discontent or jealousy. (This is not the heartburn that is caused by indigestion.)

incurred *(verb)* acquired or brought about by one's own action

magnitude *(noun)* size; extent; importance

onerous *(adjective)* burdensome; laborious; oppressive

perpetual *(adjective)* continuing indefinitely; lasting forever

perplexities *(noun)* complications; difficulties

renders *(verb)* causes to be or to become

sought *(verb; past tense of* seek*)* tried to obtain

tempered *(verb)* changed or modified, often after considering new information. (**Tempered** [adjective] *is* frequently used to describe a person's disposition; for example, a bad-tempered person is one who is unpleasant.)

testimony *(noun)*   statement or declaration of a witness, given under oath, in support of a fact or statement (usually in a court of law); proof

tranquility *(noun)*   quietness; peacefulness; calmness

tribulation *(noun)*   severe trial or trouble

wearying *(adjective)*   tiring

white elephant *(noun, idiom)*   object no longer desired by its owner. A white elephant may become burdensome or costly.

Comprehension Questions

1. Does Fitzgibbon use enumeration (classification) to
   a. restrict the topic,
   b. focus on a subject, or
   c. order the information used for development?
2. If all American youngsters who dream of becoming President read Fitzgibbon's article, what might happen to their ambitions? Why?
3. How did the first President, George Washington, feel about the job?
4. Why did John Quincy Adams say that his four years as President were the most miserable of his life?
5. What did Andrew Jackson mean by the term "dignified slavery"?
6. Why, according to James K. Polk, could a President have no leisure?
7. When did Abraham Lincoln decide to become President? What were his problems as Chief Executive?
8. Why did Grover Cleveland say that he did not want the office?
9. What was Benjamin Harrison's major complaint?
10. What was the profession of the President, according to William Howard Taft?
11. What did Woodrow Wilson feel the office of President required of its holder?
12. Why did Herbert Hoover use the term "mental wardrobe"?
13. How many hours a day did Franklin D. Roosevelt work?
14. Explain Harry S. Truman's remark that "being President is like riding a tiger."
15. How did Presidents Eisenhower and Kennedy evaluate the office?
16. What was Lyndon B. Johnson's major concern?

Topics for Critical Analysis, Discussion, and Writing

1. Look closely at the structure of Fitzgibbon's essay. The thesis and development are easily identified, but there is no conclusion at the end. Why do you suppose the author omitted it? Using the information given in the article, write a short concluding paragraph that makes some kind of judgment about the subject. Be careful not to repeat the author's words.

2. Fitzgibbon is sharing the feelings of former Presidents with those who hope to be future Presidents. What are the age and citizenship requirements for a person to hold the highest office in the United States? What qualifications (education and experience) must a prospective President have?

3. The Rose Garden is one of the best known areas of the White House grounds. It is located just outside the Oval Office of the President, and it is a pleasant and peaceful place to escape the pressures of government. In addition, social functions such as teas (and even weddings) are held there. What is the meaning of the title of the article?

4. In your own words, write about the feelings of the Presidents quoted in the article. How do they feel about the job that they worked so hard to attain? Why? Surely, they must have been warned about the demands of the office before they sought it. Prepare a brief topic outline to plan your essay. Try to cover two or three major problems identified in the article. In your essay, expand on those main ideas by giving specific examples. Be sure that your thesis answers the question.

5. Suppose this article had been written about former leaders of your country. What information would have been included? What conclusion would have been reached?

6. What do you believe are the major problems a President faces today in terms of his ability to do the job and to meet the expectations of those who elected him? Are these problems changed from those experienced by former Presidents? Why or why not?

7. Most of the difficult words that have to be defined are in the first half of the article. How can you explain this? What changes in language have occurred over a two-hundred year period? Are Presidents today better educated than their counterparts one or two hundred years ago? Is their ability to use language better or worse?

3

Narration: What's in a Story?

PURPOSE OF THE NARRATIVE: ENTERTAINMENT OR INFORMATION?

Most students know that narration, or storytelling, is used extensively in various forms of entertainment—short stories, novels, films, and television. However, the narrative is also used to give a factual account of a single experience or a series of related events in historical, biographical, or expository writing. For example, newspaper reporters use narration almost exclusively in their news and feature stories to answer the questions: Who? What? When? Where? and How? Editorial and opinion writers must answer these questions and also explore the "why" of actions, issues, and ideas in their articles. Of the three classes of writing (exposition, narration, and description), narration is the easiest to produce because it is the closest to oral communication. All we have to do is "tell what happened," something we have been trained to do since we learned to talk. This instruction was reinforced when we learned to read, and our books were full of short, simple narratives about the lives of fictional families. You should know how and when to use narration to develop a thesis in expository writing. You should also be able to analyze narration, whether fiction or nonfiction, in other people's writing so that you can understand and explain the meaning, message, theme, or importance of any reading assignment.

THE RELATIONSHIP BETWEEN PLOT AND TIME ORDER

The *plot* is the plan used by the author to select and relate the events of a story, just as the outline is used by the nonfiction writer to decide the major and minor points of an essay. Traditional plot development in a short story follows this order: (1) The characters, their surroundings, and the situation are introduced right away. (2) Something happens to start the action and provide the basis for the conflict or problem in the story. (3) The conflict is developed by a series of actions or events that complicate the story or provide suspense. (4) The final action or event, which is of greatest interest to the reader because it brings the story to a point where matters have to be settled and some resolution made, is the *climax*. (5) If the final action does not satisfactorily conclude the story (that is, explain the "why" of it), then an unraveling or clarification, a *dénouement* (from the French verb *dénouer,* to untie), is included.

Not all plot development is traditional. Many stories omit one or more of these five points or change them around because of the way time is shown. We ourselves most often relate an incident as a simple *chronology;* that is, from beginning to end, without interruption. However, sometimes we stop to include things that happened before the incident occurred so that listeners understand it better. When earlier events interrupt the present in a short story, novel, or movie, the technique is called a *flashback*. For instance, a mother who is punishing her child for eating candy just before dinner might suddenly have a flashback of her own mother scolding her for doing exactly the same thing. As she looks back at herself (in her mind's eye), for just a moment she is again a naughty child and feels everything her own child is feeling. The result is that her anger toward her child vanishes, but some kind of explanation is needed to explain the abrupt change in her attitude. The flashback provides this special insight. However, a flashback is never used to supply information that the author just forgot to include. Time order, then, is important to establish *what* happened, and *when*.

CHARACTER DEVELOPMENT

What are a character's values, motives, and attitudes? How does a character respond to other characters or to situations? How can we, as readers, evaluate or judge this character's strengths and weaknesses? In short, what kind of person is this character, and how do we know? First, we should examine *what the author tells us directly* about the character's appearance, clothing, gestures, thoughts, feelings, or behavior. Second, we should watch closely to see *what the character shows us indirectly* through dialog (conversations with other characters), interior monologs (verbalizing ideas but not speaking them aloud, or "talking to oneself"), actions, and reactions to other characters.

Read the following two passages. Decide which one "tells" and which one "shows," and explain why.

The Sound of Thunder

Allen was always **depressed** by thunderstorms, and this one had been going on all day. He watched his grandmother **dozing** peacefully in her chair by the fire, **insulated** from the noise by her deafness. A flash of lightning brightly illuminated the room and was followed a few seconds later by a loud boom. Allen tensed, unconsciously listening for the answering howls of the neighbor's terrified dogs. He felt sorry for anyone's pets stuck outside in an electrical storm. He remembered how his own dog, given away so that he could come here to live with his grandmother in her tiny house, hated thunder and used to jump into his lap and try to hide from the noise. He smiled, then, recalling how his parents always laughed when the huge dog tried to **burrow into the crook of his arm**. But his parents were sleeping, now, too. He thought of them in their rainswept graves, and he felt awfully lonely. His grandmother was good to him, but their communication was mostly unspoken because of her severe hearing loss. He missed his mother and father terribly. He missed their lively conversations and all the fun they had together. And today, probably because of the storm, he especially missed his big and timid friend, his dog.

Suddenly his thoughts were interrupted by the sound of a baby crying just outside. When he ran to the front door and threw it open, instead of an infant, he found a wet, shivering Siamese cat **yowling** insistently. She ran right through his legs straight into the living room, past his grandma's chair, and directly to the fireplace, where she **huddled** near the fire. After a minute, she shook herself violently. The cold mist from her coat flew up in his grand-mother's face, and she awoke with a start. She noticed the cat at once and reached over to give it a sympathetic little pat. Then the old woman rose with great effort from the chair and went into the kitchen. "Here's an old towel to dry that cat off with, Allen," she called.

When Allen picked up the cat and placed her on the warm **hearth**, he noticed how thin she was. He knew she must not have had much to eat for a long time. Just then, his grandmother came back from the kitchen with a freshly opened can of tuna and put it down on a piece of newspaper. The cat **devoured** the fish. Then, as she lay warming herself, Allen gently dried her fur, using care not to rub it the wrong way. The cat began to purr, pausing every little while to make hoarse **rasping** sounds of appreciation. He took her onto his lap and cupped her dark, wedge-shaped **muzzle** in his left hand as he alternately stroked her back and scratched between her ears with his right. Her round, blue eyes closed contentedly. Suddenly there was another loud thunderclap. Her eyes flew open and rolled wildly, and she stiffened with fright. Allen gently disengaged her claws from his jeans. "It's all right, kitty," he soothed, tucking her up under his chin. "I'll take care of you. You're home, now." He looked at his grandmother, standing there with the can opener still in her hand, the unvoiced question in his eyes. She nodded once and smiled.

Allen gazed contentedly at the sleeping cat. He felt happier than he had in a long time. He sat stroking his new friend, not hearing the thunder at all anymore.

Glossary

burrow into the crook of his arm *(descriptive expression)* try to find shelter or safety by pushing hard against the boy's arm at the inner part of the elbow

depressed *(adjective)* gloomy; sad; discouraged

devoured *(verb)* ate hungrily or greedily

dozing *(verb)* sleeping lightly

hearth *(noun)* stone or brick floor (of a fireplace) that extends out into the room

huddled *(verb)* hunched or drawn up because of the cold

insulated *(verb)* detached; separated

muzzle *(noun)* the mouth, nose, and jaw of an animal

rasping *(adjective)* scraping; rough; grating

yowling *(verb)* crying mournfully. Siamese cats have very loud voices.

A Matter of Discipline

Sharon D. Scull

The first thing Meg saw when she pulled into the drive was the Great Dane in the fishpond again. She screeched to a stop and jumped out of the car.

"Giant! Giant! You get out of there right now." She waved her arms violently. Giant lifted his **immense** head and **grinned** at her, water **cascading** down his face and neck as he **clambered** out of the pond, a large fish **thrashing** wildly between his teeth. "Go home! Stay in your yard!" At that moment, they both heard the familiar call.

"Giiiii—ant! Giiiii—ant! Come on home, baby."

Meg looked up the street and saw the dog's owner, whom Meg's husband called "that Great Dane of a woman who only **summons** Giant *after* he's done something really awful," standing in the weeds of her hillside yard, like a mother calling her 130 pound "baby" in from its play. "I've had enough of this," Meg said aloud, and followed the dripping dog up the street.

"Is this your dog?" Meg asked innocently.

"Of course, he's my dog. Would I be calling him otherwise?"

"I'd be really grateful if you'd keep him in your yard. Every time I come home, he's fishing in my pond. He kills at least one fish a day."

"Giant wouldn't do that. He doesn't like fish and he hates water. You don't know what you're talking about."

Meg said patiently, "Well, look at him. He's soaking wet, and he's still chewing my fish." While they watched, Giant swallowed, licked the remains of his snack from the corners of his mouth, and smiled his big doggy smile. He seemed delighted that the two women in his life had finally met. He waited happily beside Meg. "Please keep him in your yard," Meg said firmly.

"I can't do that. Our yard isn't fenced. Besides, Giant needs a lot of space to run around. That's why we moved here."

"Surely, you know about the leash law! You can't let Giant run loose all around the neighborhood—it's a matter of discipline. He's a terrible nuisance. The rest of us keep our dogs fenced, and you're going to have to do the same. Otherwise, Giant's going on a little trip to the **dog pound**."

Giant's owner **charged** down the hill. She **towered** over Meg, clenching and unclenching her fists. "Discipline! I'll show you discipline! If *anything* happens to Giant, *you will pay for it,*" she hissed. Clearly, she had never been crossed. "When Giant is on your property, you're responsible for him, and don't you forget it." She gave Meg a little push.

"Don't do that," Meg warned. "And keep your dog at home." She turned to walk away.

"Don't turn your back on *me*," shouted Giant's owner, "I'm not through talking to you!" With one easy movement she knocked the smaller woman to the street.

She must be crazy, Meg thought. She lay still even though she wasn't hurt. If I try to defend myself against this Amazon, Meg decided, she may become *really* violent. Just then, Giant sat down beside Meg and began to lick one of her hands. He whined apologetically.

"Come here, Giant," his owner screamed, but he sat down in the street by his fallen accuser, obviously moved by her **plight**. "Get away from her, Giant! Now!" Slowly, deliberately, Giant lay down, his face only inches from Meg's. He grinned **conspiratorially** and began, with great, wet, noisy **slurps**, to lick the side of her face.

The Amazon's face was purple with **fury** at Giant's disloyalty. She looks as if she's going to explode, the smaller woman thought. Her cheeks are puffed out just like a squirrel's full of nuts. Instantly, the phrase "she's **squirrely**; she's **nuts**," popped into Meg's head. She smiled at her own stupid joke, and then began to laugh aloud at the absurdity of the situation, imagining how the two of them must look to anyone watching. She laughed so hard that tears ran down her cheeks. Giant **obligingly** licked them away until her face and neck were wet with his saliva. His heavy tail thumped the pavement in a happy rhythm. The Amazon stared at them in confusion.

At last, Meg struggled up from the street, utterly spent. She leaned heavily on Giant, who had **stumbled** to his feet at the same time, nearly knocking them both over, and the two comrades **wobbled** down the hill together. Giant's owner **thundered** along behind them.

"You come back here! You can't take my dog! Stop!"

The minute they reached Meg's driveway, Giant dived into the fishpond, skillfully caught a fish in his mouth, and began to devour it. He lay half submerged in the water, joyfully looking up into their faces.

"See what I mean?" Meg murmured.

The Amazon's jaw dropped. She blushed. "Oh," she said in a **strangled** voice. "Oh, I'm so embarrassed. I've never had anything like this happen before. I don't know what to do. I . . . ." Her voice trailed off. She waited hopefully for Meg to excuse her and Giant's bad behavior.

Giant was still splashing **ecstatically**. "Go home," Meg said. "Stay in your yard." Then she looked the Amazon straight in the eye. "And take your dog with you."

Glossary

cascading *(verb)* running like a waterfall

charged *(verb)* moved forward in order to attack

clambered *(verb)* climbed awkwardly, using all four legs

conspiratorially *(adverb)* as if they had planned their actions together

dog pound *(noun)* enclosure maintained by the city and used for locking up stray animals

ecstatically *(adjective)* delightedly, rapturously; joyfully

fury *(noun)* violent anger or rage

grinned *(verb)* smiled broadly

immense *(adjective)* huge; very large

nuts *(slang)* crazy

obligingly *(adverb)* helpfully; willingly

plight *(noun)* awkward or unfortunate state or condition

slurps *(noun)* loud sounds made by an animal's wet tongue when it eats, or when it licks someone's hand or face

squirrely *(slang)* crazy

strangled *(adjective)*   choked; suppressed

stumbled *(verb)*   tripped over his own feet; missed his step

summons *(verb)*   calls

thrashing *(verb)*   moving wildly

thundered *(verb)*   ran noisily after them

towered *(verb)*   stood so high she resembled a tower

wobbled *(verb)*   shook and trembled and moved unevenly from side to side

We can see that the two passages develop character in different ways. In "The Sound of Thunder," how do we learn about Allen? What is his relationship with his grandmother? How did he get along with his parents? How did he feel about his dog? What is his reaction to the cat? How do we know? We are told what he thinks and feels and how he behaves. Dialog is minimal. On the whole, Allen seems to have many good qualities, best shown by his kind and affectionate treatment of the stray cat. But doesn't his behavior show weaknesses as well? Why does Allen assume that a beautiful cat like this one has no home? Why doesn't he mention trying to find the cat's owner, who may love the animal and be very worried about it? Are you satisfied with Allen's sense of responsibility?

In "A Matter of Discipline," the characters themselves show us, through actions, speech, and thoughts what they are like and the kinds of values they have. Is either of the women completely honest with the other? What does Meg hope to gain by asking the other woman if Giant is her dog when the answer is obvious? Could Meg's angry attitude have caused the bigger woman to feel defensive? Is the Amazon really all bad? Doesn't she change at the end of the passage? And what about Meg? Are you satisfied with her way of concluding the situation? Do you think Giant is shown convincingly?

In both passages, strengths and weaknesses "round" the characters and make them believable. Actions and behavior of real people are not always predictable. Those of fictional characters shouldn't be, either, or they risk becoming "flat," one-dimensional stereotypes; for example, the interfering mother-in-law, noble husband, perfect wife, slave-driving employer, or nosey neighbor. Well-developed characters change and grow as a narrative progresses and we learn more about them and their motives. In expository writing, you will probably be asked to analyze character more often than to create it, other than in the modes of description and process analysis.

DIALOG

If you include an anecdote in your exposition, be sure that the dialog sounds natural. A six-year-old child, for example, would greet a friend with a simple

"Hi!" or "Hello!", not with "How do you do?" Most informal speech is full of contractions and slang that are otherwise inappropriate for formal writing. Don't forget that dialog is direct speech and should be enclosed in quotation marks, but that quotation marks are not used for reported speech; for example:

"I don't have time to write a conclusion," Sarah said. (direct)

Sarah said she didn't have time to write a conclusion. (reported)

Direct speech is sometimes interrupted by explanatory nouns, pronouns and verbs (*she said; Mark answered*) that can be followed by descriptive adverbs (*angrily, happily, furiously, innocently, sharply, pleasantly, disagreeably,* etc.). But once the speakers are identified and their situation established, sometimes dialog is printed exactly as it might sound if the two people were talking together. Except for new paragraphs to indicate a change in speaker, the author includes no explanation of the speakers' actions or tones of voice. The dialog alone is strong enough to show readers what is happening. Careful choices of words and effective uses of punctuation are very important in a passage made up entirely of dialog. However, such a passage should not go on for too long without interruption; otherwise, the reader may become confused about who is saying what.

SOPHISTICATED TRANSITIONAL DEVICES

Although speakers often tell a story by using the connecting phrase "and then" over and over, writers should avoid this transition. Depending on the way time is shown, some of the following words and phrases may sometimes be used:

In a series of events: *first, second, third, fourth; first, then, next, later, much later, finally* or *at last; yesterday, today, tomorrow.*

For a flashback or some reference to the past: *Sometime before; just an hour earlier; earlier that day; a few days before; weeks ago; just last month/week/year; on my twenty-first birthday; the year we went to Europe.*

To foretell the future, in an introductory clause followed by the conditional: *afterward; much later; in the hours/days/weeks/years to come; someday; in the end.*

Years later, he *would* be sorry that he hadn't listened to his father's advice.

Within a year after they were married, she *would* regret having given up her interesting job.

To indicate two things happening at once: *meanwhile; at the same time; at that moment; in the meantime; in the interim.*

To show that one thing caused another: *since; because.*

Since you refused to return my book, I had to buy another.

To explain a result: *as a result; therefore; consequently; as a consequence; thus; accordingly.*

POINT OF VIEW

The author's point of view may be subjective (first person, "I") or objective (third person, "he/she"). The latter is favored for exposition. In fiction, if the first person is used, the story may be told by the main character or by a minor character who is involved in the story but also serves as the narrator. If the story is written in the third person, the point of view may be totally objective (with the author acting as an impartial observer and simply reporting what happens) or it may be omniscient (with the author knowing and telling all, including the thoughts of the characters). The passages about Allen and Meg, shown earlier in this chapter, are both written from an omniscient point of view to include the thoughts of the main characters. When you are writing narration, description, or exposition, use one point of view throughout; for example, don't change from third to first person in the middle of an essay.

WHAT TO INCLUDE AND EXCLUDE IN A NARRATIVE ESSAY

Do include carefully edited true stories or experiences in expository narratives, but don't just try to make up a story to use in an essay. Remember that most fiction is based, however loosely, on real events or experiences that are cleverly altered to fit into a plot plan contrived by the author. Thus, much of the "truth" of the story disappears as other characters, events, circumstances, motives, and feelings are included to enhance reader interest.

Do use some of the techniques of fiction writing discussed in this chapter in expository narrative. Your story or experience doesn't have to be completely true, either, but readers will be suspicious if you write about your recent visit to another planet or your painful, tragic death. Remember that the purpose of your story is to inform, to support your thesis and make your essay move along to its conclusion. Exclude details that make your narrative a blow-by-blow summary that takes forever to relate. For example, in the passage describing Allen and the stray cat, many unnecessary particulars have been eliminated: the kind and quantity of furniture in the room, the styles and colors of clothes Allen and his grandmother are wearing, the cause of the old woman's hearing loss, the kind of work Allen's father did, the way Allen's parents died, the names and breeds of the neighbors' dogs, the name or breed of Allen's dog, or the name he will give the cat. None of this information is important to satisfy the purpose of the narrative.

Narration can play a major or minor role in expository writing. The first essay in the text, by Jeffrey Aran, is mostly narrative. The article on marital strife by Norman Lobsenz (chapter 1) and Gerald Astor's article on body language (chapter 2) include anecdotes. Aside from chapter 3, narration is most heavily used in description (chapter 4) and process analysis (chapter 6), but it can also be found in Jim Sanderson's "househusband" article (chapter 5) and in Benjamin Stein's definition of ignorance (chapter 7). Thus, narration can be an end in itself (a story only) or it can be a means to an end (a story or anecdote that is used to support a thesis).

Whether you write to entertain or to inform, your narration should (1) answer, not raise, questions about who was involved, what happened, and when, where, and how events took place; (2) allow the reader to imagine some details (rather than making him or her read endlessly about them); and (3) illustrate some main idea that provokes thought or discussion about why you wrote it.

READINGS

The Night the President Met the Burglar

Richard C. Garvey

The author uses narration to recount a news story that was suppressed for over fifty years. The story is now noteworthy more from a human interest than from a news standpoint. The author uses both direct and reported speech in the article. Although character development is not extensive, Garvey includes sufficient details to explain the actions of the President, Mrs. Coolidge, and the burglar so that we understand the reasons for their behavior.

A **cat burglar** invaded the bedroom of the President of the United States, who confronted him, **struck a deal** with him and helped him escape.

The President and First Lady—she slept through the encounter—never notified the Secret Service and he **enjoined** a journalist friend not to print the story.

The journalist kept his word, and this is the first time the incident has been reported.

The event occurred in the early morning hours in one of the first days of

Reprinted by permission of *Newhouse News Service.*

the presidency of Calvin Coolidge, late in August, 1923. He and his family were living in the same third-floor suite at the Willard Hotel in Washington that they had occupied during his vice presidency. President Warren G. Harding's widow still was living in the White House.

Coolidge awoke to see an intruder go through his clothes, remove a wallet and unhook a watch chain.

Coolidge spoke: "I wish you wouldn't take that."

The intruder, gaining his voice, said: "Why?"

"I don't mean the watch and chain, only the charm. Take it near the window and read what is engraved on the back of it," the President said.

The burglar read: "Presented to Calvin Coolidge, **Speaker of the House**, by the Massachusetts General Court."

"Are you President Coolidge?" he asked.

The President answered, "Yes, and the Legislature gave me that watch charm. . . . I'm fond of it. It would do you no good. You want money. Let's talk this over."

Holding up the wallet, the intruder bargained: "I'll take this and leave everything else."

Coolidge, knowing there was $80 in the billfold, persuaded the intruder to sit down and talk. The young man said he and his college roommate had overspent during their vacation and did not have enough money to pay their hotel bill.

Coolidge added up the room rate and two rail tickets back to the campus. Then he counted out $32 and said it was a loan.

He then told the intruder that there probably would be a Secret Service agent patrolling the hotel corridor and asked if an escape could be made by going back along the hotel **ledge**. The man left through the same window he had entered.

The President told his wife, Grace, about the event. Later, he confided in two friends, Judge Walter L. Stevens, the family lawyer, and Frank MacCarthy, a free-lance writer and photographer.

The President held MacCarthy to silence and never told him the intruder's name. As the 25th anniversary of the event approached, 15 years after Coolidge's death, MacCarthy, by then working for the Springfield Union, asked Mrs. Coolidge to let him use the story.

She declined, saying, "There is already too much publicity given to acts of **vandalism** and violence."

MacCarthy honored her request, asking only that she review the story for accuracy and allow him to use it after her death.

Mrs. Coolidge died July 8, 1957, and MacCarthy died less than four months later without publishing his article.

MacCarthy had shared the story with me when we worked together. Because all reasons for secrecy have vanished, this report has been reconstructed from MacCarthy's own article.

I have called the young man a burglar because MacCarthy's article so identifies him, but his notes show that Coolidge said the young man repaid the $32 loan in full.

Glossary

cat burglar *(noun)* thief who enters buildings by climbing up the walls to openings in the upper stories or on the roofs

enjoined *(verb)* ordered. The President used his authority to prohibit his friend from printing the story.

ledge *(noun)* shelf-like projection, often built under windows, on the sides of buildings

Speaker of the House *(governmental term)* presiding officer of the House of Representatives

struck a deal *(idiom)* made a bargain

vandalism *(noun)* deliberate destruction or damage of property because of ignorance or meanness

Comprehension Questions

1. When did the President meet the burglar? Where? How did the intruder get in? Why wasn't the President living in the White House?
2. Which of his possessions was Mr. Coolidge most worried about losing? Why?
3. Why did the young man commit the robbery?
4. How did the President handle the situation? What kind of deal did he make with the thief?
5. How did he help the burglar escape?
6. Whom did Mr. Coolidge tell about the incident?
7. What reason did Mrs. Coolidge give for refusing to allow publication of the story fifteen years after her husband's death?
8. How did the author learn about the story, and why was he able to publish it?

Topics for Critical Analysis, Discussion, and Writing

1. In Garvey's story, the President of the United States awakened to find an intruder going through his clothes with the intention of robbing him. Why didn't Mr. Coolidge summon the Secret Service guards just outside the room?

Why did he bargain with the young man? Wouldn't it have been a good example for other thieves if Mr. Coolidge had had the burglar arrested?

2. How do you suppose this incident affected the burglar's life? What did Mr. Coolidge do for this young man that was far more important than not having him arrested or helping him to escape? Was the President's faith in the youth justified?

3. Write a narrative about this incident from the point of view of the young man. Discuss his reasons for committing the burglary and his feelings before and after he was caught. Was it in his best interests to make a "deal" with the President? Would the youth have learned more if he had been punished by the law?

4. How would you handle it if you awoke in the middle of the night to find someone methodically searching your clothes and room for valuables? Would you try to dissuade the thief? If so, how? If not, why not?

5. Are burglars today any different from those of fifty years ago? Explain.

Trial by Combat

Shirley Jackson

Using a minor theft similar to that reported in Garvey's article as the basis of her short story, the author reveals a great deal about the victim and the thief, both women. Jackson so skillfully develops the characters of Emily Johnson and Mrs. Archer that the concluding event in their strange relationship is completely unexpected. Notice that because the author uses an omniscient point of view, we know what Emily Johnson is thinking. We see both the problem and its resolution through her eyes. Watch for passages of interrupted and uninterrupted dialog.

When Emily Johnson came home one evening to her furnished room and found three of her best handkerchiefs missing from the dresser drawer, she was sure who had taken them and what to do. She had lived in the furnished room for about six weeks and for the past two weeks she had been missing small things occasionally. There had been several handkerchiefs gone, and a **service pin** which Emily wore sometimes and which had come from the **five-and-ten**. And once she had missed a small bottle of perfume and one of a set of china dogs. Emily had known for some time who was taking the things, but it was only tonight that she had decided what to do. She had hesitated about complaining to the landlady because her losses were trivial and because she had felt certain that sooner or later she would know how to deal with the situation herself. It had seemed logical to her from the beginning that the one person in the rooming house who was home all day was the most likely suspect, and then, one Sunday morning, coming downstairs from the roof, where she had been sitting in the sun, Emily had seen someone come out of her room and go down the stairs, and had recognized the visitor. Tonight, she felt, she knew just what to do. She took off her coat and hat, put her packages down, and, while a can of tamales was heating on her electric plate, she went over what she intended to say.

After her dinner, she closed and locked her door and went downstairs. She tapped softly on the door of the room directly below her own, and when she thought she heard someone say "Come in," she said "Mrs. Archer?", then opened the door carefully and stepped inside.

The room, Emily noticed immediately, was almost like her own—the same narrow bed with the tan cover, the same maple dresser and armchair; the closet was on the opposite side of the room, but the window was in the same relative position. Mrs. Archer was sitting in the armchair. She was about sixty. More than twice as old as I am, Emily thought, while she stood in the doorway, and a lady still. She hesitated for a few seconds, looking at Mrs. Archer's clean white hair and her neat, dark-blue house coat, before speaking. "Mrs. Archer," she said, "I'm Emily Johnson."

Mrs. Archer put down the *Woman's Home Companion* she had been reading and stood up slowly. "I'm very happy to meet you," she said graciously. "I've seen you, of course, several times, and thought how pleasant you looked. It's so seldom one meets anyone really"—Mrs. Archer hesitated—"really nice," she went on, "in a place like this."

"I've wanted to meet you, too," Emily said.

Mrs. Archer indicated the chair she had been sitting in. "Won't you sit down?"

"Thank you," Emily said. "You stay there. I'll sit on the bed." She smiled. "I feel as if I know the furniture so well. Mine's just the same."

"It's a shame," Mrs. Archer said, sitting down in her chair again. "I've told the landlady over and over, you can't make people feel at home if you put all the same furniture in the rooms. But she maintains that this maple furniture is clean-looking and cheap."

"It's better than most," Emily said. "You've made yours look much nicer than mine."

"I've been here for three years," Mrs. Archer said. "You've only been here a month or so, haven't you?"

"Six weeks," Emily said.

"The landlady's told me about you. Your husband's in the Army."

"Yes. I have a job here in New York."

"My husband was in the Army," Mrs. Archer said. She gestured at a group of pictures on her maple dresser. "That was a long time ago, of course. He's been dead for nearly five years." Emily got up and went over to the pictures. One of them was of a tall, dignified-looking man in Army uniform. Several were of children.

"He was a very distinguished-looking man," Emily said. "Are those your children?"

"I had no children, to my sorrow," the old lady said. "Those are nephews and nieces of my husband's."

Emily stood in front of the dresser, looking around the room. "I see you have flowers, too," she said. She walked to the window and looked at the row of potted plants. "I love flowers," she said. "I bought myself a big bunch of asters tonight to brighten up my room. But they fade so quickly."

"I prefer plants just for that reason," Mrs. Archer said. "But why don't you put an aspirin in the water with your flowers? They'll last much longer."

"I'm afraid I don't know much about flowers," Emily said. "I didn't know about putting an aspirin in the water, for instance."

"I always do, with cut flowers," Mrs. Archer said. "I think flowers make a room look so friendly."

Emily stood by the window for a minute, looking out on Mrs. Archer's daily view: the fire escape opposite, **an oblique slice of the street below**. Then she took a deep breath and turned around. "Actually, Mrs. Archer," she said, "I had a reason for dropping in."

"Other than to make my acquaintance?" Mrs. Archer said, smiling.

"I don't know quite what to do," Emily said. "I don't like to say anything to the landlady."

"The landlady isn't much help in an emergency," Mrs. Archer said.

Emily came back and sat on the bed, looking earnestly at Mrs. Archer, seeing a nice old lady. "It's so slight," she said, "but someone has been coming into my room."

Mrs. Archer looked up.

"I've been missing things," Emily went on, "like handkerchiefs and little inexpensive jewelry. Nothing important. But someone's been coming into my room and helping themselves."

"I'm sorry to hear it," Mrs. Archer said.

"You see, I don't like to make trouble," Emily said. "It's just that some-one's coming into my room. I haven't missed anything of value."

"I see," Mrs. Archer said.

"I just noticed it a few days ago. And then last Sunday I was coming down from the roof and I saw someone coming out of my room."

"Do you have any idea who it was?" Mrs. Archer asked.

"I believe I do," Emily said.

Mrs. Archer was quiet for a minute. "I can see where you wouldn't like to speak to the landlady," she said finally.

"Of course not," Emily said. "I just want it to stop."

"I don't blame you," Mrs. Archer said.

"You see, it means someone has a key to my door," Emily said pleadingly.

"All the keys in this house open all the doors," Mrs. Archer said. "They're all old-fashioned locks."

"It *has* to stop," Emily said. "If it doesn't, I'll have to do something about it."

"I can see that," Mrs. Archer said. "The whole thing is very unfortunate." She rose. "You'll have to excuse me," she went on. "I tire very easily and I must be in bed early. I'm so happy you came down to see me."

"I'm so glad to have met you at last," Emily said. She went to the door. "I hope I won't be bothered again," she said. "Good night."

"Good night," Mrs. Archer said.

The following evening, when Emily came home from work, a pair of cheap earrings was gone, along with two packages of cigarettes which had been in her dresser drawer. That evening she sat alone in her room for a long time, thinking. Then she wrote a letter to her husband and went to bed. The next morning she got up and dressed and went to the corner drugstore, where she called her office from a phone booth and said that she was sick and would not be in that day. Then she went back to her room. She sat for almost an hour with the door slightly **ajar** before she heard Mrs. Archer's door open and Mrs. Archer come out and go slowly down the stairs. When Mrs. Archer had had time to get out onto the street, Emily locked her door and, carrying her key in her hand, went down to Mrs. Archer's room.

She was thinking, I just want to pretend it's my own room, so that if anyone comes I can say I was mistaken about the floor. For a minute, after she had opened the door, it seemed as though she *were* in her own room. The bed was neatly made and the shade drawn down over the window. Emily left the door unlocked and went over and pulled up the shade. Now that the room was light, she looked around. She had a sudden sense of unbearable intimacy with Mrs. Archer, and thought, This is the way she must feel in my room. Everything was neat and plain. She looked in the closet first, but there was nothing in there but Mrs. Archer's blue house coat and one or two plain dresses. Emily went to the dresser. She looked for a moment at the picture of Mrs. Archer's husband, and then opened the top drawer and looked in. Her handkerchiefs were there, in a neat, small pile, and next to them the cigarettes and the earrings. In one corner the little china dog was sitting. Everything is here, Emily thought, all put away and very orderly. She closed the drawer and opened the next two. Both were empty. She opened the top one again. Besides her things, the drawer held a pair of black cotton gloves, and under the little pile of her handkerchiefs were two plain white ones. There was a box of Kleenex and a small tin of aspirin. For her plants, Emily thought.

Emily was counting the handkerchiefs when a noise behind her made her turn around. Mrs. Archer was standing in the doorway watching her quietly. Emily dropped the handkerchiefs she was holding and stepped back. She felt herself blushing and knew her hands were trembling. Now, she was thinking, now turn around and tell her. "Listen, Mrs. Archer," she began, and stopped.

"Yes?" Mrs. Archer said gently.

Emily found that she was staring at the picture of Mrs. Archer's husband; such a thoughtful-looking man, she was thinking. They must have had such a pleasant life together, and now she has a room like mine, with only two handkerchiefs of her own in the drawer.

"Yes?" Mrs. Archer said again.

What does she want me to say, Emily thought. What could she be waiting for with such a ladylike manner? "I came down," Emily said, and hesitated. My voice is almost ladylike, too, she thought. "I had a terrible headache and I came down to borrow some aspirin," she said quickly. "I had this awful headache and when I found you were out I thought surely you wouldn't mind if I just borrowed some aspirin."

"I'm so sorry," Mrs. Archer said. "But I'm glad you felt you knew me well enough."

"I never would have dreamed of coming in," Emily said, "except for such a bad headache."

"Of course," Mrs. Archer said. "Let's not say any more about it." She went over to the dresser and opened the drawer. Emily, standing next to her, watched her hand pass over the handkerchiefs and pick up the aspirin. "You just take two of these and go to bed for an hour," Mrs. Archer said.

"Thank you." Emily began to move toward the door. "You've been very kind."

"Let me know if there's anything more I can do."

"Thank you," Emily said again, opening the door. She waited for a minute and then turned toward the stairs to her room.

"I'll run up later today," Mrs. Archer said, "just to see how you feel."

Glossary

ajar *(adjective)*   open

an oblique slice of the street below *(descriptive term)*   a small, slanted strip of the street below. Because Mrs. Archer's view was obstructed by the fire escape, she couldn't see very much of the street.

five-and-ten *(noun)* another name for a variety store that specialized in very inexpensive merchandise; for example, Woolworth's used to be called a five-and-ten or ten-cent store.

service pin *(noun)* small, decorative pin worn by wives and mothers during World War II to show that a close relative was serving in the armed forces

Comprehension Questions

1. How long has someone been stealing from Emily? What kinds of things are taken? Why doesn't Emily complain to the landlady?
2. How does Emily know who the thief is? What does she decide to do about it?
3. What sort of person is Mrs. Archer? What does Emily learn about the older woman's family life?
4. What does Mrs. Archer learn about Emily and her husband?
5. Why does Emily tell Mrs. Archer about the thefts? What does Emily expect the older woman to do about them? What *does* Mrs. Archer do?
6. How does Emily decide to prove that she knows the thief's identity?
7. What does Emily find in Mrs. Archer's room? What does the younger woman do when Mrs. Archer returns unexpectedly? How does Mrs. Archer react?
8. Does Emily satisfactorily solve the problem of the thefts?

Topics for Critical Analysis, Discussion, and Writing

1. This story is an example of traditional plot development. In the following analysis, the numbers in parentheses are identical to those in the discussion of plot earlier in the chapter. Fill in as much information as you can to explain each stage of the plot.

(1) Emily, the thief, their surroundings, and the situation, are all introduced in the first paragraph. Who are these people? In what surroundings do they find themselves? What is the situation?

(2) Emily starts the action by going to Mrs. Archer's room. What happens there?

(3) The conflict is developed by a series of actions that complicate the story and provide suspense. List as many of them as you can.

(4) At the climax of the story, Mrs. Archer catches Emily in her room, without permission, going through her things.

(5) Explain the unraveling or *dénouement,* the strange ending of the story.

2. "Trial by Combat" is a story with a "twist"; that is, something unexpected happens at the end. Emily Johnson, who is living alone in New York in a rooming house during her husband's World War II Army duty, decides to play detective to prove that another boarder has been stealing small articles from her room. Write an essay in which you discuss Emily's behavior and reactions toward Mrs. Archer before and after she goes into the older woman's room without permission. Identify the "twist" in the story, and explain how it affects your interpretation of Emily's character.

3. Analyze Mrs. Archer's behavior. Is she an evil old woman who simply enjoys doing mischief? Is she a kleptomaniac (a person who feels compelled to steal things even though he or she doesn't need or even want them)? Is she truly in need of the articles she takes? Why doesn't she confess to stealing Emily's things when the younger woman finds them in Mrs. Archer's drawer? Can you excuse Mrs. Archer's behavior?

4. How does knowledge of Emily's thoughts affect the reader's perception of both Emily and Mrs. Archer?

5. What lesson do you think Emily learns from her experience with Mrs. Archer?

6. Write a narrative in which Mrs. Archer relates her experiences with Emily Johnson to another neighbor or to the landlady.

Dime Store Soles

Sharon Scull

In this story, Carol, a proud and spoiled teenager, learns to cope with her family's economic hard times. In the process, she learns more about herself, gains some insights into the problems of her parents, and develops ways to maintain her relationships with her peers. The story is written in the first person, from the point of view of the main character.

I was thirteen and there was a **recession** and I will always remember it as "The Year We Were Poor." Daddy looked for work every day. He haunted the employment agency and **religiously scrutinized** the want ads, but there just weren't any jobs in our small town. When our savings were gone Mother found a part time job in a drugstore "just to help out til Daddy finds something."

Reprinted by permission of the author. First published in *Pipes of Pan: An Anthology of Student Writing*, Pasadena City College, 1971.

"You're much too proud, Carol," Mother kept saying. She was doing everything possible to economize and live **frugally**, while I was desperately trying to keep up appearances.

"How can I explain to my friends that my dad can't find a job? At least they don't have to know how poor we really are!" I pretended to enjoy taking my lunch in a sack and wore my last year's clothes with an air of what-can-you-do-when-you-didn't-outgrow-a-single-thing-and-you-have-a-practical-Mom?

But there was no way to **disguise** my worn-out shoes.

Daddy always bought my shoes. He spoiled me anyway, but shoes were something extra special. The only requirement was that they fit. Mother never failed to complain about our choice and she especially disliked **loafers** because they wore out fast, which was exactly my problem. She finally noticed them herself. "Oh, dear, something will have to be done about your shoes. You have holes in both soles."

The next morning I discovered Mother's solution to the problem. She had stayed up past midnight gluing on and trimming to size some do-it-yourself half soles. The shoes were brown with leather soles and heels. The new soles were F. W. Woolworth's best **corrugated** thick black rubber.

"Oh, how could you, Mother? How can I wear those horrible looking things to school? The soles are thicker than the heels! Everyone will **make fun of** me!" Then Mother and I were both crying at once.

"Go to your room and finish dressing," Daddy said. "You've hurt your mother's feelings."

I heard her **muffled** voice through the door. "I wish we could buy her some new shoes, but we just haven't got the money. Why can't she understand?" And I heard Daddy trying to comfort her.

I looked down at the ugly dime store soles. Maybe I could pry them off. I was just beginning to get one loose when Mother came in to call me for breakfast.

"Stop that!" she snapped, and all during the meal lectured me on economy, thrift, and basic good judgment.

Squish! Flap! Squish! Flap! I walked the five long blocks to school. I knew I could get one sole off, but what if the other wouldn't come off? That would look even worse. Besides, there just wasn't time to fool with it. I was already five minutes late for my first class and I could see that the teacher was especially **crabby** this morning. A **strategically aimed** rubber band had left a large red mark on the back of his neck and he was in the process of **ferreting out the culprit** when I crept in. As if they were one, every eye fastened on me.

I squished and flapped noisily across the room, **squirming** under their scrutiny, sure that everyone was staring at my funny soles. I shrank into my seat, opened my book and tried to disappear behind it. Then the boy across from me leaned over and whispered hoarsely, "Hey, Carol, you have your shoes **retreaded**?" The class exploded with laughter; even the teacher smiled.

At the lockers my friends crowded around. "Did your mother really do that to your shoes?" someone asked. I nodded. "Why?"

"It was supposed to be a lesson not to buy loafers any more," I lied. I explained Daddy's **indulgence** and Mother's disapproval.

"Gads!" said one of the girls, "If my mother did that to me, I'd just *die*!"

"Boy, me, too," said another. "I wouldn't even come to school!"

"I'm glad I don't have *your* mother!" There was a chorus of **assent**.

I hastened to explain that it was really just a joke, that my mother hadn't done it to be mean, but everyone felt much too sorry for me to have any kind thoughts for Mother.

"How long will you have to wear them?"

"I don't know." Privately I expected it would be forever.

All day long I was called upon to write exercises on the blackboard, run errands for teachers, stand before the class to give an oral report, and do any number of things which required exposing my awful shoes to the critical eyes of my **peers**. At last it was homeroom, with only twenty minutes until dismissal. Just as I took my seat, four of the most popular boys bobbed up and chanted **in unison:**

> *"Truck tire soles, truck tire soles,*
> *May be thick, but better than holes!"*

My face flamed and I wanted to die as the laughter echoed around me. I **ducked my head** and pretended to concentrate on my homework.

I waited until everyone left, then walked home alone. I just couldn't wear those shoes to school again. I simply had to think of something. Finally, I decided to take my older, smaller loafers, with even larger holes, to school and leave them in my locker. Even though I had to curl my toes under to wear them, it would be better to have **deformed** feet than to be a **laughingstock**. Then I would wear these **clunkers** home at night and Mother would never find out.

My first period classmates were eagerly awaiting my arrival. I strolled **nonchalantly** to my seat. "Gee whiz," **bellowed** my pal across the aisle, "how come you didn't wear your **snow tires** today?" Everyone burst out laughing.

"Oh, you are just *too* funny," I said, "but if you must know, I parked them outside." The laughter became more **congenial.**

He punched my arm. "**Your old lady let up**, huh?"

"I *told* you it was a joke. You seem to think I was going to wear them the rest of my life." He grinned and punched my arm again. Then the teacher started the lesson.

At lunch I was a celebrity. A heroine. I had "suffered." My friends **jostled** each other for the privilege of sitting next to me.

"I *knew* your mother'd **let you off**," someone began. Several girls nodded wisely.

"Your mother is really a character," said another.

I made a face. "She sure is."

"Yeah, remember that **slumber party** at your house when we all ran outside in our pajamas and your mother locked us out?" Giggles. ". . . and then we climbed in your bedroom window in the dark, ever so quietly, and after we all got inside she jumped out of the closet and hollered 'AAAAaaaahh!' and scared us all out of our wits." We were all laughing.

"Gee," said the girl next to me, "I wish my mother did funny things like that."

"Boy, Carol, you must really have fun at your house!"

"Yes," I said, "I don't suppose there are very many mothers around like mine!"

I waited again after school until everyone left before I went to my locker to change into my "treads." It felt good to move my toes again. Then one of my friends rushed into the locker room. I stood up slowly and saw that **her eyes were riveted** on my feet. "How come you're wearing those crazy shoes again?"

"Oh, my mother worked so hard on them, it seems a shame to let them go to waste," I said. "Anyhow, it's raining and I'll have great **traction**."

She **shrugged**, our eyes met for a second, and suddenly everything was easy, very easy, and we were talking and laughing and walking out together, arm in arm.

Glossary

assent *(noun)*   agreement

bellowed *(verb)*   shouted loudly and powerfully (like a bull) so that the sound filled the room

clunkers *(slang)*   usually describes cars that are old, ugly, and worn out

congenial *(adjective)*   sympathetic; friendly

corrugated *(adjective)*   shaped or molded with a parallel pattern of indentations or raised areas on the surface, such as the pattern in the tread of automobile tires

crabby *(adjective)*   ill-tempered; disagreeable

deformed *(adjective)*   disfigured; misshapen

disguise *(verb)*   change the appearance of something so that it is unrecognizable

ducked my head *(idiom)*   lowered my head (to hide my face because of embarrassment)

ferreting out the culprit *(idiom)*   persistently searching for the guilty person to force him or her out of hiding. A ferret is a small, sleek animal that is easily tamed and trained to hunt rabbits and rats.

frugally *(adverb)*   inexpensively; thriftily

her eyes were riveted on *(idiom)* her attention was fixed on

indulgence *(noun)* gratification of a person's wishes; leniency; allowing a person to have or do whatever he or she wants

in unison *(idiom)* speaking the same words all together at the same time, somewhat like a musical chorus

jostled *(verb)* bumped; pushed; shoved

laughingstock *(noun)* person who is the object of everyone's ridicule

let you off *(idiom)* excused you from doing something

loafers *(noun)* moccasin-toed, close-fitting, casual leather shoes (without ties) that slip on the foot

make fun of *(idiom)* mock; ridicule; make a person the object of laughter by joking about him or her

muffled *(adjective)* made less audible

nonchalantly *(adverb)* coolly; unconcernedly; indifferently

peers *(noun)* persons of the same rank, status, or ability

recession *(noun)* temporary economic condition (instead of a full-scale economic depression) during which business activity decreases, unemployment increases, and people have less money to spend

religiously *(adverb)* conscientiously; carefully

retreaded *(verb)* resurfaced with new grooved or ridged patterned rubber. Sometimes worn automobile tires are retreaded.

scrutinized *(verb)* examined carefully or closely

shrugged *(verb)* drew up her shoulders in a gesture to show indifference or disinterest

slumber party *(noun)* party, popular with teenaged girls, to which everyone brings pajamas, blankets, and pillows to sleep overnight at one girl's house. Nobody sleeps much; instead, they talk, eat, watch television, make candy or popcorn, play cards, telephone other friends, and listen to music.

snow tires *(noun)* tires with especially deep tread to allow them to stick to slippery, snowy roads

squirming *(verb)* wriggling; twisting and turning the body. Small children squirm when their parents physically hold them too tightly; older persons squirm when they are embarrassed or uncomfortable (a physical reaction to a psychological problem).

strategically aimed *(military term)* skillfully directed

traction *(noun)* adhesive friction (like a new tire on a wet street)

Your old lady let up *(slang)* Your mother relaxed her position (that Carol had to wear the embarrassing shoes). Most women are offended if they are referred to or addressed as someone's "old lady."

Comprehension Questions

1. How old was Carol? What was her family situation? Why did her mother say that Carol was too proud?

2. What was the matter with Carol's shoes? What did her mother do about the problem? What was Carol's reaction? Whose side did her father take?

3. How did Carol's classmates react to her unusual shoes the first day that she wore them? How did Carol handle the situation? What did her classmates say about Carol's mother? Did Carol attack or defend her mother's behavior? Explain.

4. What kinds of things did Carol have to do that called attention to her shoes? What did four of the most popular boys in her homeroom do when she walked in at the end of the day? How did Carol feel?

5. How did Carol solve the shoe problem? Why did having "suffered" make Carol more popular? What was the effect on the other girls' opinion of Carol's mother?

6. Was Carol embarrassed when one of her friends found her wearing the ugly shoes again? How did she explain the situation?

Topics for Critical Analysis, Discussion, and Writing

1. Carol's feelings about her mother were ambivalent (conflicting). How did she behave toward her mother at home? What did she say about her mother to her friends at school? How can you explain this "love-hate" relationship?

2. Although Carol's father did not have a very large part in the story itself, we saw that Carol's behavior (and possibly her attitude toward her mother) and values had been shaped by her relationship with him. Explain.

3. Carol's mother criticized her daughter for being too proud; however, she encouraged her husband to be proud by saying that she went to work "just to help out," when actually her salary was supporting the family. Explain this apparent conflict.

4. Was Carol justified in fearing that everyone would make fun of her if she wore the shoes her mother had repaired? Was Carol right to lie about her problem?

5. Discuss the changes in Carol's behavior and attitude as the story progressed. Did any good come from her experiences?

6. Write a narrative account of an embarrassing experience that you had when you were a teenager. What lesson did you learn from it?

7. Examine the economic, family, and social pressures that must have been faced by Carol's parents in the story. Since events were shown through

Carol's eyes, her problem was emphasized; however, her parents' difficulties were potentially much more serious.

8. Identify the theme and discuss its importance in an essay.

9. Stories in which the main character successfully faces a frightening or emotional experience that changes him or her are called "maturation" or "coming of age" stories. Although the character is not physically older at the end of the story, he or she has learned to accept or to deal with unhappy or unpleasant situations. How did Carol "grow up" emotionally in this story?

The Helplessness That Triggers Tears

Jim Sanderson

Jim Sanderson's sensitively written column, "Liberated Male," appears regularly in newspapers. The author is unique in that he tries to show the inner feelings of men toward specific life situations and problems. For instance, in many cultures, men are not supposed to cry (except at socially approved functions such as funerals) because tears are associated with weakness. However, psychologists tell us that suppressing emotion causes stress, which in turn triggers physical health problems. In this article, Sanderson tells us that Ben's tears are appropriate to release him from the frustration and anger boiling inside him.

Ben's experience is very negative; however, it is not typical of most emergencies that occur in this country. Every day, there are radio, television, and newspaper stories about people helping each other during crises. For example, a businessman pulls a dying pregnant woman from her wrecked automobile and gives her artificial respiration until an ambulance arrives, thereby saving her baby; an entire neighborhood spends the night searching for a missing child; a truckdriver stops on a deserted highway to help an elderly woman with car trouble; a passerby rushes into a burning building to rescue a trapped infant; a bystander jumps into an icy river and risks freezing to death in order to save plane crash victims. As in other societies, many people in the United States react differently to emergency situations. Some are capable of taking command and acting instantly. Others shrink from problems because they are afraid or don't know what to do. Unfortunately, Ben encounters the latter when he needs help.

Courtesy Sun Features, Inc., Box 45, Cardiff, California 92007

Sanderson states in the beginning that he is relating a true story. There is no other thesis. The author writes objectively to report the who, what, when, where, *and* how *of his friend's experience until the final paragraph, in which the* why *of Ben's emotional outburst is evaluated. Ben's thoughts and feelings are related, and through his actions we learn a great deal about his character.*

This is a true story; it happened to a friend of mine last week.

Ben had a day off, so he drove his wife to work, took his car to the garage to be serviced and then set off on foot with his two daughters, ages 5 and 8, to do some shopping errands near his home.

He had only been in the store for a moment. As he came out his oldest daughter rushed up to him, blood **spurting** from a **wound** in her neck. It had seemed safe enough to leave them playing outside, but the girl had tripped and **impaled** herself on a sharp wire **protruding** from a waist-high decorative wire fence.

Ben dropped his packages, **smothered** the **flood flow** with his hand as best he could, swept her up in his arms and **lurched** off down the street, **yelling** for the younger girl to follow.

Several cars **cruised** up curiously along the sidewalk. "Take me to the hospital," he cried, but just as he moved toward the first car it sped away, the male driver staring straight ahead now.

He turned to the second. Two women, **horrified**, made a gesture of **helplessness**, and they too drove off. One woman turned to look back at him, her face a mask.

In desperation Ben staggered into a storefront office. It was a **chiropractor**. "Help me." The man stood there, opening his hands in **supplication**: "I can't," he said. "Please understand, I'm not a medical doctor."

With a curse Ben turned to the street again, the blood **surging out** between his fingers, his youngest daughter racing behind him, wailing.

I can't wait for an ambulance, he thought. Somebody has to drive me. The hospital emergency room must be at least a mile away. Without his car he felt **unmanned**. His daughter was not crying. She looked up at him with a strange, pale **serenity**. "Daddy, am I going to die?" she asked.

"No, damn it, you're not," he snapped. "Daddy's going to take care of you." The promise echoed hollowly in his ears. Ben was a take-charge kind of man—his entire life as a male had been built around the premise of competence and control.

He felt **terrorized** by his own helplessness. At the most **crucial** instant of his life he couldn't find the answer. He **blundered** into another store, a **draftsman's** office, and put Gina down on a table covered with **blueprints**. A woman brought him a wet paper towel to help **staunch** the blood.

And still nobody would agree to drive him to the hospital. The ambulance did come quickly, thank God, but at the hospital there was another delay. They wanted him to go to the Admissions Office to sign papers; they wouldn't start treatment until he did.

"I promised her I wouldn't leave her," he bellowed. They persisted. He turned, **raging**, to the doctor; the doctor began to work.

Gina was lucky. The wire had missed the main **artery.** The wound was cleansed and, at Ben's insistence, closed with skin tape rather than stitches, until a plastic surgeon could decide about scars. Then they walked home, all three hand in hand, quietly, totally exhausted.

Four days later at bedtime, Ben asked his wife to **massage** his back. She could feel the tenseness in his muscles. "I think I'm going to cry," he said, surprised.

"Ben," she answered softly, "let it all come out."

So, for the first time in his adult life, he did. Tears for the fear he'd felt for his child, for the shame of his helplessness and for the **panic** at not knowing instantly where to turn. Then furious rage at all the people who had turned away or found reasons why they couldn't help.

His tears released him, and they were appropriate. Without **purging** he would still be carrying this violent emotion around within. In time it would become **submerged**, piled layer on layer on top of all those other **radioactive** feelings. Destructive, deadening; forever.

Glossary

artery *(noun)*   a large, thick-walled tube that carries blood directly from the heart to the major parts of the body. If a main artery is severed, a person can bleed to death very rapidly.

blueprints *(noun)*   photographic reproductions (white writing on a blue background) of architectural or engineering drawings

blundered *(verb)*   stumbled; walked clumsily

chiropractor *(noun)*   a person who treats health problems on the basis that they are caused by interference with nerve function, and who manipulates the body joints (especially the spine) to restore normal nerve function. Chiropractors are not physicians and if they practice medicine, even if it is just helping in an emergency, they can lose their chiropractic licenses.

crucial *(adjective)*   supremely important; critical; difficult

cruised *(verb)*   drove in an unhurried way, as if for pleasure or in search of something

draftsman *(noun)*   a person who draws plans for houses or machinery

flood flow *(descriptive expression)*   flow of blood that was as fast-moving as a flood of water

helplessness *(noun)*   inability to help oneself; incompetency; ineffectiveness; weakness

horrified *(adjective)*   shocked; dismayed; disgusted

impaled *(verb)* pierced through with a sharp, pointed object

lurched *(verb)* staggered; swayed or pitched in sudden movements from one side to the other

massage *(verb)* rub or knead parts of the body to stimulate circulation and make the muscles relax

panic *(noun)* unreasoning fear

protruding *(verb)* projecting; sticking out (idiom)

purging *(verb)* cleansing; getting rid of the anger

radioactive feelings *(descriptive expression)* dangerous emotions

raging *(verb)* showing uncontrollable or violent anger

serenity *(noun)* tranquility; calmness

smothered *(verb)* covered; stifled

spurting *(verb)* gushing; squirting; being expelled suddenly and forcefully in a jet-like stream

staunch *(verb)* stop; check

submerged *(verb)* covered over; suppressed; hidden

supplication *(noun)* humble request; prayer. In this case, the chiropractor was begging Ben's forgiveness for not being able to help him.

surging out *(descriptive expression)* coming out in waves; flowing rhythmically and with increased volume

terrorized *(verb)* coerced; forced to submit to the situation

unmanned *(verb)* deprived of manly courage or self-confidence

wound *(noun)* bodily injury in which the skin is broken, cut, torn, or pierced

yelling *(verb)* shouting; crying out loudly; screaming

Comprehension Questions

1. What was the situation at the beginning of this narrative? What was Ben doing? Why didn't he have his car? Why was this important? Who was with him? Where was his wife?
2. How did Ben's daughter, Gina, get hurt? What was the nature of her injury? Was it serious?
3. What was Ben's reaction to this emergency?
4. What did the people in passing cars do when Ben asked them to drive him to the hospital? What does the author mean when he says one woman's face was a mask?
5. Why didn't the chiropractor help?

6. What did Gina think was going to happen to her? What did Ben promise her?

7. What happened in the draftsman's office?

8. What caused the delay in treatment at the hospital? How did Ben deal with the problem? What was the doctor's response?

9. Was Gina's wound serious? Why didn't the doctor use stitches to close the wound?

10. What did Ben and his daughters do after Gina's emergency medical treatment?

11. Was Ben still upset about the incident four days later? How do you know? What did he do?

12. How did his wife behave toward him?

13. What did Ben achieve by crying? What would have happened, according to the author, if Ben hadn't cried?

Topics for Critical Analysis, Discussion, and Writing

1. In the United States, anyone who gives medical aid to an injured person can be held responsible for any damage caused by his or her help, no matter how well intentioned it may be. For instance, if a person uses cardiopulmonary resuscitation (CPR) to keep an accident victim alive until an ambulance comes, but in the process breaks the victim's rib which punctures a lung and causes a long and expensive illness, an ungrateful victim may sue his or her rescuer for damages. In addition, chiropractors and other health care professionals who are not licensed physicians can get into serious trouble for giving medical care. As a result, many people are afraid to help accident victims. What are the laws in your country regarding giving help of this kind? Should the laws in the United States be changed? Why or why not?

2. Notice the economy of the article. What important details are included and what unnecessary information is excluded?

3. What is the theme or main idea of the article? What is the author's purpose in writing it?

4. Write an essay in which you discuss the appropriateness of Ben's tears. Should men be discouraged from showing their emotions openly? Is it only acceptable for women to cry? Give and discuss specific reasons that support your views.

5. Identify all the people who refused to help Ben and examine their behavior. Why didn't they help? Should Ben forgive them? What if Gina had died?

6. What would you have done if Ben had asked you for help? Would you

have driven him and his injured daughter to the hospital even if it meant getting blood on the upholstery of your new car or becoming financially liable in some way?

7. Rewrite Ben's narrative as a positive experience.

8. Write a narrative about some emergency that you or a family member faced. Was it a positive or a negative experience? Explain.

4

Description: Using the Senses and the Imagination

Description, the last of the three major forms of writing, sometimes is used to make the other two—exposition and narration—more lively and interesting. In fact, each of the three types is frequently dependent upon the others to ensure the reader's understanding and enjoyment. Most expository writing includes some narration or description; straight narration relies heavily on description and often employs exposition; description is regularly enhanced by narration and exposition. Therefore, don't feel that you must totally separate the three forms in your own essays.

There are many language devices that you can use to make descriptive prose colorful and exciting, and the most common of these are discussed in this chapter. However, an expository description, whether it is written objectively or subjectively, follows the same essay format introduced in chapter 1.

FITTING DESCRIPTION TO THE THESIS-DEVELOPMENT-CONCLUSION FORMAT

1. Proving the Thesis

Your reason for writing the essay must be stated in the thesis, and all descriptive information should support it. For instance, if you state that children reflect their parents' behavior and values, don't concentrate on the parents' physical appearances. It doesn't matter whether they are beautiful or handsome, have blue or brown eyes, or are tall or short. Instead, give and discuss examples of the attitudes or special qualities, such as kindness, honesty, and dependability (or the reverse), that make these parents good (or bad) role models for their children.

2. Ordering and Discussing Developmental Details

A descriptive essay that ignores order can be confusing and can stray from the stated purpose. Imagine that you are writing a descriptive paper explaining how you conquered a great fear. Suppose that just after you were licensed to drive, you were in a serious auto accident. Afterward, you were so afraid of driving or even riding in automobiles that you always took the bus or walked. Then, one day your favorite friends, James and Martha, convinced you to drive to the beach with them. You felt nervous and upset during the thirty-mile trip although you were somewhat relieved to be firmly safety belted to the back seat, the safest place in the car. The day passed happily—swimming, sunning, and picnicking. You stopped worrying about the long ride home. James and Martha went for a last swim, and you dozed in the warm sunshine. Frantic cries for help abruptly awoke you. Martha, caught in an undertow, was drowning. You ran for the lifeguard; James swam to help her. Martha was saved, but neither she nor James was able to drive home. The task fell to you.

How did this emergency help you conquer your fear of driving? You may order the experience chronologically—from start to finish—by describing each part of it. Did your hands perspire when James handed you the car keys? How did you feel when you slid in behind the wheel, backed the car out of the parking lot, merged into the heavy Sunday traffic, and braked violently for the first sudden stop? What thoughts ran through your mind when you saw a serious accident blocking traffic on the other side of the highway? How did you react when you finally drove into your friends' garage? On the other hand, you may choose to describe the situation spatially. Perhaps the calm, pleasant country—rolling hills, grassy meadows, and neatly planted fields—outside the car was in sharp contrast to the mood inside. Your fear and your friends' near tragedy may have combined to produce an unbearable tension that kept anyone from speaking; you were terrified of having an accident, Martha was in shock, and James was worried about you both. Another spatially organized essay might describe only your own sensations from head to toe—your head spinning, your arms feeling limp and numb, your heart pounding, your stomach churning, your legs weak, and your feet unable to respond to your brain's commands to step on the accelerator or the brakes.

Once you have established an orderly means of presenting your material, be sure that you explain or discuss it. Try to intermingle details and your analyses of them. Sometimes, you may give several details before you state their importance. There is no set rule for the amount of explanation needed for each example.

3. Concluding a Description

Use the conclusion to test the effectiveness of your evidence. This is especially important in a descriptive essay because sometimes writers get so involved in the details that they forget the purpose of the paper. If, after finishing the essay, the reader's reaction is "Nice description, but what's the point?", then something is missing. Double check the following:

1. Is the thesis clear?
2. Are descriptive details and anecdotes well chosen and their meanings thoroughly discussed?
3. Does every bit of information included support the thesis?

If your answer to all three is "yes," the conclusion probably needs rewriting to include some kind of judgment about the evidence given.

Read the following student essay. Is it an objective or a subjective account? Can you identify the thesis? Are enough details given? How are they ordered? Do they prove the thesis? Is the conclusion suitable?

Boat People

BichVan Dong

The day was coming to an end on a remote island as beautiful as a painting. The brisk, clean wind refreshed me as I sat on the earth-colored sand to admire the lovely, natural scenery. I could hear the roar of the crashing waves breaking upon the shore, smell the fresh salt in the air, and feel the moisture in the atmosphere. The fiery orange lines from the sun were radiating away from the horizon. But this calm evening was disturbed by the appearance of a small sailboat on the sea, an event that I will never forget because it symbolized the essential need of every human being for freedom.

The white spot appeared far away on the vast, blue surface. The tattery sail fluttered as if entreating someone to help. The seacoast became crowded and animated with people as the boat came within reach. Together we tried to pull it in. We discovered then that it had sailed from a great distance—all the way from Viet Nam. The boat was very battered and we wondered how it could have endured such a long trip.

I was so affected that I nearly wept when I saw nine skinny male survivors. They lay motionlessly, piled up like dead bodies. But one of them still had enough strength to speak to the camp leader. His weak voice came out through his parched, cracked lips that moved slowly, like those of a person who was half-frozen. I looked at his big, glassy eyes. They reflected such endurance and fear that I instinctively reached out to touch his hand. His skin was cold and clammy. He was barely alive. In addition, his sunken cheeks made his face more terrible than a skull. His clothes were torn and grimy and spotted with dry blood. The dirt and sweat mixed together made an unendurable fetid odor which was so strong that I almost vomited. The rest of the survivors were in the same awful condition. These nine men were sent to emergency in the sickbay. At last, they had a chance for a free life. They had survived.

After a while, the seaside became tranquil. The moon came out from behind the mountain and shone on the sea like the bright new lives of the nine piteous men.

BichVan Dong's essay chronologically recounts a brief, but memorable, incident. Every detail in the development is part of an extended example that, as a whole, provides overwhelming evidence of the intensity of the survivors' need for freedom. The author does not interrupt the description to discuss each detail, but includes so much evidence that the point of this subjective essay is unmistakable. In the conclusion, the author compares the bright light of the moon with the newly won freedom of the nine men. With light, there is hope.

LANGUAGE DEVICES

1. Careful Word Choice

The right words bring a description to life. Include specific nouns and verbs that convey exact meanings, and choose modifiers for maximum impact. This newspaper account of an attempted purse-snatching includes especially good choices of nouns and verbs. The article begins with a clear thesis and then compounds reported, objective details—the facts: who, what, when, where, and how they happened—to build to an unusual climax.

This Woman Makes Purse Grab Risky

Hell hath no fury like that of 49-year-old Wilhelmina Anderson of Pasadena, who turned an attempted purse-snatching incident into a painful lesson in good manners.

A police spokesman gave this story: Mrs. Anderson was walking to her car in the parking lot of the Lucky Market on East Villa Street in Pasadena about 1:20 p.m. Thursday when she saw a youth approaching her.

When the youth broke into a jog and grabbed her purse, she grabbed him by the shirt, threw him against a parked car, and kneed him in the groin, spilling her bag of groceries in the process.

Her anger gaining momentum, Mrs. Anderson hurled her assailant to the ground, after hitting him over the head with a bag of ice, kicked him fervently in the groin and fell upon him, striking him with a can of salad oil which had fallen from her bag of groceries.

Luckily for the youth, another shopper interceded on his behalf, pulling her from him.

Mrs. Anderson then picked up her groceries and drove away, but not before she glanced in her rear-view mirror and watched approvingly as the youth was helped to his knees, a posture befitting his rueful discovery that the 56th anniversary of women's suffrage was a poor time to misbehave.

Asked whether she thought the youth would try another purse-snatching in the near future, she allowed as how if her sore foot was any sign, he wouldn't be doing much of anything for a good while.

We aren't told the emotions of Mrs. Anderson or her attacker; but the story is compelling because the outcome is quite unexpected and the language is vivid and immediate. Notice the action words included: Mrs. Anderson **grabbed, threw, kneed, hurled, hit, kicked, struck,** and **fell upon** the youth. Furthermore, some of the nouns are very descriptive. A **jog** is a slow, steady, running pace. The **groin** is the very sensitive area where the abdomen joins either thigh. **Assailant** is a synonym for attacker. Adjectives are also used to make certain nouns more specific. An **attempted purse-snatching** incident describes both the kind of theft and its failure. The youth's **painful** lesson in **good** manners was clearly needed. Imagine the damage Mrs. Anderson could have done if she had thrown the youth against a moving vehicle instead of a **parked** car! Adverbs are used sparingly in the article. Their sole function is to intensify and qualify verbs. The victim kicked the youth **fervently.** As she drove away, she watched **approvingly** in the rear-view mirror as the youth was helped to his knees.

Reprinted by permission of the Pasadena *Star News*.

2. Sensory Details

Even more immediate are details that describe something by relating it to a sensory response—sight, sound, taste, touch, or smell. Look again at BichVan Dong's essay, "Boat People." Notice that as she was sitting on the beach looking at the scenery, she heard the waves breaking, smelled the salt air, and felt the moisture from the ocean. When she touched one of the survivor's hands, his skin felt cold and clammy, and the odor emanating from the nearly dead men was so foul that it made her sick. All of these details relate to the senses. Now, imagine paragraphs three, four, and five of the account of the purse-snatching incident written to show the youth's sensory responses. The article might have looked something like this:

According to the youth, he broke into a jog just as he approached the woman. He saw that she was pretty old and figured she was probably weak, too. Even so, his heart was pounding with excitement and nervousness. He easily grabbed her handbag because her arms were full of groceries. Then, he felt the soft, leather strap of her purse jerk out of his hand as she threw him against a parked car. Pain exploded in his neck and back. When he felt her knee crushing his groin, a hot, terrible agony surged through his body. He couldn't move. His shrill scream echoed in his ears.

Suddenly, a cold, heavy object slammed down on the top of his head, and he heard a dull thudding noise like a ripe melon cracking open on the sidewalk after being dropped from a second-story window. He woke up on the pavement. Fireworks seemed to be bursting before his eyes. He couldn't see anything else. Then she kicked him in the groin again and when he doubled up to protect himself, she grabbed a huge, heavy can and hit him with it repeatedly. He gasped under the weight of her body squashing the breath out of him and pressing him against the cement. When he could see again, her face was within inches of his. She was panting with fury, but her warm spearmint-scented breath was strangely pleasant. Her lips were moving, but he couldn't understand what she was saying. Then, before he could dodge the blow, she hit him again on the side of the face with the heavy can. He said that the last thing he remembered was the taste of salty blood as it gushed from his mouth.

Reread the passage and underline every sensory detail. You should be able to find at least one that relates to each of the senses.

FIGURATIVE LANGUAGE: WORD ARTISTRY

Adjectives and adverbs modify thinking by the process of simple addition. Figurative comparisons, however, force our minds to create images in order to evaluate similarities, either by stating directly or by merely suggesting the imaginary "picture." Because the human imagination is very active, it needs only a little help to develop a simple idea into one that is much more complex, just as an artist transforms a rough sketch into a finished painting. According to noted author Laurence Perrine, language experts have identified about 250 different figures of speech, many of which are seldom used. We will discuss only a few of the most common figurative comparisons.

1. Simile

A direct or obvious comparison, called a simile, often begins with "like" or "as." In this figure of speech, the writer compares one thing to another in very exact terms so the reader has no doubt about the similarity. If a person eats like a pig, he or she has terrible manners and probably snuffles and snorts and ingests food in a very unattractive way. To say that someone is as big as a hippopotamus is obviously not a compliment about the person's weight. Each of these examples makes a limited comparison of one quality that a human shares with an animal; however, comparisons may be made with inanimate objects, as well. Someone who is like the Rock of Gibraltar is absolutely dependable. A person who is as hard as steel is unsympathetic, unyielding, and tough. Anyone who is as sweet as honey has a sickeningly pleasant disposition. Comparisons may also be made between people. A young woman who is as delighted as a newly selected Miss America is all smiles. A young man who plays basketball just like Wilt Chamberlain is very professional. Since similes make exact comparisons of specific characteristics, there is no chance for misunderstanding and no need for guessing.

2. Metaphor

A more indirect or subtle comparison, a metaphor, uses a word or phrase with one meaning in place of another to suggest a strong likeness between them. The writer supplies the general idea, but expects the reader to imagine the exact comparison. Suppose that two young men are discussing a third friend, Bill, the youth who snatched Mrs. Anderson's purse. Joe says admiringly, "That Bill is really a tiger!" He means, of course, that Bill is fierce, strong, and fights well. He knows nothing about Bill's encounter with Mrs. Anderson, so he is shocked to hear Tom respond, "You should have seen him yesterday. He tried to steal some poor woman's purse, and after she finished with him, he was nothing more than a weak kitten." Joe is speaking of the youth's lack of physical strength. Clearly, the two friends' opinions of Bill differ greatly. By calling Bill a tiger or a weak kitten, they suggest that Bill shares the qualities for which those animals are most noted.

In telling Tom about the incident, the defeated youth may have confided that Mrs. Anderson was a wildcat without specifying whether she *looked,* *sounded,* or *fought* like a wildcat. He only suggested that she had wildcat-like characteristics. Among the possibilities are that Mrs. Anderson physically resembled a wildcat (rather unlikely), that she growled, snarled, and shrieked in such a way that she sounded like the animal, or that she was a formidable, vicious, dangerous fighter. Based on the context of the sentence (the meaning of that and related sentences), Tom probably imagined the third possibility.

When Mrs. Anderson told her husband about the experience, he might have said, "You are indeed a lioness, my dear! Good work!", indicating that his wife shared the animal's ability to defend herself against predators.

3. Symbol

Similes state exactly the comparison to be drawn; metaphors suggest a general comparison and rely on the reader's experience and imagination to provide the specifics; symbols are even more abstract and indirect. A symbol may have one or several meanings, but it is always used to represent a significant idea or value that has importance both inside and outside the reading. However, readers shouldn't give just any word symbolic value. The context of a piece of writing must signal the reader—often by repetition or emphasis—that a word is intended as a symbol. It may be an object, an action, a person, or even a name; it may reflect a state or condition; however, it must be different in kind from whatever it represents. For example, one flower can not symbolize another. In *The Little Prince,* the rose represents responsibility, not all the other roses in the garden. The wheat fields and the golden grain symbolize the color of the little prince's hair, his taming of the fox, and the lasting bond between the fox and the boy. The little prince himself stands for the good in human nature (remember, the fox has always before been hunted by men). If the owner of the wheat fields were named Mr. Hunter, his name would symbolize his and all men's behavior toward the fox.

A *universal symbol* is one that is understood by most people everywhere. For instance, the seasons are universal symbols. Spring suggests birth and rebirth, summer indicates maturity, fall is the sign of old age, and winter signals death. The rising sun symbolizes a new beginning or hope, and the setting sun signifies death or hopelessness.

A *personal symbol* is defined by individual experience; for example, the wheat fields in *The Little Prince* have constant meaning unique to the fox, but unknown to others. Individual superstitions can also cause people to create personal symbols. For instance, if you are wearing your favorite blue sweater every time something good happens, that garment may become your personal symbol for success or happiness.

A *conventional symbol* is one that varies from culture to culture, depending on custom. For example, a young Spanish woman, who was hospitalized in the United States for a very serious condition, received a beautiful chrysanthemum plant from a visitor one afternoon. (Because the flowers are long-lasting, they are frequently sent to cheer hospital patients.) The yellow blooms were sunny and gorgeous, and the visitor eagerly anticipated the young woman's pleasure. Imagine the friend's surprise when the patient began weeping so hysterically that she had to be sedated! Later, the visitor learned that chrysanthemums were commonly sent to funerals in Spain; the patient interpreted her friend's gift as a sign that she was going to die.

A well-known conventional symbol in Western cultures is the cross as the sign of Christianity. In the United States, the dove signals peace, and the hawk stands for war.

4. Personification

This comparative figure of speech gives human characteristics to nonhuman things. Personification is a favorite of poets, but you can also use this technique to make your writing lively. If taken literally, personification would be awfully silly, but when interpreted figuratively, some interesting meanings occur. Here are some examples:

The flowers breathed out their sweet perfume. (Do the flowers have lungs? No, they emit a lovely fragrance.)

The yellow daffodils nodded their heads as Carol passed by. (Do flowers have heads? No, the flower is often considered the "head" of the plant because it is at the top and is the prettiest part. Actually, when Carol walked by, a breeze probably moved the flowers.)

The wind whistled, and the rain pounded on the window. (What tune or song did the wind whistle? In reality, the wind made a whistling noise. Did the rain pound on the window with its fists or with a hammer? It did neither. The force of the raindrops against the glass sounded like hammering.)

My heart sings every time I see my sweetheart. (Does your heart actually open its mouth and sing opera? Of course not! When you see your sweetheart, you feel very happy. But the emotion is in your head, not your heart.)

ALLITERATION

Another language device that can add interest to writing, as long as it is done in moderation, is alliteration. This is the technique of repeating initial consonant sounds in two or more neighboring syllables or words in a sentence. For example, a motorcycle gang might be *w*ild and *w*icked; young sweethearts might *l*ook *l*ongingly at each other; and a cat might *p*ounce *p*owerfully on a mouse; but a little alliteration can go a long way. If you use too much, it seems strained and attracts attention. Readers are hardly able to suppress laughter when reading a sentence like "The *l*ovely *l*ady *l*ooked *l*ongingly at *L*arry as he *l*ounged *l*azily beside the *l*ake."

The most important things to remember about using language devices and figurative language are:

1. Choose precise words that convey specific meanings.
2. Select figures of speech that are noticed only because of their excellence or because they enrich meaning.
3. Use alliteration sparingly. Language devices should not be obvious, distracting, or annoying.

Examine the following passage. Identify as many of the characteristics of a good description as you can.

The Transformation

Money does make the man. That was proven to me one frosty winter day by a tramp who passed through our town. Because we aren't on the railroad, and we don't have missions or volunteer establishments to feed and house transients, we seldom see them. So this stranger was an object of curiosity.

His feet made whushing noises as he shuffled along the street. His head was bent, and he swung it slowly from side to side, like a big, shaggy pendulum, methodically searching gutters and doorways for a coin, a half-smoked cigarette, a bottle or an aluminum can that might be worth a few cents, or even a bit of discarded food. His clothes were rags—shapeless, stained, and torn. His grimy feet must have felt like blocks of ice that freezing windy morning since they were protected only by shabby, flapping sandals. He stepped into a telephone booth, visibly relieved to get out of the wind for a moment, and I saw his terrier fingers automatically explore the coin return box for forgotten change. There was nothing. He resumed his slow passage along the street. Although he was still ten or fifteen feet away from me, I could hear his teeth chattering. Involuntarily he shuddered, and a thin, high, wailing sigh escaped his lips.

Suddenly, he noticed me sitting there on the bus bench. With one quick glance, he took in everything. I was young, well fed, and alert, but most of all I was warm. I felt ashamed of my heavy wool coat and the snug boots encasing my feet and legs. For just a split second, our glances met. His eyes were mirrors reflecting such deep misery that I felt a guilty rush of sympathy. It must have shown in my expression, for he looked away at once. Then he trudged on. Impulsively, I jumped up, pretended to pick up a bill from the sidewalk, and called to him. "Just a minute, mister! I think you dropped this."

He looked hard at me for a moment. Then relief wiped the despair from his face. His shoulders straightened. Out came his cracked, dirty fist, as fast as a cat's paw, and he tried not to snatch the bill from my hand. "Thank you," he said. "I was looking for that." He was careful not to touch my gloved hand as he took the bill. Then he gave me a mock salute and a lopsided smile, and walked briskly away, his head up and his step firm.

Having a little money in his pocket again transformed this beaten derelict into a man of substance. I learned that morning that pride is the vital ingredient in self respect. Even the most pitiful persons in our society must be allowed to hold their heads high, especially since it costs the rest of us so little.

The thesis, of course, is a rephrasing of the old saying, "Money makes the man." A man with money automatically gains self-worth and earns the respect of others. The introduction explains the reason this transient was so intently observed. The essay is chronologically ordered, and language devices are used carefully.

Notice the action words and their modification. The man **shuffled**, suggesting an unsure, dragging step. He **swung** his head **slowly**, **methodically**, rhythmically, not missing a single square inch in his search for resources. His fingers **explored** the forgotten corners of the coin box. His noisily chattering teeth indicated such uncontrollable physical response to the extreme cold that the sigh **escaped involuntarily**. We learn in the next paragraph that he was too proud to let anyone know how cold and hungry he was. After he saw that the occupant of the bus bench felt sorry for him, the transient looked away at once and **trudged** on. Obviously, it was the hardest kind of labor for him to keep moving. The younger person **jumped up**, full of energy, and handed the man the bill that he had "**dropped**." Then a miraculous change occurred. The transient's shoulders **straightened**; he walked **briskly** away. He was transformed from a subhuman to a human being.

Observe the use of nouns and adjectives. A **half-smoked cigarette** or some **discarded food** would appeal only to a desperate person, to someone like this transient, dressed in **shapeless**, **stained**, **torn clothing** and wearing **flapping sandals** without socks to cover his **grimy feet**. His suffering found a natural vocal outlet, the **thin**, **high**, **wailing sigh**. When he saw the young person dressed so warmly in a **heavy coat** and **snug boots**, the transient probably felt even colder. Even though he saw through the pretense covering the gift of the money, the **beaten** man took it. And in the taking, his entire behavior changed. He was careful not to touch his benefactor's **gloved hand** with his **cracked**, **dirty fist**, but his spirit was so improved that he managed a **mock salute** and a **lopsided smile**.

Several figures of speech are included in the passage. There are some similes: **His head was like a big shaggy pendulum; his feet must have felt like blocks of ice; out came his cracked, dirty fist, as fast as a cat's paw**. We can find metaphors, too: **His clothes were rags; his terrier fingers searched the coin box** (a terrier is a hunting dog that burrows into the ground after small game animals); **his eyes were mirrors** that reflected his misery. Finally, we see that relief was personified when it **wiped the despair from his face** as the man himself might have cleansed his face with a damp cloth.

Although several examples of alliteration can be found in the essay, the most poetic occur in the last sentence, which states that even *p*itiful *p*ersons must be allowed to *h*old their *h*eads *h*igh in our society—everyone needs self-pride.

The following selections have been chosen for their descriptive qualities, for their use of language devices, or for their figurative language.

READINGS

The Brave and Ingenious Montague Stevens

Robert L. McGrath

Robert L. McGrath relies almost exclusively on language devices—careful selection of nouns, adjectives, verbs, and adverbs—to recreate the colorful and unusual Montague Stevens, a real person whose achievements became legendary in the New Mexico wilderness area of the Old West. The author includes many examples that demonstrate Stevens' ingenuity, and describes each incident with interesting "word pictures." Watch for the thesis in the sixth paragraph following the long, but lively introduction.

The two riders were nearing the **tule** on the edge of the little California lake where the **goose blind** would hide them from the **honking Canadas**. One horseman was lean, mustached and soberly dignified as he carefully analyzed a situation new to him. The other, on familiar ground, was relaxed and thoroughly at ease. Each held a loaded double-barreled shotgun across his saddle.

Without warning, the first rider's horse **bolted** into the bushes. The horseman grabbed the **muzzle** of his gun with his left hand, holding it away from him while he tried to pull up the horse with his right hand. A branch suddenly caught one hammer of the **shotgun**, pulling it back and at the same time jerking the gun around to point toward its carrier. It went off with an explosive roar.

The second rider jumped from his mount, horrified to see on the ground what was left of his companion's left arm. He bent to pick it up. The injured man, meantime, had snatched the old felt hunting hat from his head and was pressing it against the **spurting** flow of blood at his left shoulder.

Back in the saddle, the second man gently placed the shattered arm across the **pommel** in front of him, turning his horse back the way they had come.

"Ah, by Jove," said the wounded man in his **clipped British accent**, "when we get to your home, I'll bother you for that arm. That's my property!"

And thus the stage was set for one of the most colorful characters ever to come into—or out of—the West. The twenty-nine-year-old Englishman who lost his arm in the hunting accident in the fall of 1888 was a New Mexico rancher named Montague Farquhard Sheffield Stevens, who accepted his loss as a personal challenge not to allow it **to handicap** him. From that first shocking moment when he claimed the arm as "my property," Montague Stevens **steadfastly** refused to depend on others for anything a person with two arms could do.

I came to know the Montague Stevens legends as a child, for my father had grown up in the wilderness area of southwestern New Mexico where the Britisher owned extensive ranch lands. The stories my father told of hunts for mountain lions and grizzly bears, and of Stevens' pack of hunting dogs, are an **indelible** and exciting memory.

Montague Stevens, Cambridge educated, came to America on a vacation trip in 1880, hunting in the **Grand Tetons** of Wyoming after learning the fine art of rifle shooting from a professional big game hunter and a gunsmith. He returned in 1882 to begin cattle and sheep ranching in Socorro County, New Mexico. His **holdings** were eventually to **span** an area some eighty miles long, toward the Arizona border, and thirty miles wide, and his **SU brand** was a landmark in the region.

With property on both sides of the **Continental Divide**, the average altitude of his ranch land was 7,000 feet, with mountain peaks rising to 11,000 feet. Among the pine, cedar, piñon, juniper and oak trees at lower elevations, black bears thrived on piñon nuts, juniper berries and acorns. Higher up, the silvertip grizzlies **foraged**, supplementing their regular diet with an occasional cow from Stevens' herds.

A lesser man might have shrugged and accepted this as an **inevitable** law of nature. Not so with Montague Stevens. The size and strength of the grizzly embodied just one more challenge to him. He unhesitatingly hunted for the big bears—often alone except for his dogs.

Stevens had great respect for his fellowman, and he always sought the good in everyone. In most of his associations, he recognized worthy qualities, and accepted the commendable over any shortcomings. He had, however, a strict sense of justice, and more than once went to great lengths to bring **retribution** to those who failed to live up to his standards of property rights and fair play.

Perhaps the best illustration of Stevens' determination not to let his one arm create obstacles lies in some of the **unique** methods he used to overcome difficult situations. Although he was thought of as an *hombre muy curioso* (very odd man), and was even **ridiculed** by neighboring ranchers, there were frequent occasions when his genius for solving problems paid big **dividends**.

There was the time, for instance, when a band of horse thieves was **marauding** the area. Two of them, an advance party, worked for him briefly, and his cook overheard them discussing plans to run off his horses when the others reached the **spread**.

Law and order, what there was of it, was far removed from the ranch, and Stevens had to rely on his wits to save his valuable animals. His hired hands and neighbors laughed when he had all his horses rounded up and cut their tails short. They thought it a "crazy Englishman" trick.

But the laugh was on the others. The thieves did, indeed, gather Stevens' horses, but upon seeing those short tails and knowing each animal could be immediately identified, they left in disgust, stealing not one horse. Others were not so fortunate.

On another occasion, he devised a means of **breaking broncos** four at a time by using **a sweep from an old threshing machine**. By coupling the broncs with gentle horses and forcing the animals to walk around and around in a circle, he soon subdued the animals, getting them to accept saddle and rider in only a few days—far less time than the traditional "ride 'em, cowboy" practice. But his method was too extraordinary—he had to abandon it because the cowboys felt it beneath their dignity to accept horses not broken in the usual fashion.

He devised other unique ways to break his horses of bad habits. One animal was **balky**, stopping stock-still for no reason whenever it took a notion. Stevens purposely rode the horse into an icy stream where—following its custom—it stopped square in the middle. Instead of beating on it to move ahead, Stevens sat calmly in the saddle reading a newspaper, and within a few minutes, the **frigid** water swirling around the horse's knees prompted it to move on quickly. The horse was never known to balk again.

Stevens' ingenuity knew no bounds. Sometimes during bear hunts, he and his companion would lower their horses by a neck rope over the brink of a ledge, to save time in pursuing their quarry. Looping the rope around a small pine tree, they would back the horses (one had to be blindfolded) over the ledge and ease them to solid footing beneath. He also trained the horses to slide down twenty-foot embankments on their haunches, to save time on the chase.

One time he brought a fully loaded wagon to the top of a steep downward trail, only to find that the brake was broken—the drag he would normally use to keep the wagon from plunging downward on the **incline**. Although he almost never whipped his horses, this time was an exception. Tying the lines around his neck (a difficult **feat** with one hand), he suddenly **lashed out** at the animals with the whip, making them lunge down the trail at full speed. In this way, they actually outran the runaway wagon, not only saving themselves from injury but also the supplies which would have tumbled out.

Stevens devised a unique method of carrying a black bear, shot when he was alone, back to camp. Single-handed, he suspended the bear from a ten-foot-high limb of a pine tree by using two ropes attached to the **saddle horn**. Then, with the horse holding the bear suspended with one rope, he would tie the other rope to another limb, to hold the bear in place. Through a series of complicated actions, he would eventually lower the bear onto the horse's back, securing, with collars from his dogs, each of the bear's feet to a **cinch ring** on the saddle. The 300-pound bear ended up awkwardly **spread-eagled** atop the horse, but ready to be carried back to camp.

One key to Montague Stevens' success was his gentle approach to the animals he trained to help him. When it came to endurance tests for horses—and these occurred frequently on grizzly bear hunts—Stevens' philosophy was to put himself in the horse's place and act accordingly.

With dogs, cooperation was the main factor. "I try to help my dogs," he would say, emphasizing the need to convey to the dog "what you mean in a way he will understand." The result was an amazingly obedient and well-trained pack of dogs. Where others would beat their animals for **running deer** instead of bear, Stevens painstakingly trained his hounds, so they did as he wished.

Aside from the humane aspect, he felt that beating broke the dog's spirit, making him afraid. He proved his point many times by having his dogs sit in a row, each with a piece of meat on his nose, waiting for the words they wanted to hear. Only when Stevens said "Paid for!" would they toss the meat in the air, catch it and eat it.

They would also wait for hours in a particular spot when told to "Stay there!" While Stevens visited one of his sheep camps. The sheep, instinctively frightened by the dogs, remained undisturbed.

The hunting pack was **a veritable United Nations of dogdom**. There was a tiny fox terrier named Twist, whose job was to bark in the bear's face, identifying its whereabouts and often distracting it so Stevens could shoot it.

There were Russian wolfhounds, a Great Dane, an English bobtailed sheep dog, an English mastiff, a greyhound, two Scotch deerhounds, Scotch collies, and a varied assortment of other Scotch, Irish, fox and bull terriers, as well as a number of dogs of unknown origin.

Key animals to the bear hunt, however, were his bloodhounds, led by an expert called **Sleuth**, who could pick up the track of a grizzly bear after several days and follow it to its hiding place. Stevens trained some of the dogs as trail dogs, to keep in touch with both the pursuing hounds as they chased the bear, and with the riders, often left far behind as they crossed **rugged** canyons and sought their way through thickly wooded forests.

More than once, Stevens came close to being **mauled** by grizzly bears he had shot but had failed to hit in a **vulnerable** spot with the first bullet. Reloading quickly was impossible with his one arm so he carried a pistol for such emergencies. His dogs helped, too, often keeping the bears so **harassed** they could not attack the hunter.

Why did Stevens, with only one arm, insist on facing the dangers of hunting grizzly bears? Aside from the loss of cattle the bears killed, there was an even greater motive. To him, the grizzly represented the ultimate challenge—to do battle with these massive creatures was the **apex of human endeavor**. To him, it was a glorious achievement to **outwit** and conquer the big bears.

Among his most prized possessions was a collection of bullets—misshapen chunks of lead he had taken from grizzlies he had killed. They were a reminder of the excitement of the chase, of limitless energies and risks expended in pursuit of the furry giants.

Although Montague Stevens was to live more than forty years longer, he hung up his grizzly rifle for good not long after the turn of the century. His bloodhound pack, essential to his bear-hunting forays, found some poisoned meat a rancher had put out for coyotes, and all of them died. At the time, Stevens—whose fame had spread across the country—was planning to invite Theodore Roosevelt to New Mexico for a grizzly bear hunt, a hunt which never came about because of the loss of the hounds.

In typical fashion, Stevens for the rest of his days was an **ardent conservationist**, seeking to prevent the extinction of the noble grizzly he had fought so fiercely with his one arm and his **undaunted** spirit.

Glossary

apex of human endeavor *(noun)*   highest point of human effort

ardent *(adjective)*   passionate; enthusiastic; devoted

a sweep from an old threshing machine *(noun)*   long blade, mounted on a pivot, that was part of a machine used to harvest wheat or other grain. Stevens mounted the pivoting end of the blade on a stationary post, tied four horses (both wild and tame) along the length of the blade, and made the animals walk in a circle to train the wild horses.

a veritable United Nations of dogdom *(figurative expression)*   all breeds of dogs were represented

balky *(adjective)*   stubbornly resistant

bolted *(verb)*   started suddenly and ran

breaking broncos *(colloquialism)*   taming or breaking the spirit of wild horses to make them obedient

Canadas *(noun)*   Canada geese

cinch ring *(noun)*   ring at the end of the leather band that fastens the saddle on the horse

clipped British accent *(noun)*   words shortened by omitting syllables or letters and spoken with British stress and intonation

conservationist *(noun)*   person who advocates caring for and preserving natural resources

Continental Divide *(noun)*   ridge of the Rocky Mountains that separates rivers flowing to the east from those flowing to the west

dividends *(noun)*   usually sums of money, representing profits from a publicly owned company, that are divided among stockholders—thus, the term **dividends**

feat *(noun)*   accomplishment

foraged *(verb)*   searched for food

frigid *(adjective)*   extremely cold

goose blind *(noun)*   natural looking hiding place for hunters to use when shooting wild geese

Grand Tetons *(noun)*   The Teton Range, located in Grand Teton National Park in northwest Wyoming, is part of the Rocky Mountains that run from Alaska to Mexico

harassed *(verb)*   worried; troubled; tormented

holdings *(noun)*   land or property owned; sometimes financial holdings such as stock or bonds

honking *(verb)*   calling of a wild goose

incline *(noun)*   slanted surface; slope; slight hill

indelible *(adjective)*   permanent; lasting

inevitable *(adjective)*   unavoidable

lashed out *(verb)*   struck out violently

marauding *(verb)*   raiding and stealing; roving and plundering

mauled *(verb)*   injured by tearing, beating, or bruising

muzzle *(noun)*   front end of the barrel of a gun

outwit *(verb)*   overcome, or get the better of, by cleverness

pommel *(noun)*   rounded, upward projecting front part of a saddle

retribution *(noun)*   deserved punishment for wrongdoing

ridiculed *(verb)*   mocked; scorned; joked about in an unkind way

rugged *(adjective)*   rough; irregular projections and depressions; harsh

running deer *(colloquialism)*   chasing or running after deer (instead of bear)

saddle horn *(noun)*   high pommel of a Western (as opposed to an English) saddle, which is made of leather but shaped like a horn. The saddle horn is used to fasten the cowboy's rope when he is trying to tie up animals.

shotgun *(noun)*   gun used for hunting small animals at short range (distance). Instead of conventional bullets, shotguns fire clusters of small, spherical, metallic particles that cover a wider area than a single bullet.

sleuth *(noun, colloquialism)*   detective. Bloodhounds are known for their ability to follow scents.

span *(verb)*   extend or stretch over; cover

spread *(noun, colloquialism)*   Western term for ranch

spread-eagled *(verb)*   all four limbs stretched out to resemble the United States' emblem of an eagle with its wings and legs spread

spurting *(verb)*   gushing forth in a stream or jet

steadfastly *(adverb)*   firmly; constantly

SU brand *(noun)*   The letters SU were burned into the flesh of animals as a mark or brand of ownership.

to handicap *(verb)*   to disadvantage or hinder

tule *(noun)*   large bulrushes (similar to cattail or papyrus plants) found in lakes and marshes

undaunted *(adjective)*   unhesitating; unfaltering; undiscouraged

unique *(adjective)*   highly unusual; extraordinary; unequaled

vulnerable *(adjective)*   easily hurt or injured

Comprehension Questions

1. How did Stevens lose his arm? What was his reaction? How old was he at the time?
2. Was Stevens a native of the United States?
3. Where was he educated?
4. When and why did he first come to the United States? When and why did he return?
5. Describe Stevens's ranch. Where was it located? What was the altitude? What kinds of plant and animal life were found there?
6. What animal did Stevens especially like to hunt? Why?

7. What did Stevens's neighbors think of some of his ways of protecting his property and solving his ranching problems?

8. How did Stevens keep his horses from being stolen?

9. What unusual method did he use to break horses? How did the cowboys feel about this new technique?

10. How did Stevens teach his horse not to balk?

11. What timesaving "tricks" did Stevens use during bear hunts?

12. What did Stevens do when the brake broke on his fully loaded wagon just as he was about to drive it down a steep trail?

13. How did Stevens, alone and with only one arm, manage to carry a 300-pound bear back to camp?

14. What approach did Stevens use to get his trained horses and dogs to help him?

15. Why does the author say that Stevens's hunting dogs represented a "United Nations of dogdom"?

16. What animals were the most important in hunting bears? Why?

17. Why did Stevens insist on hunting dangerous grizzly bears?

18. What was the importance of his bullet collection?

19. Why didn't Stevens invite Theodore Roosevelt to a grizzly bear hunt as he had planned to do?

20. What kind of change occurred in Stevens's attitude about grizzly bears after his dogs were poisoned?

Topics for Critical Analysis, Discussion, and Writing

1. Stevens's neighbors thought he was odd because of some of the unusual methods he used to solve problems related to his ranch. He was, in fact, probably *very* different from most of the people who lived in the area. In the Old West, people had to be tough and clever (although not necessarily well-educated) to stay alive and to keep their property. Over the years, ranchers developed ranching methods that worked. Most newcomers adopted established practices; if they didn't, the old timers made fun of them or mistrusted them. Remember that even the cowboys who worked for Stevens resented changes in the traditional way of breaking horses. The most notable differences between Stevens and his contemporaries were that he was well-educated, foreign-born, and physically disabled. Write an essay in which you discuss how these three differences made Stevens a legendary figure of the Old West.

2. Why do you think Stevens became an "ardent conservationist"? Why didn't he just train new hunting dogs?

3. Analyze Stevens's reaction to the loss of his arm. How did he overcome his handicap? What might a less resourceful or strong-willed person have done?

4. Identify as many examples of Stevens's ingenuity as you can, and explain how they contributed to the legend about this unusual man.

5. Examine the language devices used in the article. Notice that the choice of words greatly affects meaning. Choose several nouns, adjectives, verbs, or adverbs that you think are especially effective, and try to find as many synonyms as possible for each. Replace the author's choices with some of the synonyms you have found. Discuss changes in the meaning of phrases or sentences.

6. Write a description of a legendary or special person that you have heard about or that you know. Choose details carefully. Make sure the language you select paints a "word picture." Follow the thesis-development-conclusion format.

Frogs

David Barton

David Barton's poem is graphic in its details. The poet-photographer is conscious of every shape, color, position, and movement of his subjects, and he describes them by using many of the language devices you have read about in this chapter. Watch for striking use of nouns, adjectives, and verbs. Observe that Barton also uses similes and metaphors to enhance his word picture.

FROGS

Wet, **wart**-conscious,
I've come to photograph
their private lives.
Some are as yellow
as a worn **mackintosh**;
some are black,
shaped like fists

and barely able to move;
all are kiss-starved
princelings of the marsh.
The marsh itself is golden,
with **reeds** and **cattails**
swaying in the flood.
The **matted marl** and
watercourse are filled
with their **plague**,
swarms sitting on each other,
swollen, **huddled** together.
Lords of the short **snort**,
brothers of the **slug**
and the **mallard duck**,
sheriffs of the marsh,
czars of the **ooze**,
gods of the **gnat** and the
dragonfly, they fill
every **nook and cranny**,
drooping like genitals,
congenitally fat,
prized for their legs
and jellied **off-spring**,
thumb-sized, stone-sized,
webbed, **mottled**, **slick**
as the fish they almost were.
I swallow hard and **grab** one.
It slips through my hands,
pulses like a heart
racing in the heat,
lets out an old angry **croak**,
and extending its leg,
wrestles free.

Glossary

cattails *(noun)*   tall, reed-like marsh plants that flower in long, cylindrical spikes that look like the tails of cats

congenitally fat *(figurative expression)*   fat from birth as a result of the prenatal environment

croak *(verb)*   deep, hoarse sound

czars *(noun)* absolute rulers; emperors with unlimited power. Czars ruled Russia until the 1917 revolution.

drooping like genitals *(figurative expression)* hanging down like external sexual organs

gnat *(noun)* extremely tiny fly

grab *(verb)* seize or grasp suddenly or forcibly

huddled *(verb)* crowded or pushed close together

mackintosh *(noun)* raincoat, usually yellow, made of rubber-coated cloth

mallard duck *(noun)* type of wild duck from which most domestic ducks have descended. The male has distinctive markings, including an iridescent, teal green head.

matted marl *(figurative expression)* wet area of clay-like earth covered with tangled stems of plants

mottled *(adjective)* spotted or blotched with different colors or shades

nook and cranny *(idiom)* corner, crack, crevice, or opening

off-spring *(noun)* child or children

ooze *(noun)* soft mud or slime; a marsh

plague *(noun)* infectious disease that often causes death; a pestilence

princelings *(noun)* young, small, or subordinate princes

reeds *(noun)* straight, tall marsh grasses

sheriffs *(noun)* law enforcement officers. Cities usually have police departments; unincorporated (county) areas often have sheriff's departments.

slick *(adjective)* slippery

slug *(noun)* snail-like creature that has no real shell. Slugs are garden pests since they eat young, tender plants.

snort *(noun)* harsh sound made by forcing breath suddenly and violently through the nostrils

swarms *(noun)* moving masses or crowds; for example, swarms of bees or mosquitoes

swaying *(verb)* moving to and fro (first in one direction, then in another)

swollen *(adjective)* increased in volume or size by inner pressure. Some frogs puff out their throats when they croak (call).

wart *(noun)* small, hard growth on the skin, caused by a virus. According to superstition, people can "catch" warts from touching frogs or their land counterparts, toads.

watercourse *(noun)* stream of water; a river or a brook

wrestles *(verb)* struggles

Comprehension Questions

1. Why has the speaker ("I" in the poem) come to the marsh?
2. What are the colors and shape of the frogs?
3. What color is the marsh? What word describes the movement of the reeds and cattails?
4. Are there many frogs in the marsh? How are they grouped together?
5. To what other creatures are the frogs "brothers"? Since these species are different, they can't really be brothers. What, then, is the relationship between them?
6. Why are frogs prized by humans?
7. What does the frog do when the speaker grabs it?

Topics for Critical Analysis, Discussion, and Writing

1. The poet describes the frogs as "kiss-starved princelings" (remember the fairy tale about the frog that turned into a handsome prince when he was kissed by the princess whom he loved?), "lords," "sheriffs," "czars," and "gods." Why are these words used in the poem? How do they indicate the social position of the frogs in the marsh?

2. Why does the poet use the words "plague" and "swarms" to refer to the number of frogs in the "watercourse"?

3. Identify several similes and metaphors in the poem, and explain what they mean.

4. Write a description of the frogs and their surroundings by "translating" the poem into prose. Be sure you write a "translation" for every line. Try to retain the same meanings, but use your own words.

5. The poet is describing an experience by using very colorful language. Which parts of the poem describe sensations of taste, touch, sight, smell, and hearing? Which of these sensory experiences would you find most memorable? Why?

6. Identify and discuss several good choices of nouns, adjectives, and verbs in the poem. What imaginary pictures do these words suggest?

7. Observe an insect, an animal, or a plant, preferably in its natural surroundings, for several minutes. Try to get as close as possible to your subject. If, for example, you are watching a spider spinning a web, you may notice its unusual design, the stylized movements of the spider at work, or even specific details about the spider's physical appearance. Write down every sensory image that occurs to you. Then, write an expository descriptive essay

about your observations. Be sure to have a thesis, development, and conclusion. Here is a sample thesis: The ugliest, most menacing spider can gracefully produce a web of amazing symmetry and unusual beauty.

Soaring on a Song

Ronald P. Pulcini

Ronald Pulcini taught English as a Second Language for sixteen years and is now a full-time writer of fiction. He lives in Montana. Pulcini describes "Soaring on a Song" as his paean (song of praise) to Los Angeles. Notice the interesting structure of the article as you read it. You will see that it is written inductively; that is, the thesis is not stated in the beginning. Instead, the images slowly build to a climax—the final image that proves his conclusion (which is also the thesis).

I am not an **avid** flyer of kites, but I do own a **box kite**, and once a year the boy in me rushes out to meet a strong wind to launch my squared-off paper **contraption**.

Echo Park has an excellent place to catch the wind, appropriately called Kite Staff by older residents. You can simply stand on the **promontory** there and let a kite go into the **updraft** of the oncoming westerly or northwesterly winds.

On a recent particularly windy early evening, I **succumbed** to the billowing howl and pulled down my kite from storage. After inspecting the **taut**, glued seams and **haphazardly** wound string, I was out the door.

The sun was **waning**, yet still had a brilliance to it in the solid clear-blue sky. A dark-green sliver of the Pacific was visible between the buildings along Santa Monica's Ocean Avenue, some 25 miles away. Off the coast, a gathering of clouds **eyed** our mountains. It was postcard time.

The hill was vacant, so I was surprised to see a dark-colored kite **hovering** steadily in one spot over the **launching** area. Suddenly it came straight down, and I thought that it must be one of those fancy Oriental creations, its **maneuvers** controlled by clever, age-old hand movements. I stopped walking, and after a moment's study discovered it actually to be a **hawk.** Hawks are not an unusual sight in the hills here in the middle of the city, but this singular appearance was spectacular and rare.

This piece first appeared in the *Los Angeles Times*. Reprinted by permission of the author.

The hawk probably was looking for something small and **scurrying** to eat. Or he may have been simply enjoying the **crisp**, **robust** wind, delighting in his fantastic **agility** and oneness with his element.

I could not continue up the hill. I looked down at my awkward box kite, and decided not to interfere with this magnificent bird's performance. With his head bent down for the search, and **talons** hanging open and ready, this supremely designed creature outdid the best of any classical fighting-kite flyer.

By moving his tail down slightly, he let the wind lift him like an express elevator. The tips of his wings—their large, thick feathers looking like fingers—opened, closed, bent up, sloped down, giving balance to his artful **acrobatics.** He soared, circled, floated and **caressed** the breezes, all the time barely flapping his wings to maintain necessary speed.

Behind him the sun continued its descent to the horizon, the sky's **pigment** thickened and the clouds turned slowly in a **kaleidoscope** of shape and color. In the middle distance, lights **winked** on in Hollywood and the mid-Wilshire corridor. Then, in an instant, when only the **mind's eye** is fast enough to click the shutter, the hawk flew right into the middle of the warm, glowing, **ochered** sun. His wings were perfectly outstretched, his head thrust proudly forward. The image seemed like an encrusted 24-karat **medallion.**

At that moment, everything came together like a perfect song: the music of the wind, the poetry of motion, the rhythm of the city, the colors of a mild winter day. Los Angeles does not need a song, it is one.

Glossary

acrobatics *(noun)* gymnastics

agility *(noun)* lightness, quickness, and ease of movement

avid *(adjective)* eager; enthusiastic

box kite *(noun)* box-shaped kite; a light frame covered with thin material or paper and meant to be flown in the wind at the end of a long string

caressed *(verb)* embraced

contraption *(noun; colloquialism)* device or gadget that one does not fully understand

crisp *(adjective)* fresh; invigorating

Echo Park *(noun)* residential section of Los Angeles. Echo Park is located in a hilly area overlooking much of the city.

eyed *(verb)* looked at

haphazardly *(adverb)* randomly; without organization or planning

hawk *(noun)* large, carnivorous bird of prey. Hawks have exceptional vision and can identify rodent-size animals from very high altitudes. Because they have a large wing spread, hawks are able to fly like gliders (motorless planes), taking advantage of the air currents.

hovering *(verb)*   suspended or fluttering in the air near one place

kaleidoscope *(noun)*   rotating tube containing mirrors that reflect bits of colored glass in continually changing symmetrical forms and patterns

launching *(verb)*   starting; sending off with force, as a rocket is launched into space

maneuvers *(noun)*   planned, controlled movements

medallion *(noun)*   large medal

mind's eye *(noun)*   imagination

ochered *(adjective)*   colored pale yellow to orange

pigment *(noun)*   coloring matter used in paints or found in the cells and tissues of plants and animals that cause them to take on color

promontory *(noun)*   high point of land that overlooks lowlands or that juts out into water

robust *(adjective)*   strong

scurrying *(adjective)*   hurrying; running quickly or hastily; scampering as rats and mice do

succumbed *(verb)*   gave in; yielded; submitted

talons *(noun)*   claws or nails of a bird of prey (or sometimes an animal)

taut *(adjective)*   tightly stretched

updraft *(noun)*   gust of wind that moves sharply upward

waning *(verb)*   becoming less bright; lessening or decreasing in brightness. **Waning** and **waxing** (increasing in brightness) are not commonly used in either speaking or writing, but they are very poetic.

winked *(verb)*   twinkled; shone with little flashes of light

Comprehension Questions

1. How often does the author fly his box kite?
2. Why does he fly the kite in Echo Park?
3. What time of day did the author leave his home to go kite flying?
4. What did Pulcini mistake for a fancy Oriental kite?
5. Why did the author decide not to fly his kite, after all?
6. Pulcini says that the bird's flight was a "performance." Explain.
7. Where did the hawk seem to be flying when it disappeared?
8. What is the meaning of the final sentence of the essay?

Topics for Critical Analysis, Discussion, and Writing

1. Identify language devices and figurative language in the article. Rewrite the most colorful sentences or passages in your own words, but try to retain the same meaning. Discuss the value of the author's word pictures in this article.

2. Pulcini is describing an experience that apparently greatly affected him. Explain his feelings about the kite and the hawk.

3. Although the author does not begin with a thesis, the entire article supports his final statement, "Los Angeles does not need a song, it is one." Thus, Pulcini's conclusion also serves as his thesis. Discuss the methods used by the author to build up to the final image that makes him realize how he feels about Los Angeles.

4. Write a description of an experience that made you realize how you felt about a city (your home town or a city you have visited). Try to introduce or make a statement about this feeling in your thesis. If you can, include figurative language. Choose nouns, adjectives, verbs, and adverbs carefully. Double check meanings in the dictionary. Be sure that you make some point about the meaning of your experience and its relationship to the city in your concluding paragraph.

5. Explain the following figurative expressions that illustrate personification:
   (a) "a gathering of clouds eyed our mountains;"
   (b) "only the mind's eye is fast enough to click the shutter."

My Mother and Miss Bean

Elmore Leppert

After more than fifty years, the author warmly remembers the wonderful day of his initiation into the adult world of understanding. Miss Bean, his fifth-grade teacher, and her strange theory about people sleeping on their stomachs remain personal symbols of a special, still treasured "moment of revelation" that Elmore Leppert shared with his mother. The author uses a variety of language devices and sensory details in his humorous essay. Details are organized chronologically to support the thesis. The short concluding paragraph is both witty and sentimental, a nice finishing touch.

This first appeared in the *Los Angeles Times* as "Remembering the Eccentric Miss Bean, Body and Soul." Reprinted from the *Los Angeles Times* by permission of the author.

Miss Bean thought that we should sleep on our stomachs.

She was my fifth-grade teacher in Michigan, and she believed that sleeping on either side caused pressure on the heart. Sleeping on the back was equally unhealthful, or so she told us, because the internal organs are attached to the backbone and are designed to hang down from it as they do in animals that walk on all fours. She implied that it would be a good thing if we all went back to walking that way. Since this was not **feasible,** at least we could sleep on our stomachs as animals do. My black cat, **E Pluribus Unum,** preferred to sleep flat on his back with all paws **dangling**. But then Pluribus was unusual in many ways that Miss Bean could not have known.

Miss Bean was a small, young woman with brightly-rouged cheeks and jet-black hair cut in the severe style called a Dutch bob. I admired her because her black eyes were so bright and her manner so lively. So, nightly, just before falling asleep, I dutifully rolled onto my stomach, though I seldom found myself in that position when I awoke next morning.

In the 1920s, grade-school teachers were, invariably, women—except for an occasional **itinerant** gym teacher—and were expected to be as **celibate** as nuns. Most of them **went on in spinsterhood** through a lifetime of selfless service, getting **wispily** thinner or **floridly** fatter, according to their natures, until they faded into retirement. And so, when word got around school that Miss Bean was going to be married to an accountant at Continental Motors, I hurried home to be the first to tell my mother.

She was standing at the kitchen table, holding on fingertips a pie-pan into which she had just pressed a freshly rolled crust, and running a knife around the edge of the pan to remove the excess dough, which dangled pale and limp and at last fell to the table with a tiny plop.

"Miss Bean is going to get married," I said.

I savored the moment of motionless silence as my mother stared at me with pale blue eyes. "To who?"

"To somebody who works at the Continental. His name is Jonathan Fish."

My mother set the pie-pan down and snorted with laughter.

"She'll be **Mrs. Bean-Fish,**" she said. "That's not a name, it's a **chowder**. With a name like that, we should invite her to dinner."

I felt a moment of panic. I enjoyed Miss Bean in the classroom, where I knew what to expect. Having her at our dinner table, subject to my mother's conversational unpredictability, might be something else again.

"She's probably busy getting ready for the wedding," I said for starters.

"She won't get married till school is out, at least until June. That's three months. No one needs three months to get ready for a wedding. Your father and I only needed three days. Anyway, if she's busy, all the more reason why she should appreciate a good dinner. She probably lives in a furnished room and eats those greasy meals at the **Athenia**. You invite her for 1 o'clock next Sunday."

"I invite her?" Already I was feeling sick with shyness. My mother knew this, of course. Her way of combating it was direct.

"If you don't, I'll come to school and walk in and invite her myself."

"You wouldn't dare!"

"Oh, wouldn't I?"

Miss Bean accepted my **mumbled** invitation the next morning with bright-eyed charm, and on the appointed day she arrived at our house promptly.

My mother had prepared her specialties: roast pork, applesauce, baked sweet potatoes, cherry pie. Miss Bean **ate with gusto** and slipped little compliments about the food into the conversation all through the meal. She and my mother found a lot to talk about, and I was **spellbound** by the sound and rhythm of their talking. The other members of my family got away from the table as soon as they politely could, and that's when Miss Bean took advantage of a pause in the conversation to ask, "Is Elmore sleeping on his stomach?"

My mother looked at Miss Bean blankly, and I felt a hollowness grow inside me. I had never mentioned this pet idea of Miss Bean's to my mother because I suspected that she might find it ridiculous. And when my mother found an idea ridiculous she said so, often implying that whoever propounded the idea was pretty silly, too.

"Miss Bean says we should sleep on our stomachs because our innards are attached to our backbones," I said.

I saw the right corner of my mother's mouth begin to twitch, as it did when she was about to laugh or say something **caustic**, or both. With my eyes I pleaded with her not to. She looked at me, and then at Miss Bean, and the twitching stopped.

"Why, yes," she said. "I have noticed that he's been sleeping on his stomach lately, but I didn't know why. I'm sure it's helping to keep his innards in the right place."

Miss Bean **beamed**. My mother turned her head away and gave me a quick wink.

It was a moment of **revelation**. I knew, suddenly, that Miss Bean's whole stomach-sleeping theory was silly, and that my mother knew it, and that, by her wink, she thought I knew it too, but we wouldn't offend our guest by revealing our superior knowledge. I felt so close to my mother, so warmed by her strength and love, that I wanted to get up and hug her then and there. Instead, I did my best to take part in polite conversation until Miss Bean thanked us a little more **effusively** than necessary and said goodbye.

She was married in June, right after school was out. Her husband got a better job with Ford and they moved to Detroit and I never saw her again.

But still, sometimes when I awake suddenly at night and find myself lying on my side, I smell varnish and the **acrid** scent of 30 children in an ill-ventilated room. I see Miss Bean, straight-backed, black-haired, bright-eyed, red-cheeked. Then I see my mother's **pixie** face. Her mouth twitches with a repressed smile and her right eye winks at me.

I feel a pressure on my heart. I roll over onto my stomach. My innards fall into place, hanging as neatly from my spine as socks on a clothesline.

Glossary

acrid *(adjective)*   sharp or irritating to the sense of smell

ate with gusto *(idiom)*   ate with great enjoyment, relish, or enthusiasm

beamed *(verb)*   smiled warmly and radiantly

caustic *(adjective)*   sarcastic; cutting; biting. Caustic remarks are often humorous, but they usually hurt or embarrass others.

celibate *(adjective)*   sexually abstinent; sexually innocent and inexperienced

chowder *(noun)*   a thick soup, usually made of vegetables, milk, and (often) clams

dangling *(verb)*   hanging and swinging loosely

effusively *(adverb)*   excessively expressive; overly demonstrative

E Pluribus Unum *(Latin term)*   out of many, one (a motto of the United States). The cat may have been given a patriotic name—or Pluribus may have been descended from many cats in the Leppert neighborhood.

feasible *(adjective)*   capable of being carried out; possible; practicable; within reason

floridly *(adverb)*   rosily. The complexions of those who became fat seemed flushed with red or pink tones.

itinerant *(adjective)*   traveling from place to place

Mrs. Bean-Fish *(special term)*   A married woman often retains her maiden name (Bean) and uses it instead of her middle name, thus, Mrs. Jonathan Bean Fish. In recent years, many women have begun hyphenating the two surnames, as in Bean-Fish; however, this was not common in the twenties.

mumbled *(verb)*   spoke indistinctly and in a low voice; muttered

pixie *(noun)*   a fairy or sprite who is full of mischief

revelation *(noun)*   sudden disclosure of something not known before

spellbound *(adjective)*   fascinated; enchanted; held as if by a magic spell

Athenia *(noun)*   local restaurant

went on in spinsterhood *(colloquialism)*   continued in an unmarried state

wispily *(adverb)*   delicately. As they grew thinner, these women seemed to become so slight and frail that they were like wisps of smoke.

Comprehension Questions

1. Why did Miss Bean feel that people should sleep on their stomachs?
2. What were Miss Bean's physical characteristics? Why did the author admire her?
3. Why was Miss Bean's forthcoming marriage so unusual?
4. Why do you think Mrs. Leppert had her son invite his teacher to dinner? What was Miss Bean's response?
5. What foods did Mrs. Leppert prepare?
6. Miss Bean asked the inevitable question, "Is Elmore sleeping on his stomach?" What reactions did that question cause in Elmore and in his mother?
7. Why and how did the author silently communicate with his mother before she answered Miss Bean's question?
8. What happened during Elmore's "moment of revelation"? What kinds of feelings did he experience? How did they affect his relationship with his mother?
9. What happened to Miss Bean?
10. What sometimes reminds the author of this incident?

Topics for Critical Analysis, Discussion, and Writing

1. Write an essay in which you describe your own "moment of revelation" when you suddenly realized that some idea or principle was not what you had been led to believe. For instance, many children in this country are taught to believe that Santa Claus brings their Christmas presents. When children learn, usually by accident, that their parents really supply the gifts, it is a "moment of revelation," but often one of disillusionment as well (unlike Leppert's experience).

2. The final paragraph of Leppert's essay is bittersweet—both sad and amusing. Analyze the meaning of each of the three sentences in the conclusion. What causes the pressure on Leppert's heart? Why does he turn over onto his stomach? Do his "innards" really change position?

3. Examine Miss Bean's theory. How much truth was in it? How many of her fifth graders do you think grew up believing it? How much influence does a grade-school teacher have on a child's life?

4. Discuss the symbolic value of Miss Bean and her "stomach sleeping theory" in the author's life.

5. Describe an incident involving your own mother that brought the two of you closer together in some way.

6. Identify language devices, sensory details, or figurative language used in the essay. Discuss their effectiveness. Why were they especially appropriate? What other words or phrases could have been used instead? Would the meaning have been changed?

5

Comparison and Contrast: Evaluating Similarities and Differences

In chapter 3 you saw that imaginative use of figurative comparisons, such as similes and metaphors, enriches ideas and makes writing or speech lively and interesting. This figurative technique is used to explain a single idea within a larger piece of writing. However, an expanded version of the comparative method, *comparison and contrast,* can be used as the basis for an entire essay showing relationships between subjects.

IDENTIFYING A COMMON PRINCIPLE

Typical college and university essay topics require that students compare and/or contrast specific ideas, theories, themes, facts, motives, characters, principles, and so on from one, two, or even several readings. Since you can find similarities and differences in practically everything—from the foods you eat and the products you buy to the friends you make and the books you read— you can usually notice the obvious ones in reading selections. With practice, you will be able to identify differences within a basic similarity and more subtle or complex comparisons and contrasts throughout a body of readings. Use classification to group and focus ideas.

DETERMINING THE PURPOSE

The simplest objective of a comparison and contrast essay is to identify similarities or differences between two subjects; for example:

George Bush and Geraldine Ferraro, experienced public servants, were vice-presidential candidates in the 1984 election. Bush, a male, advocated a conservative approach to government that would lower taxes so that people would keep more of the money they earn. Ferraro, a female, favored a more liberal approach that would continue funding essential services for people who couldn't afford them.

A more complex aim is to show that one thing or idea is better or worse than another; for instance:

In evaluating two computers, an operator may decide that a model with numerous labeled function keys is easier to use than one that requires learning many operating commands. A small, portable model with a liquid crystal display (LCD) may be more useful to a businessman than a larger, heavier unit with a conventional cathode ray tube (CRT) "television" screen.

An even more sophisticated goal is to demonstrate that both things, perhaps in different ways, represent a central theme or idea; for example:

The importance of human values is shown in John Hersey's *Hiroshima,* a book that describes the feelings and behavior of the survivors of the first of two atomic bombs deliberately dropped on Japan during World War II, and in *Fail-Safe,* a film that explains the possible effects on humans and civilization of an accidental nuclear attack.

The most complicated purpose is to compare two things by using analogy (sometimes called extended metaphor), which uses a familiar idea to *explain* (metaphor merely *describes)* an unfamiliar one; for example:

Colleges that have been forced to reduce the number and variety of course offerings because of low enrollment and lack of funds are like elegant restaurants that are beginning to go down hill. When business falls off, expensive or exotic items are gradually deleted from the menus. First to go are the appetizers, the "caviar" subjects that attract new students to the college. Then, the number of entrees, the essential "meat and potato" courses, is reduced. Obviously, diners still have adequate meals that supply nutritional necessities, just as college students still have the basic courses that fulfill minimum educational requirements—mathematics, history, English, and the rest, but the "frills" that provide breadth and a well-rounded education are no longer "served."

A good way to determine a purpose for your paper is to prepare a study sheet that identifies important differences within one or more basic similarities. Try this technique to compare and contrast "Mom, You Never Told Me. . . ." (page 7) with "Dime Store Soles" (page 85).

STUDY SHEET

Basic similarity	The main character in each reading learns an important lesson about life.	
Differences	"Mom, You Never Told Me. . . ."	"Dime Store Soles"
Main character	Jeffrey, about 18	Carol, 13
Behavior	Mature. Sensible. Uses good judgment. Takes care of house; worries about sister's nutrition; handles emergency. Responsible.	Immature. Emotional. Lacks judgment. Lies about financial difficulties (says soles are a "joke"). Proud. Causes parents to fight.
Attitudes toward parents	Embarrassed at past behavior (orange juice, sticky floor, empty refrigerator).	Feels anger at mother is justified (soles); sympathy for father's pride.
Attitudes toward others	Tolerant of and amused by sister. Sees what he was like at her age. Sees parents' side of things.	Humiliated by laughter of classmates. Feels persecuted. Sees only her problem. Hides truth.
Lessons learned	Being a parent is tough.	Being a child is hard, too, but problems can be solved.

Figure 5–1

Now, use the basic similarity plus some of the important differences as the purpose, and state your thesis exactly:

Jeffrey learns that being an adult (especially a parent) is extremely difficult and he accepts that, but Carol learns to lie to escape the realities of the adult world.

As development, expand the differences identified on the study sheet by discussing them both individually and comparatively and by adding relevant quotes from the readings to support your own ideas.

A similar comparative study sheet can be prepared for several readings; however, you may not be able to fill in all of the boxes for all of them. For instance, if you add the excerpt from *The Little Prince* to the study sheet in

Figure 5–1, you will have to leave "attitude toward parents" blank. Furthermore, the lesson learned by the prince has a broader application than the lessons learned by Jeffrey and Carol.

Let's say you have prepared a comparative study sheet that analyzes several readings. Should you try to write a little about each reading, or go into depth about one or two major points? Your decision determines the purpose, thesis, and entire direction of your essay. If the topic is not provided (maybe you are preparing the essay outside of class to fulfill an assignment), you are probably better off to narrow the focus. If you are given the topic, make certain you read it carefully. If you have any doubt about which type of development to use, ask your instructor. For a comprehensive, two-hour, final examination in the classroom, the instructor may prefer brief discussions of many similarities and differences to prove that you have read all the assignments. For other essays, the instructor may require a detailed analysis of a single contrast between only two readings.

In determining the direction of your essay, do not completely omit information that disagrees with your ideas. If you recognize a single major contrast in the midst of many, many comparisons, briefly mention it to show the reader that you are aware of it although you feel the similarities are more compelling. By acknowledging this difference, you qualify or limit its importance and impress the reader with your honesty and fairness.

ORGANIZING THE INFORMATION

There are two basic ways to organize a comparison/contrast essay: parallel order and point-by-point order. Let's use facts from the following passage to show both in topic outlines.

> Hiroshi and Noriko, both from Japan, are students at Glendale College. Hiroshi is an unusually tall and athletic young man. He has an outgoing, confident personality and a good sense of humor. His behavior is casual and relaxed. He is a regular and enthusiastic contributor to class discussions even when he has not finished the homework assignment. On the other hand, Noriko is as small and as delicate as a rare flower. She is quiet and reserved. She admits that she is shy. She behaves modestly and conservatively. She is always completely prepared for class discussions, but she never volunteers information. She waits to be called upon.

We see that within the basic similarity (both students are from Japan) are several important differences in *appearance, behavior,* and *personality.* If we organize the information from the passage in parallel order, we discuss everything about Hiroshi and then everything about Noriko in exactly the same order (but *not* in exactly the same words). The thesis acknowledges the single comparison, and all the rest of the facts are contrasts. The topic outline looks like this:

Thesis: Although Hiroshi and Noriko are both students from Japan, they are very different in appearance, behavior, and personality.

    I. Hiroshi (male)
       A. Appearance (tall, athletic)
       B. Behavior (casual, relaxed)
       C. Personality (outgoing, confident, good sense of humor)
    II. Noriko (female)
       A. Appearance (small, delicate)
       B. Behavior (modest, conservative)
       C. Personality (quiet, reserved, shy)
    III. Conclusion

If we use point-by-point organization for the information contained in the passage, we have to rearrange the material. The topic outline lists each point separately for both subjects and looks like this:

Thesis: Although Hiroshi and Noriko are both students from Japan, they are very different in appearance, behavior, and personality.

    I. Appearance
       A. Hiroshi (male, tall, athletic)
       B. Noriko (female, small, delicate)
    II. Behavior
       A. Hiroshi (casual, relaxed)
       B. Noriko (modest, conservative)
    III. Personality
       A. Hiroshi (outgoing, confident, good sense of humor)
       B. Noriko (quiet, reserved, shy)
    IV. Conclusion

Parallel order is simpler for organizing a short paper of contrast because fewer transitions are required, there is less risk of getting off the subject, and one subject can be discussed totally before going to the other. The point-by-point approach seems repetitive in a short, narrowly focused essay, but it works well to order the discussion in a longer paper with a much broader scope (see the formal research paper in chapter 9).

Regardless of the type of organization you choose, you should strive for parallel or equal development of each subject or point. The preceding two topic outlines are plans for short essays of contrast requiring a minimum of four or five well-developed paragraphs each.

Now, let's change the passage about Hiroshi and Noriko to show that they share many similarities within a basic difference.

> Hiroshi and Noriko have different personal characteristics, but they share important similarities. Both are natives of Nagasaki, Japan. In fact, their families lived in the same apartment building for eighteen years. They were playmates all during elementary school and later attended the same high school. When they met each morning in the elevator on their way to school, they talked about their favorite courses, mathematics and English. Both hoped to major in computer science in college, and both applied to study at several colleges in the United States. However, Hiroshi's father was transferred to Tokyo, and the family moved there before either Hiroshi or Noriko received any news about their applications. Thus, they were surprised to meet at the F-1 Visa Student Orientation at Glendale College. They learned that they shared the same counselor and were even registered in some of the same courses. They were both worried about speaking and understanding English, although neither had difficulty reading or writing the language. Now, they realize their ability to communicate in English is better than they thought, and they feel more confident about competing with native students.

When you use point-by-point organization for comparison only, combine the subjects (Hiroshi and Noriko) to avoid repetition, as shown in this topic outline:

Thesis: Hiroshi and Noriko have different personal characteristics; however, they share many important similarities that have contributed to their long friendship.

   I. Early childhood
      A. Born in same city
      B. Lived in same apartment building
      C. Attended same elementary school
  II. High school years
      A. Same school
      B. Both liked English and mathematics
      C. Shared computer science goals
 III. College experiences
      A. Both came to U.S. to study at Glendale College
      B. Same counselor
      C. Enrolled in same courses
      D. Both worried about English ability
 IV. Conclusion

The following outline and student essay use Jim Sanderson's "The Confessions of a Househusband" (page 138) and a reading from another text as the bases for contrasting the women of two cultures. (Notice that the student identified problems in his essay and edited his own work before submitting it for evaluation. If you have difficulty revising your work, exchange papers with a classmate. Sometimes it is easier to find someone else's errors than it is your own. See chapter 10 for more information on revision.)

Thesis: In Eastern cultures, it is forbidden for a woman to work, but in Western cultures there is no such prohibition.

    I. Western wife as breadwinner
      A. Exchange of roles with husband
      B. Too tired for family life

    II. Eastern wife as homemaker
      A. Traditional role
      B. Puts family interests first

    III. Conclusion

Two Kinds of Women

Sevak Gevorkian

In some eastern cultures, it is forbidden for a woman to work, but in western cultures there is no such prohibition. Women can work outside their homes, besides doing housework, and ~~helping~~ help their husbands. ∧ "The Confessions of a Househusband" is a story about a woman working outside and her husband taking care of ∧ the children and housework. But ∧ Mr. Akade Osman, in the essay "Should a Woman Work Outside the Home?",* tells us that a woman should take care of ∧ the housework and children. The authors of these two essays are obviously from different cultures and define the woman in different ways.

In the first essay, Lettie started to work ~~and~~ to help her family when her husband resigned his job. ~~She was going to work and~~ While she worked, John was to stay at home with the children and ~~to~~ do the housework. She came ~~back from her work~~ home late

Reprinted by permission.
*In Joy Reid, *The Process of Composition*. Englewood Cliffs, NJ: Prentice-Hall, 1982.

at night tired ~~of~~ _from_ working all day long and seemed not to want to spend ~~a night~~ _the evening_ and have dinner with John. Some days John waited for Lettie to come home, but she would call and tell _him_ ∧ that she had to entertain some business clients at a restaurant and would ~~not~~ be ~~home~~ _late at the office_. When she was ~~working,~~ she probably thought less about her husband, who was then the homemaker, and had less interest in him than he had in her. Lettie ~~was then~~ _became_ a liberated woman who was working ∧ _to support her family_ and didn't need her husband. On the contrary, John seemed to need her more ~~and have more interest in her~~.

In the second essay, a woman is considered as ∧ _a_ homemaker, and she is supposed to ~~work just~~ _stay_ at home and take good care of her family while her husband is working to earn ~~some~~ money and provide for the family financially. This kind of housewife never seems to ~~be tired~~ _tire_ of housework. She tries to fix food and get ready for her husband and when he comes home tired ~~of~~ _from_ working, she serves him his food and enjoys being with him and entertaining him. She thinks of her husband and children more than anything else and tries to do her best to satisfy them. This sort of woman is not ~~a~~ liberated ~~woman~~, and most of the main decisions in the family are made by the husband. She needs her husband more than he needs her, and life probably doesn't mean anything to her without her family.

~~These~~ two kinds of women who are discussed above have their own advantages and disadvantages. The first one is too liberated; however, the second one is a kind of slave for her husband. Ideally, a woman ~~is to~~ _should_ help her husband with anything she can, even if it is working outside. But she should always remember to put the interests of the family first.

CONSIDERING TONE AND STYLE

Gevorkian uses a reasonable tone and an objective style to contrast eastern and western views about women working outside the home. *Tone* describes the attitude projected by a speaker or writer. *Style* refers to the way that words are used to express thoughts or ideas. Happy, sad, angry, humorous, sarcastic, cruel, kind, or other feelings about a subject can be expressed easily by a speaker's tone of voice. As an example, suppose your mother asks, "Would you like to carry out the trash on your way to class this morning?" You are in a hurry, wouldn't like it at all, and want her to know that; on the other hand, you don't dare refuse, either. So you answer sarcastically, "Oh, I'd just *love* to," greatly emphasizing *love* and dropping the tone of your voice significantly to show that you really mean just the opposite. Now, you don't openly refuse, but the tone of your voice makes it clear that carrying out the trash is the last thing you want to do. You may have noticed that native English speakers have an extensive range of tonal variety that makes possible many meanings for a single phrase or sentence, as you can see in the following example (higher and lower tones are indicated by superscript and subscript; vocal stress by italics):

Native English Stress and Intonation Patterns
"Oh, I'd just   (sarcasm; doesn't want to)   *love* to."
Oh,   *love*   "   I'd just   to!" (surprised to be asked, but happy to help)
"Oh, I'd *ju*   love to." ("just" meaning "absolutely")   *ust*
just love   "Oh, I'd   to!" (would like nothing better; hoped you'd ask)

The manner of speaking—phrasing, voicing (vocal variation), gesticulation (hand or body movements), facial expression (rolling the eyes, raising an eyebrow, frowning, smiling, etc.)—indicates meaning regardless of the words chosen to convey it. On the other hand, the tone of a piece of writing is expressed *only* by the words on the page; therefore, a good writer commands a broad vocabulary and uses it to develop an original style suited to the subject and the audience. Gevorkian's style is impartial until the last two sentences when his personal views are stated openly. He has strengthened his essay by rewording some sentences. He knows that audiences become bored if they hear or read key words, phrases, and ideas over and over, so he has cut out some of the repetition. He is also aware that grammatical errors can disrupt the smooth flow of prose and detract from meaning; therefore, he has corrected even the smallest mistakes.

A variety of tones and styles is represented in the readings for this section. All the readings have been chosen to offer you practice in comparing and contrasting ideas.

The Confessions of a Househusband

Jim Sanderson

Jim Sanderson writes the column, "Liberated Male," which appears regularly in newspapers across the country. One of his constant themes is that neither sex should be bound by the stereotyped role assigned to it by society. The tone of his articles is always empathetic; Sanderson and the subjects of his essays project their own personalities into those of others (in this case, members of the opposite sex) to understand them better or to share in their emotions or feelings. (A graphic illustration of empathy is the pain a parent feels when his or her child is hurt or suffering.)

In "Confessions of a Househusband," Sanderson subtly criticizes society's definition of manliness and womanliness with the recurring inference that we should, instead, strive for humanness. This unusually insightful article tells the story of John, a man who is both secure and flexible enough to exchange jobs with his wife for a few months for the good of their family. That's when John learns what it is really like to do "women's work." Watch for contrasts in the attitudes and behavior of both John and Lettie, and try to find the reasons these changes occur.

Because John was a rising young executive, his company assumed he would not refuse a transfer across the country to corporate headquarters. It was a natural step in moving up.

But John and his wife, Lettie, had put down roots. They liked their home, their community and their life style. In the new location, it also would be difficult for Lettie to resume her own career.

John resigned his job and undertook to care for the couple's two children, ages 2 and 4, while he **pondered** a career change—possibly starting his own business. Lettie, eager to return to work, became the **breadwinner**.

"At first it seemed like a permanent vacation," John says. "No more

Courtesy Sun Features, Inc., Box 45, Cardiff, California 92007.

pressure, deadlines or crazy people to deal with. No more business trips. My time was my own, and for the first time I really got to know the kids. I loved making up games with them, and we went everywhere together. Shopping and taking care of the house was no big deal."

But after six months as the primary homemaker, John's perceptions began to change. "First of all, there was no beginning or end to the day. You're on the job all day and all night. It's hard to begin any serious adult project because you know the kids are going to interrupt you in a few minutes—you can't even count on **nap time** to read a book."

The sense of **isolation** is oppressive, John found. "Nobody knows or cares that you're alive, except for your family. You're trapped in that house, and every day is the same. You lose track of what day of the week it is. You get lonely for adult talk. I understand why people watch those dumb, slow TV **soap operas**. You can get through a screaming-child emergency and still keep up with the story."

The ex-executive felt **frustrated** by his work. "There's no sense of completion, no pride in excellence. You spend an hour shining up the kitchen and five minutes later it's a disaster again. Lettie finally began to criticize my housekeeping, so just a few minutes before she was due home I'd rush around **neating up**."

To be a good parent is one of life's most important roles, yet after six months John began to doubt himself. "Nobody ever rings any bells to tell you that you're succeeding. You don't get a raise or a promotion—or any thanks. Life with kids is always **chaotic**, and if that's your main function you begin to wonder if you're a very competent person. You think almost any **dum-dum** ought to be able to do what you do."

John never found ways to vent aggression or frustration. "You can't take it out on the kids, obviously, and Lettie comes home with her own problems. I swallowed it; I walked around with a constant low-level depression."

John's relationship with his wife also began to change. She was preoccupied with her work, and seemed to need him less, but he needed her more.

"I looked like a bum all day long but found myself shaving and putting on some decent clothes in the late afternoon. Lettie's arrival home was the highlight of the day. If she called up to say she had to work late, I'd feel **crushed**, especially if I'd put a lot of effort into dinner. But you can't really complain, can you? I'd done it often enough."

It also **bugged** John when his wife occasionally entertained business clients at a fancy restaurant and he had to stay home and eat spaghetti with the kids. "I was desperate to get out of the house. Get a baby sitter, candlelit dinner for two, cheek-to-cheek dancing. But then she'd say she was exhausted, or had to work on a report."

His wife began to appear selfish and uncaring, and John realized he was **tuning out** as she talked about her day at work. Their sex life **dwindled** down; they took turns not feeling in the mood.

Thus, when an old business associate called up to offer him a job John accepted instantly, "We're still in the process of sorting out our child-care and household duties," he says, "but obviously we'll have to share 50-50.

"I always used to praise Lettie for being a great mother and homemaker, but underneath I really felt she was **copping out**, letting herself go, and living the easy life while I **worked my butt off** to support the family. I think I almost convinced her this was true. I didn't mean to attack her self-confidence, but that's partly why she was so desperate to take an outside job.

"Life with small kids is no picnic. The pressures are there all right—they're just not very visible. When I see a woman now at the supermarket trying to cope with a couple of toddlers, I smile and say, '**Hang in there, kiddo.**'"

Glossary

breadwinner *(noun)*   person who earns the salary to support the family

bugged *(slang)*   annoyed; irritated; angered

chaotic *(adjective)*   completely disordered and confused

copping out *(slang)*   not keeping a promise; quitting, not doing one's job

crushed *(verb)*   subdued; suppressed; emotionally hurt

dum-dum *(slang)*   stupid person

dwindled *(verb)*   diminished

frustrated *(adjective)*   defeated; foiled; prevented from reaching some objective

Hang in there, **kiddo** *(slang)*   Persevere. Don't give up.

isolation *(noun)*   sense of being alone or set apart from others

nap time *(idiom)*   a certain time routinely set aside each day for brief, light sleep

neating up *(slang)*   tidying or straightening up the house

pondered *(verb)*   considered carefully; thought deeply about

soap operas *(colloquialism)*   daytime radio or television programs that are very sentimental or overly dramatic. The story moves so slowly that you can miss several programs without losing the thread of the plot. The programs received their name because many were originally sponsored by soap companies.

tuning out *(slang)*   no longer listening

worked my butt off *(slang)*   worked extremely hard

Comprehension Questions

1. John resigned his job instead of transferring with the company to a distant city. What reasons did he give?

2. What new job did John decide to take? Why?

3. What did John expect of his new job in the beginning? How did it seem after six months?

4. Why did he begin to watch soap operas?

5. Did he find satisfaction in his work? Why or why not?

6. Was Lettie satisfied with the way John did the housework? Why or why not?

7. What happened to John's relationship with his wife? Explain fully.

8. What was John's reaction when Lettie had to work late and couldn't get home in time for dinner? How did he feel when she had to entertain business clients at fancy restaurants?

9. How were the child care and household duties divided after John went back to work?

10. At the end of the article, how did John evaluate Lettie's former contributions as a homemaker?

Topics for Critical Analysis, Discussion, and Writing

1. Each of the following topics may be analyzed by using comparison or contrast. Choose one topic and prepare a well-developed essay in which you give and discuss examples to prove your statements. Be sure that you have a clear thesis. Your conclusion should evaluate the evidence you have presented.

a. Analyze John's feelings about the job of homemaking before and after he takes over for Lettie so that she can work at an outside job.

b. Examine psychological changes in John and Lettie as their new jobs begin to dominate their daily lives.

c. Explain the perception that each partner has of the other after their roles have been exchanged for about six months. How does John see Lettie? How does she view John?

How can you write a comparison/contrast essay like this one if you do not know the topics in advance? You can guess many of them based on class discussion and information given by your instructor. Then, prepare as complete a study sheet as possible (refer to Fig. 5–1) so that while you are writing you can pick out important details without rereading the article. Here is a study sheet that covers all three topics (interpretations are shown in parentheses):

John	Lettie
Thinks homemaking is easy, fun, vacation	Eager to go back to work
Totally involved in children, house	Completely preoccupied with work
Needs wife's attention, acceptance, approval more; dependent	Needs husband less; independent; breadwinner
Work never ends; no raises or promotions; no free time; no praise	Generally regular hours with established salary, regular promotions
Becomes depressed, unhappy; no outside interests; no outlets for anger and frustration; isolated	Thrives on challenges of job and stimulation of entertaining clients
Thinks Lettie is selfish, uncaring; jealous of Lettie's entertaining business clients	(May think John is boring, complaining, no longer intellectual equal)
Realizes value of Lettie's homemaking services; sees that she worked hard; feels ashamed of thinking she was lazy	(Perhaps understands how tough it is to be sole support of family; may realize how hard husband worked)

Each totally absorbed in partner's former role;
John becomes more flexible in working out
50-50 partnership. Lettie learns to assume
more financial responsibility.

2. Discuss the importance of the lesson John learns from his experiences. Explain specific instances that support your ideas.

3. Analyze the reasons for John's dissatisfaction with homemaking.

4. Sanderson's tone is clearly empathetic. Define empathy, and explain the author's use of it by discussing related examples from the article.

Working Women Happier
Than Housewives—Study

As you read this news story reporting the results of a study by Dr. Myra Marx Ferree, a sociologist, notice its relationships to Sanderson's article. John and Lettie both might have benefited from reading Dr. Ferree's findings long before they began their "great experiment." Since the article is an objective report, the tone is impartial. We don't know how the newswriter feels except by his or her choice of quotes and reported material.

CHICAGO (AP) — Housewives who work outside the home are happier than those who don't, a Connecticut **sociologist** says.

The social contact and the satisfaction of knowing a job has been well done contributed to the happiness of the women studied by the sociologist, Dr. Myra Marx Ferree of the University of Connecticut.

Writing in the September issue of *Psychology Today,* Dr. Ferree said, "These were not **glamorous**, exciting careers, but the wives who held such jobs were happier and more satisfied with their lives than the women who were full-time housewives."

While 26 per cent of full-time housewives said they were dissatisfied with their lives, only 14 per cent of those who held jobs expressed dissatisfaction.

She based her conclusions on interviews with 135 women living in a working-class community near Boston. None had preschool-age children at home. More than a third had not finished high school, but three had college degrees.

Just over half worked outside the home—in such jobs as clerks in supermarkets and department stores, waitresses, factory workers, typists, and nurse's aides. A few were bookkeepers, bank tellers and **beauticians**.

Dr. Ferree pointed out that a job "has clear requirements and clear payoffs, in money, social life and a sense of accomplishment"; it takes a woman out of the home and gives her social contact, "and the regular paycheck is proof of work well done."

"But a housewife's day is never done, and her tasks often bring neither **tangible** rewards nor social connections," she said.

"The housewives expend great effort but don't get recognition for it: their husbands accuse them of 'doing nothing all day' and in the next breath remind them that their duty is to stay home and keep house," the sociologist said.

"As a result, many housewives have an uncertain idea of what their occupation requires, and how well or poorly they are doing it," she said.

None of the women with paid jobs said she was poor at her job, while only one full-time housewife thought she was very good at it, she said.

Reprinted by permission of the Associated Press.

Dr. Ferree observed that until recent years housewives "shared a **social network** that gave them mutual support, recognition and pleasure."

She said that women "were likely to live near their mothers, other relatives, and close friends for many years and to establish **close-knit** groups. Within these groups there was no doubt whether someone was, or was not a good homemaker."

"In recent decades, however, the rise in numbers of people who move frequently and the millions of women going back to work, have made housewife networks less common and more difficult to maintain," she added.

Glossary

beauticians *(noun)*   cosmetologists; persons who do hair styling, manicuring, and so on, usually in beauty shops

close-knit *(adjective)*   closely united or joined together by social, family, or business ties

glamorous *(adjective)*   fascinating; alluring; especially attractive

social network *(special term)*   group of interconnected or cooperating individuals. The **social network** mentioned in the article is one based on friendship and mutual support. "Networking" is a term used for people who work together toward a common goal.

sociologist *(noun)*   person concerned with the science of human society, social relations, beliefs, and values

tangible *(adjective)*   can be touched or felt by touch; has material form or substance. The satisfaction of doing a good job is an **intangible** reward; a regular salary and periodic promotions are **tangible** compensations.

Comprehension Questions

1. Why were wives who worked happier than those who didn't?
2. Did the outside job have to be exciting and glamorous for the wife to like it?
3. What percentage of full-time housewives felt dissatisfied with their lives? What percentage of working wives expressed dissatisfaction?
4. What was the education of the 135 women interviewed?
5. How many worked outside the home? What kinds of jobs did they hold?
6. What were the advantages of an outside job, according to Dr. Ferree? What were the disadvantages of not working outside?
7. How did all the wives evaluate their own homemaking abilities?

8. Why was the role of housewife more rewarding in the past? What has happened to change this perception of the job?

Topics for Critical Analysis, Discussion, and Writing

1. Agree or disagree with the statement, "Housewives who work outside the home are happier than those who don't," by comparing and/or contrasting the attitudes of working and non-working wives discussed in the article. Include facts, details, and examples to strengthen your position. Does the article fairly report both sides of the situation?

2. Use information from the news story to explain John's and Lettie's feelings (in Jim Sanderson's article) about homemaking and holding a paying job.

3. Evaluate differences and similarities between the wives of your country and those of the United States regarding working outside the home. If you are a male, try to empathize with the female point of view; that is, mentally put yourself in the wife's place as you discuss the situation.

4. Why do you think so much emphasis has recently been placed on the problems and satisfactions of both working and nonworking wives?

5. Do you believe that this news story is more credible (believable) than Sanderson's article? Why or why not?

That Lean and Hungry Look

Suzanne Britt Jordan

The author is a frequent contributor to Newsweek *in which this essay first appeared. "That Lean and Hungry Look" is a humorous analysis of the obsessive concern in American society about the social importance of being thin. Throughout the article, Jordan contrasts thin and fat people, mostly by discussing differences in their appearances, attitudes, and behavior. The author's style relies heavily on slang and idioms, long strings of descriptive adjectives, alliteration, and repetition of key words for emphasis.*

Short sentences ready the reader for Jordan's equally short, amusing value judgments at the end of each paragraph. She approximates a point-by-point method of organizing her material, alternating between thin and fat people, which allows opportunities for witty comments about every point. In parallel-order development, these remarks might seem intrusive and disruptive.

Caesar was right. Thin people need watching. I've been watching them for most of my adult life, and I don't like what I see. When these narrow fellows **spring** at me, I **quiver** to my toes. Thin people come in all personalities, most of them **menacing**. You've got your "**together thin person**, your mechanical thin person, your **condescending** thin person, your **tsk-tsk** thin person, your efficiency-expert thin person. All of them are dangerous.

In the first place, thin people aren't fun. They don't know how to **goof off,** at least in the best, fat sense of the word. They've always got to be a**doing.** Give them a coffee break, and they'll jog around the block. Supply them with a quiet evening at home, and they'll fix the screen door and lick **S&H green stamps.** They say things like "there aren't enough hours in the day." Fat people never say that. Fat people think the day is too damn long already.

Thin people make me tired. They've got speedy little **metabolisms** that cause them to **bustle briskly.** They're forever rubbing their bony hands together and eyeing new problems **to "tackle."** I like to surround myself with **sluggish, inert,** easygoing fat people, the kind who believe that if you clean it up today, it'll just get dirty again tomorrow.

Some people say the business about the **jolly** fat person is a myth, that all of us **chubbies** are **neurotic,** sick, sad people. I disagree. Fat people may not be **chortling** all day long, but they're a hell of a lot *nicer* than the **wizened and shriveled.** Thin people turn **surly,** mean, and hard at a young age because they never learn the value of a hot-fudge sundae for easing tension. Thin people don't like gooey soft things because they themselves are neither gooey nor soft. They are crunchy and dull, like carrots. They go straight to the heart of the matter while fat people let things stay all **blurry** and **hazy** and **vague,** the way things actually are. Thin people want to face the truth. Fat people know there is no truth. One of my thin friends is always staring at complex, unsolvable problems and saying, "The key thing is. . . ." Fat people never say that. They know there isn't any such thing as the key thing about anything.

Thin people believe in logic. Fat people see all sides. The sides fat people see are rounded **blobs,** usually gray, always **nebulous** and truly not worth worrying about. But the thin person persists. "If you consume more calories than you burn," says one of my thin friends, "you will gain weight. It's that simple." Fat people always grin when they hear statements like that. They know better.

Fat people realize that life is illogical and unfair. They know very well that God is not in his heaven and all is not right with the world. If God was up there, fat people could have two doughnuts and a big orange drink anytime they wanted it.

Thin people have a long list of logical things they are always **spouting off** to me. They hold up one finger at a time as they **reel off** these things, so I won't **lose track**. They speak slowly as if to a young child. The list is long and full of holes. It contains tidbits like "**get a grip on yourself**," "cigarettes kill," "cholesterol clogs," "**fit as a fiddle**," "ducks in a row," "organize," and "sound fiscal management." Phrases like that.

They think these 2,000-point plans lead to happiness. Fat people know happiness is **elusive** at best and even if they could get the kind thin people talk about, they wouldn't want it. Wisely, fat people see that such programs are too dull, too hard, too off the mark. They are never better than a whole cheesecake.

Fat people know all about the mystery of life. They are the ones acquainted with the night, with luck, with fate, with **playing it by ear**. One thin person I know once suggested that we arrange all the parts of a **jigsaw puzzle** into groups according to size, shape, and color. He figured this would cut the time needed to complete the puzzle by at least 50 percent. I said I wouldn't do it. One, I like to **muddle through**. Two, what good would it do to finish early? Three, the jigsaw puzzle isn't the important thing. The important thing is the fun of four people (one thin person included) sitting around a card table, working a jigsaw puzzle. My thin friend had no use for my list. Instead of joining us, he went outside and **mulched** the boxwoods. The three remaining fat people finished the puzzle and made chocolate, double-fudged **brownies** to celebrate.

The main problem with thin people is they oppress. Their good intentions, bony **torsos**, **tight ships**, **neat corners**, **cerebral machinations**, and **pat solutions** loom like dark clouds over the loose, comfortable, spread-out, soft world of the fat. Long after fat people have removed their coats and shoes and put their feet up on the coffee table, thin people are still sitting on the edge of the sofa, looking neat as a pin, discussing **rutabagas**. Fat people are heavily into fits of laughter, slapping their thighs and **whooping it up**, while thin people are still politely waiting for the **punch line**.

Thin people are **downers**. They like math and morality and reasoned evaluation of the limitations of human beings. They have their skinny little acts together. They **expound**, **prognose**, **probe**, and **prick**.

Fat people are convivial. They will like you even if you're irregular and have **acne**. They will come up with a good reason why you never wrote the great American novel. They will **cry in your beer** with you. They will **put your name in the pot**. They will **let you off the hook**. Fat people will **gab**, **giggle**, **guffaw**, **gallumph**, **gyrate**, and **gossip**. They are generous, giving, and **gallant**. They are **gluttonous** and goodly and great. What you want when you're down is soft and **jiggly**, not muscled and stable. Fat people know this. Fat people have plenty of room. Fat people will take you in.

Glossary

acne *(noun)*   a common skin condition of adolescents and young adults, characterized by eruptions (pimples), chiefly on the face

adoing *(colloquialism)*   doing something

blobs *(noun)*   things of vague or indefinite form

blurry and **hazy** and **vague** *(adjectives)*   indistinct; indefinite; not clear

brownies *(noun)*   rich, moist, flat, chocolate cake cut into squares or oblong bars and eaten with the fingers. Double-fudged brownies contain twice as much chocolate as regular brownies.

briskly *(adverb)*   energetically

bustle *(verb)*   hurry busily; do something with much fuss and bother

Caesar *(noun)*   Julius Caesar, Emperor of the Roman Empire (49–44 B.C.)

cerebral machinations *(adjective, noun)*   intellectual plots and schemes

chortling *(verb)*   gleefully (but softly) laughing; uttering words with a snorting sound. Chortling indicates happiness or amusement.

chubbies *(noun)*   round, plump people

condescending *(adjective)*   proud; haughty; patronizing

cry in your beer *(slang)*   feel sorry for yourself

downers *(slang)*   depressants (a term used to indicate either drugs or people)

elusive *(adjective)*   hard to grasp or retain mentally

expound *(verb)*   state in detail or point by point; explain

"fit as a fiddle" *(idiom)*   in excellent health

gab *(verb)*   chatter; talk idly

gallant *(adjective)*   brave; noble; high-spirited; daring

gallumph (**galumph,** *verb*)   march or walk along with a springy step and in a self-satisfied manner

"get a grip on yourself" *(idiom)*   control yourself

giggle *(verb)*   laugh with a series of rapid, high-pitched sounds

gluttonous *(adjective)*   inclined to overeat or to eat greedily

goof off *(slang)*   waste time; avoid work; neglect duties

gossip *(verb)*   repeat and discuss idle talk and rumors about others

guffaw *(verb)*   laugh in loud, coarse bursts

gyrate *(verb)*   rotate; revolve; whirl

inert *(adjective)*   physically or mentally inactive; dull; slow

jiggly *(adjective)*   moving unsteadily in a succession of slight, quick jerks

jigsaw puzzle *(noun)* puzzle made of irregularly shaped, closely fitting pieces that, when put together, form a picture

jolly *(adjective)* good-humored or good-natured; merry; cheerful

let you off the hook *(slang)* relieve you of responsibility or blame

lose track *(idiom)* lose count; forget

menacing *(adjective)* threatening

metabolisms *(noun)* chemical and physical processes by which foods are used by the human body. Thin people are said to have efficient **metabolisms,** but the metabolic processes of fat people are supposed to be inefficient.

muddle through *(British idiom)* manage to succeed in spite of mistakes or confusion

mulched *(verb)* spread straw or leaves around the plants to prevent evaporation of water from the soil or freezing of the roots. Boxwoods can be trimmed as shrubs or allowed to grow as trees.

neat corners *(slang)* trim; smart; pleasing (generally a term of approval)

nebulous *(adjective)* unclear; vague; indefinite

neurotic *(adjective)* mentally disordered. Some common neuroses are anxiety, depression, compulsions, and obsessions. A **neurotic** person might have a compulsion to eat all the time or an obsession to eat certain kinds of foods (e.g., chocolate, bread, ice cream, and so on).

pat solutions *(adjective, noun)* solutions that seem to be exactly suitable to the situation

playing it be ear *(idiom)* deciding what to do as you go along; adjusting your actions to fit the situation. This expression is based on playing a musical instrument by ear, by remembering the tune instead of by reading the music.

prick *(verb)* puncture; pierce

probe *(verb)* explore; investigate or examine thoroughly

prognose *(verb)* forecast; predict

punch line *(noun)* the surprise last line of a joke that carries the point or makes it funny

put your name in the pot *(slang)* include you in the group

quiver *(verb)* tremble or shake (with dread, fear, anticipation, etc.)

reel off *(verb)* tell easily and quickly

rutabagas *(noun)* turnips; the large, yellow roots of these plants are used as vegetables

S&H green stamps *(noun)* trading stamps. Merchants give stamps with purchases. Stamps can be traded for gifts. During the fifties and sixties, these stamps were extremely popular.

sluggish *(adjective)* lacking energy or vigor; slow moving. (Slugs are similar to snails, but have no shells.) Slugs move slowly; the adjective **sluggish** is commonly used to describe people who share this characteristic.

spring at *(verb)* move suddenly and rapidly toward someone or something

spouting off *(verb)* speaking hastily or irresponsibly

surly *(adjective)* bad-tempered; rude; hostile; uncivil

tight ships *(Navy term)* orderly, well-run ships staffed by disciplined crews. This term describes the self-discipline used by thin people to resist fattening foods.

"together" thin person *(slang)* a person with fully developed abilities and ambitions and a well-integrated personality. A well-adjusted person can also be described as "having it all together."

torsos *(noun)* trunks of their bodies; parts of the bodies without heads or limbs

to "tackle" *(verb)* to undertake; to solve

tsk-tsk *(adjective)* disapproving or sympathetic. "Tsk-tsk" is a series of short sucking noises made between the tongue and the teeth. Meaning can only be interpreted from the context of the conversation.

wizened and shriveled *(adjectives)* dried up; withered; wrinkled

whooping it up *(slang)* creating a noisy disturbance (usually by laughing or having a good time)

Comprehension Questions

1. What types of thin people does the author identify in the first paragraph? Why does she think they need watching?

2. Why doesn't Jordan think thin people are fun? What kinds of activities do they like? How important is time to them? How do fat people feel about time?

3. How does the author contrast the movements of thin and fat people?

4. Why does Jordan not agree that "chubbies are neurotic, sick, sad people," and instead defend the "myth" of the jolly, fat person? How does she evaluate thin and fat people in the fourth paragraph?

5. Give an example of the logic used by thin people. What is the attitude of fat people toward logic? The author says that if God were "up there, fat people could have two doughnuts and a big orange drink anytime they wanted it." Explain.

6. What is the significance of the "long list of logical things" that thin people are always "reeling off" to fat people? What do fat people know about all these clichéd (overused or trite) suggestions and about life itself?

7. Reread the example of the jigsaw puzzle. Why did the three fat people have fun completing it? Why did the thin person go outside to work in the yard?

8. What is the main problem with thin people? Jordan complains about their bony bodies, self-discipline, trim appearances, careful thought processes, and unoriginal suggestions. She says they are depressing to be around. How does she contrast the behavior of fat people?

9. The last paragraph contains a long list of words beginning with the letter "g" that the author uses to describe fat people and their actions. Why does Jordan feel these characteristics are better than those of thin people?

10. Is the author thin or fat? How do you know?

Topics for Critical Analysis, Discussion, and Writing

1. Write an essay contrasting thin and fat people. Use parallel order to present your information. Your thesis should state whether you agree or disagree with Jordan's assessment of these two types of people. Include facts, details, and examples from "That Lean and Hungry Look" to support your ideas.

2. The word "stereotype" is defined as a fixed notion or conception (of a person, group, or idea) held by a large number of people and allows for no individuality. Marilyn Monroe was stereotyped as a dumb, beautiful, helpless blonde and John Wayne as a tough cowboy or military man. Common stereotypes hold that women are erratic drivers, men are able money managers, and breast-fed babies are better adjusted than their bottle-fed counterparts. Of course, we can all think of exceptions to these stereotypical ideas; therefore, such generalizations are often inaccurate. Do you think that Jordan's images of thin and fat people are stereotypical? Are there happy thin people and unhappy fat people? Why do you think the author chose to present her information the way she did?

4. Refer to Gerald Astor's article, "What Your Body Language Says About You," in chapter 2. Astor says that we can understand a great deal about a person by his or her facial expressions and bodily gestures and positions. Do you think this is true for body weight? Can we know the personality of a thin or fat person by appearance? Why or why not? Explain fully.

5. The author uses many idiomatic and slang expressions in this short article. How does this usage contribute to the style and tone of the writing?

6. In the last paragraph, Jordan says that fat people will "gab, giggle,

guffaw, gallumph, gyrate, and gossip" and that they are "generous, giving, gallant . . . gluttonous and goodly and great." Why does she overuse alliteration? What is the effect? Are these positive or negative words?

7. Contrast the author's views of thin and fat people with your own. Begin with a thesis that states whether Jordan's ideas are right or wrong. Then devote one paragraph to discussing her theories. The next paragraph should examine your own notions and show how they differ from Jordan's. The conclusion should evaluate the evidence you have presented and make a judgment about it.

Two Stories for Comparison and Contrast

"The Story of an Hour," by Kate Chopin (1851–1904) and "Miss Brill," by Katherine Mansfield (1888–1923) describe great emotional crises in the lives of two women, one married and the other single. The stories share certain similarities, but also show important differences. To encourage you to compare and contrast the readings and synthesize your ideas about them, the introductory material, the comprehension and discussion questions, and the topics for writing are presented together.

Kate Chopin, a highly skilled and widely recognized short story writer and novelist of the late nineteenth century, concentrated on developing themes that related to the experiences and problems of women. During this period, upper- and middle-income women's lives were very restricted. Women, along with any property they owned before marriage, became the property of and were controlled by their husbands when they married.

Some women, like Mrs. Mallard in the story, were invalids because no treatment for their conditions was yet known. In fact, most stylish women developed some medical problems because of their restrictive clothing. Dresses were long, with elaborate bustles that puffed out the backs of the skirts. Outer costumes were supported by several layers of petticoats and other undergarments, and the weight and bulk of all this floor-length clothing hampered movement. The fashionable hourglass figure was achieved by wearing a tightly laced corset that squeezed in the waist (the ideal of 13 inches was seldom attained, however) and pushed the extra flesh up toward the breasts or down to the hips. Corsetry also displaced the internal organs; as a result, many women were short of breath, were unable to eat even the smallest meals, suffered dizziness and fainting spells, and experienced "female problems." Women were considered weak and delicate, and being placed in the care and custody of their husbands, as Mrs. Mallard was, seemed natural and beneficial.

Lower-income women could not afford to dress stylishly, so they did not suffer from fashion-related maladies. Instead, they fell victim to accidents, illnesses, and diseases as they toiled in the factories and great homes of the wealthy. Single or married, young or old, they worked to survive. But women of Mrs. Mallard's social status (except widows and a few independent wives who wrote and sold stories, essays, poetry, and novels for income or simply for the satisfaction of having something to do) generally did not work after marriage. They were expected to show off their husbands' economic success by wearing expensive clothes, furs, and jewels and by demonstrating their educational accomplishments in music, art, needlework, and languages.

By the early twentieth century, many of the Victorian practices that kept Mrs. Mallard a social prisoner began to disappear. Married women actively participated in volunteer work for charities and social welfare organizations. Growing numbers of women earned college degrees, and professions gradually began to open to unmarried women. Miss Brill, whose story takes place not too many years after Mrs. Mallard's, shows the inner feelings of an independent, single, working woman who has the freedom Mrs. Mallard covets.

Miss Brill has no one else to direct her life, protect her health, or provide for her needs. She spends her Sundays in the park eavesdropping on the events in the lives of others. Otherwise, she has the company of her fur, which lives only in her imagination, of the semiconscious invalid to whom she reads the newspaper each week, and of her pupils.

As you read about Mrs. Mallard's and Miss Brill's reactions to their individual tragedies, remember the social forces that governed their lives, and judge their behavior accordingly.

The Story of an Hour

Kate Chopin

Knowing that Mrs. Mallard was **afflicted with** a heart trouble, great care was taken **to break to her as gently as possible** the news of her husband's death.

It was her sister Josephine who told her, in broken sentences, **veiled** hints that revealed in half **concealing**. Her husband's friend Richards was there, too, near her. It was he who had been in the newspaper office when intelligence of the railroad **disaster** was received, with Brently Mallard's name leading the list of "killed." He had only taken the time to assure himself of its truth by a second telegram, and had **hastened** to **forestall** any less careful, less tender friend in bearing the sad message.

She did not hear the story as many women have heard the same, with a **paralyzed** inability to accept its significance. She wept at once, with sudden,

First published in *Vogue*, IV (December 1894), 360.

wild abandonment, in her sister's arms. When the **storm of grief** had spent itself she went away to her room alone. She would have no one follow her.

There stood, facing the open window, a comfortable, **roomy** armchair. Into this she sank, pressed down by a physical exhaustion that **haunted** her body and seemed to reach into her soul.

She could see in the open square before her house the tops of trees that were all **aquiver** with the new spring life. The delicious breath of rain was in the air. In the street below a **peddler** was crying his wares. The notes of a distant song which someone was singing reached her faintly, and countless sparrows were **twittering** in the eaves.

There were **patches** of blue sky showing here and there through the clouds that had met and piled above the other in the west facing her window.

She sat with her head thrown back upon the cushion of the chair quite motionless, except when a sob came up into her throat and shook her, as a child who has cried itself to sleep continues to sob in its dreams.

She was young, with a fair, calm face, whose lines bespoke **repression** and even a certain strength. But now there was a dull stare in her eyes, whose gaze was fixed away off yonder on one of those patches of blue sky. It was not a glance of **reflection**, but rather indicated a **suspension** of intelligent thought.

There was something coming to her and she was waiting for it, fearfully. What was it? She did not know; it was too **subtle** and **elusive** to name. But she felt it, creeping out of the sky, reaching toward her through the sounds, the scents, the color that filled the air.

Now her **bosom** rose and fell **tumultuously**. She was beginning to recognize this thing that was approaching to possess her, and she was striving to beat it back with her will—as powerless as her two white slender hands would have been.

When she **abandoned** herself a little whispered word escaped her slightly parted lips. She said it over and over under her breath: "Free, free, free!" The vacant stare and the look of **terror** that had followed it went from her eyes. They stayed **keen** and bright. Her pulses beat fast, and the coursing blood warmed and relaxed every inch of her body.

She did not stop to ask if it were not a **monstrous** joy that held her. A clear and **exalted** perception enabled her to dismiss the suggestion as **trivial**.

She knew that she would weep again when she saw the kind, tender hands folded in death; the face that had never looked **save** with love upon her, fixed and gray and dead. But she saw beyond that bitter moment a long procession of years to come that would belong to her absolutely. And she opened and spread her arms out to them in welcome.

There would be no one to live for during those coming years; she would live for herself. There would be no powerful will bending her in that blind **persistence** with which men and women believe they have a right to impose a private will upon a fellow-creature. A kind intention or a cruel intention made the act seem no less a crime as she looked upon it in that brief moment of **illumination**.

And yet she had loved him—sometimes. Often she had not. What did it matter! What could love, the unsolved mystery, count for in face of this possession of **self-assertion** which she suddenly recognized as the strongest impulse of her being!

"Free! Body and soul free!" she kept whispering.

Josephine was kneeling before the closed door with her lips to the keyhole, imploring for admission. "Louise, open the door! I beg; open the door—you will make yourself ill. What are you doing, Louise? For heaven's sake open the door."

"Go away. I am not making myself ill." No; she was drinking in a very **elixir** of life through that open window.

Her fancy was running riot along those days ahead of her. Spring days, and summer days, and all sorts of days that would be her own. She breathed a quick prayer that life might be long. It was only yesterday she had thought with a **shudder** that life might be long.

She arose at length and opened the door to her sister's **importunities**. There was a feverish triumph in her eyes, and she carried herself **unwittingly** like a goddess of Victory. She clasped her sister's waist, and together they descended the stairs. Richards stood waiting for them at the bottom.

Some one was opening the front door with a **latchkey**. It was Brently Mallard who entered, a little travel-stained, **composedly** carrying his **gripsack** and umbrella. He had been far from the scene of accident, and did not even know there had been one. He stood amazed at Josephine's piercing cry; at Richards' quick motion to screen him from the view of his wife.

But Richards was too late.

When the doctors came they said she had died of heart disease—of joy that kills.

Glossary

abandoned *(verb)*   yielded

afflicted with *(verb)*   stricken by; suffering from; affected by; caused pain by

aquiver *(verb [obsolete])*   quivering; shaking; trembling

bosom *(noun)*   breasts; chest. Irregular breathing, caused by fear or excitement, makes the **bosom** rise and fall.

composedly *(adverb)*   calmly

concealing *(verb)*   hiding; putting out of sight; keeping from another's knowledge

disaster *(noun)* any happening that causes great harm or serious misfortune

elixir *(noun)* principle; essence

elusive *(adjective)* hard to grasp or detect

exalted *(adjective)* joyful; elated

forestall *(verb)* prevent; hinder; obstruct; intercept

grip-sack *(noun [obsolete])* small traveling bag used to hold clothing and personal articles

hastened *(verb)* hurried; moved quickly

haunted *(verb)* filled. Usually haunted is used to show the frequency of visits (of ghosts, memories, or even people); for example, a young person might haunt a video games arcade, memories might haunt a newly widowed bride, or ghosts might haunt an abandoned house.

illumination *(noun)* enlightenment; clarification; understanding

importunities *(noun)* repeated requests; continued begging or imploring

keen *(adjective)* sharp; acute

latchkey *(noun)* key to a door that opens to the outside

monstrous *(adjective)* unnatural; horrible; hideously wrong; shocking

paralyzed *(adjective)* helpless

patches *(noun)* areas (of blue sky) that are different from the surrounding areas.

peddler *(noun)* a person who goes from place to place selling small articles

persistence *(noun)* stubborn, lasting continuance. Mrs. Mallard would no longer have to obey her husband's unwelcome, persistent orders that were meant to protect her.

reflection *(noun)* serious thought

repression *(noun)* holding back or restraining of emotion or expression. The lines on Mrs. Mallard's face were probably caused by her repressing the pain she felt and trying to act as if nothing were wrong.

roomy *(adjective)* spacious; having a large capacity

save *(conjunction)* except; but

self-assertion *(noun)* declaration or affirmation to herself

shudder *(noun)* violent trembling (responding to something horrible or disgusting)

storm of grief *(figurative language)* strong outburst of emotion. Mrs. Mallard's feelings about the death of her husband are compared with the strength of a severe storm.

subtle *(adjective)* not open, direct, or obvious

suspension *(noun)*   temporary stoppage

terror *(noun)*   extreme fear

to break [it] to her as gently as possible *(idiom)*   to explain the news in a way that would upset her as little as possible

trivial *(adjective)*   unimportant; insignificant

tumultuously *(adverb)*   wildly; in a manner that shows great agitation or emotional disturbance

twittering *(verb)*   making a series of sounds common in birds—short, high-pitched chirps. People can also twitter by talking rapidly or excitedly. Mrs. Mallard hears the sparrows "talking to each other" in their nests just under the edge of the roof.

unwittingly *(adverb)*   unconsciously; unknowingly

veiled *(adjective)*   not openly discussed; hidden; obscured; disguised. A **veiled hint** is a suggestion that requires little thought or interpretation to be understood.

wild abandonment *(colloquialism)*   unrestrained emotion; utter and complete yielding to feelings

Miss Brill

Katherine Mansfield

Although it was so brilliantly fine—the blue sky powdered with gold and great spots of light like white wine splashed over the **Jardins Publiques**—Miss Brill was glad that she had decided on her fur. The air was motionless, but when you opened your mouth there was just a faint chill, like a chill from a glass of iced water before you sip, and now and again a leaf came drifting—from nowhere, from the sky. Miss Brill put up her hand and touched her fur. Dear little thing! It was nice to feel it again. She had taken it out of its box that afternoon, shaken out the moth-powder, given it a good brush, and rubbed the life back into the dim little eyes. "What has been happening to me?" said the sad little eyes. Oh, how sweet it was to see them snap at her again from the red **eiderdown**! . . . But the nose, which was of some black composition, wasn't at all firm. It must have had a **knock**, somehow. Never mind—a little **dab** of black sealing-wax when the time came—when it was absolutely necessary. . . . Little **rogue**! Yes, she really felt like that about it. Little rogue biting its tail just by her left ear. She could have taken it off and laid it on her lap and stroked it. She felt a **tingling** in her hands and arms, but that came from walking, she supposed. And when she breathed, something light and sad—no, not sad, exactly—something gentle seemed to move in her bosom.

There were a number of people out this afternoon, far more than last Sunday. And the band sounded louder and gayer. That was because the Season had begun. For although the band played all the year round on Sundays, out of season it was never the same. It was like some one playing with only the family to listen; it didn't care how it played if there weren't any strangers present. Wasn't the conductor wearing a new coat, too? She was sure it was new. He scraped with his foot and flapped his arms like a rooster about to crow, and the bandsmen sitting in the green **rotunda** blew out their cheeks and glared at the music. Now there came a little **"flutey"** bit—very pretty!—a little chain of bright drops. She was sure it would be repeated. It was; she lifted her head and smiled.

Only two people shared her "special" seat: a fine old man in a velvet coat, his hands clasped over a huge carved walking-stick, and a big old woman, sitting upright, with a roll of knitting on her **embroidered** apron. They did not speak. This was disappointing, for Miss Brill always looked forward to the conversation. She had become really quite expert, she thought, at listening as though she didn't listen, at sitting in other people's lives just for a minute while they talked round her.

She glanced, sideways, at the old couple. Perhaps they would go soon. Last Sunday, too, hadn't been as interesting as usual. An Englishman and his wife, he wearing a dreadful **Panama hat** and she **button boots**. And she'd gone on the whole time about how she ought to wear **spectacles**; she knew she needed them; but that it was no good getting any; they'd be sure to break and they'd never keep on. And he'd been so patient. He'd suggested everything—gold rims, the kind that curved round your ears, little pads inside the bridge. No, nothing would please her. "They'll always be sliding down my nose!" Miss Brill had wanted to shake her.

The old people sat on the bench, still as statues. Never mind, there was always the crowd to watch. **To and fro**, in front of the flower-beds and the band rotunda, the couples and groups paraded, stopped to talk, to greet, to buy a handful of flowers from the old beggar who had his tray fixed to the railings. Little children ran among them, **swooping** and laughing; little boys with big white silk bows under their chins, little girls, little French dolls, dressed up in velvet and lace. And sometimes a tiny **staggerer** came suddenly rocking into the open from under the trees, stopped, stared, as suddenly sat down "flop," until its small high-stepping mother, like a young hen, rushed scolding to its rescue. Other people sat on the benches and green chairs, but they were nearly always the same, Sunday after Sunday, and—Miss Brill had often noticed—there was something funny about nearly all of them. They were odd, silent, nearly all old, and from the way they stared they looked as though they'd just come from dark little rooms or even—even **cupboards**!

Behind the rotunda the slender trees with yellow leaves down drooping, and through them just a line of sea, and beyond the blue sky with gold-veined clouds.

Tum-tum-tum tiddle-um! tiddle-um! tum tiddley-um tum ta! blew the band.

Two young girls in red came by and two young soldiers in blue met them, and they laughed and paired and went off arm-in-arm. Two peasant women with funny straw hats passed, gravely, leading beautiful smoke-coloured donkeys. A cold, pale nun hurried by. A beautiful woman came along and dropped her bunch of violets, and a little boy ran after to hand them to her, and she took them and threw them away as if they'd been poisoned. Dear me! Miss Brill didn't know whether to admire that or not! And now an **ermine toque** and a gentleman in grey met just in front of her. He was tall, stiff, dignified, and she was wearing the ermine toque she'd bought when her hair was yellow. Now everything, her hair, her face, even her eyes, was the same colour as the shabby ermine, and her hand, in its cleaned glove, lifted to dab her lips, was a tiny yellowish **paw**. Oh, she was so pleased to see him—delighted! She rather thought they were going to meet that afternoon. She described where she'd been—everywhere, here, there, along by the sea. The day was so charming—didn't he agree? And wouldn't he, perhaps? . . . But he shook his head, lighted a cigarette, slowly breathed a great deep puff into her face, and, even while she was still talking and laughing, flicked the match away and walked on. The ermine toque was alone; she smiled more brightly than ever. But even the band seemed to know what she was feeling and played more softly, played tenderly, and the drum beat, "The **Brute**! The Brute!" over and over. What would she do? What was going to happen now? But as Miss Brill wondered, the ermine toque turned, raised her hand as though she'd seen some one else, much nicer, just over there, and **pattered** away. And the band changed again and played more quickly, more gaily than ever, and the old couple on Miss Brill's seat got up and marched away, and such a funny old man with long **whiskers hobbled** along in time to the music and was nearly knocked over by four girls **walking abreast**.

Oh, how fascinating it was! How she enjoyed it! How she loved sitting here, watching it all! It was like a play. It was exactly like a play. Who could believe the sky at the back wasn't painted? But it wasn't till a little brown dog **trotted** on solemn and then slowly trotted off, like a little "theatre" dog, a little dog that had been drugged, that Miss Brill discovered what it was that made it so exciting. They were all on the stage. They weren't only the audience, not only looking on; they were acting. Even she had a part and came every Sunday. No doubt somebody would have noticed if she hadn't been there;

she was part of the performance after all. How strange she'd never thought of it like that before! And yet it explained why she made such a point of starting from home at just the same time each week—so as not to be late for the performance—and it also explained why she had quite a queer, shy feeling at telling her English pupils how she spent her Sunday afternoons. No wonder! Miss Brill nearly laughed out loud. She was on the stage. She thought of the old **invalid** gentleman to whom she read the newspaper four afternoons a week while he slept in the garden. She had got quite used to the **frail** head on the cotton pillow, the **hollowed** eyes, the open mouth and the high **pinched** nose. If he'd been dead she mightn't have noticed for weeks; she wouldn't have minded. But suddenly he knew he was having the paper read to him by an actress! "An actress!" The old head lifted; two points of light quivered in the old eyes. "An actress—are **ye**?" And Miss Brill smoothed the newspaper as though it were the manuscript of her part and said gently: "Yes, I have been an actress for a long time."

The band had been having a rest. Now they started again. And what they played was warm, sunny, yet there was just a faint chill—a something, what was it?—not sadness—no, not sadness—a something that made you want to sing. The tune lifted, lifted, the light shone; and it seemed to Miss Brill that in another moment all of them, all the whole company, would begin singing. The young ones, the laughing ones who were moving together, they would begin, and the men's voices, very **resolute** and brave, would join them. And then she too, she too, and the others on the benches—they would come in with a kind of accompaniment—something low, that scarcely rose or fell, something so beautiful—moving. . . . And Miss Brill's eyes filled with tears and she looked smiling at all the other members of the company. Yes, we understand, we understand, she thought—though what they understood she didn't know.

Just at that moment a boy and a girl came and sat down where the old couple had been. They were beautifully dressed; they were in love. The hero and heroine, of course, just arrived from his father's **yacht**. And still soundlessly singing, still with that trembling smile, Miss Brill prepared to listen.

"No, not now," said the girl. "Not here, I can't."

"But why? Because of that stupid old thing at the end there?" asked the boy. "Why does she come here at all—who wants her? Why doesn't she keep her silly old **mug** at home?"

"It's her fu-fur which is so funny," giggled the girl. "It's exactly like a fried **whiting**."

"Ah, be off with you!" said the boy in an angry whisper. Then: "Tell me, **ma petite chérie**—"

"No, not here," said the girl. "Not *yet*."

On her way home she usually bought a slice of honey-cake at the baker's. It was her Sunday treat. Sometimes there was an **almond** in her slice, sometimes not. It made a great difference. If there was an almond it was like carrying home a tiny present—a surprise—something that might very well not have been there. She hurried on the almond Sundays and struck the match for the **kettle** in quite a dashing way.

But to-day she passed the baker's by, climbed the stairs, went into the little dark room—her room like a cupboard—and sat down on the red eiderdown. She sat there for a long time. The box that the fur came out of was on the bed. She unclasped the necklet quickly; quickly, without looking, laid it inside. But when she put the lid on she thought she heard something crying.

Glossary

almond *(noun)* type of tree-grown, edible nut

Brute *(noun)* cruel, unkind person lacking consciousness of or feelings for others; beast

button boots *(noun)* close-fitting, ankle-height, leather dress boots that fasten with a row of buttons (instead of laces) up the front or side. Button boots were worn before zippers were invented. This type of footwear went out of fashion around the turn of the century.

cupboards *(noun)* closets or cabinets used to hold dishes, food, and other household items

dab *(noun)* small, soft bit of something; for example, a **dab** of paint or butter. **Dab** *(verb)* means to touch or pat lightly.

eiderdown *(noun)* bed quilt stuffed with the soft breast (down) feathers of the eider duck

embroidered *(adjective)* decorated with design done with a needle and special thread. Often the stitches represent flowers or leaves.

ermine toque *(adjective, noun)* woman's white fur hat that is small, round, and close-fitting. Mansfield has personified the hat to represent the woman.

flutey **(fluty,** *adjective)* musical sound like that of a flute

frail *(adjective)* fragile, delicate, easily broken

hobbled *(verb)* walked haltingly as if disabled

hollowed eyes *(adjective, noun)* deeply set with dark shadows around them

invalid *(adjective)* weak; sickly; unwell

Jardins Publiques *(noun [French])* Public Gardens

kettle *(noun)* metal container used for boiling water

knock *(noun)* blow; hit

ma petite chérie *(French expression)* my little darling

mug *(noun, slang)* face

Panama hat *(noun)* a specially shaped straw hat designed to protect the wearer from the sun

pattered *(verb)* walked with quick, light steps

paw *(noun, colloquialism)* hand

pinched *(adjective)* thin

resolute *(adjective)* determined

rogue *(noun)* rascal; scoundrel; mischievous creature. Miss Brill uses the term affectionately as if she is dealing with a naughty but cute child.

rotunda *(noun)* round building, hall or room, often with a dome

spectacles *(noun)* eyeglasses

staggerer *(noun)* person who moves unsteadily, as though about to collapse or fall down. Children who are just learning to walk often **stagger**.

swooping *(verb)* descending suddenly and swiftly like birds **swooping** down on insects

tingling *(noun)* prickling or stinging feeling

to and fro *(adjective)* forward and backward. This is one of several expressions in English (such as "back and forth," "in and out," and "up and down") for which the word order cannot be reversed.

trotted *(verb)* moved quickly; ran

walking abreast *(verb, adjective)* walking side by side

whiskers *(noun)* hair growing from a man's face; beard

whiting *(noun)* type of European cod fish

yacht *(noun)* small ship used for pleasure cruising or racing

ye *(pronoun [obsolete])* you

Comprehension Questions and Discussion Topics

1. What sets the mood at the beginning of each story? Why is Mrs. Mallard grief-stricken? Why is Miss Brill happy?

2. Both stories include many beautifully written, figurative details about nature, which both women enjoy; however, Mrs. Mallard has a renewed appreciation for it. What does nature mean to each woman and why? How does figurative language enrich each story?

3. Both women sit alone for a good part of each story, but their reasons are different. Mrs. Mallard wants to be alone, but Miss Brill doesn't. What is Mrs. Mallard thinking about while she is locked in her room? What does Miss Brill do to amuse herself as she sits on a bench in the park?

4. Both women confuse illusion and reality. They forget what is real and try to live out their fantasies. What is Mrs. Mallard's conception of her past

and future life? Is it similar to or different from Miss Brill's "discovery" about her exciting part in the Sunday afternoon dramas at the park and her observation that there is "something funny" about many of the people there?

5. When Brently Mallard returns "from the dead," his wife is shocked. When the beautifully dressed boy and girl sit down beside Miss Brill, she is enchanted, and she eagerly awaits their conversation, but she is unprepared for their rudeness. How do these events make both women face reality at last?

6. Mrs. Mallard dies physically from the "joy that kills." What *really* kills her? On the other hand, Miss Brill dies spiritually when "she thought she heard something crying"; after all, the fur is an extension of her own personality. Explain the reason for the death in each story.

7. How important is dialog in each story? How do we learn of the feelings of the main characters?

8. Like many invalids, Mrs. Mallard thinks a great deal about herself and her problems. On the other hand, Miss Brill has both empathy and sympathy for others; for example, she is deeply involved in the discussions between the man and his wife arguing about eyeglasses and between the ermine toque and gentleman in gray. Mrs. Mallard could be described as an inwardly-directed and Miss Brill as an outwardly-directed person. Explain.

Essay Topics

Materials covered:
    Kate Chopin, "The Story of an Hour"
    Katherine Mansfield, "Miss Brill"
Instructions:
    Choose only *one* of the following topics. Each requires that you deal with both stories. Write an essay with a clear thesis, careful development, and a thoughtful conclusion. Be sure to identify the authors and stories in the first paragraph. Use a study sheet that you have prepared in advance.

1. Compare and/or contrast the characters of Mrs. Mallard and Miss Brill. How do they behave? Why?

2. Analyze the kinds of lives Mrs. Mallard and Miss Brill lead. Is one more restrictive than the other? What roles do other people play in governing the behavior of these women?

3. Both Mrs. Mallard and Miss Brill have fantasies or illusions about their lives. What does each woman dream about? What are the realities faced by each?

4. Analyze the use of figurative language, dialog, or symbols used in the stories and explain how they affect meaning.

Two Articles for Comparison and Contrast

The *Los Angeles Times* recently published these contrasting views in answer to the following question: Does marketing of alcoholic beverages on campuses encourage abuse? David Redfield, Consumer Affairs Manager for the Miller Brewing Company takes the "no" position. He contends that college marketing informs and educates consumers about alcohol use as they develop preferences for specific brands. On the other hand, Candy Lightner, President of Mothers Against Drunk Drivers (MADD), many of whose members have had children killed by drunk drivers, takes the "yes" position. She uses statistics, quotations, facts, and details to show that alcohol use should be neither endorsed nor encouraged by educational institutions.

The tone of each article is serious. Although Redfield and Lightner have entirely different motives for writing, each seems sincere. They have avoided emotional terms intended to inflame, anger, or excite the audience. Instead, the essays invite an intellectual appraisal of the merits and demerits of each side. Which position is the better one? Why?

Does Marketing of Alcoholic Beverages on Campuses Cause Abuse?

No—Ban Might Actually Increase Drinking

David Redfield

American business knows how important the college market is.

College students make up more than a third of what's called the "young adult market," consumers from the minimum drinking age to age 24 who elect to drink and who are just establishing **brand loyalties**.

The importance of these early brand decisions is obvious to manufacturers of such products as electronic equipment, automobiles and beer. So major brewers and other industries conduct extensive college promotional and advertising programs, sponsor campus events and employ student representatives.

Reprinted from the *Los Angeles Times* by permission of the author.

The activities are designed to establish a lifetime of loyalty to a specific brand for individuals who have chosen to use a specific product. For **brewers**, this means encouraging individuals of legal drinking age who choose to drink beer to use a specific brand. It does not mean encouraging non-drinkers to drink beer nor does it mean encouraging excessive or illegal use of beer or alcoholic beverages in general.

Concern About Marketing

Many university officials, industry groups and others are concerned about college marketing by the alcoholic-beverage industry. This concern legitimately stems from the growing recognition of alcohol abuse on campuses. Often, it includes a perceived link between these problems and all marketing of alcoholic beverages on campus, a perception that is not supported by the best available evidence.

In response, some have called for a **ban** on all marketing of alcoholic beverages on campuses. However, banning campus marketing would not reduce alcohol abuse any more than banning college marketing by auto makers would reduce **reckless** driving. In fact, a ban could do more harm than good.

Several facts support this assertion. First, any attempted ban on students' exposure to alcoholic beverages through advertising and marketing could impose a **"forbidden fruit"** image on alcoholic beverages. The stronger the portrayal of all alcoholic use as undesirable, the stronger the desire to taste "forbidden fruit" in a way that blurs the distinction between responsible use, which contributes to good health and social enjoyment, and excessive use, which causes serious health and social problems.

Also, at Miller Brewing Co., the college marketing staff and campus representatives promote effective alcohol education and integrate this theme into all activities. One of the ways this is accomplished is by making non-alcoholic beverages readily available at any event where our products are available.

Miller and other alcoholic-beverage industry groups also increasingly fund and promote on-campus alcohol education and awareness programs in conjunction with campus marketing activities. Bacchus (Boost Alcohol Consciousness Concerning the Health of University Students), now active on 121 campuses, and similar groups receive support from many large corporations, including the alcoholic-beverage industry. Bacchus succeeds because it is a student-based program, using peer pressure and peer education to reduce alcohol abuse by encouraging responsible decisions.

Further, much of the money Miller spends on campus marketing goes to support scholarship programs, campus charity fund-raising events, extensive social activities such as dances, film series and concerts, and athletic programs. All these activities are healthy alternatives to simply going out and getting drunk.

Banning marketing on campuses would also tend to give the false impression that excessive drinking on campus would also cease. The absence of marketing activities and programs does not mean an absence of either consumption or alcohol abuse.

Recognizing the need to define responsible alcohol-beverage marketing, the Inter-Association Task Force on Alcohol Issues last year recommended guidelines for members and schools. The task force included representatives of the American College Personnel Assn., the Assn. of College & University Housing Officers International, the National Assn. of Student Personnel Administrators and Bacchus.

Conforming to a Code

The guidelines essentially call for:

Marketing programs that conform to the **code** of student conduct at the institution where the program is being **implemented**.

Programs that do not emphasize alcohol abuse or **overindulgence**.

Letting the college or university know about the program in advance.

Not **portraying** alcoholic beverages as the solution to personal or academic problems, or as beverages that should be consumed when students must perform tasks such as operating cars or machinery.

Miller Brewing Co. immediately **endorsed** these guidelines and is encouraging distributors to do the same.

Miller believes that the key to a resolution of the campus marketing issue is responsibility on the part of alcoholic-beverage manufacturers, distributors and retailers. Campus marketing programs can be **legitimate**, worthwhile efforts. If carried out responsibly, they aren't part of the problem related to excessive use of alcohol. In many cases, they are part of the solution.

Glossary

ban *(noun)*   prohibition; official order forbidding something

brand loyalties *(special business term)*   faithfulness to particular brands of products

brewers *(noun)*   companies that make (brew) beer

code *(noun)*   set of rules of conduct

endorsed *(verb)*   gave support or approval

"forbidden fruit" *(figurative expression)*   originally the fruit of the tree of knowledge of good and evil that was forbidden to Adam and Eve in Genesis. This prohibition made the fruit seem more tempting and attractive than it really was.

implemented *(verb)*   fulfilled; accomplished; carried out

legitimate *(adjective)*   conforming to law, rules, or principles

overindulgence *(noun)*   excessively yielding to one's desires; for example, eating an entire chocolate cake instead of one or two pieces

portraying *(verb)*   describing graphically; making a word picture

reckless *(adjective)*   careless; irresponsible

Yes—Causes Drunk Driving, Academic Failure

Candy Lightner

Each year, 8,000 teen-agers and adults are killed and 40,000 more are injured in crashes involving drunk drivers. Drivers between 16 and 24 account for only 22% of all licensed drivers, yet they cause 44% of all fatal alcohol-related crashes that occur at night. Drunk driving is the leading cause of death and injury among those under 25.

It is clear that methods used to reduce drinking and driving among teen-agers have not worked. Yet alcohol continues to be promoted on campuses.

Some breweries use their own employees to **solicit** business on college campuses, while others use a **wholesaler's** employees. Normally, this is a student already attending the college who is paid a salary. One brewery reportedly employs student representatives on 550 campuses. The payment can be anywhere from $150 to $300 a month. These representatives promote the particular product of that brewing company on the campus by giving away **posters** to **dormitories, fraternities** and **sororities**; taking orders for beer, and providing beer for campus parties.

The brewers **contend** that they are trying to create brand awareness.

According to the Chronicle of Higher Education of July 21, 1982, some colleges report that as much as 80% of the vandalism on their campuses is alcohol related. More than 90% of deaths that occur on campuses are a result of **hazing** and are connected with alcohol, according to the Chronicle's surveys.

Quoting from the Chronicle article: "Some 36% of those deans surveyed by the Chronicle believe there has been an increase in the amount of excessive drinking by students over the last five years. In addition, a number of them also report increases in student behavior problems over the same period as a result of drinking: 23.8% said they had observed an increase in driving after

Reprinted from the *Los Angeles Times* by permission of the author.

drinking; 29.8% said there was more **vandalism** due to drinking, and 26.5% reported an increase in fighting as a result of alcohol use."

One study was conducted at Radford College in Radford, Va. It was determined that academic failure in as many as 60% of the cases studied was related to student drinking problems.

According to the president of Bacchus (Boost Alcohol Consciousness Concerning the Health of University Students), Gerrado M. Gonzales, assistant dean for student services at the University of Florida: "Inappropriate and irresponsible marketing promotion of beverage alcohol on college campuses is seen by many college administrators as one contributing factor to alcohol abuse among students."

Colleges are reacting by offering programs to promote safe, responsible drinking as an alternative to the typical **chug-a-lug** parties on campuses. Many colleges, in conjunction with Mothers Against Drunk Drivers, are observing alcohol awareness week, which promotes healthful products, non-alcoholic bars and programs in which sober students give **peers** who have had too much to drink a ride home.

Other colleges and universities are calling for bans on alcoholic beverages at sporting events and offering alcohol education courses. Many university communities are offering counseling for students with alcohol problems.

There is a simple solution to the problems of alcohol abuse by students: Ban alcohol on college campuses. Students in the university community are there to learn and prepare future careers, not to decide which brand of beer to drink. If this approach proves to be impossible, then some measures must be taken to control the consumption of alcoholic beverages on campus and during campus activities.

There are several actions that MADD would heartily support. First, put an end to free beer on campuses and allow no alcohol in dormitories, fraternities or sororities. Colleges and universities should not pay for alcohol to be used at parties. For those individuals living off campus, free taxi service should be provided when alcohol is part of the activities.

Responsible drinking should be encouraged by groups such as Bacchus and Students Against Drunk Drivers, and the university community should allow these groups to be highly visible. Alcohol education should be updated and become a mandatory part of college curriculums. In addition, more treatment programs should be offered such as those developed by Alcoholics Anonymous. Colleges should prominently display posters and signs about the harmful effects of alcohol and make sure students understand local ordinances and laws pertaining to drinking and driving. And, by all means, student ID cards should be checked at all campus parties.

Most important, universities and colleges should not allow brewers to have campus representatives. This totally unnecessary activity lends nothing to the educational process. Why not allow representatives of car manufacturers, gun manufacturers, tobacco wholesalers and others to hawk their wares as well?

This issue requires a long-term, serious commitment from many **segments** of society. Because higher education is so much a part of the lives of millions of students, and because schools are dedicated to educating and preparing students for future responsibilities, the university and college communities of our nation must take a leadership role in preventing alcohol abuse.

Glossary

chug-a-lug *(slang)* drinking in continuous gulps or in a single long gulp. Someone who wanted to show off might **chug-a-lug** one or more bottles of beer.

contend *(verb)* argue

dormitories *(noun)* buildings that provide housing for college students

fraternities *(noun)* groups of men joined together by common interests; college social organizations. Membership is restricted to those approved by the group. Often fraternities own houses near campus where the members live.

hazing *(noun)* initiating fellow students into fraternities or sororities by forcing them to do ridiculous or embarrassing things

peers *(noun)* persons who are equal in rank or ability

posters *(noun)* large printed cards or sheets of paper, sometimes including photographs, used to advertise or publicize information or events

segments *(noun)* sections; divisions

solicit *(verb)* seek; appeal for

sororities *(noun)* female versions of fraternities

vandalism *(noun)* deliberate, malicious destruction of or damage to property belonging to someone else

wholesaler *(noun)* business person who sells goods in large quantities, at lower than retail prices, for resale in stores

Comprehension Questions and Discussion Topics

1. The first few paragraphs of each article begin with the author's position about the need for and effects of marketing alcoholic beverages on college campuses. What is Redfield's position? How does Lightner feel? Give details.

2. How does each author assess the importance of establishing brand loyalties or creating brand awareness?

3. Colleges and universities are becoming increasingly concerned about combating alcoholism on campus, according to both articles. What are the disadvantages of uncontrolled drinking and the advantages of controlled alco-

hol use? Give as many facts, details, examples, and arguments as you can for each side.

4. How do the authors feel about completely banning alcoholic beverages at campus functions? Why?

5. Redfield calls for guidelines to govern alcoholic-beverage marketing. What are they? What actions would MADD support? Are they similar or different?

6. In their concluding paragraphs, do the authors agree or disagree? Has their fundamental difference been resolved? Has either compromised?

Essay Topics

Materials covered:
   "Does Marketing of Alcoholic Beverages on Campuses Encourage
      Abuse?"
   David Redfield, "No—Ban Might Actually Increase Drinking"
   Candy Lightner, "Yes—Causes Drunk Driving, Academic Failure"
Instructions:
   Choose only *one* of the following topics. Each requires that you write about both articles. Prepare a study sheet that shows similarities and differences between the two articles. Be sure that your essay has a thesis, adequate development, and a definite conclusion. Identify the authors and the titles of their articles in paragraph one.

1. Compare or contrast the positions taken by Redfield and Lightner. Examine the evidence presented by each. What conclusion can you reach?

2. Evaluate the purpose of each author. Does Redfield care only about marketing his company's product? Is Lightner interested only in preventing drunk driving? What other concerns does each voice?

3. Examine the advantages and disadvantages of marketing *any* product on college campuses.

6

Process Analysis: Direction or Explanation

Many of the characteristics of a narrative are included in a *process analysis,* but the purpose is to give directions about how to do something or to explain how something is or was done by someone else. Emphasis is not so much on the story being told as on the importance of the process used to achieve a certain result. Most of us would rather read a good book or magazine than read directions or explanations, but a process analysis can be entertaining and interesting if it relates an actual experience or gives a careful explanation of something the reader wants or needs to know.

Both directions and explanations should do more than list the steps used in the process. If readers are expected to follow your instructions, they want to know what happened when *you* went through the steps or why you thought the experience was important enough to write about. Was it frightening like Ken Ringle's account of a Halloween party included in this chapter? Was it satisfying? Were you able to assemble a child's bicycle using only a screwdriver? Or was it frustrating or embarrassing? Were you unable to put the bike together even though you had a full set of tools and the instructions said that "any four-year-old child can put it together in fifteen minutes"? Even if readers are merely supposed to gain a general understanding of a process without being able to do it themselves, they expect a clear and interesting discussion of it; for example, training astronauts to fly space shuttle missions, raising and salvaging sunken ships from the depths of the ocean, or building dams to control or change the course of rivers.

The process may report success (how to wash a car by hand) or failure (how the automatic car wash nearly ruined your car); it may be the major or only a minor part of your essay. However, you must state your purpose clearly in the thesis, report each step completely and correctly, and evaluate the result. Help readers get organized by categorizing steps in simple groups, such as (1) equipment, utensils, tools, supplies, or ingredients needed, (2) methods of using these items, and (3) possible problems to guard against. Be sure to define or explain unusual terms so that readers won't have to stop and look them up.

Steps should be presented chronologically, but some processes may also have to be described spatially; for instance, to wash a car by hand work from top to bottom; soap and rinse small areas at a time, and rerinse the entire car often to prevent water spotting. First, wash the top surfaces from hood to trunk. Next, do the window areas, beginning with the windshield, moving along one side, across the back, and up to the front again. Then work all the way around the car below window level, including the bumpers. Finally, wash the wheel covers and tires.

Warn of potential problems, and explain how to deal with them. If you used an abrasive cleanser instead of a mild detergent on your car and it damaged the paint, were you able to restore it with polish and wax? Give preliminary steps for processes that do not involve direct participation. Your unfortunate experience with an automatic car wash can help others. Advise readers that you should have rolled up all the windows and closed the vents *before* the car started through the wash line and was jet sprayed with soap and water, or that you should have put down the antenna *before* the blower mechanism rolled over it.

ANALYZING BY TIME

Chronological order is vital to explaining a process. People simply can't follow directions or understand explanations if the steps are out of order. Chapter 3 includes several kinds of transitional devices used (instead of "and then") to show when something happened in a narrative. Ordinal numbers (*first, second, third*) and some interrupters (*next, then, later, concurrently, simultaneously*) are useful to indicate the sequence of events in a process, but time words that definitely place the action in the past (*previous to, prior to, just before*) should be used only before beginning the first step; for example:

Prior to beginning the job, make sure you have all the equipment.

If you insert this warning *after* you have begun the process, you will seem forgetful and confused, and your directions will lack authority.

Dependent clauses linking segments of a sequence can be introduced by prepositions used as single-word adverbs (*after, before, until*) and regular adverbs (*when, while*); for example:

After (or *when*) you have thoroughly cleaned the inside, begin working on the outside.

Before moving on to the next step, double-check everything you have done so far.

Don't begin to apply the wax *until* the surface is completely free of water droplets.

Turn off the water that feeds the hose *while* you soap each section.

Be sure to use soft cloths *when* you apply wax to any painted surface.

Other useful prepositions of time cannot be used as single-word adverbs to introduce dependent adverbial clauses, but still indicate *when* or *how long: as (early/late/soon) as, in, on, to, till, up to* and *upon.*

If the sun is hot, park the car in the garage *as soon as* possible after you have finished washing it.

You should be able to complete the work *in* one hour.

I will wash the car *on* Tuesday. (I will wash the car Tuesday.)

Bake the bread *from* 45 to 55 minutes. (Bake the bread 45 to 55 minutes.)

They stayed *till* eight o'clock.

She spends *up to* three hours a night studying for this class.

Cool the cookies on a wire rack immediately *upon* removing them from the oven.

Three prepositions of time have special uses—*during, for,* and *since. During* shows the duration that the activity or event was in progress, from its beginning to its end, often without specifying the exact length of time.

George works the night shift; therefore, he always sleeps *during* his first class. (He sleeps through the entire class period.)

During Alice's first year at college, she never left the campus. (She did not leave the campus once from September until June.)

For shows a specific length of time or sometimes an appointed time:

Although Lucy has only been here *for* twenty minutes, she has to leave *for* ten minutes.

Her appointment is *for* two o'clock. (Her appointment is at two o'clock.)

Since indicates when a period of time began, but it can also show a period of time from its beginning until the present. Usually the present perfect or the present perfect progressive tenses are used with *since.*

Boris has lived in the United States *since* 1980. (He still lives here.)

At least twenty customers have been waiting for tables *since* six o'clock. (It is now eight o'clock.)

Since, used as a conjunction in the main clause with the present or perfect tense, is also used in place of *during* or *for:*

It is five years *since* I visited him. (I haven't visited him for five years.)

I have finished all my homework *since* you telephoned me an hour ago. (During the period between your telephone call and our present conversation, I finished all my homework.)

The following student essay uses many time words. Notice that the material is organized chronologically and that unusual terms are defined.

Those American Tooth Fanatics

M. Farahbakhsh

In the small village in the Middle East where I grew up, dental care was of little concern to most of us. I occasionally brushed my teeth with salt and water, but I seldom thought about it. We ate a lot of rough, hard foods, and sometimes we chewed on melon rinds, which we thought helped keep our teeth clean. Few people thought about brushing their teeth. Then, when I came to America, I met Mary, who worked for a dentist. Her teeth sparkled—she had a beautiful smile! As time went on, I learned some new and interesting things from her about teeth and some important special procedures that people should use to take care of their teeth.

One day, when I went to pick up Mary at the dentist's office, she invited me in to meet her coworkers. As I visited with them, I admitted I had never been to a dentist before. Before I knew what was happening, I ended up in one of the empty dental chairs getting an examination by Dr. Shoemaker. He checked me out and said my teeth and gums looked pretty healthy (probably because I had always had so many fresh fruits and vegetables in my diet), but that I had some rough deposits built up around the gums which made them bright red in some places. He also found lots of stains on my teeth from years of tea drinking. He said my teeth really should be "gone over" by the hygienist at once and then at regular six-month intervals. I couldn't imagine what a hygienist was and I was very worried about how it would "go over" me. "Don't look so worried," Dr. Shoemaker said. "Hygienists are professionally trained and licensed to clean, x-ray, and examine teeth. Dentists can then concentrate on doing needed repair work." Mary's coworkers laughed at my concern and said their hygienist was "the best" and "very gentle." I really didn't understand much of their explanations, but I was ashamed to say so. When I went

Reprinted by permission.

for my appointment the following Monday, my nervousness turned to embarrassment because I learned this hygienist was a *person,* my good friend, Mary, and that *she* was the one who was going to look inside my mouth. I didn't want her to see my tooth stains and red gums. But she soon made me feel comfortable. She said she was used to working in people's mouths and that it didn't bother her a bit! She explained everything using a simple vocabulary.

Mary said that everybody just naturally grows new bacteria, called *plaque,* inside their mouths every day. Plaque causes two different problems: tooth decay and gum infection, both of which can be painful and can eventually cause you to lose your teeth. Then I remembered that my father has false teeth and that my grandmother has only two teeth left. And I began to feel a growing concern for my own teeth. What if my teeth were headed in the same direction as my father's? His ended up in some dentist's garbage can! Mary assured me that I didn't need to worry about losing my teeth, ever, if I did two simple things each day.

"The first," she advised, " is brushing your teeth at least two times a day: after breakfast and before going to bed each night." She said that although toothpaste helps in the cleaning process and makes your breath smell sweet, it really isn't as important as making sure that you use a small, medium-bristle toothbrush in a gentle, scrubbing motion to get the plaque off. And she emphasized the need to tip the toothbrush bristles into the gumline crevice (the space between the tooth and the gum) as you brush, since that area collects the most plaque and food particles.

Next, she brought out a fine, little white string, called *dental floss,* that she said she used each evening to clean the sides of her teeth where the brush couldn't reach. (Another new thing for the teeth! What next? Did this Mary ever do anything except clean her teeth? I was beginning to wonder if Americans were a bunch of tooth fanatics!) "The second is using dental floss daily. It will only take you four or five minutes a day and helps prevent plaque buildup that can cause tooth loss. Also, if you don't keep your mouth clean when you are under stress, like during final examinations or when you have family or work problems, your gums can get infected and the infection smells bad. Flossing your teeth is as important for your mouth as taking a bath or shower is for your body."

Here are Mary's instructions for flossing: First, use a long piece of floss that will leave several inches exposed as you stretch it between the forefinger and thumb of each hand. Second, as you slip the floss between the teeth, curve it against the side of one tooth. Then, slip the floss gently to the bottom of the gumline crevice. Next, using pressure with the floss against the side of the other tooth, pull the floss away from the gums (this scrapes off the plaque). Finally, floss the sides of both teeth in each space, but when you switch over to the opposite side, be careful not to cut your gums. As she explained, Mary demonstrated on herself. Then, after thoroughly washing her hands, she began flossing my teeth. I felt a slight pressure between some teeth, but it didn't hurt at all. Mary said that flossing took a little practice to get good at, and that I shouldn't give up if I felt clumsy doing it at first.

I wasn't sure I wanted to spend so much time on my teeth, but I decided to try this flossing and gentle, gum-massage brushing for a little while, especially since Mary gave me samples of recommended toothpaste, toothbrush, and floss. Right away I liked the fresh, cool taste of the toothpaste; after a week I could see and feel a big change in my mouth from all this brushing and flossing. My gums no longer looked bright red on the edges. They turned a healthy, pale pink color and didn't bleed anymore, just as Mary had promised. And my mouth didn't taste like something was rotting in it when I woke up in the mornings. In almost every letter I wrote to my family, I told them more about these wonderful new ways to care for the teeth. (They began to think *I* was a tooth fanatic!)

That was six months ago, and now Mary and I are married. She still works for the dentist. I work part-time and attend college. She says I am becoming quite Americanized. However, something happened at school one day last week that reminded me I am still a foreigner. I had an appointment with an advisor who was working in the foreign students' office. When he greeted me, his breath smelled terrible. Being newly educated about teeth and gums, I wanted to share the good news with him. "Have you been under a lot of stress lately?" I asked. His eyes opened wide. "Yes, how did you know?" I explained that I could smell his mouth and that he needed to use dental floss for all the reasons Mary had given me. He thanked me for telling him, and I felt really happy, sure that Mary would congratulate me for being a good teacher. But when I told her, she was shocked. "I can't believe you said that!" Then she began laughing uncontrollably. After a while, she explained, "In this culture, the subject of bad breath is 'delicate.' It is difficult to tell another person he or she has it, but especially a complete stranger, even if you are trying to be helpful." From this experience, I concluded that Americans are fanatics about many more things than just their teeth.

ANALYZING BY SPACE

Although all processes have to be presented chronologically to make sense, some also analyze "spatially," as well. That is, they use many prepositions that indicate space, place, position, movement, and direction; for example: *above, across, against, along, among*, around, at, before, behind, below, beneath, beside, between**, by, down, from, in, in back of, in front of, inside, into, near, next to, off, on, opposite, out, out of, outside, over, past, through, throughout, to, towards, under, underneath, up.* These and other prepositions are often used as

*We live *among* the foothills. (many foothills)

**We live *between* the mountains and the beach. (two locations)

prepositional phrases and sometimes as modifiers (adverbs and adjectives) to show spatial relationships.

> We lived *near the corner*. (prepositional phrase)
>
> Children always seem to walk *behind*. (adverb)
>
> Their house was *opposite* ours. (adjective)

Occasionally, two single prepositions are combined for emphasis. In the following examples, *down* and *up* are not needed for clarity:

> Elizabeth sat *down beside/by* George.
>
> He looked *down between* his bare feet and saw a piece of broken glass.
>
> The extra car key was hidden *up under* the left front fender.
>
> The prisoner stood *up against* the wall during questioning.

In addition, some prepositions are used as separable two-word verbs (verb + direct object + preposition) which help to describe events or give directions; for example, *look up, pick up, pull up, put on, take off, tuck in.*

> *Look* the word *up* in the dictionary. (Look up the word.)
>
> I have to *pick* my son *up* at school. (I have to pick up my son.)
>
> James never *pulls* his socks *up*. (James never pulls up his socks.)
>
> *Put* this lipstick *on*. (Put on this lipstick.)
>
> *Take* your coat *off* and stay a while. (Take off your coat.)
>
> Beth likes to *tuck* her shirt *in* even though the other children wear theirs out. (Beth likes to tuck in her shirt.)

The essay that follows is a good example of a chronologically organized, spatially arranged process.

A Trip Through the Underworld

Although the women's equality movement has been **controversial** in many households, it never has been in mine. My husband has a great sense of fair play. John respects my abilities and treats me as an intellectual equal. However, I learned the true meaning of equality last summer during "the great plumbing crisis." One Saturday morning we awoke to the unseasonal melody of water rushing down our hillside. The **sprinkler system had sprung a huge leak** that was rapidly **undermining** the retaining wall, threatening our house with both landslide and flood. The only way to stop the leak was to **cap off** a pipe under the house—clearly a job for a man.

John was just **revving up the power saw** when I went outside to help. "I can't get through this crawl hole," he grumbled, pointing to a tiny screened opening, "so I'll have to enlarge it, and it will take an extra day to patch the hole in the side of the house after I get the pipe fixed." We both knew that "day" might stretch out for weeks or even months.

"Maybe we should call a plumber," I offered.

He looked really upset. "A plumber couldn't get through there, either. Go back in the house; there is nothing you can do here."

That remark made me feel rather less than equal, but I stayed where I was. "You may need me for something," I said.

Before I continue, I should explain that I am absolutely **repulsed** by insects, and I have a special dread of spiders. It has always been my belief that **hordes** of spiders with red, glowing eyes inhabit the dark and frightening underworlds of houses, where they weave sticky, **voluminous** webs in which they wait: alert, watchful, hairy, crawling, and evil. But John's tone of voice had communicated an awful desperation. It was no small matter to saw into the side of the house. "Do you want me to go under there?" I asked, sure that he would refuse.

He turned, then, and gave me a look of such gratitude that I knew I was committed. "Well, you're the right size to get through the hole, but I'm not sure you can do it, that you have the strength. . . ." His voice trailed off.

I knew he didn't mean physical strength; he meant psychological **stamina** to overcome my spider **phobia** (which he delicately avoided mentioning). He also wanted to give me a chance to save face if I felt I had spoken **rashly**. "Oh, I can do it, all right," I said confidently, but already my skin was beginning to crawl. "How hard can it be to fix one little piece of a pipe?"

John's face was completely **impassive** as he watched my extensive preparations. I tied a lightweight towel around my head and tucked the ends inside my collar. I pushed the cuffs of my sleeves down into my garden gloves and pulled the tops of my socks up over the bottoms of my jeans. I rubbed insect repellent on all exposed skin. I did all of this very slowly, like a condemned prisoner hoping for a last minute reprieve from execution. At last, I walked over to the crawl hole. The full realization of my commitment washed over me like an icy wave. I was sick with fear. Once I squeezed through that small opening, I would be in *their* world. To make matters worse, I had to **wriggle** in backwards, with a five-pound **Stilson pipe wrench** in each pocket, so I had no idea what I would land on. As I sank slowly into the **murky depths**, John's face glowed above me, framed by the sunlight pouring into the darkness. He looked like God up there. "Don't worry," he smiled, "I'll shine my light on you the whole time and tell you exactly how to do everything."

Once inside, all I could think of was getting out. I was afraid to look up, sure that *they* would be looking right back. I tried to keep my mind on my task. I had to crawl on my elbows and stomach the fifteen feet to the broken pipe because there were only eighteen inches of clearance. Rocks pierced my thin shirt and cut my elbows, and the pipe wrenches bruised my legs. I desperately wanted to stand upright, run back to the hole, and claw my way out, but the beam of light **relentlessly** drew me on in the semidarkness.

At last, I reached the trouble spot. I was to disconnect a **union** between two lengths of pipe and cap the supply line, a difficult job because that low ceiling made it hard to get enough **leverage** to manipulate the oversize wrenches. In spite of the cramped work space, everything went smoothly, and when the water was turned back on, the cap didn't leak a drop! Suddenly, I felt incredibly strong and competent. I felt I could do absolutely anything. Right then I decided to **scan** for spiders, and I didn't find even a single web! It was amazingly clean under there, and I laughed at my silly fears.

Everything was fine until I began my ascent into the sunshine. "Come out head first," John advised. I was eager to comply, but I couldn't get my **fanny** through the hole. It had gone in but wouldn't come out. I panicked! I am ashamed to admit that I immediately felt at least three million spiders crawling all over the part of me that was still trapped underneath the house. Just as tears began to well up in my eyes, John yanked me to safety. Once uncorked, I sat on the retaining wall, feeling my strength **ebbing**, hardly listening to John's **profuse** praise of my mighty deed. I was watching a giant spider sunning itself on the wall about ten feet from the edge of the opening. John looked embarrassed, but not until much later did he confess that he had seen the spider crawl away from the access hole just before I went inside but couldn't see any others around and didn't want to alarm me.

I gained some important insights from this little test. Equality is both physical and intellectual. It means doing my share of the dirty jobs, taking occasional risks, and conquering some irrational fears. For the first time in our marriage, I was able to fix something that my husband couldn't, but I paid a high emotional price for my success. I discovered a truth that every soldier learns in basic training: People, men or women, do what they have to do. It is not a question of equality, but a test of spirit and determination.

Glossary

cap off *(verb)*   fasten an end piece on a pipe to seal it

comply *(verb)*   obey

controversial *(adjective)*   disputed

ebbing *(verb)*   declining; slipping away

fanny *(noun, slang)*   buttocks

had sprung a huge leak *(idiom)*   had developed a serious leak

hordes *(noun)*   swarms; masses

impassive *(adjective)*   without expression; blank

leverage *(noun)*   mechanical advantage or increased power of action

manipulate *(verb)*   manage; use

murky depths *(figurative expression)*   dark, gloomy innermost part

phobia *(noun)*   persistent, unreasonable, excessive fear of something

profuse *(adjective)*   abundant; extravagant

rashly *(adverb)*   hastily

relentlessly *(adverb)*   harshly; pitilessly

reprieve *(noun)*   postponement; delay

repulsed *(verb)*   repelled or disgusted

revving up the power saw *(slang)*   accelerating the motor of the power saw

scan *(verb)*   look hastily

sprinkler system *(noun)*   watering system composed of many pipes that have separate sprinkler "heads" to spray water on specific areas of the yard or garden, all sprinklers are controlled by a few valves

stamina *(noun)*   endurance; strength

Stilson pipe wrench *(noun)*   Stilson is a brand name for a large steel tool used for holding and turning pipes.

undermining *(verb)*   wearing away or weakening the base of a foundation

union *(noun)*   pipe connection

voluminous *(adjective)*   bulky; webs of great magnitude

wriggle *(verb)*   twist and turn the body

"Those American Tooth Fanatics" and "A Trip Through the Underworld" analyze lessons learned from experience. The former, a chronological account, gives explicit instructions about how to care for teeth. The latter account is both chronological and spatial and describes how a woman conquered her fears and shouldered her share of the emergency home repair burden. Write a short practice essay about some process that you think is useful, interesting, or entertaining. Use the following procedure:

1. Include a statement that explains your purpose in the first paragraph. Give just enough background to introduce the reader to your subject. What was the situation? What problems did you face?

2. Examine and discuss facts, details, and examples to prove your point(s) in the development paragraphs. How or in what order did things happen? Why?

3. Evaluate the evidence in your conclusion. Does it prove the thesis? What is important about it? Can others benefit from your experience? Are you a better or worse person because of gaining new insights? Are your values changed? What lesson did you learn?

How to Write with Style

Kurt Vonnegut

Kurt Vonnegut is a contemporary American author and novelist. His imaginative treatment of the responses of ordinary people to extraordinary situations has earned him well-deserved literary recognition. Vonnegut's fiction points out the absurdity of society's expectations and the futility of our attempting to satisfy them. His most successful characters are those who say "yes" to the inner voice that guides them along the path toward individuality.

Vonnegut's unique writing style has won him critical acclaim. The article (on pages 182–83), which discusses the process of writing, contains Vonnegut's advice on how to use ideas, language, and punctuation effectively to write any-thing with style.

Glossary

any which way *(slang)*   with no logical order

band saw *(noun)*   saw consisting of an endless toothed steel band passing over pulleys and used to saw metal or wood

chowderhead *(noun, slang)*   person who is stupid or uses poor judgment

egomaniac *(noun)*   person who is extremely conceited or selfish

eloquence *(noun)*   fluent, graceful, powerful, or persuasive speech or writing

freaks *(noun)*   persons who are abnormal in appearance or behavior

frisky *(adjective)*   lively; playful

galvanized *(adjective)*   plated with zinc

glittering *(adjective)*   shining brilliantly; sparkling

guts *(noun, slang)*   inner strength, courage

higgledy-piggledy *(colloquialism)*   in a jumbled confusion; disorderly

hollows of Appalachia *(special expression)*   communities tucked into areas between the mountains of the Appalachian Range in the eastern United States

How to write with style

By Kurt Vonnegut

International Paper asked Kurt Vonnegut, author of such novels as "Slaughterhouse-Five," "Jailbird" and "Cat's Cradle," to tell you how to put your style and personality into everything you write.

Newspaper reporters and technical writers are trained to reveal almost nothing about themselves in their writings. This makes them freaks in the world of writers, since almost all of the other ink-stained wretches in that world reveal a lot about themselves to readers. We call these revelations, accidental and intentional, elements of style.

These revelations tell us as readers what sort of person it is with whom we are spending time. Does the writer sound ignorant or informed, stupid or bright, crooked or honest, humorless or playful – ? And on and on.

Why should you examine your writing style with the idea of improving it? Do so as a mark of respect for your readers, whatever you're writing. If you scribble your thoughts any which way, your readers will surely feel that you care nothing about them. They will mark you down as an egomaniac or a chowderhead – or, worse, they will stop reading you.

The most damning revelation you can make about yourself is that you do not know what is interesting and what is not. Don't you yourself like or dislike writers mainly for what they choose to show you or make you think about? Did you ever admire an empty-headed writer for his or her mastery of the language? No.

So your own winning style must begin with ideas in your head.

1. Find a subject you care about

Find a subject you care about and which you in your heart feel others should care about. It is this genuine caring, and not your games with language, which will be the most compelling and seductive element in your style.

I am not urging you to write a novel, by the way – although I would not be sorry if you wrote one, provided you genuinely cared about something. A petition to the mayor about a pothole in front of your house or a love letter to the girl next door will do.

2. Do not ramble, though

I won't ramble on about that.

3. Keep it simple

As for your use of language: Remember that two great masters of language, William Shakespeare and James Joyce, wrote sentences which were almost childlike when their subjects were most profound. "To be or not to be?" asks Shakespeare's Hamlet. The longest word is three letters long. Joyce, when he was frisky, could put together a sentence as intricate and as glittering as a necklace for Cleopatra, but my favorite sentence in his short story "Eveline" is this one: "She was tired." At that point in the story, no other words could break the heart of a reader as those three words do.

Simplicity of language is not only reputable, but perhaps even sacred. The *Bible* opens with a sentence well within the writing skills of a lively fourteen-year-old: "In the beginning God created the heaven and the earth."

4. Have the guts to cut

It may be that you, too, are capable of making necklaces for Cleopatra, so to speak. But your eloquence should be the servant of the ideas in your head. Your rule might be this: If a sentence, no matter how excellent, does not illuminate your subject in some new and useful way, scratch it out.

5. Sound like yourself

The writing style which is most natural for you is bound to echo the speech you heard when a child. English was the novelist Joseph Conrad's third language, and much that seems piquant in his use of English was no doubt colored by his first language, which was Polish. And lucky indeed is the writer who has grown up in Ireland, for the English spoken there is so amusing and musical. I myself grew up in Indianapolis, where common speech sounds like a band saw cutting galvanized tin,

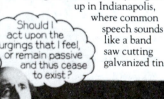

"Keep it simple. Shakespeare did, with Hamlet's famous soliloquy."

"Be merciless on yourself. If a sentence does not illuminate your subject in some new and useful way, scratch it out."

and employs a vocabulary as unornamental as a monkey wrench.

In some of the more remote hollows of Appalachia, children still grow up hearing songs and locutions of Elizabethan times. Yes, and many Americans grow up hearing a language other than English, or an English dialect a majority of Americans cannot understand.

All these varieties of speech are beautiful, just as the varieties of butterflies are beautiful. No matter what your first language, you should treasure it all your life. If it happens not to be standard English, and if it shows itself when you write standard English, the result is usually delightful, like a very pretty girl with one eye that is green and one that is blue.

I myself find that I trust my own writing most, and others seem to trust it most, too, when I sound most like a person from Indianapolis, which is what I am. What alternatives do I have? The one most vehemently recommended by teachers has no doubt been pressed on you, as well: to write like cultivated Englishmen of a century or more ago.

6. Say what you mean to say

I used to be exasperated by such teachers, but am no more. I understand now that all those antique essays and stories with which I was to compare my own work were not magnificent for their datedness or foreignness, but for saying precisely what their authors

meant them to say. My teachers wished me to write accurately, always selecting the most effective words, and relating the words to one another unambiguously, rigidly, like parts of a machine. The teachers did not want to turn me into an Englishman after all. They hoped that I would become understandable – and therefore understood. And there went my dream of doing with words what Pablo Picasso did with paint or what any number of jazz idols did with music. If I broke all the rules of punctuation, had words mean whatever I wanted them to mean, and strung them together higgledy-piggledy, I would simply not be understood. So you, too, had better avoid Picasso-style or jazz-style writing, if you have something worth saying and wish to be understood.

Readers want our pages to look very much like pages they have seen before. Why? This is because they themselves have a tough job to do, and they need all the help they can get from us.

7. Pity the readers

They have to identify thousands of little marks on paper, and make sense of them immediately. They have to *read*, an art so difficult that most people don't really master it even after having studied it all through grade school and high school – twelve long years.

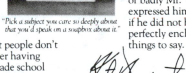

"Pick a subject you care so deeply about that you'd speak on a soapbox about it."

So this discussion must finally acknowledge that our stylistic options as writers are neither numerous nor glamorous, since our readers are bound to be such imperfect artists. Our audience requires us to be sympathetic and patient teachers, ever willing to simplify and clarify – whereas we would rather soar high above the crowd, singing like nightingales.

That is the bad news. The good news is that we Americans are governed under a unique Constitution, which allows us to write whatever we please without fear of punishment. So the most meaningful aspect of our styles, which is what we choose to write about, is utterly unlimited.

8. For really detailed advice

For a discussion of literary style in a narrower sense, in a more technical sense, I commend to your attention *The Elements of Style*, by William Strunk, Jr., and E.B. White (Macmillan, 1979). E.B. White is, of course, one of the most admirable literary stylists this country has so far produced.

You should realize, too, that no one would care how well or badly Mr. White expressed himself, if he did not have perfectly enchanting things to say.

intricate *(adjective)* hard to follow or understand because of complicated structure

locutions *(noun)* forms or styles of speech or written expression. Words, phrases, or expressions of the sixteenth century are still used in these isolated Appalachian communities.

monkey wrench *(noun)* wrench (tool) with one adjustable, movable jaw used to turn nuts, bolts, pipes, etc.

nightingales *(noun)* type of European thrush (bird). The male is known for its beautiful night song.

piquant *(adjective)* agreeably sharp in taste

pothole *(noun)* deep, round hole (in the street) that makes driving dangerous

profound *(adjective)* having deep intellectual meaning

ramble *(verb)* talk or write aimlessly without definite direction or connection of ideas

reputable *(adjective)* respectable; well thought of by others

sacred *(adjective)* holy; respected and revered as a holy thing; worshiped

scribble *(verb)* write hastily, carelessly, messily, or illegibly

seductive *(adjective)* inviting; enticing; tempting

soar *(verb; figurative expression)* fly; sail; glide along high in the air

unambiguously *(adverb)* not having more than one meaning; clearly; definitely

vehemently *(adverb)* passionately; fervently; intensely; with great feeling

wretches *(noun)* miserable, unhappy persons

Comprehension Questions

1. Why are newspaper reporters and technical writers different from other kinds of writers? How do tone and style tell us "what sort of person it is with whom we are spending time"?

2. Why should you examine and improve your own writing style?

3. What is "the most damning revelation you can make about yourself"? How can you begin to develop your own style?

4. How does choosing a subject you care about affect your writing?

5. What does the author mean when he says not to ramble? Does he take his own advice?

6. What kind of language should you use in your writing?

7. When should you cut?

8. Which writing style is most natural for you? Should you try to copy another author's style? Why or why not?

9. How can you best say what you mean? How did Vonnegut's teachers help him to become an effective writer? What elements of style are important if you want to be understood? What do readers expect from your pages?

10. Vonnegut says, "Pity the readers." Why?

11. What does the audience require that writers be and do? What would most writers rather do? What does Vonnegut mean when he says, "That is the bad news"?

12. What is the good news?

13. Why does Vonnegut suggest that you read *The Elements of Style* by Strunk and White?

Topics for Critical Analysis, Discussion, and Writing

1. Why did the International Paper Company ask Kurt Vonnegut to write this article?

2. What kind of language does Vonnegut use in his writing? Does he "practice what he preaches" (do what he advises) in his writing style? Give examples and discuss them.

3. Vonnegut says his English teachers wanted him to write unambiguously and accurately. Why? What were his reactions then and now? What are your reactions to the suggestions of your English teachers? Do you think you can improve your own style? If so, how?

4. Discuss the relationship between the writer and the reader. Who has more responsibility? Explain.

5. Examine the process that *you* use to write an essay.

6. Evaluate Vonnegut's advice about writing, point by point. Then review the suggestions for revision shown in Chapter 10. Based on evaluations that you have received on your essays, try to identify specific suggestions that you think will help you the most as you write your next essay.

7. Vonnegut emphasizes the need for writers to observe the rules of grammar, style, and punctuation if they want to be understood. Write an essay in which you defend or attack his advice.

8. Analyze the importance of writing well in college.

Make Your Kids' Halloween What It Should Be—A Night of Sheer Terror

Ken Ringle

Ken Ringle writes for The Washington Post. *This article, about a childhood Halloween party, illustrates both the internal and external processes of terror. The gradual buildup of Ringle's own fears is tightly coupled with the progress of the party itself. Obviously, the experience influenced Ringle's life. He not only recalls it vividly after thirty years, but also states that nothing ever frightened him again. Although he doesn't give all the details of the party preparations, he includes enough facts to show the illusion and reality of the "actors" and the scare they gave the children.*

Halloween, a contraction of "all hallow even," means "Holy Eve," the evening of October 31, which is followed by a Christian festival, All Saints Day. But even before the Christian era, pagan peoples held autumn festivals celebrating the harvest and honoring various gods and goddesses. Some cultures believed that the dead roamed the night before the festival began, and bonfires were lighted to scare them away. Later, Halloween became a night for fun and frolic with much attention to superstition and folklore. Young people began to dress in costumes and to wear grotesque masks as they gathered to celebrate. Now masked and costumed Halloween celebrants go from house to house "trick or treating." Halloween costume parties, at which children play old-fashioned games, are common. Sometimes parents add a little excitement to parties by staging terrifying events, like some of those that Ringle saw as he stumbled through his basement.

Ringle's thesis is that Halloween ought to really frighten children by making them use their imaginations ("the real Halloween process requires a trick or treat of the mind"). His essay is organized chronologically, but also includes spatial suborganizations; for example, the arrival of the party guests at the front door of his house and their journey through the basement.

Many people, I realize, are depressed or **disgusted** by Halloween, and by the **whiney** little wretches who **yammer** at their door and then dive with both greasy hands into the popcorn bowl.

But those who allow the **tacky** reality of Halloween to **intrude** on their spirits have only themselves to blame. They need to concentrate on making Halloween what it should be—a night of **sheer terror** for all children.

Fright is truly **splendid** for the very young, and they don't get much of it these days. What they get instead is a **mind-numbing** diet of televised **yucks** and violence that **saps** the imagination and cheapens the soul.

Pry beneath that **veneer** of **Gong Show** sophistication with a good scare and you can liberate the same **snakepit** of **tribal anxieties** that once was the **playpen** of the **brothers Grimm**.

Children love you to do this, as the unending popularity of horror movies testifies. But the made-in-Japan **explicitness** of a foam-rubber **Godzilla** never really gets the juices flowing. Neither does getting beaten up at school.

The real Halloween process requires a **trick or treat** of the mind.

I learned the fine art of true Halloween terror from my parents when, **goaded** by an **obnoxious** neighbor child's **assertion** that "there's nothing scary about Halloween," they decided to throw a party. The boy's name was Alec.

I was eight years old at the time. My parents had always had a fondness for **masquerade** parties. I remember my father stepping out once, when I was about five, in some **Khayyam** Arab costume he had picked up in the Middle East, complete with artificial beard. I told him he looked just like Jesus.

But there was nothing Christlike in the party preparations that Halloween three years later. My mother **conjured up** a witch outfit out of a black skirt and **conical** paper hat, then **distressed** me by blacking out several teeth with construction paper.

My father, who detested the boy named Alec, silently made himself up into a blood-chilling pirate, complete with earring and eyepatch, and went around sharpening his Naval Academy sword.

The house was entirely dark when the children began to arrive. They would act like **your basic giggling children** until they got to the front **stoop**. Then my father would jerk open the door with the sword in his hand, grab them by the shirtfront and **hurl** them bodily onto the front stairs. To wait. In the dark.

When Alec **swaggered** up to the door, my father jerked him inside by the neck, pushed the blade of the sword against his throat and—leaning down inches from his face—hissed slowly: "One word out of you, you filthy little **bilge rat**, and I'll cut your liver out and make you eat it."

Then he threw Alec on the stairs where the rest of us were huddled, scarcely daring to breathe.

My sister and I knew some friends of our parents were coming to help with the party, but they had arrived by way of the basement door, and God only knew what they were doing down there. From time to time, as we waited, we heard long, **blood-curdling** screams, occasional **sobs** and **whimpers** and a lot of weeping. We didn't like it at all.

Then, after what seemed like hours squeezed up into tiny balls of fright in the dark, a **snaggle-toothed** witch emerged from the basement stairs carrying a single candle.

"Welcome then, my precious ones," my mother the witch **cackled**, in a **voice like chalk on slate**. "Who will be the first?"

My sister and I, as it turned out, were the last, due to some **demented** parental notion of party manners. This meant we had to sit there in the dark, our imaginations **galloping**, listening to the screams, until Mother had led everyone else, one at a time, downstairs to what once had been our good old familiar basement.

By the time my turn came (no one else was left), I didn't know what was down there, and I had no desire to find out. I was too scared to move. Mother eventually had to drop the witch voice and remind me that, after all, I was her own flesh and blood. That somehow made it worse. Finally I agreed to go, but only after she had taken the black paper off her teeth.

There were no lights on in the basement either. Total silence. Then, as we rounded the corner into the **washroom**, came the sound of **moaning**. Seated atop a stool, **heaving** in the candlelight, sat a man with his hands clutched to his face. Through his fingers poured what looked like blood. It dripped on the basement floor.

"My eyes!" he cried. "What have they done to my eyes?"

"Someone tore out his eyes," explained my mother, matter of factly. "I wonder where they can be?"

She began searching around on the floor, bending low in the candlelight, then led me into a tiny concrete room. A long, terrible scream sounded in the basement hallway.

"Not here," she said, ignoring a **corpse** on the bed with a knife **jutting** from its back.

"Not here," she said as she looked into the shower, where a body swung from a hangman's noose. "Not here." From the hallway a sound of weeping.

We crept on through another small doorway into the back of the hall. My mother raised her candle, and there in the flickering light hung a **gore-stained** sheet. Above its edge, suspended by long hair from a hook in the ceiling, hung the head of a woman. Just the head.

Down the hall we wandered until my mother stopped before an old, peeling Thermos jug I knew from a hundred picnics.

"What have we here?" she asked. "Put your hand in and see."

I reached down and, in the icy liquid within, felt the sickening **clamminess** of something **clotted**, round and **spongy**: the blind man's eyes.

Then, right at my ear, came the loudest scream of all, as if the soul had been torn out of something just inches away. I turned and **glimpsed** in the candlelight the running figure of a woman, red hair streaming, eyes glazed with madness, face as pale as death. She disappeared in the darkness. A door slammed shut.

Another door opened. Lights.

In the basement playroom, barely containing their **manic** laughter and fright-turned-relief-that-it's-over, stood the rest of the neighborhood kids.

"Jeez," said young neighbor Alec as he shakily reached for a doughnut and cider. "Did you see that head?"

The party was so perfect my parents never gave another. They knew it couldn't measure up. It was such a success that two of the acting principals are still known familiarly in our family, 30 years later, as "the corpse" and the "bodiless head." The blind man and the screamer now live in Mexico, but we still get Christmas cards from them.

As for the kids, I doubt if any of us has really been frightened of anything since. And that, of course, is the real value of Halloween: discovering that the blind man's eyes that scare you today, turn out tomorrow to be peeled grapes.

Glossary

assertion *(noun)* declaration; positive or definite statement

bilge rat *(adjective, noun)* rat that lives in the rounded, lower part of the hull or hold of a ship where stagnant, dirty water collects

blood-curdling *(adjective)* frightening; terrifying

brothers Grimm *(noun, adjective)* Jakob, 1785–1863, and Wilhelm, 1786–1859, German writers of fairy tales

cackled *(verb)* laughed by making shrill, broken sounds like those made by a hen

clamminess *(noun)* unpleasant moistness, coldness, and stickiness

clotted *(adjective)* soft lumpy area formed by the thickening of liquid

conical *(adjective)* cone-shaped

conjured up *(verb)* called up or summoned as if by magic

corpse *(noun)* dead body

demented *(adjective)* insane; mad; mentally deranged

disgusted *(adjective)* sickened by dislike or distaste

distressed *(verb)* caused [him] anxiety, suffering, or worry

explicitness *(noun)* preciseness; clarity; definiteness

galloping *(verb)* operating, running, or working at a fast pace

glimpsed *(verb)* caught a brief, quick, incomplete view

goaded *(verb)* driven to act; urged on

Godzilla *(noun)* giant, lizard-like monster that attacked Japan in the horror movie *Godzilla*

Gong Show *(noun)* former television show that presented amateur performers in competition for a modest prize. They were judged on their talent by a panel of "experts." A gong was sounded when a performer was really terrible (as most were), and he or she had to leave the stage. Ringle is being sarcastic when he says the show was sophisticated.

gore-stained *(adjective)*   stained with thickened lumps of blood shed from a wound

heaving *(verb)*   breathing heavily and groaning with great effort and pain

hurl *(verb)*   throw or fling violently or forcefully

intrude *(verb)*   force itself into their thoughts without being invited or welcomed

jutting *(verb)*   sticking out; projecting

Khayyam *(adjective)*   flowing; romantic. Omar Khayyam (1050?–1123?) was a Persian poet, mathematician, and astronomer.

manic *(adjective)*   wild; violent; mentally disordered

masquerade *(adjective)*   costume

mind-numbing *(slang)*   anesthetizing; rendering the mind incapable of thinking

moaning *(adjective)*   low, mournful sound of pain or sorrow

obnoxious *(adjective)*   unpleasant; objectionable; offensive

playpen *(noun)*   small, portable enclosure in which a baby can be safely left to stand, crawl, or play. Ringle suggests that today's children passively experience so much visual stimulation through television that they are unable to imagine anything; however, after a good scare, the atmosphere becomes as creative as it was for the Grimm brothers.

saps *(verb)*   weakens; exhausts

sheer *(adjective)*   absolute; unqualified; utter; pure; complete

snaggle-toothed *(adjective)* broken-toothed or crooked-toothed; having one or more teeth that stick out from the others

snakepit *(noun)*   place of horror and confusion (refers to the movie, *The Snakepit,* which was set in a mental hospital where patients were mistreated)

sobs *(noun)*   short, gasping breaths that occur during crying or weeping

splendid *(adjective)*   magnificent; worthy of high praise

spongy *(adjective)*   soft; elastic; moisture-soaked; sponge-like

stoop *(noun)*   porch or platform with steps

swaggered *(verb)*   walked boldly and arrogantly as if he were superior to everyone else

tacky *(adjective)*   lacking in good taste; in poor taste. Ringle means that for most people Halloween has deteriorated into a night where greedy children come to the door and demand treats; the excitement and mystery are gone.

terror *(noun)*   intense fear

tribal anxieties *(adjective, noun)*   psychic or superstitious fears experienced by members of a social group

trick or treat *(special expression)* traditional greeting used by costumed children as they go from door to door on Halloween. The treat (usually candy) originally ensured that no tricks (soaping windows, overturning flowerpots, etc.) would be played. Today, children are more interested in treats than tricks.

veneer *(noun)* attractive, but superficial, appearance or display; outward appearance

voice like chalk on slate *(figurative expression)* voice that sounded screechy or scratchy. His mother's voice had the same effect as the sound of someone scraping a fingernail on a chalkboard.

washroom *(noun)* laundry room

whimpers *(noun)* low, whining, broken sounds made during crying or out of fear

whiney (**whiny,** *adjective*) characteristically high-pitched, nasal tone used to complain or beg in a childish way

yammer *(slang)* talk loudly; complain; whine; nag

your basic giggling children *(special expression)* typical nervously laughing children

yucks *(slang)* laughs

Comprehension Questions

1. How do many people feel about Halloween trick or treaters? What does Ringle say Halloween ought to be? Why?
2. Why don't the young get frightened much these days?
3. What is Ringle saying in paragraph four?
4. How does Ringle know that children love to be frightened? What does he mean when he says that horror movies and getting beaten up at school "never really get the juices flowing"?
5. What does the real Halloween process require? Explain.
6. Why did Ringle's parents give a Halloween party when he was eight years old?
7. What costumes did his parents wear?
8. What did the children see when they walked up to the house? What happened when they got to the front stoop? Where were they left to wait once they got inside? What sorts of sounds did they hear from time to time?
9. How did Ringle's father treat Alec when the boy arrived?
10. Who was the first "character" to emerge from the basement? How was she dressed? What was her task?

11. Why were Ringle and his sister the last to go through the process? What effect did this have on them? How did Ringle feel when his turn came?

12. Describe the four creatures that were waiting for him in the darkness. What was in the Thermos jug?

13. Why did all the activities occur in the dark? What happened when the lights went on?

14. Why didn't Ringle's parents ever give another Halloween party?

15. What was the effect of that party on the children? What is the real value of Halloween?

Topics for Critical Analysis, Discussion, and Writing

1. Analyze Ringle's idea that children love to be frightened. If this is so, why are frightening dreams called "bad" dreams (nightmares)? Is it ever really fun to be scared? Explain.

2. Use an experience from your childhood to develop a process analysis. Explain how to do something or how something is done. Be sure that you have a thesis, clearly organized development, and a conclusion.

3. Discuss the moral or lesson in Ringle's essay. How important is it for people to know the difference between illusion and reality?

Too Scared to Die

Robert L. McGrath

Robert L. McGrath, whose father was a Colorado farmer, writes short stories, articles, and books on a variety of subjects. His interest in and knowledge of the Old West can be seen in his account of the legendary Montague Stevens (chapter 4) and in this historical article that describes the process used by Truman C. Everts to stay alive in the wilderness for thirty-seven days—without his horse, camping equipment, food supplies, gun, or eyeglasses—after he became separated from the main party of the "Yellowstone Expedition of 1870."

The article on Everts grew out of a research project that McGrath undertook in 1951 when he was working on a Master's Degree at the University of Southern California. The project culminated in a radio series based on explorations in the United States. Exploration naturally falls into the category of process analysis;

Reprinted by permission of the author. First published in *PEN*.

Montana Historical Society

Truman C. Everts

however, the article also works as narration or description, proving again that a piece of writing often has more than one application. The thesis occurs well into the article, after a long description that shows how Everts became lost and explains the purpose of his expedition. The author states, "And he resolved that he would not give up. He would not let this perilous situation overcome him." Then we learn exactly how Everts managed to survive.

The lone horse and rider moved slowly through the **tangle** of downed pine trees, making their own trail. The man peered anxiously ahead through his thick-lensed glasses, one hand cupped to his ear to catch whatever sound the forest might give up. It was early morning, shortly after sunup.

Suddenly, without warning, the horse **surged** forward, jumping over a fallen log, and as he did so, a low limb brushed against the horseman, scratching his face and sweeping his **spectacles** off. Almost unseated, the rider jerked the reins angrily.

"**Whoa!** Whoa! I say!" The horse stopped, and the man swung down stiffly.

Dropping the reins, the man turned back to search for his glasses, bending low and spreading his hands across the forest floor in hopes of locating those all-important lenses. He had moved only a short distance when the horse **snorted,** jumped, and crashed away through the trees.

"Whoa! Whoa, there!" It was a desperate shout, for the horse carried everything the man needed for survival in this wilderness—blankets, extra clothing, matches, a gun.

Forgetting his search, the man plunged **headlong** after the horse, which by now could be identified only by the sound of crashing brush. Time and again, the man fell, for he could not see well enough to avoid fallen tree limbs and other **debris**. The sun was high overhead before he finally gave up; he could neither see nor hear the horse. He was completely alone, he was lost, he was terror-stricken.

This man was Truman C. Everts, former **assessor** for the state of Montana. Twenty days before, on August 22, he had departed with eighteen other men from Fort Ellis, Montana on what was known as the "Yellowstone Expedition of 1870." It was the first time anyone other than **trappers** and Indians had entered the area of what is now Yellowstone National Park, and during those twenty days, the members of the party were already—as one of them wrote later—"completely surprised and **captivated** with the wonders of nature."

For more than fifty years, trappers had brought back wild tales of spouting **geysers**, colorful **canyons**, boiling mud pools, and other unbelievable phenomena. These stories had been laughed at, thought to be outright lies. The party of which Everts was a member had decided to find out the truth, once and for all.

To their amazement, they had discovered hot springs, a huge geyser which they at first thought was a forest fire, and the Grand Canyon of the Yellowstone River, along with its crashing waterfalls. They saw a **sulphur** mountain, a mud volcano, other wonders. And on September 9, on the rough southern side of Yellowstone Lake, Truman Everts became separated from the rest of the party.

He spent that night in relative comfort; he had blankets, his horse, and although without food, he was sure the rest of the group would return for him the next day. But the next day was the **fateful** one when his horse ran away with his **gear,** when he lost his all-important spectacles, when he realized he was lost in **timber** so thick that every tree looked alike, especially to a person as near-sighted as Everts.

"They'll find me," he kept telling himself. "They have to find me!" But he began walking this way and that, searching for some clue that would tell him which way he should go.

Suddenly, the gloom of the forest became deeper. Night fell with frightening swiftness, and with it came the bone-chilling frost of the 7,700-feet altitude. Hungry, cold, panic-stricken, this timid man faced the terrors of the unknown in **abject** misery. The howl of distant **coyotes** sent **shivers** down his spine. A mountain lion screamed, and Everts' teeth **chattered**.

Then he thought of home, his daughter, his friends. And he resolved that he would not give up. He would not let his **perilous** situation overcome him. He would keep his faith—in his companions, in God.

Meantime, the other members of the expedition were becoming more and more alarmed about the **plight** of the missing Everts. The first night, they didn't worry. He would turn up soon, they were sure. But when they back-tracked the next day and failed to locate him, their concern grew with each passing hour.

For a full week, the group tediously tried to find the missing Everts. They put up signs, they made fires, they shot their guns, but at no time did they find any sign of the missing man. After almost two weeks, they concluded he had been killed or had headed back the way they came, so they moved on up the west side of Yellowstone Lake and in the general direction of home, sad and gloomy at having lost one of their party.

On the third morning of his **desolation**, Truman Everts struck out in the direction he thought the party would have taken. Actually, he was going almost directly away from their route, but late in the day—hungry and ex-hausted—he stumbled onto a tiny lake in a deep valley surrounded by lofty mountains. It was a beautiful spot, but Everts' **nearsightedness** kept him from appreciating it. There were ducks and swans on the lake, trout in it, and all types of game surrounding it. But this despondent man was starving, in the midst of all this plenty.

Although fearful of hostile Indian attack when the trip began, Everts now would have welcomed the sight of any human being, Indians included.

Looking out over the lake, he was sure he saw a boat coming across it, and he hastened to where he thought it would land. But instead of coming in to shore, the boat suddenly took wing and flew off. It was not, Everts realized now, a boat—it was a huge **pelican**. His poor eyesight left him like a stricken wanderer chasing a **mirage** in the desert.

Near the edge of the lake, Everts now found growing a **thistle** with a root like a **radish.** Desperate for food, he tried eating these roots, and found them wholesome and nourishing. At least, with them, he would keep from starving, and he busied himself with **laying in** a good supply.

Toward dusk, a strange sensation came to him, as though he were being watched by angry eyes. Not trusting his own vision, he wasted no time in going to a nearby tree and climbing into its branches. He was none too soon. Almost immediately, a huge mountain lion began pacing around the base of the tree, coughing and **yowling**. For hours, Everts sat in the tree and shivered from cold and fear. Finally, the big cat disappeared as quietly as it had come, and the man—half-dead with stiffness and chill, climbed down.

The next day it snowed, and miraculously, a small **benumbed** bird fell into Evert's hands. He killed and ate it on the spot. He discovered then that he could stay warm by going to the hot springs at the edge of the lake. Throwing together a shelter of broken pine **boughs** near one of these bubbling mini-ature geysers, he cooked his thistle roots in the boiling water of the spring. The steam **soaked** his clothing, but at least he was warm.

For several days, he was content to wait there at the spring, knowing he must leave if he were ever to find his way home. He desperately needed fire—otherwise, he would surely freeze.

One afternoon, after a storm, the clouds abruptly opened up, and the sun lighted the surface of the lake like a mirror. Everts thought of how the sun would **kindle** fires by use of a burning glass. If only he had—but he did! His hand went to his pocket, came out with the little pair of **opera glasses** he'd used to look over the **terrain** before he became lost. In his confusion, he had forgotten all about them.

Finding a piece of soft dry wood, he focused the rays of the sun on it through the small field glass. A blessed sight—smoke, coal, flame! He could hardly believe it. If he could keep this fire going, his danger of freezing to death would be over.

After seven days, Everts **ventured forth from** the little lake, heading in the direction he believed to be home. Although he frequently burned his hands, and though the smoke turned his face the color of an Indian's, he carried a burning **brand** with him, in order to make certain he would always have a fire.

At the end of one long day's journey, in raw cold weather, he laid the brand down to gather some dry sticks. When he returned, the flame was gone. And hope went with it. The sun was almost down, with broken clouds surrounding it. Everts watched and prayed. If only he could get the benefit of a few rays of that sinking sun. Then the clouds parted, and for an instant the sun peeped through. Everts focused his lens. Would it work? Smoke, coal, saved again! He built the fire up big, thankful for that brief instant of sunlight.

Where at first he had been able to keep moving at night to avoid freezing, now he had to depend on the fire, for he was getting weaker each day. But he pushed on, covering as much ground every day as he could. If it was clear, he would let his brand go out, and rely on his lens to start a fire before nightfall.

After one such day, he found himself on a high **plateau**, in early afternoon, and it was already turning bitter cold. He reached for his lens. Not there! He must have left it where he had stopped the night before. Wearily, Everts retraced his steps. Without that lens. . . . He refused to think what would happen.

He found his way back before sunset. There! There it was, lying on the ground where he had slept. He had wasted a whole day's time because he had failed to make sure that precious glass was in his pocket.

On the shore of the Yellowstone Lake, he discovered one of the campsites where the entire party had stopped before he became lost. He also found a gull's wing, freshly torn off through some unknown accident, and he stripped off the feathers, pounded it up—bones and all—and boiled it in a tin can left at the campsite.

The result was a delicious bowl of soup, the only appetizing meal Everts had. After **savoring** it, he lay down and slept the rest of that day and all night.

And he pushed on again early the following morning, carrying his fire brand and as many thistle roots as he could handle.

Tempted to give up time and again, Everts felt some inner force that moved him to keep pushing forward. His hopes, often dim, told him he would yet win. But his **waning** strength took him a shorter distance each day, and every night seemed colder, more **bleak** than the one before.

At last he came to another high plateau, open country, where he could see a vague outline of distant hills. He knew he would find help there—if only he could reach them.

His thistle supply was **dwindling**. His clothes were **tattered**. If he could hold out for two or three more days, perhaps he could make it. He had visions; he "saw" wild animals; he lost all sense of time; he imagined that he had "companions" and he **babbled** constantly at them.

At last, near death, he stumbled and fell against a rock. He felt he could never rise again. He "saw" a mountain lion, crouched, ready to **devour** him, and he was worried that his former companions would never find even a trace of his body. He was ready to give up.

Then, **out of the blue**, a voice!

"Are you Mister Everts?"

"Yes," the stricken man faltered. "All that is left of him!"

And Truman C. Everts, lost for thirty-seven days in the Yellowstone wilds, collapsed into the arms of two men who leaped from their horses to grasp him. It was October 16, 1870.

When the Yellowstone exploration party had returned home, they had organized a relief expedition to search for the missing man. The two who found him were experienced mountain **scouts**, who took him to the nearest house and sent for a doctor. Everts was soon on the way to complete recovery.

In fact, this remarkable man lived for thirty-one more years, **passing on** at the age of eighty-five. His demonstration of human courage and divine faith in the face of **insurmountable** odds is one of the most thrilling and unusual achievements in our country's history.

His reward still stands today—the bold and lofty rampart that faces Mammoth Hot Springs from across the Gardiner River in Yellowstone National Park. Although not really a mountain, it is ten miles from where the wanderer was finally found and is known as Mount Everts—a fitting **monument** to the man who was, in his own words, "too scared to die."

Glossary

abject *(adjective)*   wretched; the worst; total

assessor *(noun)*   person who sets values on property to determine the amount of property taxes to be paid

babbled *(verb)*   talked foolishly or incoherently [to] them

benumbed *(verb)*   made numb physically

bleak *(adjective)*   gloomy; harsh; hopeless; unpromising

boughs *(noun)*   branches

brand *(noun)*   burning or partially burned stick

canyons *(noun)*   long, deep, narrow valleys, often with streams flowing through them

captivated *(adjective)*   figuratively taken or held captive by the beauty, excellence, or charm of something

chattered *(verb)*   clicked together rapidly when the lower jaw trembled from cold

coyotes *(noun)*   small wolves

debris *(noun)*   bits and pieces of rocks, plants, and decaying leaves

desolation *(noun)*   loneliness; misery

devour *(verb)*   eat hungrily or greedily; consume with great appetite

dwindling *(verb)*   shrinking; diminishing

fateful *(adjective)*   significant; decisive; important; consequential

gear *(noun)*   clothing and equipment

geysers *(noun)*   springs from which columns of boiling water and steam are spouted or projected into the air at intervals. More cold spring water is then heated geothermally until it boils and spouts again; the process repeats itself endlessly.

headlong *(adverb)*   head first; recklessly; rashly

insurmountable *(adjective)*   impossible to overcome

kindle *(verb)*   ignite; start

laying in *(verb)*   gathering; collecting; amassing

mirage *(noun)*   optical illusion in which a distant object, such as an oasis in the middle of the desert, seems to be nearby, floating in the air, or inverted. A mirage can also be something that appears real, but isn't, such as water far ahead on a long, straight, hot road.

monument *(noun)*   structure (statue, building, pillar, etc.) built to honor the memory of someone; for example, the Washington and Lincoln monuments in Washington, D.C. honor the first and sixteenth presidents of the United States.

nearsightedness *(noun)*   inability to see distant objects clearly; myopia

opera glasses *(noun)*   small binoculars (two small, attached telescopes) that allow both eyes to see distant images as if they were close. Usually opera glasses are used in theaters.

out of the blue *(idiom)*   without warning; unexpectedly; from nowhere

passing on *(verb, idiom)*   dying

pelican (noun) water bird with a pouch (for scooping up and storing fish) that hangs from its large lower bill

perilous *(adjective)* dangerous; risky

plateau *(noun)* elevated level land; table land

plight *(noun)* condition; dangerous situation

radish *(noun)* plant with a sharp-tasting, edible root. Radishes are usually eaten raw, alone or in salads.

savoring *(verb)* relishing or enjoying the taste

scouts *(noun)* persons especially trained to find animals or people in the wilderness

shivers *(noun)* trembling sensations; nervous thrills

snorted *(verb)* forced breath suddenly and violently through his nostrils so that they vibrated and made a harsh sound

soaked *(verb)* thoroughly wet

spectacles *(noun)* eyeglasses

sulphur (**sulfur,** *noun*) greenish-yellow chemical element. The mountain was either composed of or covered with this substance.

surged *(verb)* moved suddenly with heavy, violent force

tangle *(noun)* snarl; intertwisted, confused mass of things; for example, a **tangle** or snarl of traffic, a **tangle** of hair, or a **tangle** of weeds

tattered *(adjective)* torn and ragged

terrain *(noun)* physical characteristics of the ground or earth

thistle *(noun)* plant with prickly leaves and dense, fluffy flowers

timber *(noun)* trees; forests

trappers *(noun)* persons who use traps to catch fur-bearing animals

ventured forth from *(idiom)* risked leaving

waning *(adjective)* diminishing; declining

Whoa! *(imperative)* Stop! (used for horses and mules, not for people)

yowling *(verb)* howling; crying mournfully

Comprehension Questions

1. How did Everts lose his horse? Why was this loss so important? What did Everts do to try to recapture the animal? Was he successful?
2. What job did Everts hold? Why had he gone on the "Yellowstone Expedition of 1870"? What natural wonders did the members of the expedition see in the Yellowstone area?

3. When did Everts become separated from the rest of the party? Why wasn't he worried at first? How did he feel after his horse ran away? What was the most important personal item he lost?

4. Why was Everts afraid the second night? What made him decide not to give up?

5. How long a time did the other members of the expedition spend trying to find Everts? What measures did they take? What was the result?

6. What did Everts do on the third day to try to find his comrades? What mistake did he make? Why couldn't he appreciate the beauty of the valley and the abundance of game animals in the valley he found?

7. What was the "mirage" he saw, and what caused him to see it?

8. What was the importance of the thistle Everts found?

9. What caused Everts to feel that he was being watched? Explain the incident.

10. How did he catch the bird the next day? How did he prepare the bird so that he could eat it?

11. What uses did Everts make of the hot springs? What happened to his clothing? How long did he stay at the spring? Why did he have to leave it? What did he need to keep from freezing if he left the spring? How did he get it?

12. How many days after he successfully built a fire did Everts wait to leave the lake area? How did he make sure he would have a fire every night? Why didn't he just rely totally on his lens?

13. Why couldn't Everts continue to keep moving at night to avoid freezing? What did he do to keep warm? How did he lose and then regain his lens?

14. Why was Everts's discovery of one of the expedition's campsites important? How did he find the ingredients for and prepare "the only appetizing meal" that he had during his ordeal?

15. What happened to Everts mentally as his physical condition weakened?

16. Who found Everts? How did they happen to be searching for him?

17. What was Everts's reward for his courage, faith, and determination?

Topics for Critical Analysis, Discussion, and Writing

1. How important was chance in Everts's ordeal? Discuss specific examples of chance occurrences (for instance, losing his horse, supplies, eyeglasses, lens, and sense of direction; finding food, warmth, and the deserted campsite and being found by scouts) that both harmed and helped him. Is it possible to eliminate totally the element of chance from our lives? Be realistic in your answer.

2. Describe fully the physical and psychological elements of the process that Everts used to stay alive. Which form of process analysis is this article?

3. Exploration and discovery have been an important part of history from ancient times until the present. Explorers have expanded our world by traveling to its most distant points, climbing its highest peaks, descending to the depths of its oceans, and journeying into outer space.

In the United States, the Lewis and Clark Expedition, led by Meriwether Lewis (1774–1809) and William Clark (1770–1838) from 1804–1805, made new scientific and geographical findings during its 6,000 mile exploration of the Northwest American continent from the frontier to the Pacific Ocean. Zebulon Pike (1779–1813) explored the Arkansas River in his expedition of 1806. During that trip, he first saw the mountain which is now named for him, Pikes Peak, in Colorado.

In Africa, David Livingston (1813–1873) explored from the Atlantic to the Indian Oceans and from the Cape nearly to the equator. He discovered Victoria Falls; Lakes Nyasa, Mweru, and Bangweulu; and the upper course of the Congo River (which he thought was the Nile because it flowed northward). Henry Stanley (1841–1904) discovered that it was indeed the Congo River when he followed it westward where it eventually emptied into the sea. During this expedition (1874–1877), Stanley traveled completely across the equatorial region of Africa and was instrumental in opening that area to trade and commerce.

In Asia, in May 1953, Edmund Hillary and Tensing Norkay were the first men to reach the summit of Mt. Everest, the world's highest mountain at 29,028 feet above sea level.

In the oceans, Charles William Beebe (1877–1962), in 1930, made his first underwater descent in a bathysphere (depth sphere). Bathyspheres had become so sophisticated by 1960 that August (Jacques) Piccard (1884–1963) and Donald Walsh were able to dive almost seven miles to the bottom of the Pacific Ocean. Television personality Jacques Cousteau is a contemporary undersea explorer.

In space, Yuri Gagarin, in Vostok 1, was the first to orbit the earth on April 12, 1961. The first men to land on the moon, July 16, 1969, were Neil Armstrong and Edwin Aldrin, Jr., on the Apollo 11 mission.

Choose one of these explorers and write a process analysis that tells "how it was done." You should be able to find full accounts of all these adventures and discoveries in an encyclopedia or a biographical dictionary in the library. *Be sure to write in your own words.* If you use any quoted material from a reference book, include the title and author of the article, the name of the book, the year of publication, and the page numbers in parentheses after the first quotation. Subsequent quotations from the same source should be followed by page numbers in parentheses.

4. Write a process analysis that gives explicit instructions about how to do something; however, avoid simply listing directions. Instead, include a thesis explaining your purpose. Develop it through narrative or description, mak-

ing sure you include all the steps in chronological order. Don't forget a conclusion.

A New England Nun

Mary E. Wilkins Freeman

Mary E. Wilkins Freeman (1851–1930) was born and lived for nearly half a century in a small New England town like the one in the story. Unmarried and dependent on her parents for a living, she only began to write seriously in her late twenties after their deaths. By 1895, she was widely recognized as a specialist in stories about small-town life and characters. With this recognition came financial security. She did not marry until the age of forty-nine.

The story of Louisa Ellis clearly pictures social expectations in a small New England town near the end of the nineteenth century. The only socially acceptable role for a woman is marriage. Great store is placed on honor, so we understand why Louisa and Joe intend to keep their promise to marry even though their feelings and life circumstances have changed during the fourteen years that Joe has been away "earning his fortune." Louisa's activities, unlike those of her neighbors, have not been restricted by the demands of a husband and children during all this time; therefore, she has had the leisure to engage in activities that give her pleasure and allow her independence. She is naturally loath to surrender her freedom to Joe, and she is apprehensive about her future relationship with his cranky, demanding, old mother. On the other hand, a new love, for another woman, has been kindled in Joe's heart. But Joe intends to "do the right thing" and go through with his marriage to Louisa. The story describes the process of Louisa's discovery and resolution of her real feelings about Joe, her planned marriage, and his love for Lily.

It was late in the afternoon, and the light was waning. There was a difference in the look of the tree shadows out in the yard. Somewhere in the distance cows were **lowing** and a little bell was tinkling; now and then a farm-wagon **tilted** by, and the dust flew; some blue-shirted laborers with shovels over their shoulders **plodded** past; little swarms of flies were dancing up and down before the peoples' faces in the soft air. There seemed to be a gentle stir arising over everything for the mere sake of **subsidence**—a very **premonition** of rest and hush and night.

This soft **diurnal** commotion was over Louisa Ellis also. She had been

From Mary E. Wilkins Freeman, *A New England Nun and Other Stories*, 1891.

peacefully sewing at her sitting-room window all the afternoon. Now she **quilted** her needle carefully into her work, which she folded precisely, and laid in a basket with her thimble and thread and scissors. Louisa Ellis could not remember that ever in her life she had mislaid one of these little feminine **appurtenances**, which had become, from long use and constant association, a very part of her personality.

Louisa tied a green apron round her waist, and got out a flat straw hat with a green ribbon. Then she went into the garden with a little blue crockery bowl, to pick some **currants** for her tea. After the currants were picked she sat on the back door-step and stemmed them, collecting the stems carefully in her apron, and afterwards throwing them into the hen-coop. She looked sharply at the grass beside the step to see if any had fallen there.

Louisa was slow and still in her movements; it took her a long time to prepare her tea; but when ready it was set forth with as much grace as if she had been a **veritable** guest to her own self. The little square table stood exactly in the centre of the kitchen, and was covered with a starched linen cloth whose border pattern of flowers **glistened**. Louisa had a **damask** napkin on her tea-tray, where were arranged a cut-glass tumbler full of teaspoons, a silver cream-pitcher, a china sugar-bowl, and one pink china cup and saucer. Louisa used china every day—something which none of her neighbors did. They whispered about it among themselves. Their daily tables were laid with common crockery, their sets of best china stayed in the **parlor** closet, and Louisa Ellis was no richer nor better bred than they. Still she would use the china. She had for her supper a glass dish full of sugared currants, a plate of little cakes, and one of light white biscuits. Also a leaf or two of lettuce, which she cut up daintily. Louisa was very fond of lettuce, which she raised to perfection in her little garden. She ate quite heartily, though in a delicate, pecking way; it seemed almost surprising that any considerable bulk of the food should vanish.

After tea she filled a plate with nicely baked thin corn-cakes, and carried them out into the back-yard.

"Cæsar!" she called. "Cæsar! Cæsar!"

There was a little rush, and the **clank** of a chain, and a large yellow-and-white dog appeared at the door of his tiny **hut**, which was half hidden among the tall grasses and flowers. Louisa patted him and gave him the corn-cakes. Then she returned to the house and washed the tea-things, polishing the china carefully. The twilight had deepened; the chorus of the frogs floated in at the open window wonderfully loud and shrill, and once in a while a long sharp **drone** from a tree-toad pierced it. Louisa took off her green gingham apron, disclosing a shorter one of pink and white print. She lighted her lamp, and sat down again with her sewing.

In about half an hour Joe Dagget came. She heard his heavy step on the walk, and rose and took off her pink-and-white apron. Under that was still another—white linen with a little cambric edging on the bottom; that was Louisa's company apron. She never wore it without her calico sewing apron over it unless she had a guest. She had barely folded the pink and white one with methodical haste and laid it in a table-drawer when the door opened and Joe Dagget entered.

He seemed to fill up the whole room. A little yellow canary that had been asleep in his green cage at the south window woke up and fluttered wildly, beating his little yellow wings against the wires. He always did so when Joe Dagget came into the room.

"Good-evening," said Louisa. She extended her hand, with a kind of **solemn cordiality**.

"Good-evening, Louisa," returned the man, in a loud voice.

She placed a chair for him, and they sat facing each other, with the table between them. He sat bolt-upright, toeing out his heavy feet squarely, glancing with a good-humored uneasiness around the room. She sat gently erect, folding her slender hands in her white-linen lap.

"Been a pleasant day," remarked Dagget.

"Real pleasant," Louisa assented, softly. "Have you been **haying**?" she asked, after a little while.

"Yes, I've been haying all day, down in the ten-acre lot. Pretty hot work."

"It must be."

"Yes, it's pretty hot work in the sun."

"Is your mother well to-day?"

"Yes, mother's pretty well."

"I suppose Lily Dyer's with her now?"

Dagget colored. "Yes, she's with her," he answered, slowly.

He was not very young, but there was a boyish look about his large face. Louisa was not quite as old as he, her face was fairer and smoother, but she gave people the impression of being older.

"I suppose she's a good deal of help to your mother," she said, further.

"I guess she is; I don't know how mother'd get along without her," said Dagget, with a sort of embarrassed warmth.

"She looks like a real capable girl. She's pretty-looking too," remarked Louisa.

"Yes, she is pretty fair looking."

Presently Dagget began fingering the books on the table. There was a square red autograph album, and a Young Lady's Gift-Book which had belonged to Louisa's mother. He took them up one after the other and opened them; then laid them down again, the album on the Gift-Book.

Louisa kept eying them with mild uneasiness. Finally she rose and changed the position of the books, putting the album underneath. That was the way they had been arranged in the first place.

Dagget gave an awkward little laugh. "Now what difference did it make which book was on top?" said he.

Louisa looked at him with a **deprecating** smile. "I always keep them that way," murmured she.

"You do beat everything," said Dagget, trying to laugh again. His large face was flushed.

He remained about an hour longer, then rose to take leave. Going out, he stumbled over a rug, and trying to recover himself, hit Louisa's work-basket on the table, and knocked it on the floor.

He looked at Louisa, then at the rolling spools; he ducked himself awkwardly toward them, but she stopped him. "Never mind," said she; "I'll pick them up after you're gone."

She spoke with a mild stiffness. Either she was a little disturbed, or his nervousness affected her, and made her seem **constrained** in her effort to reassure him.

When Joe Dagget was outside he drew in the sweet evening air with a sigh, and felt much as an innocent and perfectly well-intentioned bear might after his exit from a china shop.

Louisa, on her part, felt much as the kind-hearted, long-suffering owner of the china shop might have done after the exit of the bear.

She tied on the pink, then the green apron, picked up all the scattered treasures and replaced them in her work-basket, and straightened the rug. Then she set the lamp on the floor, and began sharply examining the carpet. She even rubbed her fingers over it, and looked at them.

"He's tracked in a good deal of dust," she murmured. "I thought he must have."

Louisa got a dust-pan and brush, and swept Joe Dagget's track carefully.

If he could have known it, it would have increased his **perplexity** and uneasiness, although it would not have disturbed his loyalty in the least. He came twice a week to see Louisa Ellis, and every time, sitting there in her delicately sweet room, he felt as if surrounded by a **hedge** of lace. He was afraid to **stir lest** he should put a clumsy foot or hand through the fairy web, and he had always the consciousness that Louisa was watching fearfully lest he should.

Still the lace and Louisa commanded **perforce** his perfect respect and patience and loyalty. They were to be married in a month, after a singular courtship which had lasted for a matter of fifteen years. For fourteen out of the fifteen years the two had not once seen each other, and they seldom exchanged letters. Joe had been all those years in Australia, where he had gone to make his fortune, and where he had stayed until he made it. He would have stayed fifty years if it had taken so long, and come home feeble and tottering, or never come home at all, to marry Louisa.

But the fortune had been made in the fourteen years, and he had come home now to marry the woman who had been patiently and unquestioningly waiting for him all that time.

Shortly after they were engaged he had announced to Louisa his determination to strike out into new fields, and secure a **competency** before they should be married. She had listened and **assented** with the sweet serenity which never failed her, not even when her lover set forth on that long and uncertain journey. Joe, **buoyed up** as he was by his sturdy determination, broke down a little at the last, but Louisa kissed him with a mild **blush**, and said good-by.

"It won't be for long," poor Joe had said, **huskily**; but it was for fourteen years.

In the length of time much had happened. Louisa's mother and brother had died, and she was all alone in the world. But greatest happening of all—a subtle happening which both were too simple to understand—Louisa's feet had turned into a path, smooth maybe under a calm, serene sky, but so straight and **unswerving** that it could only meet a check at her grave, and so narrow that there was no room for any one at her side.

Louisa's first emotion when Joe Dagget came home (he had not apprised her of his coming), was **consternation**, although she would not admit it to herself, and he never dreamed of it. Fifteen years ago she had been in love with him—at least she considered herself to be. Just at that time, gently acquiescing with and falling into the natural drift of girlhood, she had seen marriage ahead as a reasonable feature and a probable desirability of life. She had listened with calm **docility** to her mother's views upon the subject. Her mother was remarkable for her cool sense and sweet, even temperament. She talked wisely to her daughter when Joe Dagget presented himself, and Louisa accepted him with no hesitation. He was the first lover she had ever had.

She had been faithful to him all these years. She had never dreamed of the possibility of marrying any one else. Her life, especially for the last seven years, had been full of a pleasant peace, she had never felt discontented nor impatient over her lover's absence; still she had always looked forward to his return and their marriage as the inevitable conclusion of things. However, she had fallen into a way of placing it so far in the future that it was almost equal to placing it over the boundaries of another life.

When Joe came she had been expecting him, and expecting to be married for fourteen years, but she was as much surprised and taken aback as if she had never thought of it.

Joe's consternation came later. He eyed Louisa with an instant confirmation of his old admiration. She had changed but little. She still kept her pretty manner and soft grace, and was, he considered, every **whit** as attractive as ever. As for himself, his **stent** was done; he had turned his face away from fortune-seeking, and the old winds of romance whistled as loud and sweet as ever through his ears. All the song which he had been **wont** to hear in them was Louisa; he had for a long time a loyal belief that he heard it still, but finally it seemed to him that although the winds sang always that one song, it had another name. But for Louisa the wind had never more than murmured; now it had gone down, and everything was still. She listened for a little while with half-**wistful** attention; then she turned quietly away and went to work on her wedding-clothes.

Joe had made some extensive and quite magnificent alterations in his house. It was the old **homestead**; the newly-married couple would live there, for Joe could not desert his mother, who refused to leave her old home. So Louisa must leave hers. Every morning, rising and going about among her neat **maidenly** possessions, she felt as one looking her last upon the faces of dear friends. It was true that in a measure she could take them with her, but, robbed of their old environments, they would appear in such new **guises** that they would almost cease to be themselves. Then there were some peculiar features of her happy solitary life which she would probably be obliged to relinquish altogether. **Sterner** tasks than these graceful but half-needless ones would probably **devolve upon** her. There would be a large house to care for; there would be company to entertain; there would be Joe's **rigorous** and **feeble** old mother to wait upon; and it would be contrary to all thrifty village traditions for her to keep more than one servant. Louisa had a little still, and she used to occupy herself pleasantly in summer weather with distilling the sweet and aromatic essences from roses and peppermint and spearmint. By-and-by her still must be laid away. Her store of essences was already considerable, and there would be no time for her to distil for the mere pleasure of it. Then Joe's mother would think it foolishness; she had already hinted her opinion in the matter. Louisa dearly loved to sew a linen seam, not always for use, but for the simple, mild pleasure which she took in it. She would have been loath to confess how more than once she had ripped a seam for the mere delight of sewing it together again. Sitting at her window during long sweet afternoons, drawing her needle gently through the dainty fabric, she was peace itself. But there was small chance of such foolish comfort in the future. Joe's mother, **domineering, shrewd** old matron that she was even in her old age, and very likely even Joe himself, with his honest masculine rudeness, would laugh and frown down all these pretty but senseless old maiden ways.

Louisa had almost the enthusiasm of an artist over the mere order and cleanliness of her solitary home. She had throbs of genuine triumph at the sight of the window-panes which she had polished until they shone like jewels. She **gloated** gently over her orderly bureau-drawers, with their exquisitely folded contents **redolent** with lavender and sweet clover and very purity. Could she be sure of the endurance of even this? She had visions, so startling that she half **repudiated** them as indelicate, of coarse masculine belongings strewn about in endless litter; of dust and disorder arising necessarily from a coarse masculine presence in the midst of all this delicate harmony.

Among her forebodings of disturbance, not the least was with regard to Cæsar. Cæsar was a veritable **hermit** of a dog. For the greater part of his life he had dwelt in his secluded hut, shut out from the society of his kind and all innocent canine joys. Never had Cæsar since his early youth watched at a **woodchuck**'s hole; never had he known the delights of a stray bone at a neighbor's kitchen door. And it was all on account of a sin committed when hardly out of his puppyhood. No one knew the possible depth of remorse of which this mild-**visaged**, altogether innocent-looking old dog might be capable; but whether or not he had encountered remorse, he had encountered a full measure of **righteous retribution**. Old Cæsar seldom lifted up his voice in a growl or a bark; he was fat and sleepy; there were yellow rings which looked like spectacles around his dim old eyes; but there was a neighbor who bore on his hand the imprint of several of Cæsar's sharp white youthful teeth, and for that he had lived at the end of a chain, all alone in a little hut, for fourteen years. The neighbor, who was **choleric** and smarting with the pain of his wound, had demanded either Cæsar's death or complete ostracism. So Louisa's brother, to whom the dog had belonged, had built him his little kennel and tied him up. It was now fourteen years since, in a flood of youthful spirits, he had inflicted that memorable bite, and with the exception of short **excursions**, always at the end of the chain, under the strict guardianship of his master or Louisa, the old dog had remained a close prisoner. It is doubtful if, with his limited ambition, he took much pride in the fact, but it is certain that he was possessed of considerable cheap fame. He was regarded by all the children in the village and by many adults as a very monster of **ferocity**. St. George's dragon could hardly have surpassed in evil repute Louisa Ellis's old yellow dog. Mothers charged their children with solemn emphasis not to go too near to him, and the children listened and believed greedily, with a fascinated appetite for terror, and ran by Louisa's house **stealthily**, with many **sidelong** and backward glances at the terrible dog. If **perchance** he sounded a hoarse bark, there was a panic. Wayfarers chancing into Louisa's yard eyed him with respect, and inquired if the chain were stout. Cæsar **at large** might have seemed a very ordinary dog and excited no comment whatever; chained, his reputation overshadowed him, so that he lost his own proper outlines and looked darkly vague and enormous. Joe Dagget, however, with his good-humored sense and shrewdness, saw him as he was. He strode **valiantly** up to him and patted him on the head, in spite of Louisa's soft **clamor** of warning, and even attempted to set him loose. Louisa grew so alarmed that he desisted, but kept announcing his opinion in the matter quite forcibly at intervals. "There ain't a better-natured dog in town," he would say, "and it's downright cruel to keep him tied up there. Some day I'm going to take him out."

Louisa had very little hope that he would not, one of these days, when their interests and possessions should be more completely **fused** in one. She pictured to herself Cæsar on the rampage through the quiet and unguarded village. She saw innocent children bleeding in his path. She was herself very fond of the old dog, because he had belonged to her dead brother, and he was always very gentle with her; still she had great faith in his ferocity. She always warned people not to go too near him. She fed him on **ascetic fare** of corn-mush and cakes, and never fired his dangerous temper with heating and **sanguinary** diet of flesh and bones. Louisa looked at the old dog **munching** his simple fare, and thought of her approaching marriage and trembled. Still no anticipation of disorder and confusion in lieu of sweet peace and harmony, no forebodings of Cæsar on the rampage, no wild fluttering of her little yellow canary, were sufficient to turn her a hair's-breadth. Joe Dagget had been fond of her and working for her all these years. It was not for her, whatever came to pass, to prove untrue and break his heart. She put the exquisite little stitches into her wedding-garments, and the time went on until it was only a week before her wedding-day. It was Tuesday evening, and the wedding was to be a week from Wednesday.

There was a full moon that night. About nine o'clock Louisa **strolled** down the road a little way. There were harvest-fields on either hand, bordered by low stone walls. **Luxuriant** clumps of bushes grew beside the wall, and trees—wild cherry and old apple-trees—at intervals. Presently Louisa sat down on the wall and looked about her with mildly sorrowful **reflectiveness**. Tall shrubs of blueberry and meadow-sweet, all woven together and tangled with blackberry vines and horsebriers, shut her in on either side. She had a little clear space between them. Opposite her, on the other side of the road, was a spreading tree; the moon shone between its boughs, and the leaves twinkled like silver. The road was bespread with a beautiful shifting **dapple** of silver and shadow; the air was full of a mysterious sweetness. "I wonder if it's wild grapes?" murmured Louisa. She sat there some time. She was just thinking of rising, when she heard footsteps and low voices, and remained quiet. It was a lonely place, and she felt a little timid. She thought she would keep still in the shadow and let the persons, whoever they might be, pass her.

But just before they reached her the voices ceased, and the footsteps. She understood that their owners had also found seats upon the stone wall. She was wondering if she could not steal away unobserved, when the voice broke the stillness. It was Joe Dagget's. She sat still and listened.

The voice was announced by a loud sigh, which was as familiar as itself. "Well," said Dagget, "you've made up your mind, then, I suppose?"

"Yes," returned another voice; "I'm going day after to-morrow."

"That's Lily Dyer," thought Louisa to herself. The voice embodied itself in her mind. She saw a girl tall and full-figured, with a firm, fair face, looking fairer and firmer in the moonlight, her strong yellow hair braided in a close knot. A girl full of calm **rustic** strength and bloom, with a masterful way which might have beseemed a princess. Lily Dyer was a favorite with the village folk; she had just the qualities to arouse their admiration. She was good and handsome and smart. Louisa had often heard her praises sounded.

"Well," said Joe Dagget, "I ain't got a word to say."

"I don't know what you could say," returned Lily Dyer.

"Not a word to say," repeated Joe, drawing out the words heavily. Then there was a silence. "I ain't sorry," he began at last, "that that happened yesterday—that we kind of let on how we felt to each other. I guess it's just as well we knew. Of course I can't do anything any different. I'm going right on an' get married next week. I ain't going back on a woman that's waited for me fourteen years, an' break her heart."

"If you should **jilt** her to-morrow, I wouldn't have you," spoke up the girl, with sudden **vehemence**.

"Well, I ain't going to give you the chance," said he; "but I don't believe you would, either."

"You'd see I wouldn't. Honor's honor, an' right's right. An' I'd never think anything of any man that went against 'em for me or any other girl; you'd find that out, Joe Dagget."

"Well, you'll find out fast enough that I ain't going against 'em for you or any other girl," returned he. Their voices sounded almost as if they were angry with each other. Louisa was listening eagerly.

"I'm sorry you feel as if you must go away," said Joe, "but I don't know but it's best."

"Of course it's best. I hope you and I have got common-sense."

"Well, I suppose you're right." Suddenly Joe's voice got an undertone of tenderness. "Say, Lily," said he, "I'll get along well enough myself, but I can't bear to think—You don't suppose you're going to fret much over it?"

"I guess you'll find out I **sha'n't** fret much over a married man."

"Well, I hope you won't—I hope you won't, Lily. God knows I do. And—I hope—one of these days—you'll—come across somebody else—"

"I don't see any reason why I shouldn't." Suddenly her tone changed. She spoke in a sweet, clear voice, so loud that she could have been heard across the street. "No, Joe Dagget," said she, "I'll never marry any other man as long as I live. I've got good sense, an' I ain't going to break my heart nor make a fool of myself; but I'm never going to be married, you can be sure of that. I ain't that sort of a girl to feel this way twice."

Louisa heard an exclamation and a soft **commotion** behind the bushes; then Lily spoke again—the voice sounded as if she had risen. "This must be put a stop to," said she. "We've stayed here long enough. I'm going home."

Louisa sat there in a daze, listening to their retreating steps. After a while she got up and **slunk** softly home herself. The next day she did her housework methodically; that was as much a matter of course as breathing; but she did not sew on her wedding-clothes. She sat at her window and meditated. In the evening Joe came. Louisa Ellis had never known that she had any diplomacy in her, but when she came to look for it that night she found it, although **meek** of its kind, among her little feminine weapons. Even now she could hardly believe that she had heard **aright**, and that she would not do Joe a terrible injury should she break her **troth-plight**. She wanted to sound him without betraying too soon her own inclinations in the matter. She did it successfully, and they finally came to an understanding; but it was a difficult thing, for he was as afraid of betraying himself as she.

She never mentioned Lily Dyer. She simply said that while she had no cause of complaint against him, she had lived so long in one way that she shrank from making a change.

"Well, I never shrank, Louisa," said Dagget. "I'm going to be honest enough to say that I think maybe it's better this way; but if you'd wanted to keep on, I'd have stuck to you till my dying day. I hope you know that."

"Yes, I do," said she.

That night she and Joe parted more tenderly than they had done for a long time. Standing in the door, holding each other's hands, a last great wave of regretful memory swept over them.

"Well, this ain't the way we've thought it was all going to end, is it, Louisa?" said Joe.

She shook her head. There was a little quiver on her placid face.

"You let me know if there's ever anything I can do for you," said he. "I ain't ever going to forget you, Louisa." Then he kissed her, and went down the path.

Louisa, all alone by herself that night, wept a little, she hardly knew why; but the next morning, on waking, she felt like a queen who, after fearing lest her **domain** be wrested away from her, sees it firmly insured in her possession.

Now the tall weeds and grasses might cluster around Cæsar's little hermit hut, the snow might fall on its roof year in and year out, but he never would go on a rampage through the unguarded village. Now the little canary might turn itself into a peaceful yellow ball night after night, and have no need to wake and flutter with wild terror against its bars. Louisa could sew linen seams, and distil roses, and dust and polish and fold away in lavender, as long as she **listed.** That afternoon she sat with her needle-work at the window, and felt fairly steeped in peace. Lily Dyer, tall and erect and blooming, went past; but she felt no qualm. If Louisa Ellis had sold her **birthright** she did not know it, the taste of the **pottage** was so delicious, and had been her sole satisfaction for so long. Serenity and placid narrowness had become to her as the birthright itself. She gazed ahead through a long reach of future days strung together like pearls in a **rosary**, every one like the others, and all smooth and **flawless** and innocent, and her heart went up in thankfulness. Outside was the **fervid** summer afternoon; the air was filled with the sounds of the busy harvest of men and birds and bees; there were **halloos**, metallic clatterings, sweet calls, and long hummings. Louisa sat, prayerfully numbering her days, like an **uncloistered** nun.

Glossary

appurtenances *(noun)*   equipments; accessories

aright *(adverb)*   correctly

ascetic *(adjective)*   austere; plain

assented *(verb)*   agreed; consented; concurred

at large *(idiom)*   free; not confined; loose

birthright *(noun)*   right or rights a person has as a result of being born into a particular family

blush *(noun)*   redness of face showing embarrassment

buoyed up *(verb)*   encouraged; cheered up

choleric *(adjective)* quick-tempered; irritable

clamor *(noun)* outcry; complaint

clank *(noun)* sharp, short, metallic sound

commotion *(noun)* disturbance; noisy movement

competency (**competence,** *noun*) means of earning a living

consternation *(noun)* great fear or shock that causes helplessness or bewilderment

constrained *(adjective)* forced; unnatural

cordiality *(noun)* warmth; friendliness

currants *(noun)* small, berry-like fruits that grow on bushes

damask *(adjective)* linen woven with a reversible pattern

dapple *(noun)* spots

deprecating *(adjective)* belittling; disapproving

devolve upon *(verb)* be assigned to; be passed on or down to

diurnal *(adjective)* daily; daytime

docility *(noun)* obedience

domain *(noun)* territory or land

domineering *(adjective)* arrogant; overbearing; tyrannical

drone *(noun)* continuous, monotonous humming or buzzing sound

excursions *(noun)* trips. Caesar was held by the chain even when taken for brief walks.

fare *(noun)* food

feeble *(adjective)* weak; frail

ferocity *(noun)* fierceness; cruel violence; savagery

fervid *(adjective)* hot; impassioned; fervent

flawless *(adjective)* without defect or fault

fused *(verb)* united; joined

glistened *(verb)* shone; sparkled with reflected light

gloated [over] *(verb)* exulted over; looked and thought with pleasure about

guises *(noun)* ways; manners; aspects; disguises. They would seem to have different identities in new surroundings.

halloos *(noun)* shouts; calls

haying *(verb)* cutting or mowing grasses used to feed animals

hedge *(noun)* fence made of closely planted bushes or shrubs. Awkward Joe felt "hedged in" by all of Louisa's delicate, feminine possessions.

hermit *(noun)* recluse; person who lives alone in a lonely or secluded place

homestead *(noun)* place of his family home, including land, house, and outbuildings

huskily *(adverb)* hoarsely

hut *(noun)* crudely built little house

jilt *(verb)* reject a suitor or lover after having previously accepted him or her

lest *(conjunction [obsolete])* for fear that

listed *(verb [obsolete])* liked; chose; wished

lowing *(verb)* mooing (a sound made by cows)

luxuriant *(adjective)* vigorously growing; abundant

maidenly *(adjective)* suitable for a maiden (unmarried woman)

meek *(adjective)* gentle [this usage is obsolete]; weak

munching *(verb)* chewing steadily

on the rampage *(idiom)* behaving wildly and violently

parlor *(adjective)* old-fashioned sitting room; formal room used for entertaining

perchance *(adverb [obsolete])* accidentally; by chance; possibly

perforce *(adjective [obsolete])* necessarily

perplexity *(noun)* confusion; puzzlement; bewilderment

plodded *(verb)* walked heavily and laboriously

pottage *(noun)* thick soup or stew made of vegetables and meat. This term is used figuratively as a metaphor for Louisa's unmarried state.

premonition *(noun)* advance warning; foretelling

quilted *(verb)* ran her needle in and out of the cloth but did not draw the thread through so that stitches were formed

redolent *(adjective)* fragrant; sweet-smelling

reflectiveness *(noun)* thoughtfulness; contemplation

repudiated *(verb)* refused; rejected; denied

retribution *(noun)* deserved punishment for evil done

righteous *(adjective)* morally right, fair, and just

rigorous *(adjective)* strict; harsh; severe

rosary *(noun)* string of beads used by members of several faiths to count each prayer as it is said

rustic *(adjective)* simple; plain

sanguinary *(adjective)* bloody. She thought red meat would make the dog bloodthirsty (eager for bloodshed).

sha'n't *(verb [obsolete spelling])* shan't; shall not

shrewd *(adjective)* cunning, keen-witted, or clever in dealing with others

sidelong *(adjective)* directed toward the side

slunk *(verb)* walked in a furtive, sneaky way

solemn *(adjective)* serious; grave

stealthily *(adverb)* secretly; furtively; slyly

stent (**stint**, *noun [obsolete]*) assigned task or period of work

sterner *(adjective)* harder; more severe; more demanding

stir *(verb)* move

strolled *(verb)* walked in a slow, leisurely manner

subsidence *(noun)* settling things down

tilted *(verb)* went shakily by

troth-plight *(noun [obsolete])* betrothal; agreement to marry

uncloistered *(adjective)* unconfined. Members of religious orders are sometimes confined to monasteries or convents for prayer and meditation.

unswerving *(adjective)* unchanging; undeviating

valiantly *(adverb)* courageously; bravely

vehemence *(noun)* force; feeling; passion

veritable *(adjective)* true; actual

visaged *(adjective)* faced

whit *(noun)* bit

wistful *(adjective)* longing; yearning; wishful

wont to *(verb)* accustomed to

woodchuck *(noun)* large rodent (up to 21 inches from head to tail tip) with coarse reddish-brown fur; known for burrowing (digging) and hibernating (sleeping in winter)

Comprehension Questions

1. The story begins at the close of a typical day. What has Louisa been doing all afternoon? How does she dress to pick the currants? How does she prepare them? How does she fix and arrange her afternoon tea? What kinds of foods does she eat? How do these details establish the type of person Louisa is and the kind of life she leads?

2. How many aprons does Louisa wear? Why?

3. What details about Joe Dagget show that he is out of place in Louisa's environment? How does the canary react when Joe enters? How does Louisa react when he picks up the books on the table? What happens when he knocks her work basket to the floor? What does Louisa do after he leaves?

4. Why does Dagget "color" (blush) when Louisa asks about Lily Dyer?

5. How long is Joe's visit? How does he feel when he is inside Louisa's house?

6. How determined is Joe to honor his promise to marry Louisa? How long was he away making his fortune?

7. How did Louisa's mother influence her daughter's agreeing to marry Joe? Did Louisa's views of marriage to Joe change over the years? How did Joe feel about her when he returned after all those years?

8. Where will the newlyweds live and under what circumstances? How do these arrangements suit Louisa? What problems does she foresee? With whom? Why?

9. What does Louisa like about her solitary home?

10. What concerns does she have about Caesar? Why? What crime did the dog commit in puppyhood? Was his punishment realistic? What is Caesar's reputation? Is it justified? What does Louisa feed the dog? Why? What does Louisa fear Joe Dagget will do with Caesar after the wedding? What terrible picture keeps recurring in her mind?

11. How does Louisa happen to overhear Joe's conversation with Lily? What does Louisa learn about them? What are Lily's plans? How does Joe feel about her decision? What is happening during the "soft commotion behind the bushes"? What does Lily's final remark tell you about her character?

12. What are Louisa's reactions to her discovery about Joe and Lily? Why doesn't she mention Lily when she tells Joe of her decision? How does Joe respond? How do they part?

13. Why does Louisa cry that night? How does she feel the next morning? What fears are quieted? What lies ahead for her? Is she satisfied with her decision?

Topics for Critical Analysis, Discussion, and Writing

1. Discuss several examples that prove that Joe and Louisa would have been incompatible if they had married.

2. The process by which Louisa arrives at her decision not to marry Joe is mostly psychological and gives the reader many insights into Louisa's character. From the moment of his return, she has doubts that she can adjust to married life with Joe, but these concerns build gradually as the story progresses chronologically. Discuss the important steps in Louisa's decision-making process and explain why each serves to develop her character.

3. Write a process analysis in which you describe the means by which you or someone in your family made an important decision. Be sure that you organize the essay chronologically and that you include a thesis and conclusion.

4. Examine the importance of the dog and the canary in the story. What do the animals tell us about the humans?

7

Definition: Clarifying and Expanding Meanings

When you first started to learn English, you probably used a dual-language dictionary exclusively. Although your vocabulary and writing soon became much more sophisticated, sometimes your essays contained many "wrong words" because they were shown in your dictionary as correct definitions. Now you know that all meanings for English words are not translated accurately (especially if the dictionary is compiled and printed in a foreign country), and that you must use an English-only college-level dictionary to double check all dual-language definitions. Furthermore, effective communication with another person requires that key words or terms mean the same thing to both of you. Meaning can be achieved by strict adherence to the *dictionary definition* or by cultural association, but on many occasions a more comprehensive explanation called *extended definition* is necessary.

DICTIONARY DEFINITION

Dictionary definitions best explain concrete words or terms not subject to argument. These definitions reinforce existing understanding or offer new information by supplying a broad range of meanings; for example, *Webster's New World Dictionary of the American Language,* second edition, shows nine different ways of using the adjective *rude:*

> (1) crude or rough in form or workmanship [a *rude* hut] (2) barbarous or ignorant [*rude* savages] (3) lacking refinement, culture, or elegance; uncouth, boorish, coarse, vulgar, etc. (4) discourteous; unmannerly [a *rude*

reply] (5) rough, violent, or harsh [a *rude* awakening] (6) harsh in sound; discordant; not musical [*rude* tones] (7) having little skill or development; primitive [*rude* drawings] (8) not carefully worked out or finished; not precise [a *rude* appraisal] (9) sturdy; robust; rugged [*rude* health].

But note that synonyms (and antonyms) refer to the most common usage relating to human behavior shown in (3) and (4):

> SYN.—*rude,* in this comparison, implies a deliberate lack of considera-tion for others' feelings and connotes, especially, insolence, impudence, etc. [it was *rude* of you to ignore your uncle]; *ill-mannered* connotes ignorance of the amenities of social behavior rather than deliberate rude-ness [a well-meaning but *ill-mannered fellow*]; *boorish* is applied to one who is rude or ill-mannered in a coarse, loud or overbearing way; *impolite* implies merely a failure to observe the forms of polite society [it would be *impolite* to leave so early]; *discourteous* suggests a lack of dignified con-sideration for others [a *discourteous* reply]; *uncivil* implies a disregarding of even the most elementary of good manners [her *uncivil* treatment of the waiter]—ANT. *polite, civil.*

Some dictionary definitions use *classification* to categorize a word or term and to explain how it differs from others in the same group. If we use this method to define only a few of the many fermented alcoholic beverages that exist, such as beer, brandy, whiskey, and wine, we can see that even though they are all members of the same general class, they differ greatly in ingre-dient content, preparation method, and alcohol content:

Fermented Alcoholic Beverages

Beer	Brandy	Whiskey	Wine
made of grains, hops	made of wines (grapes, other fruits)	made of grains	made of grapes, other fruits
Brewed	Distilled	Distilled	Filtered, Clarified
3–10% normal alcohol range	25–50% normal alcohol range	40–60% normal alcohol range	7–12% normal alcohol range

EXTENDED DEFINITION

Extended definition goes beyond the dictionary to explain a word or term that is abstract, controversial, technical, or cultural. *Definition* is an expository technique that often includes one or more of the other forms of exposition we have already studied. *Classification,* a necessary part of many dictionary definitions, can be expanded to explain more about a word or term in relation to others in its class or group; for instance, an extended definition of *brandy,* one of the fermented alcoholic beverages discussed in the preceding paragraph, may include important details about related beverages (whiskey, wine, and beer) in the same category and may use *comparison and contrast* to show similarities and differences in their use (brandy as an elegant after-dinner liqueur; beer as a thirst quencher on a hot day; whiskey as a cocktail or before-dinner drink; wine served with luncheon or dinner). *Process analysis* can show the means (steps) used to reach an end (the term being defined); for example, the steps used in making your own peach brandy may be the best way to define its character. *Narration* is frequently used to clarify meaning; for instance, you can define brandy by showing its effects on the human body. An obvious result is, of course, intoxication, and everyone knows anecdotes about people who deliberately or accidentally drink too much. A less common consequence is allergic reaction. Although the distilling process purifies the product, it does not remove allergens. To illustrate this, you might reveal that you instantly developed a severe facial rash the first and only time you had peach brandy (unfortunately, during a toast to your new husband or wife at your wedding), and that your reaction is captured forever in your wedding photographs.

Meanings of common *abstract words* used in this country, like *love, pride,* and *ethics,* are closely tied to cultural values that you may not understand or that may be interpreted differently in your country. The word *love,* for example, may not exist in your language, or it may mean *respect* or *passion; pride* may refer to *arrogance;* and *ethics* may translate as *courtesies.* Obviously, these differences in meaning require thorough explanation.

Opinion words, which can be invitations to argument, should be carefully defined. Such words as *gorgeous, handsome, clever, stupid, cruel,* and *nice* are subjective judgments that may not be shared by others. *Controversial terms,* too, need definition because they frequently reflect individual biases and prejudices; for example, *male supremacy, women's equality, job discrimination,* and *nuclear arms proliferation.*

Technical terms are found in every specialized field of work. In the exploration of space, terms like *lift off, payload capability, mission control,* and *touch down* have specific meanings. Teachers use *holistic grading;* dentists can now do *bonding* to make cosmetic tooth repairs; the police need a *search warrant* to enter your home; psychologists bring patients together for *group therapy,* but also refer to *bonding* between mother and infant; and lawyers prepare *living wills.*

In addition to culture-based values that can affect definitions of abstractions, judgments, and opinions, specific *cultural terms* exist. These are often slang expressions, like the "burnt idea" in Benjamin Stein's article included in this chapter. Remember that slang is meant to be a "coded" sublanguage used by special groups (dictated by age, economics, social status, etc.) to limit or control communication of certain ideas so that their real meanings are not generally understood. As soon as a slang expression is so well-defined that it is commonly used, it is replaced by a new "coded" term.

DENOTATION AND CONNOTATION

Denotation is the explicit, specific meaning of a word, such as in a dictionary definition. For example, if Elizabeth introduces Jack to you at a party as her *sweetheart,* you can safely assume that they are in love with each other.

In contrast, the same assumption cannot be made about a soccer player who calls the coach a *sweetheart.* When the exact definition of a word does not fit the intended meaning, the writer or speaker may be using *connotation* to suggest meaning derived from association. In slang, a *sweetheart* is a very agreeable person or an excellent thing; thus, your uncles, aunts, cousins, friends, teachers, doctors, and dentists can all be *sweethearts,* as can your new sports car, the family dog, your neighborhood, a football game, etc. The expression "a sweetheart of a ———" is also common; for example, "He's a sweetheart of a mechanic," or "It's a sweetheart of a motorcycle."

Remember, too, that a word can have both denotative and connotative meaning at the same time; for instance, *New Year's Eve,* literally the evening before New Year's Day, often connotes celebration and even romance because partygoers (especially younger men and women) "ring out the old and bring in the new" with symbolic kisses. So if someone tells you in April that he or she would like to spend New Year's Eve with you, take it as a positive, definite sign of romantic interest.

Connotation often uses metaphor to suggest meaning. Suppose you do make that date in April for New Year's Eve. By December, you are ready to make a serious commitment, and you plan to announce your engagement at a New Year's Eve party to which you have been invited. The party begins well; everyone is dancing with everyone else and having a wonderful time, but when the magical midnight moment arrives, you and your sweetheart aren't dancing together. You look up just in time to see your intended kissing someone else. You are furiously jealous! What was to be a special shared moment for the two of you has become a betrayal. You break away from your partner and go off to collect your coat. You intend to leave—alone. You won't listen when your sweetheart tries to explain that the kiss meant nothing, that it was a spontaneous reaction to the clock striking midnight. "I'm glad I found out in time," he or she says, "what a jealous wet blanket you are," and walks away. The denotative meaning of "wet" is to be soaked with water or some liquid. The definition of "blanket" is "a large rectangular piece of soft, loosely woven fabric, used for a bedcovering." Since you are literally neither of these, you conclude that your friend means something else. A *wet blanket,* in slang, is a person who habitually discourages or whose presence prevents others from enjoying themselves. Your sweetheart means that your unwarranted jealousy spoiled the evening and your relationship as effectively as a wet blanket would have put out a fire.

Euphemism, too, connotes meaning by substituting pleasant sounding words or terms for their more direct or distasteful counterparts. For example, many people in this country are uncomfortable when they have to talk seriously about death. Although people mention death all the time—"I'll die if I eat even one more bite" ("I'm too full to eat any more"); "That joke was so funny it nearly killed me" ("That was a terribly funny joke"); "She nearly died when the teacher called on her" ("She was very embarrassed when the teacher asked her the answer"); "I'm dead" (I'm tired); or "My parents will kill me if I get home late" ("I will get in trouble if I get home late")—this sort of exaggeration is rarely taken literally. However, when people have to acknowledge a real death, they often talk around it. Here is the experience of one international student:

> Yesterday when I was waiting for the bus, an old man came and sat on the bench beside me. He seemed worried and upset, and he kept sighing and touching his handkerchief to his eyes. Finally, I asked, "Is something wrong?"
>
> He looked at me strangely. "Well, you could say so," he answered, "I just lost my wife."
>
> "Well, I've lived here for five months now, and I know this city pretty well," I said. "Shall I help you find her?" I smiled cheerfully and spoke enthusiastically, knowing my parents would want me to help this old gentleman.
>
> But he replied angrily. "I guess you don't understand that my wife is dead, young man."
>
> How could I have known what he meant?

The old man could have said his wife had *passed away, passed on,* or *gone to meet her maker,* but the student might not have understood those expressions, either.

Euphemisms are regularly used instead of the correct anatomical names for the private parts of the body or the medical terms for bodily functions; in fact, most people in this country shrink from using even the word *toilet* in public. Instead, they ask the location of the *restroom* (obviously not with resting in mind), the *men's or ladies' room,* the *powder room* (where women supposedly go *only* to freshen their makeup), or the *bathroom* (certainly not for a bath). Other euphemisms transform a *second-hand car* into a *previously owned automobile;* make a *lie* into a *fib* or an *exaggeration;* and change *old* to *mature* and *ugly* to *unattractive* or *plain.*

WRITING AN EXTENDED DEFINITION

As with all expository essays, base a paper of definition on a thesis which states the term to be defined and takes some position about it. Use language appropriate to your audience.

In your first paragraph, try to clear up any confusions that may exist about the word or term itself; for example, if the meaning today is different from that of the time of its origin, include a brief explanation. *The Oxford English Dictionary* and many other unabridged dictionaries provide detailed *etymologies* (histories) of the origins and development of words, terms, or phrases in English and in languages (such as Greek, Latin, and French) from which the English was derived. An example is the word *chauvinism,* which derives from Nicolas Chauvin, an excessively patriotic and devoted soldier in Napoleon's First Republic and Empire. Initially these qualities were celebrated and admired; but after the fall of Napoleon, old soldiers who remained loyal to the emperor were ridiculed for their *chauvinism.* As time went on, the term was used to describe blind enthusiasm for national glory or militant, fanatical patriotism. Today *chauvinism* is most commonly used to describe an unreasoning devotion to one's own sex accompanied by a feeling of superiority over and contempt for the opposite sex; thus, we have both *male* and *female chauvinists.* The former joke that women can't even balance their checkbooks, let alone understand the family's finances. The latter laugh about men who are so helpless around the house they not only can't operate a can opener, but also can't even identify one.

Avoid *circular definitions,* using a form of the word or the word itself as a part of the definition, as in "Chauvinism is being chauvinistic," or "Happiness is when people feel happy." In fact, make a note *never* to use "is when" in relation to a term you are defining. Don't forget to acknowledge other members of the class that includes your term; for example, if you are defining *governor* as the elected head of any state government in the United States, don't forget that a governor is also commonly appointed by the British to administer a dependency, town, or province. Another type of governor is one who serves on a Board of Governors, such as for a hospital or a university. Be sure to exclude these closely related terms by giving differentiating information so that the reader will know that *your* governor is one of several.

Don't be afraid to use negation in your definition, either in stating what the word *doesn't* mean or in explaining that many people don't know the meaning and why. In the student essay on alcoholism that follows, the author has used the latter technique to show that people from many age groups are unable to define the word or comprehend its significance.

Pay attention not only to what the word denotes, but also to *how it works* or *what its causes and effects are.* Although the student writer candidly admits that the cause of alcoholism is not positively known, she offers some possible explanations in the form of questions. She also provides many facts about the ways alcoholism works its damage on the internal organs and she carefully examines the effects of alcohol—both on the alcoholic and on others with whom he or she comes in contact.

Finally, be sure that your conclusion refers to the thesis and takes into consideration all the proofs you have submitted in your extended definition. Falkenhagen concludes her essay on alcoholism with suggestions for solving the problems alcoholism causes and a call to continue the fight against this disease.

Alcoholism

Rose Falkenhagen

Everyone knows what alcohol is. Even young children know it is an adult beverage used frequently at the dinner table or at parties. But not everyone knows what alcoholism is. And many adults and young people who abuse alcohol are not even aware of the true significance of alcoholism. They do not know that it is an insidious, debilitating disease that adversely affects many areas of the body, destroys family ties, breaks up friendships, and wreaks havoc on society.

Alcoholism is one of the oldest diseases known to man. It is also one of the most complex. We don't know what causes it. Is it a person's genetic makeup? Is it the family's lifestyle? Is it environment? Why is it that one person consumes a great deal of alcohol and never becomes alcoholic while another person drinks very little and is overcome by the disease? There are many factors to consider, but one fact is quite clear. A person who drinks alcohol frequently and in considerable quantities is certainly more likely to become habituated or addicted than a light drinker.

Alcoholism is also one of the most destructive diseases. Prolonged use can cause a variety of serious illnesses. It can irritate the stomach and cause gastritis or more serious ulcers. It can cause malnutrition because the appetite becomes depressed. It can also damage the cardiovascular system. Even cancer of the mouth, pharynx, larynx, and esophagus can be caused from heavy alcohol use, especially if the drinker also smokes. Excessive alcohol use can cause temporary or permanent psychotic conditions. Taken in combination with another drug, such as phenobarbital (a barbiturate), it can be deadly. But

Reprinted by permission of the author.

cirrhosis of the liver, an irreversible degeneration of the liver cells, is the most destructive disease of all because without a liver, the human body simply ceases to function. The combination of all these diseases can only add up to a significantly shortened life span for the heavy drinker. These are the effects of alcohol on the abuser.

But what about the parents, the spouse, the children, or even the unborn children of the abuser? The grief and anguish heaped upon these innocent victims can never be measured. The physical and mental abuse many families endure for years does irreparable damage. Battered spouses and children are not a pretty sight. But at least these external conditions can be identified and are treatable. Emotional scars are invisible and often incurable. The unborn fetus is yet another victim. It can be born with a number of birth defects, such as stunted growth; malformation of facial features, extremities, and heart; and even mental retardation.

Society also pays a continuing price as it is a fact that half of the children of alcoholic families themselves become alcoholics. Society pays for it in the workplace, within the community, and on the highways. A drunk is unable to perform to capacity on the job, to be a good parent, or to be part of the community. But worst of all, the drunk behind the wheel or walking across the street is responsible for one-half of all traffic fatalities in the U.S. That's about 12,000 deaths a year. Unfortunately, about 75% of these deaths include innocent victims.

Alcoholism will continue to be a major problem in our society. But as we learn more about the disease and are able to communicate about it more openly, perhaps alcoholics and their victims will seek help earlier. Many communities now have free counseling centers available to the public. More education about the dangers of alcoholism will help young people learn restraint. Because alcohol is here to stay and is a drug that must be treated with caution and respect, the fight against alcoholism must be continued.

READINGS

The "Astonishing Ignorance" of Some Teenagers

Benjamin J. Stein

Benjamin Stein has worked as a government trial lawyer, a speech writer for Presidents Nixon and Ford, a newspaper columnist, a movie script writer, and a novelist. His nonfiction focuses on politics, economics, business, and current events requiring a wide range of knowledge and an excellent command of language. In the following article, Stein defines ignorance, *a controversial term, by giving examples of teenagers' lack of knowledge or awareness of anything that goes beyond day-to-day life in Los Angeles. Stein's conversations with these young people are related in a narrative, anecdotal format, and he makes liberal use of repetition for effect. He condemns our educational system for its negligence and shows how ignorance works to make individuals unfit to protect and defend a free society.*

As you read the last few paragraphs of the article, try to determine the author's purpose in writing it (surely not just to relate examples of the painful ignorance of these young people). Does his critical tone (attitude) affect your understanding of the material?

For an interesting dramatic effect, two students should read the article aloud as a dialog between Stein and the students. Underline all student responses, many of which are shown in parentheses.

I spend a lot of time with teenagers. Besides employing three of them part time, I frequently conduct focus groups at Los Angeles-area high schools to learn about teenagers' attitudes toward movies or television shows or nuclear arms or politicians. I meet the friends of the teenagers who work for me. I make it my business not only to meet those young people but also to ask them about their lives and about what they know. In the course of two years of this kind of inquiry, I have collected a mass of data about how teenagers see business (very negatively), how they feel about the likelihood of nuclear war (terrified), how they like Richard Gere (a lot), and how they feel about American cars (extremely negative).

But all of these specific attitudes **pale** into insignificance compared with something else I have learned of: the astounding level of ignorance of the Southern California teenager. No amount of preparation could possibly cushion the blows of unawareness of even the most elementary current events, history, politics, economics or just what goes on each day in the world outside of Los Angeles that **lurks** in the cheerful minds of these children. I have not figured out a way to **quantify** this ignorance, but I can offer a few examples that might just make you wonder where all that money for public education is going.

Recently, a 19-year-old junior at the University of Southern California sat with me while I watched "Gaudalcanal Diary" on television. It goes without saying that the child had never heard of **Guadalcanal**. More surprisingly, she did not know who the United States was fighting against in the Pacific. ("The Germans?") She was genuinely shocked to learn that all those little people on that island were Japanese and that the United States had fought a war against them. ("Who won?")

Another student at U.S.C. did not have any clear idea when World War II was fought. She believed it was some time this century. (She is a journalism major.) She also had no clear **notion** of what had begun the war for the United States. ("Pearl Harbor? Was that when the United States dropped the atom bomb on Hiroshima?") Even more astounding, she was not sure which side Russia was on and whether Germany was on our side or against us.

In fact, I have not yet found a single student in Los Angeles, in either college or high school, who could tell me the years when World War II was fought. Nor have I found one who could tell me the years when World War I was fought. Nor have I found one who knew when the American Civil War was fought.

Not one could name all the presidents since World War II. Only one could even place the correct decade in which Dwight D. Eisenhower was president. Not one could tell me who Martin Luther King Jr. was except that he was black. A few have known how many U.S. senators California has, but none has known how many Nevada or Oregon has. ("Really? Even though they're so small?")

Of the (at least) 12 I have asked, none has known within 40 million what the population of the United States is. Only two could tell me where Chicago is, even in the **vaguest** terms. (My particular favorite geography lesson was from the junior at the University of California at Los Angeles who thought that Toronto must be in Italy. My second-favorite geography lesson is from the junior at U.S.C., a pre-law student, who thought that Washington, D.C., was in Washington State.) None had even the vaguest idea of where New England is and several had never heard of Vermont or Connecticut and could not identify them as states of the Union.

Not so long ago, I watched a television news show about the so-called "lifting" of **martial law** in Poland. On the screen were pictures of Poles in large pen-like enclosures rounded up after martial law was imposed. One of my assistants, a junior at U.S.C., stared at the screen open mouthed.

"What's going on there?" she asked. "Why are those people in that big cage?"

I explained that they had been imprisoned as the result of a **crackdown** by the Communist government. "Why don't they just leave and come to L.A.?" she asked. I explained that they were not allowed to leave.

"They're not?" she said. "Why not?"

I explained that in **totalitarian** states, citizens usually could not emigrate.

"They can't?" she said. "Since when? Is that something new?"

After some explanation of that, she asked who "that guy in uniform" (Wojciech Jaruzelski) was. I explained that he is the **dictator** of Poland. "He is?" she asked. "Why does he do that?"

She then expressed amazement that there were such things as nonfree countries in the world. She had never known that before. She was amazed that there was a whole **array** of countries around Russia that are controlled by Russia. ("There are? Why doesn't Reagan make them stop?") She was also amazed that people could be and were put in prison for expressing political views in Russia. ("What a **burnt idea**."). Finally, she wondered why she had never been told about this subject before.

Of the teenagers with whom I work, none had ever heard of Vladimir Ilyich Lenin. Only one could identify Josef Stalin. (My favorite answer: "He was president just before Roosevelt.") Only two could even approximately identify Thomas Jefferson. Only one could place the date of the Declaration of Independence. None could name even one of the first 10 amendments to the Constitution or connect them with the Bill of Rights. Only one knew roughly when the Great Depression was. None could say even approximately when Lyndon B. Johnson was president.

Only a few could articulate in any way at all why life in a free country is different from life in an un-free country. None had ever heard of the **Warsaw Pact**. None could tell me what **NATO** stood for. ("Aren't they the ones who put up the space shuttle and all those things?")

On and on it went. On and on it goes. I have mixed up episodes of ignorance of facts with ignorance of concepts because it seems to me that there is a connection. If a student has no idea when World War II was and who the combatants were and what they fought over, that same human being is likely to be ignorant of just what this society stands for. If a young woman has never heard of the Bill of Rights, that young woman is unlikely to understand why this is a **uniquely** privileged nation with uniquely privileged citizens, young and old. If a student has never heard of the Warsaw Pact and has no idea what the Russian system is all about, the student is unlikely to understand why **sacrifice** is necessary to defend this society.

The examples here could be repeated almost endlessly. (One night in 1982, I watched a television mini-series about Adolf Hitler. In the series, a demented, defeated Hitler rants that he never wanted war, that it was forced on him by Russia and England. One of my friends at U.C.L.A. said to me while watching, "Why did Russia and England do that?" The point is that in a state of such astonishing ignorance, young Americans may well not be prepared for even the most basic national responsibility—understanding what the society is about and why it must be preserved. The kids I saw (and there may be lots of others who are different) are not mentally prepared to continue the society because they basically do not understand the society enough to value it.

None of this means that the children in my circle are bad children or **inherently flawed**. Far from it. They are fine human beings. Their comments often bring tears of joy to my eyes. Recently, two of them read an article in the newspaper about a militantly **anti-Semitic** organization. One of them pointed at the word "anti-Semite" and said, "What's this word?" I explained that it was someone who hated Jews. The girl looked at me with genuine amazement and asked, "Why would anyone do that?" The other girl said, "What is it again? I never heard of that."

I respectfully suggest that we should be happy and proud to have such **gilded**, innocent children in our midst. But unless they are given some concept of why the society must be protected and defended, I fear that they will learn too soon about a whole variety of ugly ideas they did not want to know about. If we are going to upgrade our educational system, if we are going to start teaching again, I hope we will begin by instructing young Americans with historical facts and with concepts about why the society is worth preserving. People who do not value what they have rarely keep it for long, and neither will we.

Glossary

anti-Semitic *(adjective)*   having or showing prejudice against Jews; discriminating against or persecuting Jews

array *(noun)*   impressive display; orderly grouping or arrangement

burnt idea *(slang)*   extreme view; intolerable, outrageous, or terrible idea

crackdown *(noun)*   implementation of stricter means of discipline or punishment

dictator *(noun)*   ruler with absolute power and authority

flawed *(adjective [derived from status verb])*   defective; faulty

gilded *(adjective)*   thinly applied, bright, attractive outer golden finish that covers an unattractive, inner substance

Guadalcanal *(noun)*   largest of the Solomon Islands (British protectorate) located in the southwest Pacific. During World War II, the United States and Japan fought a bloody battle there.

inherently *(adverb [modifying adjective])*   naturally; characteristically; basically

lurks *(verb)*   exists undiscovered and unobserved; is present but not readily noticeable

martial law *(noun)*   temporary rule over civilian population by military authorities because of war or breakdown of civil authority

NATO (**North Atlantic Treaty Organization,** *special term*)   mutual defense pact between western European powers and the United States

notion *(noun)*   general idea; belief, opinion, or view

pale *(verb)*   weaken; become unimportant

quantify *(verb)*   measure

sacrifice *(noun)*   the act of giving up something valued for the sake of something more important

totalitarian *(adjective)*   type of state in which a political party or group is in complete control of the government. **Totalitarian** governments are dictatorships that do not permit individual rights and freedoms to citizens.

uniquely *(adverb)*   singularly; extraordinarily; unusually

vaguest *(adjective)*   least clearly stated; least precise

Warsaw Pact *(special term)*   mutual defense pact between eastern European powers and the Soviet Union

Comprehension Questions

1. Why does the author spend so much time with teenagers? What has he learned about how they feel and what they know? What subjects are important to them?

2. Stein writes of the "amazing ignorance" of these high school and college students. In what subject areas does he find their knowledge substandard?

3. How many of the author's questions can *you* answer?
   a. Stein uses World War II as a major reference for many historical contexts. Do you know (1) when the war was fought and its duration? (2) the war relationship between Germany and Japan? (3) what happened at Pearl Harbor and when? (4) whose side Russia was on?
   b. Do you know the dates (years) for the American Civil War? World War I?
   c. Can you name all the U.S. presidents since World War II?
   d. Who was Martin Luther King, Jr.? (Note that a national holiday honors his memory each January.)
   e. How many U.S. senators does each state have? Why might the students have expected the number to be related to the size or population of the states?

    f. Where is Chicago? Toronto? Washington, D.C.? New England? Vermont? Connecticut?

    g. The concept of totalitarianism is important in the article. The author uses Russia and its satellite states (formerly independent countries now part of the Soviet Union) as examples. Explain the policies of these countries toward individual freedoms and emigration.

    h. Who was Lenin? Stalin?

    i. When was Franklin D. Roosevelt president?

    j. What is the date of the Declaration of Independence?

    k. What is the connection between the Bill of Rights and the first ten amendments to the Constitution?

    l. When was the Great Depression? How long did it last?

    m. How does life in a free country differ from life in a non-free country?

    n. What is the Warsaw Pact? What is NATO? What is their relationship?

    o. Did Russia and England force Germany into World War II? Explain.

    p. What is the significance of anti-Semitism in contemporary society, both in the United States and the world?

4. What will happen to our society if children are not taught the historical facts and concepts necessary to protect and defend it?

Topics for Critical Analysis, Discussion, and Writing

    1. In his essay, Stein does not include a dictionary definition of ignorance. Instead, his extended definition uses specific examples of teenagers' lack of knowledge of commonly understood concepts and widely known historical facts to support his thesis, which occurs in the second paragraph: Southern California teenagers exhibit an astounding level of ignorance about "even the most elementary current events, history, politics, and economics" (which causes the author to question the value of public education). Presenting one instance of ignorance after another, Stein catalogs the educational deficiencies of these young people. He concludes by warning that allowing such ignorance to continue jeopardizes preservation of our free society. Write your own definition of ignorance, and include a dictionary definition that relates to your thesis. Use examples of ignorance about any subject; for example, the value of money, the rights and obligations of citizens, the freedom of choice, the responsibilities of parenthood, the importance of a college education, the dangers of living alone, or the proper limits of government.

    2. Write an extended definition of one of the following words or terms: *democracy, totalitarian rule, dictatorship, republic, monarchy, anarchy, theocracy, parliamentary government, martial law, freedom of speech.*

    3. Defend or attack Stein's definition of ignorance.

4. Stein relates many different examples of ignorance, but each incident occurred with a different student. Thus, the essay is a composite of individual experiences which are relatively minor when they occur singly, but seem absolutely staggering when they are combined. When this essay was discussed in a college Humanities class composed of freshmen and sophomores (also from the Los Angeles area), all students easily knew *most* of the information Stein found so sadly lacking in teenagers of his acquaintance. The students seriously questioned whether young people were as ignorant of historical facts and important concepts as Stein claimed, and challenged his indictment of teenagers as ignorant because he attributed all weaknesses to most young people. Do you think Stein's treatment of the subject is fair? Explain your answer in detail.

5. Examine the tone and style of Stein's article. What attitude does the author project? How does his writing style affect the "message"?

Why I Want a Wife

Judy Syfers

Judy Syfers's article first appeared in Ms., *a magazine devoted to women's issues. The author defines* wife *by enumerating the qualities and duties of the "ideal" home companion; however, Syfers does not necessarily say that a wife must be a woman although she acknowledges that she is a wife and mother. (As a matter of fact, Sanderson's househusband, in chapter 5, can be compared in many ways with Syfers's "wife.") Instead, Syfers reasons that if* wife *is defined by economic, physical, social, and sexual responsibilities, then a person of either sex should be able to do the job—and "who wouldn't want a wife?"*

As you read the article, pay special attention to the author's angry, sarcastic tone. The wife that the article defines is a voiceless, formless, compliant servant, an object that is acted upon by everyone else. This wife is never allowed to have intellectual or career pursuits, and never permitted to satisfy basic wants and needs. The article establishes the basic dissatisfactions that can result when the needs of only one marriage partner are considered in a relationship.

Notice also the very consistent style. The pronouns she *and* her *are conspicuous by their absence, and Syfers uses repetition for effect with the phrase, "I want a wife who . . ."*

Reprinted by permission of the author.

I belong to that classification of people known as wives. I am a Wife. And, not altogether incidentally, I am a mother.

Not too long ago a male friend of mine appeared on the scene fresh from a recent divorce. He had one child, who is, of course, with his ex-wife. He is obviously looking for another wife. As I thought about him while I was ironing one evening, it suddenly occurred to me that I, too, would like to have a wife. Why do I want a wife?

I would like to go back to school so that I can become economically independent, support myself, and, if need be, support those dependent on me. I want a wife who will work and send me to school. And while I am going to school I want a wife to take care of my children. I want a wife to keep track of the children's doctor and dentist appointments. And to keep track of mine, too. I want a wife who will wash the children's clothes and keep them **mended**. I want a wife who is a good **nurturant** attendant to my children, who arranges for their schooling, makes sure they have an adequate social life with their **peers**, takes them to the park, the zoo, etc. I want a wife who takes care of the children when they are sick, a wife who arranges to be around when the children need special care, because, of course, I cannot miss classes at school. My wife must arrange to lose time at work and not lose the job. It may mean a small cut in my wife's income from time to time, but I guess I can **tolerate** that. Needless to say, my wife will arrange and pay for the care of the children while my wife is working.

I want a wife who will take care of *my* physical needs. I want a wife who will keep the house clean. A wife who will pick up after me. I want a wife who will keep my clothes clean, ironed, mended, replaced when need be, and who will see to it that my personal things are kept in their proper place so that I can find what I need the minute I need it. I want a wife who cooks the meals, a wife who is a *good* cook. I want a wife who will plan the menus, do the necessary shopping, prepare the meals, serve them pleasantly, and then do the cleaning up while I do my studying. I want a wife who will care for me when I am sick and sympathize with my pain and loss of time from school. I want a wife to go along when our family takes a vacation so that someone can continue to care for me and my children when I need a rest and change of scene.

I want a wife who will not bother me with **rambling** complaints about a wife's duties. But I want a wife who will listen to me when I feel the need to explain a rather difficult point I have come across in my course of studies. And I want a wife who will type my papers for me when I have written them.

I want a wife who will take care of the details of my social life. When my wife and I are invited out by my friends, I want a wife who will take care of the **babysitting** arrangements. When I meet people at school that I like and want to entertain, I want a wife who will have the house clean, prepare a special meal, serve it to me and my friends, and not interrupt when I talk about the things that interest me and my friends. I want a wife who will have arranged that the children are fed and ready for bed before my guests arrive so that the children do not bother us. I want a wife who takes care of the needs of my guests so that they feel comfortable, who makes sure that they have an ashtray, that they are passed the **hors d'oeuvres**, that they are offered a second helping of the food, that their wine glasses are **replenished** when necessary, that their coffee is served to them as they like it.

And I want a wife who knows that sometimes I need a night out by myself.

I want a wife who is sensitive to my sexual needs, a wife who makes love passionately and eagerly when I feel like it, a wife who makes sure that I am satisfied. And, of course, I want a wife who will not demand sexual attention when I am not in the mood for it. I want a wife who assumes the complete responsibility for birth control, because I do not want more children. I want a wife who will remain sexually faithful to me so that I do not have to **clutter up** my intellectual life with jealousies. And I want a wife who understands that *my* sexual needs may entail more than strict adherence to **monogamy**. I must, after all, be able to relate to people as fully as possible.

If, by chance, I find another person more suitable as a wife than the wife I already have, I want the liberty to replace my present wife with another one. Naturally, I will expect a fresh, new life; my wife will take the children and be solely responsible for them so that I am left free.

When I am through with school and have a job, I want my wife to quit working and remain at home so that my wife can more fully and completely take care of a wife's duties.

My God, who wouldn't want a wife?

Glossary

babysitting *(adjective)*   child care

clutter up *(verb; also **clutter**)*   disorder; confuse; jumble up

hors d'oeuvres *(noun [French])*   appetizers served just before a meal, often with cocktails

mended *(adjective)*   in good condition or repair

monogamy *(noun)*   practice of being married to one person at a time

nurturant *(adjective)*   physical, nutritional, educational, and developmental. **Nurturant** attendant appears to be a way of specifying *mother* without identifying the sex of the person.

peers *(noun)*   equals; children of the same age and circumstances

rambling *(adjective)*   aimless; disconnected

replenished *(verb)*   refilled

tolerate *(verb)*   allow; permit; bear; not interfere with

Comprehension Questions

1. What made the author suddenly want to have a wife?
2. Why does Syfers want to go back to school? Who should pay for it? How?
3. What kinds of wifely responsibilities are involved in caring for the children?
4. What kinds of physical needs will Syfers's wife be sure to take care of?
5. Is Syfers willing to listen to complaints about a wife's duties? What should a wife be willing to do instead of complaining?
6. What kinds of details should a wife be able to arrange to assure that the partner's social life is satisfactory?
7. How should a wife feel when the partner goes out alone?
8. What sexual attitudes should a wife exhibit to make the partner happy?
9. Is the position of a wife a secure one, according to Syfers?
10. What should the wife do after the partner has finished school?

Topics for Critical Analysis, Discussion, and Writing

1. Examine the author's tone in the article. What is her attitude about wives? Do you think she enjoys being one? Why or why not?

2. Why do you think Syfers wrote this article?

3. Who would want a wife like the one she describes? Who would want to be a wife like this?

4. The term *double standard* is defined as a system or code that is applied unequally; in particular, a stricter code of behavior for one sex than for the other. Find as many examples as you can of a double standard of behavior in the article.

5. Syfers defines *wife* by giving numerous examples of the many tasks and obligations a wife is expected to fulfill. Use the same format, tone, and style to write an extended definition entitled "Why I Want a Husband." Your essay should not use the pronouns *he, his,* or *him.*

Blimps

The Goodyear Tire & Rubber Company

In its extended definition of the technical word blimp, *Goodyear not only gives the dictionary definition, but also the etymology of the word. The article includes a fascinating history of the development and use of lighter-than-air craft. Goodyear uses narration to relate how the blimp came to have its unusual name and classification. The article also uses comparison and contrast to differentiate between the three kinds of airships.*

Of all the words that have entered the English language because of man's development of powered flight, the term "blimp" seems to hold exceptional fascination for etymologists, those **savants** who study the origin and history of words.

A blimp is defined as a non-rigid airship with the shape of its envelope, or bag, entirely maintained by the internal pressure of the lifting gas.

So how did such a flying machine come to be known as a blimp?

For years, The Goodyear Tire & Rubber Company of Akron, Ohio, a pioneer in the production of lighter-than-air craft in the United States, has been telling people that "blimp" is a contraction of the military designation of the World War I British airship known as "Balloon, Type B, limp."

That wasn't just Goodyear's story. It has always been the most popular and widely accepted account of how the word came into being. Even dictionaries list this as the probable origin of the word.

The man who burst the historical bubble—or balloon, if you will—is Dr. A. D. Topping, an expert on the history of lighter-than-air craft. Dr. Topping serves as editor and historian of The Lighter-Than-Air Society, which draws its membership from all over the world. Topping claims that the British never had an airship with a "limp" designation before, during or after World War I, nor did they have anything referred to as "Type B." After considerable research on the subject, the LTA historian says he believes the truth about the origin of the word "blimp" can be found in the pages of the British magazine, *The Aeroplane*. The credit, according to Topping, must go to Lt. (later Air Commodore) A. D. Cunningham of the Royal Navy Air Service, who, in December 1915, was commanding officer of the British airship station at Capel.

On Sunday, December 5, 1915, Lt. Cunningham was conducting his weekly inspection of the airship station. One of his stops was a large shed, or hangar, which housed His Majesty's Airship SS-12 (the SS for Submarine

A cartoon depicting the origin of the word "blimp."

Scout). The shed was constructed with a deep **recess** in the floor to accommodate the airship car, permitting crewmen and others to walk along the floor at the same level as the bag of the airship.

During his inspection of the SS-12, Cunningham broke the **solemnity** of the occasion by playfully **flipping** his thumb at the gasbag. He was rewarded with an odd noise that **echoed** off the **taut** fabric.

Cunningham smiled, then orally imitated the sound that his thumb had drummed out of the airship bag: "Blimp!"

According to the account in *The Aeroplane,* the commanding officer then "**straightened his face**—and so did the midshipman commanding the SS-12, the first airship to be called Blimp."

While the word "blimp" is now common to our language, the type of aircraft which it describes is not. Airships have three classifications: rigid, semi-rigid and non-rigid.

Rigid airships, such as the Graf Zeppelin, the Hindenburg and the Goodyear-built Akron and Macon, had metal frameworks within their envelopes to maintain their shape. The lifting gas was contained in a series of separate cells within these frameworks.

In semi-rigid construction, the airship had a rigid or jointed **keel** which ran the length of the envelope. This keel and the pressure of the lifting gas gave the envelope its shape.

In non-rigid models, such as the Enterprise, Columbia, America and Europa, the envelope shape is maintained entirely by the internal pressure of the lifting gas.

It is equally correct to refer to a blimp as a dirigible, for by definition a dirigible is "a lighter-than-air craft that is engine-driven and steerable." Only a rigid airship is a zeppelin, while blimps, dirigibles and zeppelins all can correctly be called airships.

With the development of the gas-tight bag, the gas valve and other devices, ballooning came into its own in the 19th century. Balloons found great favor as aerial observation posts in the American Civil War and the Franco-Prussian War.

The first power-driven balloon, a 145-foot dirigible, was built in 1851 by French inventor Henri Giffard. Power was supplied by a three-horse-power steam engine.

The first rigid airship, with an interior framework to maintain its shape, was built in 1898 by Austrian David Schwartz. Powered by a 12-horse-power engine with a belt drive, the airship crashed on its maiden flight.

It remained for Count Ferdinand von Zeppelin, a retired German cavalry general, to develop the first practical rigid airship in 1900. His work, until his death in 1917, established Germany as a lighter-than-air power. The industry which he founded produced 115 rigid airships between 1900 and 1918. Many were military ships which terrorized the British Isles with bombing raids during World War I.

Non-rigid airships also came into their own during World War I, along with the familiar, **sausage-shaped** observation and **barrage balloons**. America's first military airship, a non-rigid type, had been built in 1908 by Army Signal Corps Major Thomas S. Baldwin.

Goodyear built its first airship envelope in 1911, a big, 400,000-cubic-foot bag ordered by a lighter-than-air enthusiast named Melvin Vaniman. He planned to fly across the Atlantic Ocean. His attempt proved disastrous. A spark from an engine set fire to a hydrogen-filled bag, plunging the airship into the ocean just off the New Jersey coast. Vaniman and several crewmen were lost.

Goodyear established its reputation as a leader in lighter-than-air during World War I, producing more than 1,000 balloons and approximately 100 non-rigid airships for the Allies.

The most popular period for airships were the years between World War I and World War II when Germany, France, Great Britain and the United States all had rigid airships. Goodyear's fleet of commercial blimps, as many as six operating at one time, also was born during this period. Popularity of airships hit its peak in the 1930's. The global passenger and freight-carrying feats of Germany's Graf Zeppelin and Hindenburg, and the nationwide flights of the Navy's Goodyear-built Akron and Macon captured the imaginations of people the world over.

Goodyear pioneered the use of helium in 1925 when the first of its commercial airships, the Pilgrim, was inflated with *nonflammable* gas. Until that time, hydrogen was the most frequently used lifting agent, but it is highly flammable. A cubic foot of hydrogen can lift about 10 percent more weight than a cubic foot of helium, but the latter has a greater safety advantage.

Popularity of the rigid airships came to an end in the late 1930s with the loss of the Akron, Macon and Hindenburg within a period of 37 months. However, these tragedies were, in part, responsible for the accelerated development of the non-rigid airships, particularly for the Navy.

In spite of this, the Navy had only 10 non-rigid airships in operation when Pearl Harbor was attacked on December 7, 1941. By the end of the war, the Navy had 168 airships in operation. Most of them were constructed by Goodyear. In fact, blimps of Goodyear's commercial fleet also were **"drafted"** into the Navy to serve chiefly as training craft. The Navy airships compiled an astonishing record during the war, especially in the role of aerial escorts for **convoys**.

Goodyear resumed its commercial airship operation after World War II. With the **advent** of the Korean conflict, the Navy once again stepped up its airship operations. The last airships built by Goodyear for the Navy were four huge ZPG-3W type non-rigid airships for use in the early warning defense network. These airships were retired from service by the Navy after more sophisticated early-warning equipment was developed.

A modern blimp.

The Enterprise, based in Pompano Beach, Florida; the America, based in Houston, Texas; and the Columbia, based in Los Angeles, California, are the only lighter-than-air craft known to be operating in the United States today. The Rome-based Europa plies the skies of Western Europe and England.

When you see the Goodyear blimp over the skyline, it is more than likely on a mission to promote **conservation** or other activities in the public interest made at the request of an agency of the government, an environmental group or some civic organization.

Approximately 75 percent of all night sign messages flown by the blimp are public service in nature. These range from conserve energy reminders and gas-saving tips to ecology-oriented messages and the support of worthy causes. And during the daylight hours the ship regularly lends its services to such things as air and noise pollution studies, traffic surveys, marine life aerial studies, projects by law enforcement agencies to improve methods of patrol, or the production of educational television programs.

Each of the airships carries approximately 8,000 passengers annually, a remarkable figure when the limited capacity of only six at one time is considered. The guests who have been for a ride on a Goodyear blimp include presidents, congressmen, city and state officials, astronauts, authors and scientists. Goodyear airships, past and present, have operated for more than five decades without a single passenger fatality.

Glossary

advent *(noun)*   coming; arrival

barrage balloons *(noun)*   numbers of anchored balloons with cables or nets attached to entangle low-flying, attacking airplanes

conservation *(noun)*   official care and protection of natural resources, such as lakes, rivers, and forests

convoys *(noun)*   groups of ships traveling together for mutual protection, usually escorted by protecting warships on the seas (and in these cases, blimps overhead)

drafted *(verb)*   selected for some special use

echoed *(verb)*   repeated or reflected

flipping *(verb)*   moving with a quick jerk; flicking or snapping

keel *(noun)*   chief steel piece extending along the entire length of the airship to support the frame

nonflammable *(adjective)*   not easily set on fire; not readily or quickly burned

recess *(noun)*   hollow place in a flat surface

sausage-shaped *(adjective)*   rounded but elongated in shape

savants *(noun [French])*   learned persons; important scholars

solemnity *(noun)*   seriousness; ceremonial mood; ritual observance

straightened his face *(slang [British])*   erased his smile (in keeping with the serious occasion)

taut *(adjective)*   tightly stretched; strained

Comprehension Questions

1. What is the dictionary definition of *blimp?*

2. How did this lighter-than-air craft come to be known as a blimp?

3. What are the three classifications of airships? Describe the characteristics of each type and explain how each operates.

4. What is a dirigible? What is a zeppelin?

5. What developments allowed ballooning to become popular in the 19th century? What use was made of ballooning during the American Civil War and the Franco-Prussian War?

6. When was the first power-driven balloon built and by whom? What kind of engine was used?

7. Who built the first rigid airship? When? What kind of engine did it have? What happened to the craft?

8. Who developed the first practical rigid airship? When? What was the significance of his work? What was the major application of rigid airships during World War I?

9. Who built the first non-rigid military airship in America? When? What were the main uses of non-rigid airships during World War I?

10. What was the most popular period for airships? What was the role of rigid airships? What happened to the Akron, Macon, and Hindenburg? How did these events affect development of new lighter-than-air craft?

11. How many non-rigid airships did the Navy have in operation when Pearl Harbor was attacked? What was the role of these craft during World War II?

12. What was the intended use of the last airships built by Goodyear for the Navy? What happened to them?

13. What commercial airships are in operation today? Where are they based? What are their main functions?

14. How many passengers are carried annually by each airship? What is the passenger capacity of each craft? What types of passengers have been for blimp rides? What is the safety record of the blimps over the past fifty years?

Topics for Critical Analysis, Discussion, and Writing

1. What is the purpose of the article? Why is the thesis a question? Is it satisfactorily answered? Would you have used this thesis? Does Goodyear give enough facts, details, statistics, and examples to answer your questions? Does the conclusion tie in with the thesis?

2. What is the value of the anecdote about the origin of the word *blimp*? Would the information have been better related in another way? Explain.

3. Blimps are almost an endangered species of aircraft because so few still exist. As you read, blimps today are used mostly for public service activities rather than for military or commercial purposes. Blimps are the dinosaurs of the air and someday will probably disappear altogether, but the story of their development and their uniqueness assures them an important niche in the history of modern aircraft. Using the Goodyear tribute to the blimp as a model, write an extended definition about an endangered species of animal that you would like to have remembered. In January 1985, in the United States alone, the Fish and Wildlife Service listed 823 species in danger of extinction, and extensive efforts are being made by wild life enthusiasts to save many of them. The highly publicized series of attempts by biologists to save the California condor is an example. Many countries have similar lists of endangered species; for instance, the African elephant, Siberian tiger, African gorilla, Peruvian condor, Chinese leopard, and Chinese giant panda.

4. Choose an important technological advance or an unusual invention (such as computers, satellite transmission of communications, nuclear power, robotics, supersonic aircraft, etc.) and write an extended definition about it. Your thesis should state your reason for writing. Give the dictionary definition of your technical term. If the term is a member of a class, differentiate between it and the other members. If the term involves a process, as computers and satellite communications do, explain it. Examine controversial aspects of such terms as nuclear power. If the history of your term is interesting, include it. Be sure your conclusion makes a point that relates to the thesis.

That Purr-fect Pet Might Terrorize Its Way into Your Heart

Jenny Campbell

Jenny Campbell is a newspaper staff writer and artist whose occasional human interest pieces examine subjects common to most readers. Even if you are not a cat lover, you can identify with the accommodations most people make to keep their pets happy. This essay, written as part of a general campaign to convince readers to adopt homeless cats from animal shelters, defines by including many examples of behavior, characteristics, and idiosyncrasies of a typical cat—in other words, how a cat works . . . its way into your home and heart.

There's no such thing as indifference when cats are involved. They're either **nurtured** or hated.

And no other animal can inspire the range of emotions a cat can.

It's already the middle of Adopt-a-Cat month, when shelters and humane societies across the country urge the public to adopt homeless **strays**. And time is running out for prospective adoptive cat-owners. It's time to abandon that **wishy-washiness** before it's too late for Snowball's newborns.

So if you're thinking about picking up a new bundle of fur, but you've never had the pleasure of knowing one before (no one really *owns* a cat), here are a few tips about the species that might help you better understand your new addition.

For one thing, you should know that cats are able to change their weight and size to fit any situation.

You'll find that a 5-pound cat can drape itself over your legs at night and suddenly—miraculously—become a 45-pound mass. It's like falling into **quicksand**, and you may find yourself experiencing nightmares that you've lost the use of your legs.

The cat, of course, is bothered by little. It not only will remain **unperturbed** when you wake up in a panic, but it will resist moving when you kick with your weighted legs. This nighttime exercise, however frustrating, is very good for the old stomach muscles.

You'll also discover that a 15-inch-long cat can curl up next to you, stretch out and become so large that it forces you slowly across your bed until you're sleeping on the outside 4½ inches of your king-size mattress.

On the other hand, you'll be astonished to find that the same cat can reduce itself to the thickness of cardboard to hide in your suitcase when it sees you packing for a trip.

Cats also are supposed to be tremendous climbers.

Reprinted by permission of Pasadena Star-News.

This may be a myth, however. I've had to rescue my own cat from trees, roofs, building ledges, telephone poles and other frighteningly high places. Sometimes I wonder if I suffer from much worse **acrophobia** than my feline friend.

And if they *do* attempt to jump from those **lofty perches**, it's OK, because they always land on their feet, right? Not always. Cats have been known to land on their backs, sides and heads. Being the only animal with an ego, however, they will always act as though they'd done it on purpose, for the drama.

Cats also are adventuresome, and always willing to try new things. I've found my cat, Splat (so named when I lived on a busy street), swinging from the shower curtain **a la Tarzan**; riding on my dog's back as she galloped down the hallway in a panic; and sitting atop the buttons on my **cable TV box**, changing the channels with her hind leg and watching the flashing screen below.

Of course, there are certain disadvantages to owning a cat. For one thing, canned cat food smells worse than just about anything in the world—with the possible exception of a **catbox** left untended for more than 72 hours.

Also, small **tumbleweeds** of cat fur will show up continuously on your dark clothing and furniture. And many cats suffer an inability to distinguish an expensive sofa from a $10 scratching post.

But for the most part, if you decide that now is the time to make one of Snowball's kittens yours, the new pet will no doubt be a **cherished** addition to your home. Contrary to what non-believers will tell you, cats can be very loving, loyal pets; they show their affection in subtle but very significant ways.

So try to think of it as a token of supreme affection when you step on the dead mouse your new pet has laid so carefully next to your bed.

After all, it's only because you're loved.

Glossary

acrophobia *(noun)*   abnormal fear of being in high places

a la Tarzan *(slang)*   in the manner of Tarzan, a character in Edgar Rice Burroughs's novels about a man who was brought up by and lived among the apes in the jungle

cable TV box *(special term)*   special box installed by the subscription television company used with the subscriber's television set to adapt it for cable service

catbox *(noun)*   litter tray, usually filled with a special mixture of diatomaceous earth and deodorants, and used by indoor cats as toilets

cherished *(adjective)*   loved; held dear; protected

lofty *(adjective)* very high

nurtured *(verb)* cared for by providing a beneficial environment (food, affection, comfort, etc.)

perches *(noun)* resting places or positions, especially high ones such as tree branches or roofs

quicksand *(noun)* loose, wet, deep sand which easily engulfs a person, an animal, or an object. Unaided escape or removal is nearly impossible.

strays *(noun)* homeless wanderers

tumbleweeds *(noun)* thistle or similar plants that break off near the ground and then are blown about by the wind

unperturbed *(verb)* not confused; undisturbed

wishy-washiness *(noun, colloquialism)* indecisiveness

Comprehension Questions

1. Why isn't it possible to be indifferent toward cats?
2. What is the purpose of Adopt-a-Cat month? What is the purpose of the article?
3. How does the author explain a cat's ability to change its weight? Is the effect on their human owners good or bad?
4. What are the advantages (for the cat) and disadvantages (for the human) when the cat changes its size?
5. How and why does the cat change its shape?
6. Are cats really good climbers? Explain by relating the author's experiences.
7. Although most people think a cat always lands on its feet when it jumps from heights, Campbell says this is not true. Explain, and describe the cat's reaction.
8. In what ways are cats adventuresome?
9. What are the four major disadvantages of owning a cat?
10. How do cats show their loyalty, love, and affection? Give a specific example.

Topics for Critical Analysis, Discussion, and Writing

1. Rewrite the article as a more traditional extended definition of cats. Include the dictionary definition. Use classification or comparison and contrast to differentiate between various members of the class. Consider narration or process analysis as vehicles for explanation. (Relate an interesting

anecdote or explain how you taught your cat to do something.) Make certain that you have a thesis and a conclusion.

2. The author seems to find more disadvantages than advantages in owning a cat; yet, her tone and concluding paragraphs clearly indicate that she is a cat lover. Explain.

3. Here is a different version of Campbell's article. Compare or contrast the tones and styles of the two versions. Which do you like better? Why? What mood does Campbell's version project that you don't find in this one? Do the two versions contain essentially the same information?

Adopt a stray cat this month to save it from a needless death. If you are unfamiliar with cats, here are some facts about them. Cats are lightweight animals that can seem very heavy when they sleep on your legs. Cats also crowd you when they are allowed to sleep on your bed. And they like to hide in your suitcase when you are packing for a trip. Although cats can climb well, they often don't know how to get back down from high places and they have to be rescued. But they are more adventurous when they are closer to the ground and frequently do naughty things like swinging on the shower curtain or riding on the back of the dog. The disadvantages of cat ownership are putting up with the nasty-smelling cat food and equally odorous catbox, the cat hairs that cling to clothing and furniture, and the damage caused by the cat scratching your furniture. However, all these problems are unimportant because when a cat loves you, it subtly shows its affection by leaving gifts beside your bed. Being loved by a cat is pretty special, so special that you'll be glad you saved a homeless kitten from the jaws of death.

8

Logical Argument: The Heart of Critical Thinking

Of all the writing techniques presented in this text to help you improve your critical skills, *argument* is the most sophisticated. Argument is always based on controversial issues—points, matters, or questions that are disputed or undecided. An argumentative essay requires more than simply stating the thesis, adequately supporting it, and reaching an appropriate conclusion. In addition, you must try to get the reader to accept or even adopt your views about the subject. Use any appropriate form of writing, such as comparison, contrast, definition, description, or cause and effect, to present your argument.

LOGICAL ARGUMENT

Argument is intended to *convince* an opponent to overcome doubts about your side of an issue by offering logical proofs in a reasonable way. The word *logic*, introduced by the ancient Greeks, is still used today to describe the process of correct reasoning used to evaluate any proposition. Plato (c. 428–348 B.C.) and Aristotle (384–322 B.C.) taught their students to think clearly and critically about implications and contradictions of evidence presented in arguments and to use valid *induction* and *deduction* to reach conclusions.

Induction uses many specifics to reach a generalization. For example, if you were a poor hitter in baseball, if you could scarcely return a service in tennis, if you could rarely complete a volley in ping pong, and if you had trouble driving a golf ball, you might *infer* or decide that you are not suited to any sport that requires hitting a ball with a piece of equipment like a bat, racquet, paddle, or club. This generalization might lead you to decline an invitation to play racquetball, even though you had never tried it.

You *think* inductively during prewriting when you link similar or parallel ideas or fit many pieces of evidence together to form some kind of pattern allowing you to reach a generalization or thesis. You can also *write* inductively. For instance, an argument presented to a hostile audience may have a better chance of success if your position is not openly stated in the beginning. But beware! Inductive essays are difficult to write because of the danger of wandering from the subject. Be sure you have a thesis even though you wait until the end to state it. Make each piece of evidence that follows the introduction stronger and more compelling than its predecessor, so that the total accumulation of proof erases the reader's doubts about the merits of your position.

Deduction uses generalities derived from induction as the bases for reasoning. This process is comparative and draws on past experience; for example, since you are not able to hit a golf or tennis ball, you might generalize that you aren't good at ball games of any kind, citing football, soccer, volleyball, handball, and basketball as evidence. From this, a reader may generalize that you are poor at *all* sports. But this logic may be faulty because you may be an excellent swimmer, runner, bicycler, or skier.

This text concentrates on the deductive method of writing an argument by suggesting that essays begin with a preliminary judgment (a thesis or premise) about an issue and conclude with a refined judgment that evaluates the proofs offered in support of the thesis. A good argument should include facts, examples, details, or statistics which can be readily observed by the reader or are attributed to some knowledgeable authority; for example, a hospital emergency room physician who has treated hundreds of automobile accident victims would be a good authority for the argument that both drivers and passengers should fasten seat belts to prevent death or serious injury. Conversely, this physician would be a poor authority to support an argument that everyone should buy a new car every year. An automobile manufacturer would be a more logical choice to supply data for this argument.

The *dialectic method* of argument is based on contrasts. The *thesis* states one position and the *antithesis* the opposite. After each is discussed fully, the *synthesis* (conclusion) reaches a moderate view somewhere between the two extremes. Here is an example of the dialectic method:

I. Citizens have the right to revolt if they believe their taxes are unreasonably high.

II. On the other hand, citizens should realize that they must pay high taxes to provide essential services (street lights, road repairs, police protection, etc.).

III. Citizens should be willing to pay reasonable taxes, but should insist on limits.

Analyzing alternatives is another logical way to argue. This type of argument examines all possible solutions to a particular problem, eliminates undesirable alternatives, and ranks other possibilities in the order of their desirability. Here is an example:

The problem: Several neighbors who live on a short, private street are frequent victims of burglary.

Each family submits one suggestion for the most efficient, practical, and economical way to jointly protect community property. The alternatives are:

1. Killer watchdogs could patrol the neighborhood to frighten and discourage strangers from entering the street.
2. Laser cannons, mounted at the entrance to the street, could be programmed to fire at unauthorized intruders.
3. Armed security guards could patrol the neighborhood twenty-four hours a day.
4. Residents could wire explosives to their valuable items.
5. Burglar alarms with piercing sirens and the capacity to notify police could be installed in all homes.
6. Residents could form a Neighborhood Watch program with the help of the police department.

Analysis of alternatives shows that they range from the truly unworkable to the definitely practical. Killer dogs might attack harmless strangers or even neighborhood children. Laser cannons could fire at innocent people—delivery persons, visitors, and children's playmates. If valuables such as jewelry were wired with explosives, owners might forget to disarm the explosive devices when reaching for necklaces or rings and blow themselves up. Conversely, armed security guards could be given explicit instructions that would allow them to be selective in their methods of protection, but the cost would be prohibitive. Less expensive burglar alarms would cause no physical harm and would call the police for help when an intruder tried to break in, but if an electronic system malfunctioned and caused false alarms, the property owner could be charged a fee for each one. A Neighborhood Watch program would be free of cost, but would be effective only if some of the residents were always at home to call the police if they saw anything suspicious.

Recommendations weigh the pros and cons of the acceptable alternatives. If the neighborhood is deserted for several hours every day when residents are away at work and school, either costly security guards or less expensive alarm systems would be best. But if several adults are usually at home, the Neighborhood Watch would be effective and cheap.

COMMON LOGICAL FALLACIES

Fallacies, or mistakes in logic, are caused by faulty or misleading reasoning. An argument that includes such errors is not sound. There are many, many kinds of logical fallacies. Only the most common are discussed here.

1. *Sweeping generalizations* fail to qualify an assertion that can't possibly apply to the entire population. Often such a statement begins with "All" or "Everyone," but sometimes these words are only implied when the writer or speaker refers to a general class. Here are some examples:

All Americans like hot dogs.

Everyone has a home computer.

Men are stronger than women.

People are so selfish!

Nobody would buy an ugly car like that.

"Some" or "Many" should be used unless the claim truly applies to everyone.

2. *Hasty generalizations* are errors caused by jumping to conclusions (making quick judgments) about an entire group based on a single experience. A restaurant owner who discharged a cook for gross incompetence would be guilty of hasty generalization if he or she then insisted that all cooks were worthless.

3. *Rationalizing* is simply making excuses; for example, "I got a speeding ticket for driving 75 mph in a 35 mph zone on Main Street today. The policeman would have given a warning to an older person, but he cited me because I'm a student." The driver ignores the fact he or she was traveling 40 mph in excess of the speed limit.

4. *Non sequiturs* (Latin for "that which does not follow") occur when a person jumps from a basic premise to a conclusion without explaining the intermediate logic used to reach it; for example, "The Ritz is my favorite restaurant. I always eat at the Savoy." A confused reaction to these seemingly connected, but obviously contradictory, statements is predictable: "I'm sorry, I don't follow your reasoning. If you like the Ritz so much, why do you always eat at the Savoy?" The logical process looks something like this:

The Ritz is my favorite restaurant. (*but*)

The food there is too expensive. (*and/or*)

No one will ever go there with me. (*and/or*)

The Ritz has no parking facilities available. (*and/or*)

Reservations must be made weeks in advance. (*so/therefore*)

I always eat at the Savoy.

Another cause of non sequiturs is failure to show some logical connection between one sentence or clause that is supposed to be the result of another. Examples:

> When Elizabeth Taylor married Richard Burton, she became a British citizen. She owned one of the biggest diamonds in the world. (What's the connection between citizenship and ownership?)

> Richard Nixon liked to eat catsup on his cottage cheese, and he was the first President of the United States to resign his office. (Was his taste in food the cause of his resignation?)

5. *Oversimplifying* applies a simple or incomplete answer to a complex problem. For instance, explaining that health care costs so much in the United States because doctors and hospitals want to make a lot of money is an over-simplification. The explanation fails to take into account that because people are now living much longer, they must expect increased medical costs. Further, doctors fear malpractice suits, so they often order many expensive laboratory tests to support their diagnoses. Finally, health care services pass along to the patients the costs of sophisticated medical equipment and of increasingly expensive malpractice insurance.

6. *False dilemmas* try to block an opponent's recognition of other alternatives that exist. A genuine dilemma allows only two options: it is an "either/or" situation. Neither alternative is acceptable, but one must be chosen. When a salesperson warns parents, "Without a home computer, your kids will never master mathematics," he or she is ignoring the fact that many schools have terminals for children to use, and that most schools have other successful methods for teaching the subject.

7. *Appeals to illegitimate authority* use well-known, important, or respected persons or occupations to "sell" unrelated ideas or products. For example, unidentified physicians endorse filtered cigarettes: "Doctors everywhere testify that Carcinorettes contain less tar than any other cigarette on the market." (Which doctors? No ethical physician would advertise any product.) Here is an *appeal to an irrelevant authority:* "Mary Smith, local veterinarian, supports Joe Doaks for election to the School Board." (What is the connection between veterinary medicine and school administration?)

8. *Ignoring the question* is a technique that pretends to answer an opponent's charges, but actually changes the subject. A politician might state, "In reply to my opponent's criticism that I do not support increasing government benefits for widows and orphans, I want to go on record as advocating that gasoline taxes be used to build a new public swimming pool to benefit the entire community."

9. *Begging the question* tries to prejudice the reader by stating an unproved assumption as if it were a fact. Examples:

"The total lack of morality in this country can be directly traced to the bad influence of television." (Is there really a *total* lack of morality? If there were, would television be its sole cause?)

"The reason our high school graduates can neither read nor write is the weakening of the high school programs in the last two decades." (Can *none* of them read or write?)

"The insane idea that the welfare system should be restructured is causing many problems in Washington, D.C." (Who says the idea is insane?)

10. *Circular argument* restates the initial assumption instead of giving proof. For instance, "Sherlock Holmes was a brilliant detective because he was so intelligent." Since "brilliant" and "intelligent" are synonymous, no cause is given. A valid argument might be that Holmes was a brilliant detective because he understood logic and psychology.

11. *Argument ad hominem* (Latin for "argument to the man") uses false statements that damage the character or reputation of an opponent to distract the audience from the real issues by questioning the opponent's credibility or morals. When politicians use this technique, it is called "mudslinging." A candidate for political office might try to discredit a competitor by stating, "I certainly don't want to say that my opponent is lying on this issue; check the record yourselves." (The implication is that you will agree that he or she is lying once you have seen the facts.)

Closely related to *argument ad hominem* are two commonly used fallacies. The first, *name calling,* uses insults to try to beat down an opponent. For instance, a conservative banker and a liberal social worker might argue angrily over the need to raise taxes to provide more help for the needy. The banker might call the social worker a "radical extremist," which sounds immoderate, unreasonable, and even dangerous. In return, the social worker might call the banker a "Wall Street profiteer," which makes him or her seem greedy and unscrupulous.

The second, *appeal to emotion,* plays on people's fears and feelings. As an example, after World War II, the American mood was vehemently anti-communist. Joseph McCarthy (U.S. Senator from 1946 until 1957) began a series of investigations of the political activities of influential citizens, alleging that they were or had once been communists or communist sympathizers and therefore disloyal to the United States. Many Hollywood writers, directors, and actors were summoned to testify before the Senate Un-American Activities Committee (chaired by McCarthy). Those who protested or resisted the senator's methods because they believed their civil rights were being violated were labeled "communists" or "subversives" even though the charges against them were not proved. Because of fear of guilt by association, many were blacklisted and unable to work in the film industry for years. "McCarthyism" or "McCarthy witch hunt" are still common terms that describe the use of "scare" tactics and name calling to intimidate others. But these names can also be misused to turn others against a person making a just accusation.

12. *Slanting* takes several forms. One is deliberate misrepresentation by making a true statement in such a way that it is misleading. For instance, in the twelfth-century story *The Romance of Tristan and Iseult,* the lovers carry on an adulterous relationship because they have accidentally drunk a love potion. Iseult is married to King Mark (Tristan's uncle). To prove her innocence of deliberate wrongdoing (remember, the potion was the cause of her liaison with Tristan), Iseult undergoes the Ordeal by Iron, a test requiring that she walk nine steps without her hands being burned by the red-hot iron she has to hold in them. She successfully completes this test after swearing an oath that no man except her husband (the king) and the poor beggar (Tristan in disguise) who carried her across the stream had ever held her in his arms. (Iseult isn't lying, is she? Does that mean she is telling the truth?)

The *slanted question* is just as deceiving; for example, "When did you stop cheating on your taxes?". (Maybe you have never done such a thing in your life, but the question suggests that you have always cheated on your taxes and that the speaker is surprised that you have finally stopped.)

Gossip magazines and newspapers frequently use another form of slanting. They attract and deceive readers by quoting out of context or by omitting or rearranging facts; thus, the printed story may be completely different from what actually happened. The next time you are waiting in the check-out line at the supermarket, you might see something like this:

Headline on the magazine cover: PALACE GARDENER REAL FATHER OF BABY PRINCE

The article inside: Because their royal highnesses, the Prince and Princess are required to attend so many state functions, they are often away from home for hours at a time. Although the baby prince is looked after by several devoted nursemaids, he is occasionally left for an hour or so in the care of Hiram Higby, a trusted gardener on the royal estate. While Higby tends to his duties, the baby snoozes in his pram. Higby, who has ten children of his own, jokingly describes himself as "a real dad, all right," and confides to his friends that "I don't mind being a father to one more, especially one as well behaved as the bonny baby prince!"

Here is another example of material taken out of context to mislead the reader: "Edward and Sarah Andrews announced today that they will divorce. Their stormy six-year marriage has been marked by many trial separations. Lawyers for the couple cited irreconcilable differences as the cause of the split. Mrs. Andrews has long been a close friend of Henry Smith, the rich, glamorous playboy." (The last sentence suggests that whatever is going on between Mrs.

Andrews and Mr. Smith is the *real* cause of the "stormy" marriage and its subsequent breakup.)

13. *Faulty causation* totally ignores logic. Chance or coincidence is sometimes mistaken for true cause and effect: "If I hadn't worn my blue dress, Adam would never have asked me to marry him!" (Does he want to marry you or your blue dress?)

Hasty or *sweeping generalizations* fail to consider all evidence before relating cause and effect.

One event may be thought to cause another simply because it occurred first. This is called the *post hoc* fallacy (*post hoc, ergo propter hoc,* Latin for "after this, therefore because of this"): "My mother telephoned me last night while I was cooking dinner, so the meat burned." (Don't blame your mother. You could have removed the meat from the broiler while you were talking to her.) "I went to France last summer; of course, the value of the dollar immediately declined." (Really? Because *you* went abroad?)

Omissions in a chain of causes and effects can be confusing, too. Causal analysis should explain the *why* of any effect. Identify the most immediate cause and work backward to the underlying or ultimate cause (the reverse order may also be used). In a long chain of events, each cause becomes the effect of the deeper cause:

Effect: The engine of my new car overheated and caught fire.

Causes: There was no oil in the engine.   (immediate)

The garage mechanic forgot to replace the drain plug when the oil was changed.   (deeper)

The mechanic was working on three cars at the same time.   (deeper)

Another mechanic was unable to come to work that day; the garage failed to hire a substitute, but tried to get the usual amount of work done.   (ultimate)

PERSUASION

Argument may originate with an opinion about some issue, but it must use sound logic and include proof (facts, examples, statistics, or details) to reach a reliable conclusion and *convince* the reader or listener. On the other hand, persuasion is meant to *convert*. It may use some logic, but it often relies heavily on opinion, emotion, distorted facts, logical fallacies, or unreliable sources.

Most individuals occasionally use their persuasive skills on relatives and friends. However, *propaganda* is a more sophisticated form of persuasion that is regularly used by certain elements of society—governments, elected officials, businesses, non-profit organizations, and others—to promote certain ideas or practices or to defeat opponents. The aim of propaganda is to affect the emotions of audiences to achieve a targeted goal. Our highly developed media communications systems—radio, television, and print—make it easy for propagandists to reach huge numbers of people with their messages, whether they are single one-minute spot announcements on radio or television or well-placed publicity releases or advertisements in newspapers and magazines. As critical thinkers, you should be alert to both obvious and subtle attempts to affect, influence, or direct your ideas, beliefs, or behavior.

In 1937, the Institute for Propaganda Analysis published a list of seven devices that were (and still are) commonly used in propaganda to fool people by distorting logic. Propagandists do not present claims for you to examine intellectually; they send emotional messages for you to act upon. If you become familiar with these seven propaganda devices and understand the logical fallacies they contain, you can easily recognize propaganda.

1. The Name Calling Device (see *argument ad hominem*). Propagandists attach labels to causes or individuals that they wish to discredit. During the Viet Nam War, the labels "hawk" and "dove" were used to show how people felt about the war. Initially, hawks had good motives. They were patriotic. They wanted to halt the spread of communism and were willing to sacrifice American lives and resources to do it. Later, hawks seemed unreasonable and their ideas became increasingly unpopular because they advocated more and more U.S. involvement in the war and seemed to disregard both human and monetary costs. Doves, in the beginning, were soft on communism and unpatriotic. In the end, doves seemed totally reasonable in their demands that the United States end the war to save both American and Vietnamese lives. Other common labels such as "big business," "working people," "special interests," and "women's equality" can be good or bad, depending on who is making the claim and who is listening to it.

2. The Glittering Generalities Device (see *sweeping generalizations* and *hasty generalizations*). This propaganda technique overgeneralizes and arouses emotions, often by using "virtue" (good) and "vice" (bad) words or phrases. Most people find "good" words like *honor, freedom, truth, duty, human right, fair play, social justice, public service, generosity, motherhood,* and *democracy* very appealing because they suggest noble ideals to live by. On the other hand, "bad" words like *human suffering, imperialists, colonialists, Wall Street profiteers,* and *warmongers* produce anger and sometimes violence. Both vice and virtue words may have a wide range of meaning within a specific group.

Here are some excerpts from Woodrow Wilson's speech of April 2, 1917, in which he asked Congress to declare war against Germany. An excerpt from the response of Senator George W. Norris immediately follows. Identify as many vice and virtue words and phrases as possible:

. . . Property can be paid for; the lives of peaceful and innocent people cannot be. The present German submarine warfare against commerce is a warfare against mankind.

It is a war against all nations. American ships have been sunk, American lives taken, in ways which it has stirred us very deeply to learn of, but the ships and people of other neutral and friendly nations have been sunk and overwhelmed in the waters in the same way. There has been no discrimination. The challenge is to all mankind. Each nation must decide for itself how it will meet it. The choice we make for ourselves must be made with a moderation of counsel and temperateness of judgment befitting our character and our motives as a nation. We must put excited feeling away. Our motive will not be revenge or the victorious assertion of the physical might of the nation, but only the vindication of right, of human right, of which we are only a single champion. . . .

Just because we fight without rancor and without selfish object, seeking nothing for ourselves but what we shall wish to share with all free peoples, we shall, I feel confident, conduct our operations as belligerents without passion and ourselves observe. . . . the principles of right and of fair play we profess to be fighting for. . . .

. . . There are, it may be, many months of fiery trial and sacrifice ahead of us. It is a fearful thing to lead this great peaceful people into war, into the most terrible and disastrous of all wars, civilization itself seeming to be in the balance. But the right is more precious than peace, and we shall fight for the things which we have always carried nearest our hearts,— for democracy, for the rights of those who submit to authority to have a voice in their own Governments, for the rights and liberties of small nations, for a universal dominion of right by such a concert of free peoples as shall bring peace and safety to all nations and make the world itself at last free. To such a task we can dedicate our lives and our fortunes, everything that we are and everything that we have, with the pride of those who know that the day has come when America is privileged to spend her blood and her might for the principles that gave her birth and happiness and the peace which she has treasured. God helping her, she can do no other.

Excerpt from the response of Senator George W. Norris of Nebraska:

To whom does the war bring prosperity? Not to the soldier who for . . . $16 per month shoulders his musket and goes into the trench, there to shed his blood and to die if necessary; not to the broken-hearted widow who waits for the return of the mangled body of her husband; not to the mother who weeps at the death of her brave boy; not to the little children who shiver with cold; not to the babe who suffers from hunger; nor to the millions of mothers and daughters who carry broken hearts to their graves. War brings no prosperity to the great mass of common and patriotic citizens. It increases the cost of living of those who toil and those who already must strain every effort to keep soul and body together. War brings prosperity to the stock gambler on Wall Street—to those who are already in possession of more wealth than can be realized or enjoyed. . . .

Their object in having war and in preparing for war is to make money. Human suffering and the sacrifice of human life are necessary, but Wall Street considers only the dollars and the cents. . . . The stock brokers would not, of course, go to war, because the very object they have in bringing on the war is profit, and therefore they must remain in their Wall Street offices in order to share in that great prosperity which they say war will bring. The volunteer officer, even the drafting officer, will not find them. They will be concealed in their palatial offices on Wall Street, sitting behind mahogany desks, covered up with clipped coupons—coupons soiled with the sweat of honest toil, coupons stained with mothers' tears, coupons dyed in the lifeblood of their fellow men.

We are taking a step today that is fraught with untold danger. We are going into war upon the command of gold. We are going to run the risk of sacrificing millions of our countrymen's lives in order that other countrymen may coin their lifeblood into money. And even if we do not cross the Atlantic and go into the trenches, we are going to pile up a debt that the toiling masses that shall come many generations after us will have to pay. Unborn millions will bend their backs in toil in order to pay for the terrible step we are now about to take. We are about to do the bidding of wealth's terrible mandate. By our act we will make millions of our countrymen suffer, . . . and all because we want to preserve the commercial right of American citizens to deliver munitions of war to belligerent nations.

3. The Transfer Device (see *appeals to illegitimate authority*). With this method, the propagandist uses the authority or prestige of an individual or an institution to persuade others to accept an idea, product, or program that is unrelated to the authority's area of expertise. Church groups advocate tax reform. A former vice presidential candidate speaks candidly with her daughter about women's issues as part of a soft drink commercial. Obviously, any concept *appears* more worthy if it is presented or supported by a respected authority.

Symbols, too, are widely used as a visual means of propaganda. Clyde R. Miller, in his article, "How to Detect Propaganda" (Ford and Turpin, *Language in Uniform* [New York: Odyssey, 1967]), points out that "the cross represents the Christian Church. The flag represents the nation. Cartoons featuring Uncle Sam represent a consensus of public opinion. These symbols stir emotions.

At their very sight, with the speed of light, is aroused the whole complex of feelings we have with respect to church or nation. A cartoonist by having Uncle Sam disapprove a budget for unemployment relief would have us feel that the whole United States disapproves relief costs."

4. The Testimonial Device (see *appeals to illegitimate authority*). Testimonials, both positive and negative, are frequently used because people tend to believe that "experience is the best teacher," so when a famous film star, whose appearance shows that he clearly enjoys his food and drink, assures you in rich, mellow tones that a well-known wine maker "sells perfection, not just ordinary wine," you pay attention. But is he worth listening to? Actually, he may know nothing at all about wine making. However, you can be sure he is earning a lot of money for making the commercial. If you want the wine, buy it for that reason, not because of the movie star's pitch. Otherwise, a consumers' research organization is a better source of information about almost all products than the famous men and women employed to advertise them. As for political, social, and economic issues, such as nuclear disarmament, prayer in schools, and import quotas, you are better off to research them yourself before making a decision or judgment. Remember that many testimonials are based on anticipated gain—of money, power, or advantage.

5. The Plain Folks Device (see *hasty generalizations*).   This technique is a favorite of politicians to win your trust and your votes by showing that they are "just like everyone else." How often have you read about or seen news reports showing candidates picnicking with farm families in Iowa, putting on hard hats to inspect a major construction project in New York, or having a Mother's Day dinner with the residents of a retirement home in Florida? Former President Carter used this technique regularly by staying overnight in the homes of "typical" American families when he visited different parts of the country. Commercial ventures do the same thing with "family-owned and produced" products—yogurt, beer, and wine. If individuals (rather than large companies) stand behind the product, somehow it seems safe and good. It is even better if more than one generation seems to be involved—Grandma's Pie Shop or Pop's Orangeade.

6. The Card Stacking Device (see *begging the question, faulty causation, false dilemma, slanting,* and *ignoring the question*).   Card stacking is used intentionally to deceive people so that they will support a cause or ideal in which the propagandist strongly believes or from which he or she will realize financial gain. The device is full of half-truths, outright lies, omissions, and distortions. Certainly, Hitler used card stacking in his campaign to rid Germany and the rest of Europe of Jews. The same technique was used during World War II to explain relocation of American citizens of Japanese ancestry. Sometimes sales representatives are so eager or under so much pressure to make sales that they, too, "load the deck," as in the example of the low-mileage, green and white, ten-year-old used car driven by a little old lady from

Pasadena only once a week to the market six blocks away from her home. It is only after you buy the car that you learn its true past history from its real former owner, Green & White Taxi Co.

7. The Band Wagon Device (see *sweeping generalizations*).   Propagandists employ this device to persuade the masses to buy products, believe ideas, or commit actions. Many people feel more comfortable doing what everybody else is doing than thinking for themselves. Advertisers exert influence by using symbols to illustrate qualities that people admire; for instance, certain expensive makes of automobiles have become status symbols, and people who own them are supposed to be privileged and special, so that you and millions like you want to buy one. Never mind if the car is expensive to repair and in the shop half the time. A more harmful use of this technique is to persuade people to believe and practice certain ideas. Propaganda is used to prejudice people against certain groups on the basis of religion, race, sex, political belief, occupation, etc. For instance, during the women's suffrage movement which culminated in the Nineteenth Amendment to the Constitution, people who spoke out in favor of women's voting rights were vilified in many of the newspapers. Cartoons showed suffragists wrecking homes, destroying the traditional family, and taking over the nation. Finally, propaganda is used to influence people to commit actions. In the 1980 election, voters were warned that they would "throw their votes away" on third-party (Independent) candidate John Anderson; anybody who wanted his or her vote to count was advised to vote for a Democrat (Jimmy Carter) or a Republican (Ronald Reagan).

If you are asked to change your opinion about anything, evaluate the information you are given. Does it include one or more of the seven devices favored by propagandists? If so, remember that it may be intended to pull on your emotions and control your thoughts and actions.

WRITING AN ARGUMENT

When you write an argument, remember that critical thinkers try to see an issue in its broader context rather than in isolation, to use logical proofs to support a position, and to recognize and avoid fallacies and propaganda techniques. Critical thinkers are well-informed about both sides of an issue, understand weaknesses in their own and their opponents' arguments, and recognize points on which a compromise can be reached. An argumentative essay should include the following information:

1. The first paragraph (a) identifies the issue, (b) briefly explains both sides of the argument, and (c) includes a thesis that states the side of the argument the essay defends.
2. Subsequent paragraphs (a minimum of two) develop the argument logically by discussing and using verifiable evidence.

3. The penultimate (next to last) paragraph anticipates (mentions) and refutes counter arguments that opponents might use in reacting to the proofs presented.

4. The concluding paragraph reexamines the essay's position on the issue and reevaluates its correctness. The paper may end with a warning, prediction, or value judgment.

Many sophisticated arguments contain these four elements in combination or in slightly different order, which in no way diminishes their merit. However, until you are skilled at judging the content of your own arguments, use the four point format to double check your writing.

READINGS

Smoking Bans: Meant to Protect or to Force Beliefs on Others?

In 1983, San Francisco voters adopted legislation regulating smoking in offices. In 1985, the Los Angeles City Council passed a law that limits smoking to certain designated areas in all enclosed public places—offices, restaurants, and elevators, for example. The two articles that follow were written before either the San Francisco or the Los Angeles measures were adopted. Lewis C. Solmon and William L. Weis, the authors, are university professors who are authorities on the subject of the rights of individuals in regard to the issue of whether smoking should be allowed in enclosed public places, specifically the workplace. Both authors express their personal views, not necessarily those of the institutions with which they are affiliated. Dr. Solmon, of the Graduate School of Education at the University of California, Los Angeles, is also a consultant to the Tobacco Institute. He opposes prohibition or regulation. Dr. Weis, of the Albers School of Business at Seattle University, has authored many articles about the smoking issue. He favors a strict smoking policy. Evaluate their essays as logical arguments. Note that comprehension questions and topics for critical analysis, discussion, and writing are combined to help you synthesize your findings.

Arguments in Favor of Bans Are Full of Holes

Lewis C. Solmon

In a society where individual freedom of action is a basic right, and where **productivity** is a major concern, laws that make smoking illegal in most enclosed places are **ill-advised**. In the first place, such ordinances may be unenforceable, or enforceable only at great cost—both monetary and social. Second, once the principle of legislating behavior becomes established, where does it stop? Will the Los Angeles City Council next try to reduce heart attacks by passing a law limiting consumption of red meat, which may increase **cholesterol**?

Some might argue that, because of economies of scale in collecting and **disseminating** information, the government would be the logical body to administer measures relating to smoking and health. But the public appears to be well aware of the smoking and health **controversy**. Because consumers are making choices that some believe are a risk to their health does not necessarily imply that they have inadequate knowledge.

We must avoid falling into the trap of thinking that if consumers do not respond to a piece of information, they do not have enough information or do not understand what they have.

Since the practice of smoking has not declined as certain groups would like, they are offering new types of "information" to **foster** such a result. These groups are trying to convince employers that corporate profits will decline (by as much as $4,600 per smoker per year) if smokers are hired. Such arguments are without merit.

It is **alleged** that smokers are absent from work more than nonsmokers. It is not clear, however, that a statistical **correlation** between smoking and absenteeism really exists. But even if it does, the connection between smoking and absenteeism is unproven and improbable. Numerous factors have been associated with absenteeism, including age, sex, family responsibilities, personal problems, use of drugs, type of employment, job responsibilities, job satisfaction and **commuting time**.

More specifically, many studies have reported a higher incidence of smoking among **blue-collar workers** than among **white-collar workers**. Therefore, if relatively low-paid assembly-line workers are more inclined to skip work occasionally than are top executives, a correlation between smoking and absenteeism would be observed. Actually, however, the absenteeism probably would be linked to boredom, lack of commitment to the employer, low pay and so on.

Reprinted by permission of the author. Dr. Lewis C. Solmon is Professor and Associate Dean at the Graduate School of Education at UCLA.

Merely Using Benefit

Unionized workers negotiate a benefits package that includes salary, insurance, vacations and sick leave. To get more of one benefit (e.g., sick leave) implies giving up some of another (e.g., salary). To take advantage of the total benefits package, workers must use what is theirs. Thus, workers tend to use all their vacation time and all their sick leave. If unionized smokers are entitled to more sick leave than are nonunionized managers who smoke less, they will be observed to take more sick days. But this is not the result of smoking. Rather, it is due to the **trade-off** between sick leave and relatively lower wages.

Companies **incur** costs for all benefits they offer, and allowable sick leave is more costly than any other benefit. Workers who take more than their allowable sick leave see their salaries reduced and so they, not their employers, incur the costs. In sum, there is no proof that absenteeism is caused by smoking.

Another claim frequently put forth as a cost of smoking is time lost on the job while smokers put down their pens or tools to light up. This argument assumes that smokers are able to take more leisure time at work than are nonsmokers. But nonsmokers may spend time drinking coffee, **gossiping** or **daydreaming**. And productivity should not be measured by minutes worked per day, but by **output**. It is well-known that work breaks, regardless of how they are spent, can increase total productivity.

Bid to Reorient Behavior

My own studies show that other alleged costs to companies from hiring smokers are equally invalid. This general line of argument is an example of efforts by anti-smoking groups to disseminate faulty information in an attempt to **reorient** behavior in a direction other than the one being chosen by informed citizens.

It has also been argued that workplace smoking bans will improve employee **morale**. Employers who seek **optimal** impact from expenditures to improve morale must determine the costs and benefits of various ways to achieve this goal. Before blindly **implementing** workplace smoking bans, they must ask what is the evidence that this is a more effective means of improving morale than would be **piping in music**, buying new furniture, giving longer coffee breaks to all employees or increasing salaries. Moreover, since about 50 million Americans are smokers, it should be obvious that a smoking ban is bound to offend a substantial portion of any firm's employees.

And, if substantial numbers of workers in a particular trade or profession are excluded from hiring consideration because they smoke, there are **inherent** inefficiencies. The situation, from an economic efficiency perspective, is not different from that which exists when blacks, women or other subgroups are systematically excluded for reasons unrelated to job performance.

It is the job of public officials to make sure that accurate information, not data contrived to foster certain behavior, is available, and then allow firms and individuals to act freely according to their informed **cost-benefit analyses**.

Glossary

alleged *(verb)*   declared; stated positively

blue-collar workers *(noun)*   semiskilled or unskilled industrial workers

cholesterol *(noun)*   fatty deposits that build up in the arteries and block or slow blood circulation

commuting time *(adjective, noun)*   the time spent in traveling back and forth from home to work

controversy *(noun)*   dispute; quarrel; disagreement

correlation *(noun)*   relationship; connection

cost-benefit analyses *(special expression)*   evaluations of relationships between costs to the company and benefits to the employee

daydreaming *(verb)*   having waking, but dreamlike, imaginings or thoughts

disseminating *(verb)*   spreading

foster *(verb)*   promote; stimulate; develop

gossiping *(verb)*   repeating talk or rumors about other people

ill-advised *(adjective)*   unwise

implementing *(verb)*   putting into effect; providing means for carrying out

incur *(verb)*   acquire; take on

inherent *(adjective)*   naturally existing; basic; inborn

morale *(noun)*   confidence; enthusiasm; spirit

optimal *(adjective)*   most favorable or desirable

output *(noun)*   work done or produced

piping in music *(idiom)*   installing a sound system to play recorded music

productivity *(noun)*   production of goods or services that have economic value

reorient *(verb)*   readjust; redirect

trade-off *(noun)*   exchange

white-collar workers *(noun)*   professional or semiprofessional workers

Curbs Give a Boost to Productivity, Morale

William L. Weis

On Tuesday, the voters of San Francisco will decide whether to protect one of the most basic of all civil rights: the right to pursue one's **livelihood** in a safe and healthful environment.

Fortunately, with or without legal **mandate**, a growing number of conscientious employers—including Merle Norman Cosmetics, Unigard Insurance Group and Campbell Soup Co.—are recognizing that **untrammeled** smoking in the workplace constitutes a fundamental conflict with human rights, and they are responding with policies that either **ban** or severely curtail smoking in their organizations. This **trend** toward more and stronger smoking restrictions is certain to continue because of growing awareness of both the **adverse** health effects from working in a smoky environment and the substantial **incremental** costs associated with smoking on the job.

Despite confusion created by tobacco propaganda, no one's rights are **abridged** unreasonably by a smoking ban at the workplace. All employees enjoy the same rights, which are, by reason, restricted to behaviors that do not **infringe upon** the rights of colleagues to a comfortable, healthful work environment. Similar behavioral restrictions apply to singing and whistling on the job (nonhealth-related irritants) and to **using nondesignated unplumbed repositories when nature calls** (both a health **hazard** and irritant). Normal employees comply easily with these behavioral constraints without feeling, in the words of the Tobacco Institute, like "second-class citizens."

Probably the most persuasive evidence arguing in favor of smoking restrictions is the **cumulative** result of several major employee surveys showing that smoking is a prime source of **impaired** morale among workers. **Comprehensive surveys** conducted earlier this year at Pacific Telephone and Pacific Northwest Bell, for example, document that nearly 80% of their employees (both smokers and nonsmokers) want to see smoking either banned or confined to separate smoking areas. Even a majority of smokers at both companies favor a complete ban or separate areas, confirming that the so-called controversy over workplace smoking restrictions is not a **feud** between "anti-smokers" (a term **coined by** the Tobacco Institute) and smokers, but between employees, both smokers and nonsmokers, and the American tobacco industry.

Another reason commonly cited by employers who have already banned or **curtailed** smoking on their premises is that enlightened organizations feel that they should no longer impose on their employees an environment that is known to be **contaminated** by **hazardous** substances. Reasonable men and

Reprinted by permission of the author. Dr. William L. Weis is Associate Professor at the Albers School of Business at Seattle University.

women now recognize that involuntary smoking (i.e., breathing smoke of one's co-worker) is a serious health hazard and that forcing employees to assume that hazard is an **unconscionable** accommodation to a minority of the work force. (Government reports indicate that an estimated 31% of employed Americans smoke.)

Employers who have imposed workplace bans have, for the most part, been especially sensitive to the problems encountered by smokers when faced with temporary withdrawal from a very powerful drug addiction (nicotine, according to U.S. Surgeon General C. Everett Koop, is the most addictive drug in the United States). But the mandate to protect employees from exposure to a **toxic** substance **supersedes** the desire to accommodate an addictive behavior in the workplace, when that behavior threatens the health and comfort of co-workers.

Perhaps the reason cited least often for restricting or prohibiting smoking in the workplace—but, **paradoxically**, a reason that has attracted considerable interest in the popular press—is to take advantage of the substantial cost savings available to a smoke-free business. Employers who have implemented strong smoking policies—policies that ban smoking on company premises *and* restrict hiring to applicants who agree to be nonsmokers during working hours—are reporting positive and **envious** productivity effects from the smoking restrictions.

These benefits accrue from such factors as lower rates of absenteeism and **turnover**; reduced costs for fire, life, industrial accident and health insurance; lower expenditures for routine cleaning and maintenance, property damage and equipment and furniture replacement; greatly reduced rates of working-age **mortality** and early retirement; elimination of a major drain on employee efficiency—the frequent informal smoke break, and reduced risk of costly **litigation** initiated by employees whose health is damaged by working in a smoky environment.

These factors alone can deliver cost savings measurable in terms of thousands of dollars per smoker per year to an organization that becomes totally smoke-free. Nevertheless, the most important benefit of a workplace smoking policy is enhanced employee morale. The direct costs associated with workplace smoking are collectively **dwarfed** by the indirect costs owing to impaired morale when employees are forced to tolerate what most believe today is an unjust, if not inhuman, imposition of irritating and toxic air contamination in their work areas.

Impediment to Sales

The trend toward workplace bans is considered by the tobacco industry to be a major **catalyst** in **eroding** the social acceptability of smoking, and hence an **impediment** to tobacco sales. The industry's argument bridges **absurdity** with **vulgarity**. On the absurd side, it states that higher absenteeism is a cost-free factor for businesses, since sick-leave benefits are a fixed component of employee compensation packages. Economists whose thinking extends beyond grammar school analysis recognize that excess rates of absenteeism, regardless of the structure of sick-leave benefits, represent an incremental cost of doing business, if only from necessitating an **inflated** work force.

Moving toward vulgarity, the industry enlists a **debased**, Tobacco Institute tactic by stating that refusing to hire smokers constitutes a situation that "is not different from that which extends when women, blacks or other subgroups are systematically excluded for reasons unrelated to job performance."

Not different? Employment discrimination on the basis of sex and race is illegal in this country, and immoral to most of its citizens. Selective hiring based on achieved qualities, on the other hand, is both expected and considered vital in a competitive economy. For the tobacco industry to **trivialize** the moral **depravity** of racism and sexism is a **vile affront** to every American who has been a victim of racial and sexual prejudice, and to every individual with a moral conscience.

The San Francisco ordinance, should it become law, will neither convey nor withdraw **preferential rights**. It will merely guarantee that all employees who wish to work in a safe, smoke-free environment will be entitled to that basic right.

Regardless of legal mandate, many enlightened, conscientious business organizations now have or are planning a strict smoking policy. Smoking is no longer considered an appropriate behavior in most professional work environments, and that attitude is extending rapidly to other work settings where employee health, morale and productivity are deemed more important than accommodating addictive behavior.

Glossary

abridged *(verb)*   reduced; shortened; lessened

absurdity *(noun)*   foolishness; nonsense

adverse *(adjective)*   unfavorable; harmful

affront *(noun)*   insult; offense

ban *(noun)*   prohibition; order forbidding something

catalyst *(noun)*   agent acting as a stimulus in bringing about some result

coined by *(verb)*   made up or invented by

comprehensive surveys *(adjective, noun)*   detailed studies including or dealing with all of the relevant or important details

contaminated *(verb)*   polluted; made impure; infected

cumulative *(adjective)*   increasing in effect

curtailed *(verb)*   reduced the amount permitted

debased *(adjective)*   lowered in value, dignity, or quality; cheapened

depravity *(noun)*   corruption; wickedness

dwarfed *(verb)*   made smaller

envious *(adjective, obsolete)*   enviable; so good that others are jealous

eroding *(verb)*   causing gradual deterioration of

feud *(noun)*   bitter quarrel that lasts a long time

hazard *(noun)*   risk; danger

hazardous *(adjective)*   dangerous; risky; perilous

impaired *(adjective)*   damaged; weakened; worsened; reduced

impediment *(noun)*   obstruction

incremental *(adjective)*   increased. In mathematics, the quantity by which a variable increases is called an increment.

infringe upon *(verb)*   break in on; trespass on

inflated *(adjective)*   swollen; enlarged; increased beyond normal

litigation *(noun)*   processes of carrying on lawsuits

livelihood *(noun)*   means of living

mandate *(noun)*   order; command

mortality *(noun)*   death (rates)

paradoxically *(adverb)*   seemingly contradictory to common belief

preferential rights *(adjective, noun)*   rights that confer special privileges or advantages on a certain group

supersedes *(verb)*   takes the place of; replaces

toxic *(adjective)*   poisonous

trend *(noun)*   general tendency; inclination

trivialize *(verb)*   treat as unimportant

turnover *(noun)*   number of new workers hired to replace those who have left during a given period of time

unconscionable *(adjective)*   not guided by conscience; unscrupulous; unreasonable; immoral

using nondesignated, unplumbed repositories when nature calls *(colloquialism)*   using toilets that are not marked as to which sex may use them and that have no connections to incoming water or outgoing sewer pipes

untrammeled *(adjective)*   unrestrained; unconfined; uncontrolled

vile *(adjective)*   evil; wicked; sinful; degrading; repulsive; disgusting

vulgarity *(noun)*   lack of sensitivity, culture, refinement, and good taste

Comprehension Questions

1. What is the issue? What is Solmon's position? What position does Weis take?

2. Every citizen is entitled to individual freedom of action—unless that freedom takes away someone else's basic rights. How does each author use the idea of basic freedom to support the ideas in his essay?

3. Solmon says that smokers are well aware of the health dangers that government studies have linked to smoking, but they choose to take the risk and smoke anyway. What is Weis's response? Is the risk assumed solely by the smokers?

4. Does Solmon agree that smokers are absent from work more often than nonsmokers? What type of worker does he say has a higher incidence of smoking? How does this relate to the type of work done? Why does Solmon say workers use all their sick leave benefits if they are not really sick? Employee absenteeism costs the company money, Solmon says. What kinds of activities cause employees to lose time on the job? Who pays for the time loss?

5. Does Weis agree with Solmon that when employees use their sick leave benefits, the employer doesn't have additional expense because sick leave is a fixed cost? What does Weis mean when he says excessive absenteeism causes the work force to be inflated? Who pays for this?

6. Weis states that employers save a substantial amount of money when smoking is not permitted in the workplace. What kinds of direct costs are reduced? Does Solmon agree that it costs the employer more to employ smokers than nonsmokers? Why does he say people use this kind of argument?

7. Both authors discuss preferential hiring (hiring only nonsmokers). Does Weis agree with Solmon's position that excluding smokers from the work force is the same as excluding blacks, women, or other subgroups for reasons unrelated to job performance? Explain.

8. Do Solmon and Weis differ on whether a smoking ban will improve employee morale in the workplace? Explain their positions.

9. What percentage of employed Americans smoke? Why is this figure important in evaluating the argument?

10. Both essays begin with a discussion of basic rights. Do the authors get back to this concept in their conclusions?

Topics for Critical Analysis, Discussion, and Writing

1. Identify the four points of argument in each essay. (Remember that the first point names the issue, briefly mentions each side, and includes a thesis that takes a position relating to one side or the other.)

2. Evaluate the credibility of each author as an authority on the subject of smoking in the workplace.

3. Examine the tone (attitude) of each author. What kind of language is used by each? Why?

4. Discuss the evidence used by each author to support his position. Identify any logical fallacies or propaganda techniques that you believe are used to get the message across.

5. Argue for or against smoking bans in the workplace. Use evidence from the Solmon or Weis articles to support your position. Identify your sources in the essay; for example:

> Weis states that "an estimated 31% of employed Americans smoke," an important fact in determining whether a smoking ban would cause extreme hardship.

> According to Solmon, "many studies have reported a higher incidence of smoking among blue-collar workers then among white-collar workers," but he believes it is impossible to correlate absenteeism and smoking.

6. Write an argument in which you defend or attack smoking in one of the following situations: (a) in restaurants; (b) on commercial airliners; (c) on city buses; (d) in hospitals; (e) in any public waiting area; for example, a ticket line at the movies.

We Should Cherish Our Children's Freedom to Think

Kie Ho

Kie Ho, who grew up in Indonesia and is now a Southern California business executive, argues in the following article that the educational system in the United States is the best in the world because it teaches students to think and to experiment with ideas. The author criticizes educational systems that rely solely on memorization and rote learning, because those methods stifle creative impulses. As you read the article, compare or contrast the educational system of your country with that of the United States.

Americans who remember "the good old days" are not alone in complaining about the educational system in this country. Immigrants, too, complain, and with more up-to-date comparisons. Lately I have heard a Polish refugee

This article first appeared in the *Los Angeles Times*.

express dismay that his daughter's high school has not taught her the difference between Belgrade and Prague. A German friend was furious when he learned that the mathematics test given to his son on his first day as a freshman included multiplication and division. A Lebanese boasts that the average high-school graduate in his homeland can speak fluently in Arabic, French and English. Japanese businessmen in Los Angeles send their children to private schools staffed by teachers imported from Japan to learn mathematics at Japanese levels, generally considered at least a year more advanced than the level here.

But I wonder: If American education is so tragically inferior, why is it that this is still the country of **innovation**?

I think I found the answer on an **excursion** to the Laguna Beach Museum of Art, where the work of schoolchildren was on exhibit. Equipped only with colorful yarns, foil paper, felt pens and crayons, they had transformed simple paper lunch bags into, among other things, a waterfall with flying fish, **Broom Hilda the witch** and a house with a woman in a **skimpy** bikini hiding behind a swinging door. Their public school had provided these children with opportunities and direction to fulfill their creativity, something that people tend to dismiss or take for granted.

When I was 12 in Indonesia, where education followed the Dutch system, I had to memorize the names of all the world's major cities, from Kabul to Karachi. At the same age, my son, who was brought up a Californian, thought that Buenos Aires was Spanish for good food—a plate of tacos and burritos, perhaps. However, unlike his counterparts in Asia and Europe, my son had studied *creative* geography. When he was only 6, he drew a map of the route that he traveled to get to school, including the streets and their names, the buildings and traffic signs and the houses that he passed.

Disgruntled American parents forget that in this country their children are able to experiment freely with ideas; without this they will not really be able to think or to believe in themselves.

In my high school years, we were models of dedication and obedience; we sat to listen, to answer only when asked, and to give the only correct answer. Even when studying word forms, there were no alternatives. In similes, pretty lips were *always* as red as sliced pomegranates, and beautiful eyebrows were *always* like a parade of black clouds. Like children in many other countries in the world, I simply did not have a chance to choose, to make decisions. My son, on the contrary, told me that he got a good laugh—and an A—from his teacher for concocting "the man was as nervous as **Richard Pryor** at a **Ku Klux Klan** convention."

There's no doubt that American education does not meet high standards in such basic skills as mathematics and language. And we realize that our youngsters are ignorant of Latin, put Mussolini in the same category as Dostoevski, cannot recite the **Periodic Table** by heart. Would we, however, prefer to stuff the developing little heads of our children with hundreds of geometry problems, the names of rivers in Brazil and 50 lines from "The Canterbury Tales"? Do we really want to **retard** their impulses, frustrate their opportunities for self-expression?

When I was 18, I had to memorize Hamlet's "To be or not to be" soliloquy flawlessly. In his English class, my son was assigned to write a love letter to Juliet, either in Shakespearean **jargon** or in modern **lingo**. (He picked the latter; his Romeo would take Juliet to an arcade for a game of **Donkey Kong**.)

Where else but in America can a history student take the role of Lyndon Johnson in an open debate against another student playing Ho Chi Minh? It is unthinkable that a youngster in Japan would dare to do the same regarding the role of Hirohito in World War II.

Critics of American education cannot grasp one thing, something that they don't truly understand because they are never deprived of it: freedom. This most important measurement has been omitted in the studies of the quality of education in this century, the only one, I think, that extends even to children the license to freely speak, write and be creative. Our public education certainly is not perfect, but it is a great deal better than any other.

Glossary

Broom Hilda the witch *(special expression)*   comic strip character

disgruntled *(adjective)*   discontented; displeased

Donkey Kong *(special term)*   video game

excursion *(noun)*   short pleasure trip

innovation *(noun)*   introduction of new methods, customs, or devices

jargon *(noun)*   language or dialect (Shakespeare's time was 1564–1616)

Ku Klux Klan *(special term)*   secret organization of white men begun in the South after the Civil War to maintain white supremacy

lingo *(noun)*   language or dialect

Periodic Table *(special term)*   the arrangement of the chemical elements according to their atomic numbers

retard *(verb)*   slow the advance of; hinder; delay

Richard Pryor *(noun)*   black male film actor

skimpy *(adjective)*   not quite large enough in size

Comprehension Questions

1. What are some of the complaints of immigrants about the educational system in the United States? What do parents want their children to learn?

2. What kinds of innovation did the author observe on a visit to an art museum? Why were the exhibits important?

3. What educational techniques were stressed in Indonesia? How did they differ from American educational methods?

4. What happens to children who are not able to experiment freely with ideas? How important is choice in the educational system?

5. The author concedes that "American education does not meet high standards in such basic skills as mathematics and language," but states that "it is a great deal better than any other." How can you explain this apparent contradiction?

Topics for Critical Analysis, Discussion, and Writing

1. How well-qualified is the author to evaluate the educational system of the United States in relation to those of other countries?

2. Identify the four points of argument in the article. Are any of them combined? What is the result?

3. Discuss the evidence (the visit to the museum, the author's own and his son's chidhood experiences, examples from literature and other cultures) given in support of the thesis. What do they suggest about the author?

4. Argue for or against the following statement:

The American educational system is better than any other for preparing students to enter colleges and universities.

Make up a study sheet comparing and contrasting the American system with your own. Based on your findings, take a position and defend your thesis.

5. A critical thinker is able to see an individual problem within a broader context. Does Ho do this? Explain.

Tolerance and Truth in America

Edward M. Kennedy

The following is an excerpt from Senator Kennedy's remarks at Liberty Baptist College on October 3, 1983. Kennedy, a liberal Democrat who has represented the state of Massachusetts in the Congress for many years, was surprised when he mistakenly received a computer-generated membership card for Dr. Jerry Falwell's ultraconservative Moral Majority. Since Kennedy's and Falwell's ideas are in direct opposition, the Senator was again surprised when, after the incident was reported to the press, he was told to keep the card and was invited to speak sometime at Liberty Baptist College. In turn, Falwell and his Moral Majority were surprised when the Senator quickly accepted the invitation.

Kennedy's speech was delivered to a full house—the entire student body was required to attend—and took as its major theme the necessity for separation of church and state, which is required by the Constitution. The Senator also focused on the need for recognition of basic truths and for tolerance of the beliefs of others in order to "ensure that no one is ever denied his or her personal rights and freedoms."

I have come here to discuss my beliefs about faith and country, **tolerance** and truth in America. I know we begin with certain disagreements; I strongly suspect that at the end of the evening some of our disagreements will remain. But I also hope that tonight and in the months and years ahead, we will always respect the right of others to differ—that we will never lose sight of our own **fallibility**—that we will view ourselves with a **sense of perspective** and a sense of humor. After all, in the New Testament, even the **disciples** had to be taught to look first to the beam in their own eyes, and only then to the **mote** in their neighbor's eye.

I am mindful of that **counsel**. I am an American and a Catholic; I love my country and treasure my faith. But I do not assume that my **conception** of patriotism or policy is invariably correct—or that my convictions about religion should command any greater respect than any other faith in this **pluralistic** society. I believe there surely is such a thing as truth, but who among us can claim a **monopoly** on it?

There are those who do, and their own words testify to their intolerance. For example, because the Moral Majority has worked with members of different denominations, one Fundamentalist group has denounced Dr. Falwell for **hastening** the **ecumenical** church and for "**yoking** together with Roman Catholics, Mormons, and others." I am relieved that Dr. Falwell does not

This speech was given by Senator Edward M. Kennedy at Liberty Baptist College on October 3, 1983.

regard that as a sin—and on this issue, he himself has become the target of narrow prejudice. When people agree on public policy, they ought to be able to work together, even while they worship in **diverse** ways. For truly we are all yoked together as Americans—and the yoke is the happy one of individual freedom and mutual respect.

But in saying that, we cannot and should not turn aside from a deeper, more pressing question—which is whether and how religion should influence government. A generation ago, a presidential candidate had to prove his independence of undue religious influence in public life—and he had to do so partly at the insistence of **Evangelical Protestants**. John Kennedy said at that time: "I believe in an America where there is no (religious) **bloc** voting of any kind." Only twenty years later, another candidate was appealing to an evangelical meeting as a religious bloc. Ronald Reagan said to 15 thousand evangelicals at the roundtable in Dallas: "l know that you can't endorse me. I want you to know that I endorse you and what you are doing."

To many Americans, that pledge was a sign and a symbol of a dangerous breakdown in the separation of church and state. Yet this principle, as vital as it is, is not a simplistic and rigid command. Separation of church and state cannot mean an absolute separation between moral principles and political power. The challenge today is to recall the origin of the principle, to define its purpose, and refine its application to the politics of the present.

The founders of our nation had long and bitter experience with the state as both the agent and the **adversary** of particular religious views. In colonial Maryland, Catholics paid a double land tax, and in Pennsylvania they had to list their names on a public roll—an ominous precursor of the first Nazi laws against the Jews. And Jews in turn faced discrimination in all the thirteen original colonies. Massachusetts exiled Roger Williams and his congregation for **contending** that civil government had no right to enforce the Ten Commandments. Virginia **harassed** Baptist **preachers**—and also established a religious test for public service, writing into the law that no "Popish followers" could hold any office.

But during the Revolution, Catholics, Jews and non-conformists all **rallied** to the cause and fought **valiantly** for the American **commonwealth**—for John Winthrop's "city upon a hill." Afterwards, when the Constitution was ratified and then amended, the **framers** gave freedom for all religion—and from any established religion—the very first place in the Bill of Rights.

Indeed the framers themselves professed very different faiths—and in the case of Benjamin Franklin, hardly any at all. Washington was an **Episcopalian**, Jefferson a **Deist**, and Adams a **Calvinist**. And although he had earlier opposed toleration, John Adams later contributed to the building of Catholic Churches—and so did George Washington. Thomas Jefferson said his proudest achievement was not the Presidency, or writing the Declaration of Independence, but drafting the Virginia **Statute** of Religious Freedom. He stated the vision of the first Americans and the First Amendment very clearly: "The God who gave us life gave us liberty at the same time."

The separation of church and state can sometimes be **frustrating** for women and men of deep religious faith. They may be tempted to misuse government in order to **impose** a value which they cannot persuade others to accept. But once we succumb to that temptation, we **step onto a slippery slope** where everyone's freedom is at risk. Those who favor **censorship** should recall that one of the first books ever burned was the first English translation of the Bible. As President Eisenhower warned in 1953, "Don't join the bookburners . . . The right to say ideas, the right to record them, and the right to have them **accessible** to others is unquestioned—or this isn't America." And if that right is denied, at some future day the **torch** can be turned against any other book or any other belief. Let us never forget: Today's Moral Majority could become tomorrow's **persecuted** minority.

The danger is as great now as when the founders of the nation first saw it. In 1789, their fear was of **factional strife** among dozens of denominations. Today there are hundreds—and perhaps thousands of faiths—and millions of Americans who are outside any **fold**. Pluralism obviously does not and cannot mean that all of them are right; but it does mean that there are areas where government cannot and should not decide what it is wrong to believe, to think, to read and to do. As Professor Laurence Tribe, one of the nation's leading constitutional scholars has written, "Law in a **nontheocratic state** cannot measure religious truth"—nor can the state impose it.

The real **transgression** occurs when religion wants government to tell citizens how to live **uniquely** personal parts of their lives. The failure of **prohibition** proves the **futility** of such an attempt when a majority or even a substantial minority happens to disagree. Some questions may be **inherently** individual ones or people may be sharply divided about whether they are. In such cases—cases like Prohibition and abortion—the proper role of religion is to appeal to the conscience of the individual, not the **coercive power** of the state.

But there are other questions which are inherently public in nature, which we must decide together as a nation, and where religion and religious values can and should speak to our common conscience. The issue of nuclear war is a compelling example. It is a moral issue; it will be decided by government, not by each individual; and to give any effect to the moral values of their **creed**, people of faith must speak directly about public policy. The Catholic bishops and the Reverend Billy Graham have every right to stand for the **nuclear freeze**—and Dr. Falwell has every right to stand against it.

There must be standards for the exercise of such leadership—so that the obligations of belief will not be **debased** into an opportunity for mere political advantage. But to take a stand at all when a question is both properly public and truly moral is to stand in a long and honored tradition. Many of the great evangelists of the 1800's were in the forefront of the **abolitionist movement**.

In our own time, the Reverend William Sloane Coffin challenged the morality of the war in Vietnam. Pope John XXIII renewed the gospel's call to social justice. And Dr. Martin Luther King, Jr., who was the greatest **prophet** of this century, awakened our national conscience to the evil of **racial segregation**.

Their words have blessed our world. And who now wishes they had all been silent? Who would bid Pope John Paul to quiet his voice about the oppression in Eastern Europe; the violence in Central America; or the crying needs of the landless, the hungry, and those who are tortured in so many of the dark political prisons of our time?

President Kennedy, who said that "No religious body should seek to impose its will," also urged religious leaders to state their views and give their commitment when the public **debate** involved **ethical issues**. In **drawing the line between imposed will and essential witness**, we keep church and state separate—and at the same time, we recognize that the City of God should speak to the civic duties of men and women.

There are four tests which draw that line and define the difference.

First, we must respect the **integrity** of religion itself.

People of **conscience** should be careful how they deal in the word of their Lord. In our own history, religion has been falsely **invoked** to **sanction** prejudice and even slavery, to condemn labor unions and public spending for the poor. I believe that the prophecy—"The poor you have always with you" is an **indictment**, not a commandment. I respectfully suggest that God has taken no position on the Department of Education—and that a balanced budget constitutional amendment is a matter for economic analysis, not heavenly appeals.

Religious values cannot be excluded from every public issue—but not every public issue involves religious values. And how ironic it is when those very values are denied in the name of religion—for example, we are sometimes told that it is wrong to feed the hungry—but that mission is an explicit **mandate** given to us in the 25th chapter of **Matthew**.

Second, we must respect the independent judgments of conscience.

Those who proclaim moral and religious values can offer counsel, but they should not casually treat a position on a public issue as a test of **fealty** to faith. Just as I disagree with the Catholic bishops on **tuition tax credits**—which I oppose, so other Catholics can and do disagree with the **hierarchy**, on the basis of honest conviction, on the question of the nuclear freeze.

Thus, the controversy about the Moral Majority arises not only from its views, but from its name—which, in the minds of many, seems to imply that only one set of public policies is moral—and only one majority can possibly be right. Similarly, people are and should be **perplexed** when the religious **lobbying group** Christian Voice publishes a **Morality Index** of congressional voting records—which judges the morality of senators by their attitude toward Zimbabwe and Taiwan.

Let me offer another illustration. Dr. Falwell has written—and I quote:

"To stand against Israel is to stand against God." Now there is no one in the Senate who has stood more firmly for Israel than I have. Yet I do not doubt the faith of those on the other side. Their error is not one of religion, but of policy—and I hope to persuade them that they are wrong in terms of both America's interest and the justice of Israel's cause.

Respect for conscience is most in **jeopardy**—and the harmony of our diverse society is most at risk—when we re-establish, directly or indirectly, a religious test for public office. That **relic** of the colonial era, which is specifically prohibited in the Constitution, has reappeared in recent years. After the last election, the Reverend James Robison warned President Reagan not to surround himself, as Presidents before him had, "with the counsel of the ungodly." I utterly reject any such standard for any position anywhere in public service. Two centuries ago, the victims were Catholics and Jews. In the 1980's, the victims could be atheists; in some other day or decade, they could be the members of the Thomas Road Baptist Church. Indeed, in 1976 I regarded it as unworthy and un-American when some people said or hinted that Jimmy Carter should not be President because he was a **Born Again Christian**. We must never judge the fitness of individuals to govern on the basis of where they worship, whether they follow Christ or Moses, whether they are called "Born Again" or "ungodly." Where it is right to apply moral values to public life, let all of us avoid the temptation to be self-righteous and absolutely certain of ourselves. And if that temptation ever comes, let us recall Winston Churchill's humbling description of an intolerant and inflexible colleague: "There but for the grace of God—goes God."

Third, in applying religious values, we must respect the integrity of public debate.

In that debate, faith is no substitute for facts. Critics may oppose the nuclear freeze for what they regard as moral reasons. They have every right to argue that any negotiation with the Soviets is wrong—or that any **accommodation** with them sanctions their crimes—or that no agreement can be good enough and therefore all agreements only increase the chance of war. I do not believe that, but it surely does not violate the standard of fair public debate to say it.

What does violate that standard, what the opponents of the nuclear freeze have no right to do, is to assume that they are **infallible**—and so any argument against the freeze will do, whether it is false or true.

The nuclear freeze proposal is not **unilateral**, but **bilateral**—with equal restraints on the United States and the Soviet Union.

The nuclear freeze does not require that we trust the Russians, but demands full and effective **verification**.

The nuclear freeze does not concede a Soviet lead in nuclear weapons, but recognizes that human beings in each great power already have in their fallible hands the overwhelming capacity to remake into a pile of radioactive **rubble** the earth which God has made.

There is no morality in the mushroom cloud. The black rain of nuclear ashes will fall alike on the just and unjust. And then it will be too late to wish that we had done the real work of this atomic age—which is to seek a world that is **neither red nor dead**.

I am perfectly prepared to debate the nuclear freeze on policy grounds, or **moral** ones. But we should not be forced to discuss **phantom** issues or false charges. They only **deflect** us from the urgent task of deciding how best to prevent a planet divided from becoming a planet destroyed.

And it does not advance the debate to contend that the arms race is more divine punishment than human problem—or that in any event, the final days are near. As Pope John said two decades ago, at the opening of the second Vatican Council: "We must beware of those who burn with **zeal**, but are not **endowed with** much sense . . . We must disagree with the prophets of doom, who are always forecasting disasters, as though the end of the earth was at hand."

The message which echoes across the years since then is clear: The earth is still here; and if we wish to keep it, a prophecy of doom is no alternative to a policy of arms control.

Fourth and finally, we must respect the motives of those who exercise their right to disagree.

We sorely test our ability to live together if we too readily question each other's integrity. It may be harder to restrain our feelings when moral principles are at stake—for they go to the deepest **wellsprings** of our being. But the more our feelings diverge, the more deeply felt they are, the greater is our obligation to grant the sincerity and essential decency of our fellow citizens on the other side.

Those who favor **E.R.A.** are not "anti-family" or "**blasphemers**" and their purpose is not "an attack on the Bible." Rather we believe this is the best way to fix in our national **firmament** the ideal that not only all men, but all people are created equal. Indeed, my mother—who strongly favors E.R.A.— would be surprised to hear that she is anti-family. For my part, I think of the amendment's opponents as wrong on the issue, but not as lacking in moral character.

I could multiply the instances of name-calling, sometimes on both sides. Dr. Falwell is not a "**warmonger**"—and "liberal clergymen" are not, as the Moral Majority suggested in a recent letter, equivalent to "Soviet sympathizers." The critics of official prayer in public schools are not "**Pharisees**"; many of them are both **civil libertarians** and believers, who think that families should pray more at home with their children, and attend church and **synagogue** more faithfully. And people are not "sexist" because they stand against abortion; they are not "murderers" because they believe in free choice. Nor does it help anyone's cause to shout such **epithets**—or try to shout a speaker down—which is what happened last April when Dr. Falwell was hissed and **heckled** at Harvard. So I am doubly grateful for your courtesy here today. That was not Harvard's finest hour, but I am happy to say that the loudest applause from the Harvard audience came in defense of Dr. Falwell's right to speak.

In short, I hope for an America where neither **fundamentalist** nor **humanist** will be a dirty word, but a fair description of the different ways in which people of good will look at life and into their own souls.

I hope for an America where no president, no public official, and no individual will ever be deemed a greater or lesser American because of religious doubt—or religious belief.

I hope for an America where the power of faith will always burn brightly—but where no **modern inquisition** of any kind will ever light the fires of fear, coercion, or angry division.

I hope for an America where we can all contend freely and vigorously—but where we will treasure and guard those standards of **civility** which alone make this nation safe for both democracy and diversity.

Twenty years ago this fall, in New York City, President Kennedy met for the last time with a Protestant assembly. The atmosphere had been transformed since his earlier address during the 1960 campaign to the Houston Ministerial Association. He had spoken there to allay suspicions about his Catholicism—and to answer those who claimed that on the day of his baptism, he was somehow disqualified from becoming President. His speech in Houston and then his election drove that prejudice from the center of our national life. Now, three years later, in November, 1963, he was appearing before the Protestant Council of New York City to reaffirm what he regarded as some fundamental truths. On that occasion, John Kennedy said: "The family of man is not limited to a single race or religion, to a single city or country . . . The family of man is nearly 3 billion strong. Most of its members are not white—and most of them are not Christian." And as President Kennedy reflected on that reality, he restated an ideal for which he had lived his life—that "the members of this family should be at peace with one another."

That ideal shines across all the generations of our history and all the ages of our faith, carrying with it the most ancient dream. For as the apostle Paul wrote long ago in **Romans**: "If it be possible, as much as it **lieth** in you, live peaceably with all men."

I believe it is possible; the choice lies within us; as fellow citizens, let us live peaceably with each other; as fellow human beings, let us strive to live peaceably with men and women everywhere. Let that be our purpose and our prayer—yours and mine—for ourselves, for our country, and for all the world.

Glossary

abolitionist movement *(historical term)* organized activities of groups of citizens working to abolish (put an end to) slavery in the United States

accessible *(adjective)* obtainable; available

accommodation *(noun)* adjustment or adaptation to the beliefs of others

adversary *(noun)* opponent; enemy

bilateral *(adjective)* affecting both sides equally

"blasphemers" *(noun)* people who curse or speak irreverently of God

bloc *(noun)* group of voters who forget their political parties and join together to support some common goal related to religion, employment, etc.

Born Again Christian *(special expression)* person who publicly acknowledges sinfulness and accepts Christ as his or her personal savior. The individual is spiritually reborn through a conversion experience and makes a deep commitment to his or her (often evangelical) faith.

Calvinist *(noun)* believer in the theology of John Calvin, who emphasized predestination (God planned or ordered everything before it happened) and salvation only by God's grace (only God could save sinners; people couldn't help themselves). Calvinists followed a strict moral code.

censorship *(noun)* removal or prohibition of reading materials because they are objectionable—morally or politically. The moral or political ideals of the group in control determine what materials are censored. Most Americans oppose censorship because it limits or curtails individual rights and freedoms.

civility *(noun)* politeness

civil libertarians *(noun)* people who believe in an individual's freedom to think, speak, write, and act as he or she wishes as long as the public welfare is not harmed

coercive power *(political expression)* ability to make citizens comply with government demands through use of force or legal authority

commonwealth *(noun)* democracy or republic

conception *(noun)* mental impression; general idea or notion

conscience *(noun)* knowledge of right and wrong and the desire to do right

contending *(verb)* asserting; stating as a fact

counsel *(noun)* advice

creed *(noun)* statement of religious belief

debased *(verb)* lowered (in value, character, or dignity)

debate *(noun)* discussion; argument; contest

deflect *(verb)* turn

Deist *(noun)* individual who believed in the existence of God based on logical reasoning, not on revelation by or authority of the Bible. Deism was a doctrine of the 17th and 18th century that God created the world and its natural laws but took no further part in its functioning.

Disciples *(noun)*   followers of Jesus Christ, especially the Apostles

diverse *(adjective)*   different; dissimilar

drawing the line between imposed will and essential witness *(special expression)*   limiting the power of the individual (or group) to influence the state, but still allowing the free expression of beliefs. The state cannot force citizens to follow certain ideas, just as individuals holding private opinions cannot force the state to accept and adopt them even though the state encourages religious leaders to speak out on issues. Kennedy is saying here that some balance must be maintained between the responsibilities of the state and the exercise of individual rights. Church and state must be separate; on the other hand, religious beliefs can't help influencing political decisions.

ecumenical *(adjective)*   unified Christian church including all denominations (subdivisions)

endowed with *(verb)*   provided with; given

Episcopalian *(noun)*   member of a Protestant church who believes the authority to govern the church lies in a group of bishops, rather than a single individual as the Pope of the Roman Catholic Church

epithets *(noun)*   descriptive names or titles used to characterize some person or thing, such as the terms "sexist" and "murderers" used in the article

E.R.A. *(noun)*   Equal Rights Amendment

ethical issues *(adjective; noun)*   questions or disagreements about the standards of conduct or code of behavior of a particular society

Evangelical Protestants *(adjective; noun)*   members of Christian churches, as Baptist or Methodist, that emphasize spreading the teachings of the Gospels (Matthew, Mark, Luke, and John, the first four books of the New Testament of the Bible)

factional strife *(political term)*   fighting between small groups of people within a larger group or population because of political, religious, or social differences

fallibility *(noun)*   tendency to be mistaken, deceived, or inaccurate

fealty *(noun)*   loyalty; duty; allegiance

firmament *(noun)*   sky (poetic)

fold *(noun)*   group or organization with common aims, goals, or interests

framers *(noun)*   writers, designers, or creators of the Constitution

frustrating *(verb)*   upsetting because they are prevented or blocked from achieving their objectives

fundamentalist *(noun)*   person whose religious beliefs are based on a literal interpretation of the Bible

futility *(noun)*   worthlessness; hopelessness; complete failure

harassed *(verb)* tormented; troubled; worried

hastening *(verb)* causing something to happen faster; accelerating; speeding up

heckled *(verb)* annoyed or taunted a speaker by interrupting with questions or critical comments

hierarchy *(noun)* governmental system (church, state, military, etc.) arranged in graded ranks

humanist *(noun)* person who believes that humans are capable of fulfilling their ideals and behaving ethically and rationally without intervention of supernatural forces

impose *(verb)* force others to accept

indictment *(noun)* accusation; charge. A formal, written indictment charging a person with committing a crime is part of the legal process of criminal justice. The term is also used to indicate a moral wrong.

infallible *(adjective)* never wrong; incapable of error

inherently *(adverb)* basically; naturally existing

integrity *(noun)* strong moral principles; sincerity; honesty

invoked *(verb)* put into use

jeopardy *(noun)* danger; peril

lieth *(verb, obsolete)* lies

lobbying group *(political term)* special interest group that tries to influence legislation or government decisions

mandate *(noun)* command; order

Matthew *(noun)* first book of the New Testament of the Bible

modern inquisition *(adjective; noun)* suppression of ideas or harsh punishment of those who differ or disagree. The original inquisition of the Roman Catholic Church began in the 13th century to discover and punish heretics (those who opposed church doctrines).

monopoly *(noun)* exclusive possession or control of something

Morality Index *(special term)* list that ranks the morality of each congressman according to the moral standards of a single group (rather than the standards of the nation)

mote *(noun)* speck or particle of dust

neither red nor dead *(special expression)* Americans who favor nuclear disarmament by the United States, whether the Soviet Union disarms or not, sometimes use the slogan, "Better red than dead," meaning they prefer to live under communism rather than to die in a nuclear war. Kennedy says the two governments must try to reach agreement on arms control so that the false dilemma will no longer exist.

nontheocratic state *(special term)* country or state governed by those not claiming to rule with God's authority

nuclear freeze *(political term)* proposal that the nuclear powers stop building nuclear arms (as opposed to *nuclear disarmament,* a proposal that the nuclear powers gradually decrease the number of nuclear weapons)

perplexed *(verb)* confused; puzzled; uncertain

persecuted *(adjective)* cruelly oppressed for reasons of race, religion, politics, etc.

phantom *(adjective)* ghost; illusory; nonexistent

Pharisees *(noun)* persons who observe the laws but don't really believe in them; hypocrites

pluralistic *(adjective)* allowing for and favoring the preservation within the nation of groups distinctive in ethnic origin, cultural patterns, religion, etc.

preachers *(noun)* clergymen (often called ministers)

prohibition *(noun)* the period between 1920 and 1933 when the manufacture, transport, and sale of alcoholic beverages was prohibited by Federal law

prophet *(noun)* spokesman for a cause, group, or movement; in this case, King, a minister, led black people in nonviolent marches and demonstrations to protest racial inequality in the United States

racial segregation *(adjective; noun)* separation or isolation of minority racial groups from the main mass or group of the population. Certain areas of the United States, especially in the deep South, maintained separate social facilities and schools for blacks and whites.

rallied *(verb)* came together to work for a common cause

relic *(noun)* object or custom that has survived from the past

Romans *(noun)* book in the New Testament of the Bible, a message from the Apostle Paul to the Christians of Rome

rubble *(noun)* debris or broken ruins of buildings caused by man-made or natural disaster. Kennedy's point is that a full-scale nuclear war could destroy every structure and change the world into a huge mass of radioactive rubble in which no one could survive.

sanction *(verb)* authorize; permit

sense of perspective *(idiom)* ability to see ourselves in a true (rather than a distorted) relationship

statute *(noun)* law passed by a legislative body and published in a formal document

step onto a slippery slope *(colloquialism)* place ourselves in a dangerous position

synagogue *(noun)* building used for religious worship by Jews

tolerance *(noun)* freedom from prejudice; respect for (if not acceptance of) others' beliefs, views, or practices that differ from one's own

torch *(noun)* device that produces a flame and can be used for starting a fire.

transgression *(noun)* act of breaking a law or commandment; going beyond accepted limits or boundaries

tuition tax credits *(political term)* proposed credits against income tax for parents who pay private school tuition fees for their children rather than sending them to public (tax supported) schools

unilateral *(adjective)* occurring on or affecting one side only

uniquely *(adverb)* extraordinarily. Religion is subject to individual choice and is an extremely private matter.

valiantly *(adverb)* courageously; bravely

verification *(noun)* confirmation or proof

"warmonger" *(noun)* person or agency that tries to bring about war

wellsprings *(noun)* sources

yoking *(verb)* joining; linking

zeal *(noun)* intense enthusiasm or devotion

Comprehension Questions

1. What is the subject of Kennedy's speech?
2. What right must we respect in others? What must we recognize in ourselves?
3. What kinds of people believe that they have a monopoly on truth? Why are they wrong?
4. Why did John Kennedy appear before a group of Evangelical Protestants? Why did Ronald Reagan appeal to a similar group twenty years later? What did Reagan's pledge mean to many Americans?
5. What church-state conflicts did the founders of the nation experience? What did the framers of the Constitution give to the citizens of the new nation?
6. Why can separation of church and state be frustrating for persons of deep religious faith? What are they tempted to do about it? Why can their actions be dangerous?
7. What is the limitation of government in a nontheocratic state?
8. When does the "real transgression" occur? What is the proper role of religion?

9. What examples does Kennedy give of the kinds of questions that are affected by religious values?

10. What are the four tests which can be used in "drawing the line between imposed will and essential witness"?

11. What is meant by the integrity of religion? How has religion been misused in the past? How is it misused today?

12. What is the role of conscience and why are independent judgments important? What is the controversy about the views and name of the Moral Majority? What is Dr. Falwell's position on Israel? Why does Kennedy seem to disagree?

13. What is Kennedy's position on a religious test for public office?

14. Why is the integrity of public debate so important? Explain the nuclear freeze example that Kennedy uses.

15. Why is the right to disagree so fundamental in the United States? What does Kennedy say happens to an argument when the opponents use "name calling" (*argument ad hominem*)? What examples of name calling does Kennedy give?

16. What kind of America does Kennedy hope for? Where does the choice lie? How should we try to live?

Topics for Critical Analysis, Discussion, and Writing

1. Define and discuss *tolerance* and *truth* as they are used in Kennedy's speech.

2. Explain separation of church and state. Why and how did the founding fathers and framers of the Constitution insist on this concept? Under what circumstances can religion and religious values influence government? What are the dangers of religious bloc voting? What point does Kennedy try to make by giving examples of John Kennedy and Ronald Reagan?

3. Kennedy asserts that individual values cannot be imposed on others without risking everyone's freedom. He uses issues from past and present as evidence. How effective is his argument?

4. *Respect* is a key word in Kennedy's argument. What values does he say we should respect in others? Why?

5. Kennedy identifies weaknesses in the arguments of his opponents. Find the examples he presents of logical fallacies and related propaganda techniques, such as *appeal to illegitimate authority, argument ad hominem, card stacking,* etc. Does Kennedy use these methods himself?

6. Go to the library and look up Dr. Falwell's position on some of the issues identified by Kennedy. Once you know both sides of the argument, defend or attack one of the following statements from Kennedy's speech:

"Today's Moral Majority could become tomorrow's persecuted minority."

"The real transgression occurs when religion wants government to tell citizens how to live uniquely personal parts of their lives."

"There are other questions which are inherently public in nature, which we must decide together as a nation, and where religion and religious values can and should speak to our common conscience."

"Respect for conscience is most in jeopardy—and the harmony of our diverse society is most at risk—when we re-establish, directly or indirectly, a religious test for public office."

"In that [public] debate, faith is no substitute for facts."

"The more our feelings diverge, the more deeply felt they are, the greater is our obligation to grant the sincerity and essential decency of our fellow citizens on the other side."

Begin your essay by briefly describing Kennedy's theme, identifying him as the author of the speech, and giving its title. Choose a statement with which you strongly agree or disagree. Be sure your thesis clearly expresses your view or opinion of the statement. After that, stick to the facts. Prove your point without using logical fallacies or propaganda techniques. Be sure that you include a counter argument in which you anticipate and refute objections or contradictions to your evidence. Your conclusion should refer to (but not restate) the thesis.

7. Discuss Kennedy's tone or attitude. How does it affect the audience? Why?

8. How does Kennedy's speech relate to Kie Ho's essay, "We Should Cherish Our Children's Freedom to Think"?

Dying: Who Lives, Who Dies, Who Decides, and Who Pays the Bills?

Do incurably ill people have the right to die? If so, at what point in a person's life may he or she decide to end it? Is extreme physical suffering an acceptable reason for ending a person's life? Does age make a difference? Should only the wishes of the individual be honored? Does the family have any say? Should people have to die as punishment for killing others? How should society deal with people who want desperately to live but are condemned to die because they have committed terrible crimes? Does a criminal convicted of a capital offense deserve a humane, painless death? Should the criminal be made to suffer as much as the victim did? These are some of the questions that are explored in the following cluster of articles. Comprehension questions follow each article; however, topics for critical analysis, discussion, and writing combine ideas from all four readings.

Society Confronted with Painful Choices

Patricia O'Brien

In this article, O'Brien comments on the long, unsuccessful court fight of Elizabeth Bouvia to compel a hospital to help her die by keeping her comfortable while she starved to death. Bouvia's wishes were in direct conflict with the major aim of the medical profession—preserving life. In contrast, O'Brien notes that two people who wanted very much to live were executed by the state in the same week that it decided not to help Bouvia die. The author thoughtfully discusses this irony and explains the reasons for these decisions.

In the latest of the painful **dilemmas** over an individual's right to die, a woman in California suffering from **cerebral palsy** has been denied state help in painlessly starving herself to death. In effect, the California Supreme Court **condemned** Elizabeth Bouvia to live.

Has she then "lost," and has an unfeeling state "won"?

The answer to that, in the sometimes **heartbreaking tangle** that surrounds today's **moral** choices, is as complicated as the problem.

Reprinted by permission of Knight-Ridder Newspapers.

Bouvia is a pretty, 26-year-old woman who **persevered** for years through the **grueling chore** of trying to build a life for herself. Severely **disabled**, she is at this point able to move only her head and one hand.

Even so, she managed to earn a bachelor's degree in social work from San Diego State University. She even married.

She did the kind of things those of us who can walk and talk and live normal lives think of as very admirable, even as we extend our pity. She did them for the same fundamental reasons that most severely disabled people will **heroically extend themselves**: She wanted to have at least some portion of the satisfactions and challenges that give life **texture** and meaning.

Apparently, Bouvia tired of the struggle. Her marriage failed. She was unable to find work. When her disabilities grew worse, to the point where she became unable to feed herself without assistance, Bouvia asked the court to take the **unprecedented** action of ordering a hospital to help her die.

What Bouvia wanted, and was **denied**, was the ability to end her life because of its **meager** quality.

What she needed, and did not get, was society's cooperation.

In handing down his opinion, Judge John H. Hews **acknowledged** that Bouvia has a fundamental right to choose death. But, he said, "this right has been overcome by the strong interest of the state and the society (for) preservation of life."

It's worth noting that Hews' decision came in the same week when two human beings who **petitioned** the courts for life were executed by the state.

When viewed through the eyes of opponents of the death penalty, then, the state's insistence on the preciousness of life in this case holds a certain **irony**.

And yet that insistence, as **contradictory** as it may seen to some, is a **legitimate** effort to hang onto a social moral code in matters of life and death—even if that moral code gets harder and harder to define.

More and more, the people who make up what we call "society"—courts, hospitals, doctors, parents—find themselves **confronted with** making life and death choices.

Who has the right to decide if an infant born with severe disabilities should be allowed to die? Who has the right to **unhook** the **intravenous solution** that keeps a terminal cancer patient alive?

Without clear-cut and shared understandings of what is "right" and what is "wrong," all we can do is, keep **stumbling** along in our search to make moral sense out of a fast-changing world where these decisions have become technologically possible.

Elizabeth Bouvia wanted to die. But by asking for the state's cooperation, she asked for more than the state can—or should—give. She wanted the state to take on the power of deciding her life was worthless, and that is too large a power to delegate.

Glossary

acknowledged *(verb)*   admitted, recognized; affirmed

cerebral palsy *(medical term)*   central nervous system disorder resulting from brain damage before or after birth and characterized by paralysis or defective motor ability

condemned *(verb)*   doomed. The high court inflicted the penalty of life on Bouvia, exactly the opposite of the penalty of death imposed upon a criminal who has committed a capital offense.

confronted with *(verb)*   faced with; face to face with; opposed by

contradictory *(adjective)*   contrary; inconsistent; false

denied *(verb)*   refused

dilemmas *(noun)*   arguments requiring choices between two equally un-acceptable and unpleasant alternatives

disabled *(adjective)*   incapacitated; crippled; lacking normal functioning of the limbs and body

grueling chore *(adjective, noun)*   exhausting task

heartbreaking *(adjective)*   overwhelmingly sad or disappointing

heroically extend themselves *(special expression)*   courageously enlarge or expand their abilities; bravely make themselves work or try very hard

intravenous solution *(medical term)*   fluids (containing nutrients, anesthetics, etc.) that are slowly dripped directly into a vein through a special needle

irony *(noun)*   a combination of circumstances or a result that is opposite of what is expected or considered appropriate

legitimate *(adjective)*   reasonable; logically correct; conforming to established rules, standards, and principles

meager *(adjective)*   poor; inadequate; not full or rich

moral *(adjective)*   relating to, dealing with, or capable of making the distinction between right and wrong

persevered *(verb)*   continued in her effort or course of action in spite of difficulty and opposition

petitioned *(verb)*   formally asked (in writing)

stumbling *(verb)*   blundering; proceeding in a confused manner

tangle *(noun)*   confused, intertwisted mass of things; confused condition

texture *(noun)*   character; structure

unhook *(verb)*   remove; unfasten

unprecedented *(adjective)* unheard of; having no precedent or parallel. No court decision of this kind had ever been made before.

Comprehension Questions

1. How did Elizabeth Bouvia hope to end her life? Why did she want to die? Give details.
2. What was the California Supreme Court's decision? What reason was given?
3. Who ends up making the moral life or death choices? What is the role of technology?
4. Who should have the power to decide whether a life is worthless?

Beyond the *Right* to Die, Will It Become a *Duty* to Die?

Arthur D. Silk

Here is a physician's view of who should decide whether a terminally ill person should live or die. In his argument, Dr. Silk examines the problems of prolonged suffering, extended medical treatment, financial drain, guilt, and decision making.

It is morally terrifying to me to consider **legislating** "the right to die."

No one has the right or desire to extend life simply to **prolong** suffering, but economic pressures are beginning to **erode** humanitarian considerations. Medical economists have calculated that 60% or more of an individual's entire lifetime medical expense is generated in the last year of life. It follows, then, that if we could predict that terminal period (and eliminate or ignore it) we could find the **long-sought** magic that would immediately and **drastically** cut **soaring** medical expenses.

Since it is not given to the best of our **medical prognosticators** to predict with certainty and finality just when that last 12 months will begin or end, and because our **Judeo-Christian ethic** is dedicated to the **sanctity** of life, we physicians, with the **endorsement** of society, keep trying to extend, as well as to improve, life. But, as several sociologists familiar with the British

Reprinted by permission of the author. This first appeared in the *Los Angeles Times*.

hospice movement have asked, if the right to die is **legitimized by statute**, how long will it be before the *right* to die becomes the *duty* to die?

Committees of physicians are already legally required to decide what medical and surgical procedures should be done, whether they may be done in a hospital, and how long the hospital **convalescence** may take. Is it too much to imagine that, **empowered** by right-to-die laws, the duties of these committees will extend to the judgment of who shall live and who shall die?

The moral **precedent** for such decisions is already taken for granted by **triage physicians** in war and disaster—those who assign the priorities for medical treatment on the basis of **urgency** or chance of survival. It would be such a little step, and with such big **potential** for **massive** financial savings, to allow a committee to decide that a patient beyond a certain stage of **colon** or breast cancer could not be treated. Would we apply a different standard to those whom we choose to condemn by **benevolent** neglect if they were over 70 or under 35, if they were rich and famous or poor and unknown?

Indeed, how long would it take before the **stricken** individual, feeling comfortable and **functional** but sensing the emotional and financial drain on his loved ones, became sufficiently **guilt-ridden** to request the right to die **prematurely**?

Prematurely! Ah, **there's the rub**. We're all going to die—some gracefully and without suffering, some after **protracted,** painful and **debilitating** treatment. **In retrospect**, it is easy to make decisions when we have seen the quality of a life **deteriorate**. But who among us can sufficiently **codify** the stages of the quality of life to make the decision in advance to **extinguish** it? Would we be successfully transplanting kidneys, hearts and livers today if we had legislated the right to die 20 years ago?

What is the answer? How do we let go of our relatives and friends without guilt or sin or unnecessarily prolonged suffering? We do it in the same way in which we have done it over the years. First a caring physician establishes **rapport** with the patient and his family. Together they make a compassionate, *unwritten* decision to stop trying. Lawyers and legislators have no part in life's final drama.

Glossary

benevolent *(adjective)* kindly; charitable

codify *(verb)* systematically arrange laws or rules

colon *(noun)* part of the large intestine extending to the rectum

convalescence *(noun)* gradual recovery period after illness

debilitating *(adjective)* weakening; enfeebling

deteriorate *(verb)* worsen; lower in quality; depreciate

drastically *(adjective)* severely; harshly

empowered *(verb)* given power or authority

endorsement *(noun)* written approval or support; sanction

erode *(verb)* wear away; weaken; disintegrate

extinguish *(verb)* put an end to; destroy

functional *(adjective)* able to perform normal activities

guilt-ridden *(adjective)* obsessed or dominated by self-reproach resulting from the belief or feeling of having done a wrong

hospice movement *(medical term)* effort to establish special homes or shelters to take care of the needs of and supply comforts to the dying

in retrospect *(idiom)* reviewing the events of the past

Judeo-Christian ethic *(special term)* system of morality based on Jewish-Christian teachings from the Old and New Testaments of the Bible

legislating *(verb)* making or passing laws approving or disapproving certain actions

legitimized by statute *(legal term)* made legal by law; sanctioned by legal action

long-sought *(adjective)* long searched for or looked for

massive *(adjective)* larger or greater than normal; extensive

medical prognosticators *(noun)* doctors who can foretell or predict a patient's medical future by physical signs and indications

potential *(noun)* unrealized or undeveloped possibility

precedent *(noun)* existing practice based on earlier legal decisions that serve as examples to justify actions or behavior

prematurely *(adverb)* before the proper or usual time

prolong *(verb)* lengthen or extend

protracted *(adjective)* lengthened; drawn out; prolonged; extended

rapport *(noun, French)* close or sympathetic relationship

sanctity *(noun)* sacredness; holiness

soaring *(adjective)* elevated or rapidly rising above usual and ordinary levels

stricken *(adjective; alternate past participle of strike)* afflicted (by wounds or illness)

there's the rub *(from Shakespeare, Hamlet)* there's the obstacle, hindrance, or difficulty

triage physicians *(medical term)* physicians who, faced with huge numbers of injuries or illnesses, must choose whom to treat based on who has the best chance of survival

urgency *(noun)* need for action; necessity; importance

Comprehension Questions

1. How does Silk feel about legislating "the right to die"?
2. What is the relationship between economic pressures and humanitarian considerations?
3. By what means does Silk say that medical expenses could be "immediately and drastically cut"? Does Silk find this solution acceptable? Why or why not?
4. Since triage (war and disaster) physicians must assume the moral right to decide who lives and who dies, why shouldn't all physicians do this?
5. What moral problems does Silk foresee with legislating the right to "premature" death? Would the same standards apply to all? What effect would guilt have on the patient?
6. Who decides when to "let go" of a relative or friend? What is the role of lawyers and legislators?

Are We Squandering Millions on the Dying?

Daniel S. Greenberg

Greenberg makes several compelling points about health care costs in the article that follows. Better health care affords people longer, more productive lives but also allows expensive, prolonged processes of dying. Although Medicare (national health insurance for Social Security recipients) picks up the bills, Greenberg comments that the money might be better used for others who depend on federal funding for health care.

Is the American medical system **squandering** billions in **scarce** resources on well-intentioned but **futile** treatment of dying elderly patients? The question is both ugly and beyond precise knowledge, given the hopes and **anxieties** that accompany serious illness and the occasional recovery of seemingly **terminal** patients.

As the **recession** and government **cutbacks impinge on Medicare** funding, however, several recent studies have found that this federal program for the elderly has quietly evolved into an expensive system of in-hospital deathbed finance. That finding contains powerful **implications** for the

Reprinted by permission of the author. Daniel S. Greenberg is editor and publisher of *Science and Government Report,* an independent, Washington-based newsletter, and he writes a syndicated newspaper column on health and science policy.

hospice movement and political demands to **restrain** the rapid rise of Medicare expenditures, which continue to **outrun** the general rate of inflation.

Thus, a staff analysis conducted last year in the Department of Health and Human Services noted "the increasingly **intense** use of Medicare services as death approaches."

Over 20% of Medicare's $49 billion in 1982 was spent on patients in the last six months of life, with a large proportion of that money spent in the final 30 days. The analysis concludes, "The amount of Medicare expenditure for persons in the last year of life **brings home** the reality that Medicare, by its very nature, is a program involved with dying." The study adds, "Some have questioned the appropriateness of the hospitals as a place to **render** care to the dying . . . (but), as long as **third-party insurance** pays most of the bills, physicians and family can avoid the difficult decision of terminating active care even when it is likely to be of little benefit."

There are circumstances, of course, in which costly **intensive care** does prove effective, but, as economic necessity forces closer examination of health-care **tactics,** there is reason to doubt the **efficacy**—as well as the humanity—of a substantial portion of the **commonplace** use of high-technology medical care.

A 1980 study of the final two weeks of hospital treatment for a group of terminally ill cancer patients found that "**diagnostic** and **therapeutic** services were given to nearly all . . . until the day of death." The study, conducted for the department by SRI International, cautiously observes that because these and other Medicare **beneficiaries** "died, despite the treatment received, it is reasonable to question whether scarce resources were most appropriately used." It points out, too, that medical care is tied to "a **reimbursement system** where more treatment generates more reimbursement and a **peer-review system** where most treatment is, by definition, better."

The **impulse** to "do everything"—though, in fact, nothing effective can be done—is understandable and deeply imbedded in medical ethics and public expectations. What the analysts of Medicare's billions for terminal care are inviting attention to are some **unpalatable** realities. Medically, the system frequently doesn't work; economically, we can no longer afford it, since it is consuming resources that could produce worthwhile medical results.

Anyone who doubts the latter point might consider how far those billions could go in **alleviating** the medical scarcities that hard times and federal economizing have brought to the inner city.

Glossary

alleviating *(verb)*   lessening; reducing, decreasing

anxieties *(noun)*   worries (especially about the future)

beneficiaries *(noun)*   persons repaid by Medicare for their medical expenses

brings home *(idiom)* clearly shows, emphasizes

commonplace *(adjective)* common; ordinary

cutbacks *(noun)* reductions (in funding)

diagnostic *(adjective)* evaluative. Diagnostic studies help the physician decide the nature of patient's disease or condition.

efficacy *(noun)* effectiveness; power to produce effects or results

futile *(adjective)* useless; hopeless; ineffective

impinge on *(verb)* have a bad effect on or cut into (the amount of money available)

implications *(noun)* inferences or conclusions reached after logical examination of all the facts

impulse *(noun)* sudden desire to act, often without conscious thought

intense *(adjective)* very strong; extreme

intensive care *(medical term)* especially attentive care given to very ill or recovering patients

Medicare *(noun)* national health program which pays for certain medical and hospital expenses for elderly people. Costs are paid by the federal government, mostly from Social Security funds.

outrun *(verb)* run faster than; exceed

peer-review system *(medical term)* procedure by which medical colleagues of equal rank and stature examine and judge the need for or kind of treatment a physician orders or arranges for a patient

recession *(noun)* temporary lessening of business activity during a period when business has generally been increasing

reimbursement system *(insurance term)* method for paying back money spent by individuals for medical treatment

render *(verb)* give or provide

restrain *(verb)* control; limit; restrict

scarce *(adjective)* hard to get; not plentiful

squandering *(verb)* spending or using wastefully or extravagantly

tactics *(noun)* methods used to gain an end; procedures used to reach an objective

terminal *(adjective)* dying; in the final stages of a disease for which there is no cure, such as cancer

therapeutic *(adjective)* designed to cure, speed healing, or preserve health

third-party insurance *(special term)* organization other than the principals (patient and physician) that pays most of the costs for procedures and care ordered by the physician.

unpalatable *(adjective)* unpleasant or unacceptable

Comprehension Questions

1. Is Medicare wasting money on the dying elderly? Give both sides of the argument as stated in the article.

2. When does the use of Medicare services become intense?

3. Given the enormous expense of hospital care for the dying, why do physicians and families continue to use these institutions?

4. What is Greenberg's conclusion about the effectiveness of intensive care treatment for the dying?

5. Why is such costly care (tests and treatment using sophisticated equipment) given to dying people until the day of death?

6. Ethically, we want to spare no expense to try to save a loved one. What are the medical and economic realities?

Why Fret Over Killers

Mike Royko

This article deals with a slightly different aspect of dying—enforcement of the death penalty for conviction of a capital crime. As you read Mike Royko's views, examine the roles of the state and of the individual. How are they different from or similar to those in the three preceding articles?

There has been some anxious **wringing of hands** because Jimmy Lee Gray apparently suffered some discomfort when he departed this world the other day.

Jimmy Lee, in case you missed the story, was executed in Parchman, Miss. He was a murderer.

In Mississippi, they execute killers by strapping them into a chair and dropping **cyanide** crystals into a pan of water and **sulfuric acid** under the chair.

This is supposed to do the job quickly and with a minimum of suffering.

However, this was not the case with Jimmy Lee. He moaned and **convulsed** and **thrashed** about for several minutes before his end came.

His lawyer was upset by the way Jimmy Lee died, and so were many of the kindly souls who oppose the death penalty in any form.

But they've overlooked something unusual about Jimmy Lee's death.

And that is the fact that this is one of those **rare** times when a killer got exactly what he **dished out**.

Jimmy Lee was executed for the crime of **smothering** a 3-year-old girl. He did this after **raping** her.

It can be assumed that the little girl also gasped for breath and suffered when she was deprived of air. The difference is that the little girl did nothing to deserve her suffering and death.

Actually, most methods of executing killers are far more merciful than the methods used by the killers to earn their places on Death Row.

Many killers torture and torment their victims, subjecting them to long, painful deaths. They sometimes kill entire families, forcing them to endure the **unspeakable** horror of seeing each other die.

On those rare occasions when these killers are punished, they get far better treatment than their victims did. In most states, they're strapped into a chair and, after a couple of quick jolts of electricity, it's all over. In other states, gas or a firing squad is used.

All of these are faster and less painful than death by **bludgeoning**, stabbing and torture—frequently accompanied by sexual abuse.

So I really don't see why there is this **heartfelt** concern for how killers are executed.

In Illinois, for example, there is a minor controversy stirring. It has been proposed that the electric chair be replaced by a **lethal** injection. A doctor sticks a needle into **Mad Dog Jack**'s arm and—zap—Mad Dog Jack is gone. Some **tender hearts** oppose the injection method because it is so clinical and impersonal. It's so simple, they say, that it devalues human life.

That just proves that you can't please some people. They don't like the electric chair because smoke curls out of the killer's ears. And they don't like the idea of an injection because it makes the whole thing seem so routine and simple.

I suspect that most of these objections really have nothing to do with how the execution is performed. It's the idea of the death penalty itself that bothers these people.

My feelings are similar up to a point. I really don't care how the execution is performed, either. I just want it done.

My only objection to the death penalty is that it isn't carried out nearly as often as it should be.

When I think of the thousands of inhabitants of **Death Rows** in the hundreds of prisons in this country, I don't react the way the kindly souls do— with **revulsion** that the state would take these human lives.

My reaction is: What's taking us so long? Let's get that electric current flowing. Drop those **pellets** now!

Whenever I argue this with friends who have opposite views, they say that I don't have enough regard for that most marvelous of miracles—human life.

Just the opposite: It's because I have so much regard for human life that I favor **capital punishment**. Murder is the most terrible crime there is. Anything less than the death penalty is an insult to the victim and society. It says, in effect, that we don't value the victim's life enough to punish the killer fully.

Some people say that life in prison—with no hope of release—is an even more terrible punishment than death.

If I thought that were true, I'd be in favor of it. But I think that argument is a joke. If life in prison were so unbearable, we'd see a lot more **lifers slinging** a belt across a pipe and hanging themselves.

But we don't. That's because they prefer life—even in prisons—to a hole in the ground.

The kinds of two-legged animals who commit terrible murders are very **adaptable**. In prison, they're provided with food, **lodging**, medical care, recreation, entertainment and a social structure of sorts. If they're **enterprising**, they find drugs and sexual companionship.

Consider the recent murders on Chicago's Far North Side. The home of a married couple was invaded. The husband—a decent man—was beaten to death with a bat. The wife was raped and killed. Their small son survived a beating.

Two brothers have been charged with the crime. Apparently they were looking for something to steal, and tossed in the murders as an afterthought. The police apparently have more than enough evidence—including confessions—to get a conviction.

If they're convicted, any judge who gives them less than the death sentence should spend the rest of his life in **Traffic Court**. He should also have to explain to that little boy why the lives of two killers are more precious than those of his parents.

In the game of golf there is an old saying for those times when a bad shot takes a **miraculous** bounce off a tree or a rock and winds up in or near the **hole**.

The saying is: "It's not how—it's how many."

That's my feeling about the death sentence: "It's not how—it's when."

Glossary

adaptable *(adjective)*   able to adjust to new or changed circumstances

bludgeoning *(verb used as noun)*   beating given with a short club or a blunt, heavy object

capital punishment *(noun)*   the death penalty. A person is killed as punishment for his or her crime.

convulsed *(verb)*   shook violently; had spasms

cyanide *(noun)*   potassium cyanide or sodium cyanide; extremely poisonous, white crystalline compounds with an odor of bitter almonds

Death Rows *(noun)*   extra secure sections of prisons where condemned criminals are kept until they are executed

dished out *(verb; slang)*   gave. During his execution, the murderer suffered the same pain he caused his victim.

enterprising *(adjective)*   energetic; willing to try new or risky projects

heartfelt *(adjective)*   sincere; deeply felt

hole *(noun; golf term)*   small, round cup sunk into a green (an especially well-tended lawn-like area of a golf course). The object of the game is to hit the ball into the hole.

lethal *(adjective)*   fatal; deadly

lifers *(noun; slang)*   people sentenced to life imprisonment

lodging *(noun)*   living quarters; a place to live

Mad Dog Jack *(colloquialism)*   Royko's "nickname" for a fictional killer whose behavior is as vicious and dangerous as that of a dog infected with rabies

miraculous *(adjective)*   marvelous; supernatural; like a miracle

pellets *(noun)*   small balls of some compressed substance, such as clay, paper, medicine, or poison

raping *(verb)*   forcing another person to have sexual intercourse

rare *(adjective)*   unusual; uncommon; infrequent

revulsion *(noun)*   extreme disgust

slinging *(verb)*   throwing; flinging

smothering *(verb)*   suffocating; killing by keeping a person from getting enough air to breathe

sulfuric acid *(noun)*   oily, colorless, corrosive liquid. In the execution Royko describes, sulfuric acid was used with cyanide pellets and water to form deadly cyanide gas.

tender hearts *(idiom)*   sensitive, sympathetic, or compassionate people

thrashed *(verb)*   moved violently or wildly

Traffic Court *(noun)*   lower-level court that handles only traffic violations committed on local streets and highways

unspeakable *(adjective)*   so bad or evil that description is impossible

wringing of hands *(idiom)*   clasping and twisting of the hands to show distress

Comprehension Questions

1. Why were Jimmy Lee Gray's lawyer and others upset about the way he died?

2. What are Royko's feelings about Gray's death?

3. How does Royko compare or contrast the methods of execution with those of murder?

4. How does Royko react to those who are opposed to capital punishment?

5. What is prison like for a "lifer"? What does Royko think about this kind of treatment for murderers?

6. What is Royko's feeling about the death sentence?

Topics for Critical Analysis, Discussion, and Writing

(These topics combine ideas from all four articles and require that you use all your analytical skills. Read each topic carefully several times before you begin discussing it or writing about it.)

1. The legislation of death is a stated or implied topic of all four articles. O'Brien concludes that a citizen who decides that life is worthless and wants to die should not expect the state to accept responsibility for carrying out that action. On the other hand, Royko approves existing legislation calling for the state to carry out the death penalty in convictions for capital crimes regardless of the feelings of the individual or the public. Both cases are fairly uncommon. But the terminal illnesses discussed by Silk and Greenberg occur frequently. Silk states that "life's final drama" should not be subject to legislation, but should be handled by an unwritten agreement between family members and the attending physician. However, Greenberg implies that "drastically soaring medical costs" will eventually cause some kind of legislation to control Medicare expenditures.

Write an argument in which you defend or attack legislation of death. Use information from the articles to support your ideas. Take into account that some people want to die; others do everything possible to stay alive. Does the value placed by the individual or by society on human life affect your position?

2. The authors examine the morality of choices made in life or death issues. Although each situation is different and discussed from a different perspective, all involve making choices and accepting responsibility. Execution of a convicted criminal is a form of punishment; turning off the life support systems of a terminally ill patient can be considered an act of mercy or of murder. The state is obligated to do everything possible to protect and preserve life (as in the Bouvia case); conversely, some murderers are executed. In addition, the economic realities of health care costs for the terminally ill raise the possibility of legislation that threatens to shorten life for those solely dependent on Medicare. What is the difference between the right to die and the duty to die? What are the emotional, social, and economic obligations of individuals to society?

After you have thought about some of these questions, discuss them informally with other class members. Jot down notes that relate to the questions. Then write a brief paragraph to answer each one. Refer to the articles for supporting materials. Then argue for or against the following statement:

The reason for committing any action determines its morality.

3. Write an argument in which your thesis supports or opposes one of the following statements:

    a. Human life should be preserved at all costs.

    b. The state should not determine who lives and who dies.

    c. Terminally ill patients must consider their families.

    d. In some instances, shortening or ending human life is acceptable.

Give and discuss details and examples from the readings. Be sure to include a counter argument and refutation before you conclude.

4. Identify the writing techniques (narration, description, comparison/contrast, etc.) used by each author and explain whether these methods are effective in advancing their arguments.

5. Rank the arguments from most to least convincing. How important are your personal beliefs in deciding which argument is best? Reexamine the articles for form, style, and content. Do you still agree with your evaluation? Why?

9

Learning to Do Research: From Informal Project to Formal Research Paper

What is a term paper? Why do instructors in other disciplines, such as history, anthropology, psychology, astronomy, political science, biology, sociology, economics, geology, and business assign them? Why are these papers so often a large part of the final grade? Why don't all instructors explain exactly how to do term papers? Why do ESL students find these assignments so difficult?

A library research or term paper is *not* a report; it is a long, original, thesis-based essay supported by information found in books, periodicals, newspapers, pamphlets, and other reference materials available in the library. Instructors assign term projects because they want students to study a single topic in depth and to think independently and critically about the information presented in the course instead of simply memorizing facts from the reading assignments and class lectures in order to pass examinations. Often the term paper heavily influences the final grade because instructors want students to show that they can apply the ideas, theories, and facts of one situation to another by means of comparison and contrast, cause and effect, argument, or other forms of analysis. Few ESL students are able to plunge right into freshman composition (the course in most colleges and universities in which library research methods and writing techniques are emphasized) during their first semester or quarter of college, but they do enroll in a wide variety of other academic subjects that require research papers. Therefore, many instructors of advanced or transitional ESL courses try to cover the fundamentals of library research.

Your instructor may ask you to do a full-length paper or a shorter essay based on your research. Regardless of the size of your assignment, any written work that you do must follow certain guidelines. First, base your paper on a thesis. Second, interpret facts or examples that you include; don't just report them. Third, avoid including your beliefs or opinions; instead, make statements that you support with information collected from knowledgeable sources or experts in the field. Fourth, write in your own words unless you are quoting from a source; be sure that all quoted material is copied *exactly,* including punctuation, and that it is enclosed in quotation marks. Fifth, *never* copy or even paraphrase ideas or information from other authors in your paper without identifying the source, or you will be guilty of plagiarism (see chapter 1). Stealing someone else's writing is a very grave offense that can cause serious trouble.

CHOOSING A TOPIC

Whether you are given a list of topics prepared by your instructor or make up a list yourself, try to identify several possible choices. Then, do some preliminary checking to see what reference materials are available for each one. If everyone in your class is working on the same few assigned topics, there may not be enough information to go around in your college or university library. However, your local public library may have the resources that you need. Most libraries in the United States are organized similarly, although some are more complete than others, and most offer a basic selection of indexes and other reference materials.

One way to focus your research is to phrase your topic in the form of a question. Your affirmative or negative answer is your position. This is especially effective for dealing with current events or issues; for example:

> *Topic:* Smoking
> Should smoking be permitted in the workplace?
> Should smoking be prohibited in restaurants?

> *Topic:* Drunk Driving
> Should a drunk driver be tried for murder if he or she causes the death of another motorist or a pedestrian?
> Should a person convicted more than once of drunk driving be prohibited from owning or driving an automobile?

> *Topic:* Gun control
> Should the ownership of handguns be strictly controlled?
> Should every citizen have the right to own a handgun?

Your thesis should be a complete sentence that answers the question, not just "yes" or "no"; for example:

> In order to protect the health of all employees, smoking should not be permitted in the workplace.

Persons convicted more than once of drunk driving should never be allowed to own or operate an automobile again.

Private ownership of handguns can never be effectively controlled because criminals don't obey the law.

Direct your research toward proving your answer, but don't forget that you must know both sides of the issue to argue your point intelligently. For ideas about the smoking issue, refer to the Solmon–Weis arguments in Chapter 8 and to student essays in Chapter 10. Then consult medical, nursing, or psychological journals, popular periodicals (magazines), newspapers, books, and encyclopedias. Be sure that the information is up-to-date and only about the subject. For instance, don't include information on legalized smoking of marijuana in your paper, because you will change the focus from smoking in the workplace or in restaurants to smoking controlled substances. For information on the drunk driving issue, see the David Redfield and Candy Lightner articles in chapter 5, and consult newspapers, periodicals, and pamphlets. Additional sources are publications of insurance companies and legislative offices. For examples of treatment of the gun control issue, examine the sample student papers in this chapter.

Another good technique to help establish a research focus, if you are not dealing with an already narrow controversial subject, is classification. Let's say you are asked to research American authors, and you choose one included in this textbook, for instance, Shirley Jackson. Instead of telling her life story, discuss a major theme that Jackson uses throughout several of her works. Literary criticism, biography, periodicals, and journals provide helpful information. Or, suppose you research a past or present congressman, such as George Norris or Edward Kennedy, whose remarks are included in chapter 8. Instead of examining their entire political careers or personal lives, discuss their positions on a single continuing issue or problem, note changes over a period of time, and explain reasons for them. Government publications (such as the *Congressional Record* and Senate Committee Reports), *Vital Speeches,* newspapers, books, and periodicals are useful reference materials.

LOCATING SOURCES

All of the resources mentioned in the preceding paragraph can be found very easily if you know how to use the library. Since you probably have a limited amount of time to spend on your research project, the few minutes you take to learn about your college or university library are worthwhile. Clearly, the best person to teach you is a qualified librarian.

Marshall E. Nunn is a reference librarian at Glendale Community College, in Glendale, California. He often helps international students with research projects, so he is familiar with the difficulties they have trying to find and use materials in unfamiliar library systems. He has also served abroad as a librarian for the United States Information Service. The following article offers ESL students suggestions for efficient use of library resources and effective communication with library staff.

International Students and the American College Library

Marshall E. Nunn

As international students in American colleges, you will have many opportunities to use academic (college and university) libraries. College instructors will tell you how important it is for you to learn how to use the library and will expect you to master this important skill on your own. Don't worry! There are many librarians and library assistants who are eager and willing to help you.

Differences Between U.S. and Foreign Libraries

When you enter an American library for the first time, you may find its organization bewildering, unfamiliar, and complex. In fact, everything about your college or university library may be different from libraries in your home country.

One important difference is in the *classification* system used to organize and arrange materials on library shelves. American libraries use either the Dewey Decimal or Library of Congress classification systems (both explained further later), which are not widely used overseas. Another is in the wide variety of resources available in "open stacks" (shelves accessible to all library users) and by special request through librarians. A third is in the concept of self service. Library users locate and check out most of their own materials themselves.

Different Kinds of American Libraries

In addition to *academic libraries,* designed to serve college students, faculties, and staffs, there are several other kinds you should know about. *Public libraries* exist in cities and towns all across America. Their use is generally

Reprinted by permission of the author.

free to the people who live in the communities they serve. Their collections and services are designed to meet the needs of a broad cross section of the public, but you will find that they can often supplement your college library's services and holdings. *Research libraries* are similar in many ways to academic libraries, but serve only researchers, scholars, and advanced (graduate) students who must show a real need to get permission to use them. *Special libraries* provide information and services to people working in particular fields, such as business, medicine, or law. *Government libraries* are maintained by federal and state governments. The Library of Congress, in Washington, D.C., is the best-known and largest of this kind. Its first responsibility is to provide information to members of the U.S. Congress. It also functions as a *national library,* as it provides many services to all kinds of libraries throughout the country. (Do not use *school libraries* in elementary, middle or junior high, and high schools because the information they contain is not written at the college level.)

Responsibilities of Library Users

Certain responsibilities go along with the privilege of using any library in the United States. Learn the rules and regulations. These are usually published in a *library handbook* available upon request. Although library rules vary, certain basic ones apply to all: Return materials you borrow on time. Take reasonable care of these materials so that they are not lost, damaged or stolen, and promptly pay any fines or charges if they are. Remember that your library card is for your use only; don't lend it to anyone else to use. Respect the needs of others to use limited library resources such as reserve or reference books, and make photocopies of pages that you wish to write on or keep.

Effective Communication with the Library Staff

International students say that communicating with the staff is their most serious problem in using the college library. Regional accents or dialects of library employees and foreign accents of ESL students sometimes cause confusion in their understanding each other. If the library staff can not understand what you need, because of your pronunciation, accent, or limited vocabulary, try writing your question on a piece of paper. Feel free to ask the librarian to speak slowly, repeat, or demonstrate instructions. *Never* be afraid to seek help. In fact, many reference librarians have large signs on their desks with this single word, "ASK!"

You can save time on library research if you ask a librarian for help when you first begin to work on your topic. For example, if you want to locate materials in the printed card or computer catalog on the subject of "gun control," ask the reference librarian to go with you to the catalog and show you how to look up this subject. Then ask for an explanation of the various signs and symbols on the entries in the catalog. After this, request directions for finding these materials in the library. Refer often to the library handbook so that you learn to find materials by yourself.

While you should not hesitate to approach the reference librarian for help, remember that this person is a highly-educated professional, and is not a clerk to be ordered about. Be careful not to treat the librarian as an inferior or a servant who will do your library assignments for you. He or she won't do that, but will show you how to do them.

Efficient Use of Resources

You will learn from reading the college library handbook that the library is a vast storehouse of knowledge. Your ability to find the key that unlocks its hidden treasures can measure your success in many college courses. Although you have some help from librarians and other library personnel, you are expected to find this key by yourself. The next step in your orientation is to take a tour of the facility, which can be guided by a library employee or self guided using audio cassettes.

Let's take our own tour of a typical college library, keeping a special eye out for ways to locate various materials on our assigned topic of "gun control."

Nearest the entrance is the *Circulation* or *Loan Desk*. Here you obtain your library (borrower's) card, check out and return materials, pay fines for late or "overdue" items, and ask about materials that are not in their assigned places on the shelves.

The *public catalog,* also located near the entrance, may take three possible forms: (1) the traditional *card catalog,* an arrangement of cabinets containing drawers filled with three-by-five inch cards filed alphabetically by author, title, and subject (illustrated in Figure 9–1); (2) the more modern *computer catalog,* which lists material by author, title, subject, *and* call number (computerized libraries ask that you read instructions for operating terminals before you begin your search); (3) a combination of both card and computer catalogs.

Whatever its form, you must learn to use the public catalog because it lists all the books and many other types of materials (periodical titles, maps, films, and other media materials) in the library. It also gives you the coded information, the *call number,* which tells the location of the material in the library. This code appears in the upper left-hand corner of each card filed in the card catalog or in the first or second line of data for each entry shown on the computer screen. Under the subject heading, "gun control," is a "cross reference" card or entry indicating that material on this subject is listed under the subject heading "Firearms—laws and regulations."

Periodical or magazine *titles* owned by your library may appear in the public catalog, but individual articles in these publications do not. Pamphlets and government publications, both excellent sources of material on current topics, are not listed in the public catalog.

Write down the authors, titles, and call numbers of books that you want

Author Card

```
363.33
S555g    Shields, Pete
              Guns don't die—people do / Pete
         Shields.—New York: Arbor House,
         c1981.
              191 p.: charts, forms; 22 cm.
              Bibliography: p. 191.


              1. Firearms—Law and legislation.
         I. Title

              09   FEB   82        7802302      CGNA dc        81–67522
```

Subject Card

```
         FIREARMS—LAW AND LEGISLATION.
363.33
S555g    Shields, Pete
              Guns don't die—people do / Pete
         Shields.—New York: Arbor House,
         c1981.
              191 p.: charts, forms; 22 cm.
              Bibliography: p. 191.

              1. Firearms—Law and legislation.
         I. Title

              09   FEB   82        7802302      CGNA dc        81–67522
```

Title Card

```
              Guns don't die—people do
363.33
S555g    Shields, Pete
              Guns don't die—people do / Pete
         Shields.—New York: Arbor House,
         c1981.
              191 p.: charts, forms; 22 cm.
              Bibliography: p. 191.

              1. Firearms—Law and legislation.
         I. Title

              09   FEB   82        7802302      CGNA dc        81–67522
```

Figure 9–1

to find. If the library uses a card catalog, the circulation desk will have to check the library records to find out when books that are not on the shelves will be returned. In a computer catalog, this information is instantly available to you on the screen.

Before you try to locate books in the library, you should know a little more about call numbers and the two major classification systems used by American libraries to organize their materials. Practically all public and many small college libraries use the *Dewey Decimal Classification*. It is a clear, easy way of dividing knowledge into ten large categories, each of which is then subdivided. The main classes and examples of subjects that fall under them are as follows:

000–099   General (encyclopedias, periodicals)

100–199   Philosophy (ethics, psychology)

200–299   Religion (Bible, mythology)

300–399   Social Sciences (economics, law, political science)

400–499   Linguistics (dictionaries, grammar)

500–599   Pure Science (astronomy, chemistry, mathematics)

600–699   Applied Science (agriculture, engineering)

700–799   Arts and Recreation (music, painting)

800–899   Literature (English, French, German, Italian, Spanish)

900–999   History (biography, geography)

For example, the "Dewey number" for American history is 973; and the number for the American Civil War is 973.7. You do not have to memorize the "Dewey numbers" (they are usually posted in the library), but you should have a general idea of the number assigned to each of the ten broad categories. Remember, too, that most public and some small college libraries do not assign "Dewey numbers" to fiction books (novels and short stories), but shelve them alphabetically by the author's last name in a special section.

In contrast, large college, research, and special libraries use the Library of Congress (sometimes abbreviated *LC*) system of classification, which is longer and more complicated than the Dewey. The LC system divides knowledge into 21 main subjects which are identified by letters, not numbers. So the books are arranged from A to Z, rather than from 000 to 999. LC call numbers are combinations of letters and numbers. But this classification number, whether Dewey or LC, is only part of a book's call number. To shelve all books on the same subject together in an orderly way, catalog librarians add a second or third line which identifies the author's last name and the subject through the combination of a capital letter and a few numbers. For the book *Guns Don't Die—People Do,* by Pete Shields, the call numbers look like this:

Dewey

363.33	category and broad subject classification
S555g	author's last name and specific subject

LC

KF3941	classification
S5	author designation
1981	edition

These call numbers are written on labels that are placed on the *spines* of the books (the narrow, outside edges that face you as they stand upright on the shelves).

Most library books are part of the *circulation collection,* which means you can borrow them if you have a library card. But none of the books in the *reference collection,* the next stop on your tour, may be removed from the library. Their name indicates that you *refer* to them, rather than read them all the way through. Reference books—dictionaries, encyclopedias, yearbooks, almanacs, handbooks, bibliographies, atlases, directories, and biographical source books—can be used to find specific items of information. The reference librarian may suggest that you consult the recently published *Encyclopedia of Crime and Justice* for material on "gun control," but advise you that regular encyclopedias are better sources for the history of gun control laws in the United States. He or she can save you a lot of time by directing you to a recently published *bibliography* (printed list of books) on your subject.

Your next stop is the *Reserve Desk,* where materials for *limited loan* are placed and where you must ask for them. They are marked "Reserve" in the public catalog and on the materials themselves and their use is restricted to the library or extremely short loan periods, perhaps overnight. Some instructors ask that certain materials relating to their courses be placed on reserve so that all enrolled students have an opportunity to use them.

You are now ready to search for material on "gun control" in some important *nonbook* sources, materials not printed between the covers of books. They include periodicals or magazines, newspapers, pamphlets, maps, microfilm and microfiche, and media or audio-visual materials. Let's begin in the *Periodical Room.*

Literally hundreds of periodical articles on your subject have been published over the years, and you can locate them all in the *periodical indexes* which have two forms: print and microfilm. Although there are many printed periodical indexes that the reference librarian can show you in the college library, the most widely used, and the one most popular with the general public and beginning college students, is the *Readers' Guide to Periodical Literature.* It has been published continuously, first in paper issues and later in bound volumes, since 1905. It indexes, or lists, articles in about 150 popular periodicals by author, title, and subject, but most students look up practically all of their material under subject. Before you use the *Readers' Guide,* read the instructions and the list of abbreviations in the front of the book. The reference librarian will explain anything you don't understand.

To find articles on "gun control," look under that subject in the most recent paper issues of the *Readers' Guide* (for material on the history of this subject, search through older issues of this index). When you look under "gun control," you find a cross-reference (as you did in the card catalog) to the heading "Firearms—laws and regulations," which lists periodical articles on the subject. (See Figures 9-2a and 9-2b for sample entries.)

A far faster and easier way to find recent periodical articles on your subject is to use *The Magazine Index,* which includes over 670,000 articles in more than 400 magazines printed during a four-year period. This index is a type of *microfilm reader;* it magnifies material that has been photographed, reduced, and stored on rolls of film. Directions for use are posted on the unit. Most libraries update the index every month or two to include the most recent four-year period.

Special Services

College libraries offer many special services and some equipment that you can use to great advantage. These include coin-operated typewriters and copying machines, conference rooms for group study, computerized literature searching, and interlibrary loans. Some libraries have microcomputers for student use, and many can arrange telefacsimile transmission of documents (a process by which pages of text are sent by wire or satellite from one library to another). Two of these services deserve special mention.

One is computerized literature searching, which can save you hours of time because you can locate material in any library that is a member of the service. You can make an appointment with the reference librarian for an *online search* of *databases* likely to contain material on a particular subject. "Online" means the computer that contains the information you need is accessible over telephone lines to a user with a computer terminal and the proper password. "Database" refers to information files which are stored in a computer and which can be made accessible to a user. These data are continuously updated. This kind of search is incredibly fast and efficient. It is also expensive. Your library has to pay for it and must pass the charge on to you in most cases. Ask about the cost in advance.

The other is interlibrary loans, which enable you to borrow material from another library when your library does not have it. Again, the reference librarian can arrange this service for you. If you need a periodical article, the lending library sends your library a photocopy of it. You must then pay a fee to your library to cover the cost of duplicating, processing, and mailing the material. Get an estimate of the fee before you request an article. Usually there is no charge for borrowing books, but the length of time you may keep them is

The boxed item shows a cross reference to firearms.

Negotiable instruments
Securities
Stock exchanges
Stocks
Taxation
United States—Appropriations and expenditures
United States—Economic conditions
United States. Dept. of the Treasury
    See also subhead Finance under various subjects

British Columbia
The school board takeover [budget battle results in firing of Vancouver trustees] J. O'Hara. il *Macleans* 98:10-11 My 20 '85

Canada
    See also
Banks and banking—Canada
Budget—Canada
Debts, Public—Canada

Great Britain
    See also
Securities—Great Britain

Italy
    See also
Money—Italy
Securities—Italy
Stock exchanges—Milan exchange

Finance, International
    See also
Debts, External
Inflation (Finance)
International Monetary Fund

Finance, Personal
    See also
Children—Cost of raising
Investments
Loans, Personal
Saving and savings
Youth—Economic conditions
Money talk. A. Williams. *Saturday Evening Post* 257:40+ My/Je '85

Finance Committee *See* United States. Congress. Senate. Committee on Finance

Finance companies
    See also
Beneficial Corporation

Accounting
A balance-sheet buster from the FASB [finance subsidiaries] S. Weiss. il *Bus Week* p107 Je 10 '85

Japan
The plight of the spendthrift in thrifty Japan [loan sharks] R. Phalon. il *Forbes* 135:50+ My 20 '85

Financial Accounting Standards Board
A balance-sheet buster from the FASB [finance subsidiaries] S. Weiss. il *Bus Week* p107 Je 10 '85
Pass that peace pipe [compromise proposal on pension liability] J. Andresky. il *Forbes* 135:196 My 20 '85

Financial analysts *See* Investment advisers
Financial consultants *See* Investment advisers
Financial guaranties *See* Securities—Guaranty
Financial institutions
    See also
Banks and banking
Brokers
Finance companies
Investment trusts
Savings and loan associations

Acquisitions and mergers

Canada
The Bronfman empire's reach. R. McQueen. il pors *Macleans* 98:42-3 My 6 '85

Investments
    See Institutional investments

Laws and regulations
The debanking of Canada [views of R. Bandeen] P. C. Newman. il por *Macleans* 98:41 My 6 '85

Sears, Roebuck and Co.
Financial statements
    See also
Bush, George, 1924-—Financial disclosure
Congressmen—Financial disclosure
Corporation reports
Reagan, Ronald, 1911-—Financial disclosure

Fines (Penalties)
CAFE: it's no cheap lunch in Detroit [Corporate Average Fuel Economy] *U S News World Rep* 98:56 My 13 '85
Chrysler vs. GM, Ford on fuel rule fines [Corporate Average Fuel Economy standard] M. Crawford. *Science* 228:307 Ap 19 '85
Close the doors on CAFE standards. M. Copulos. il *Consum Res Mag* 68:16-18 My '85
Ford and GM want a federal bailout on fuel economy [Corporate Average Fuel Economy Standard] *Consum Rep* 50:262 My '85

Fingernail manicuring *See* Manicuring
Finishes and finishing
    See also
Furniture—Finishes and finishing

Fink, Robert A.
Great blue heron [poem] *Blair Ketchums Ctry J* 12:71 Ap '85

Fiorentino, Linda
    about
Leggy Linda Fiorentino says Gotcha! to some of the silver screen's cutest virgin hunks. D. Donahue. il pors *People Wkly* 23:53-4+ My 27 '85

Fire engines
    See also
American La France
Emergency One (Firm)
The limits of tradition [fire truck market] J. Merwin. il *Forbes* 135:112+ My 20 '85

Fire extinction
    Equipment
    See also
Fire engines

Fire on the mountain [television program] *See* Television program reviews—Single works

Fire prevention
    See also
Old age homes—Fires and fire prevention
Stadiums—Fires and fire prevention

Fire trucks *See* Fire engines
The fire unleashed [television program] *See* Television program reviews—Single works

Firearms
    See also
Air guns
    Laws and regulations
Endangered tradition. D. E. Petzal. See issues of Field & Stream beginning March 1985
Shooting down gun myths [Second Amendment] R. J. Spitzer. *America* 152:468-9 Je 8 '85
Firearms industry
    See also
Weatherby, Inc.

Fires
    See also
Brush fires
Casinos—Fires and fire prevention
Colleges and universities—Fires and fire prevention
Old age homes—Fires and fire prevention
Stadiums—Fires and fire prevention

Firewood storage *See* Woodbins, racks, etc.
Firing of employees *See* Employees—Dismissal
Firing of teachers *See* Teachers—Dismissal
First aid in illness and injury
    See also
Burns and scalds
Until help arrives [farm accidents] A. Hannay. il *Blair Ketchums Ctry J* 12:79-83 My '85

Figure 9–2a

The boxed item is an article on gun control.

Guidance *See* Counseling

Guidance, Vocational *See* Vocational guidance

Guidebooks

Mr. Chow libel award overturned on appeal [Guide Gault-Millau restaurant review suit] J. Mutter. *Publ Wkly* 227:18 Ap 12 '85

Bibliography

Big Bend to Piney Woods: a roundup of guides for the Texas traveler. J. F. King. il *Sierra* 70:88-91 My/Je '85

Guided missile industries

See also
    General Dynamics Corp.
    McDonnell Douglas Corp.

Guided missiles

Continuing the acquisition of the Peacekeeper missile [message to Congress and summary of report, March 4, 1985] R. Reagan. *Dep State Bull* 85:57-9 Ap '85

The importance of the MX Peacekeeper missile [statement, February 26, 1985] G. P. Shultz. *Dep State Bull* 85:23-5 Ap '85

Old Titan missiles given new life [proposals to convert into expendable launchers] il *Space World* V-5-257:32-3 My '85

Accidents and explosions

Army alters Pershing 2 to prevent accidents. *Aviat Week Space Technol* 122:24 My 6 '85

Costs

Half full [Senate limits deployment of MX] *Time* 125:22 Je 3 '85

Defenses

Downing Street muddle [views of G. Howe on the Strategic Defense Initiative] *Natl Rev* 37:18 My 3 '85

Europe leaders expect international participation in Defense Initiative. M. Feazel. *Aviat Week Space Technol* 122:101+ My 27 '85

House panel cuts Strategic Defense by $1.24 billion [Armed Services Committee] E. Kozicharow. *Aviat Week Space Technol* 122:23 My 20 '85

New gains could cut antimissile laser costs [Strategic Defense Initiative] P. Mann. *Aviat Week Space Technol* 122:97+ My 20 '85

News conference: January 9, 1985 [excerpts] R. Reagan. *Dep State Bull* 85:5-7 Mr '85

Nuclear strategy: can there be a happy ending? [Strategic Defense Initiative] F. C. Iklé. *Foreign Aff* 63:810-26 Spr '85

The president's Strategic Defense Initiative [text of pamphlet] *Dep State Bull* 85:65-72 Mr '85

SDI Office pushes innovative science, technology research. P. J. Klass. *Aviat Week Space Technol* 122:225+ Ap 29 '85

SDI Organization moves to promote non-U.S. share of research work. E. Kozicharow. *Aviat Week Space Technol* 122:215-21 Ap 29 '85

Spark for technology [Strategic Defense Initiative] W. H. Gregory. *Aviat Week Space Technol* 122:11 My 27 '85

Star Wars at the summit [Bonn summit] H. Quinn. il por *Macleans* 98:32-3 My 6 '85

Star Wars grants attract universities. R. J. Smith. *Science* 228:304 Ap 19 '85

Star Wars: lasers can guide electrons. J. Raloff. il *Sci News* 127:230 Ap 13 '85

Star Wars once funny, now frightening. H. Brown. *Bull At Sci* 41:3 My '85

Understanding treaties [Strategic Defense Initiative and treaty limiting anti-ballistic-missile systems] *Natl Rev* 37:15-16 My 17 '85

Wagons hitched to Star Wars [possible participation by NA...

Guided missiles, Russian

A new Soviet missile angers the White House [tests of the SS25 violate SALT II] R. J. Smith. il *Science* 228:155-7 Ap 12 '85

Guiding of telescopes *See* Telescopes—Control

Guillou, Ruth

about

How's your pickup? L.A.'s Freeway Singles Club offers a smooth way to get your love life in gear. J. Pilcher. il por *People Wkly* 23:104-5 My 27 '85

Guilt

Tired of hearing mothers ask, What did I do wrong?, Lynn Caine wrote a book saying Knock it off! [interview] J. Stark. il por *People Wkly* 23:112+ My 27 '85

What are nonconfessing Catholics doing with their guilt? E. C. Polomsky. il *U S Cathol* 50:30-6 Ap '85

Guitar music

Henry Kaiser's solo on Omaha—a guitar transcription. S. Vai. *Down Beat* 52:56-7 My '85

Guitarists

See also
    Kaiser, Henry
    Mack, Lonnie
    Remler, Emily

Gulbenk Collection *See* Antiques—Collectors and collecting

Gulf & Western Industries, Inc.

Golden parachutes come to publishing. J. Mutter. il *Publ Wkly* 227:14+ Ap 5 '85

P-H Canada faces U.S. ownership review. B. Slopen. *Publ Wkly* 227:12 Ap 5 '85

Gulf Canada Limited

A developer strikes oil [Olympia & York buyout of Gulf Canada] R. Laver. il *Macleans* 98:44 Je 3 '85

What the Reichmanns see in Canada's oil patch. B. Javetski and others. il *Bus Week* p62-3 Je 10 '85

Gulf of Mexico

See also
    Helicopter airlines—Gulf of Mexico

Gulf Resources & Chemical Corp.

He who lives by the raid . . . [dissident shareholders stage proxy] J. R. Norman. *Bus Week* p114+ My 20 '85

Gums

Diseases

See also
    Dental plaque

Gun control legislation *See* Firearms—Laws and regulations
Guns (Small arms) *See* Firearms

Gurney family

about

The Gurneys: perfect together. L.-M. Singer. il pors *World Tennis* 32:49-51+ Ap '85

Guterman, Gerald

about

Selling the dream. A. D. Frank. il por *Forbes* 135:96-7 Je 3 '85

Guyer, Murphy

about

Eden Court [drama] Reviews
    N Y il 18:101-2 My 27 '85. J. Simon

Gwaltney, Eugene C.

about

Like the kid at F.A.O. Schwarz. R. Behar. il por *Forbes* 135:162 My 20 '85

Gwynn, Robin

England's 'first refugees'. il *Hist Today* 35:22-8 My '85

Gymnastics

Mary Lou Retton: life after the Olympics. pors *Teen* 29:94+ My '85

The naked sport. G. Norman. il *Esquire* 103:185-6+ My '85

Gypsum industry

Figure 9–2b

often very limited. A service similar to interlibrary loans is provided by University Microfilms International Article Clearinghouse. This electronic mail service ships listed articles from more than 7,300 periodicals within 48 hours of order. Ask the librarian about the cost of this service.

Write all required information for each periodical you wish to see on separate *periodical call slips,* provided by the library, and ask the clerk at the *Periodical Services Desk* to find the materials for you. Be sure to include the full (not abbreviated) name of the periodical, volume number, date, and page numbers of the article you wish. Most college libraries do not allow you to check these periodicals out of the building, so you may have to photocopy materials from them to use at home.

Your next stop is the *Newspaper Room.* Much valuable material on "gun control" appears in newspapers, and you can find it in printed and microfilmed indexes similar to those for periodicals. Articles in *The New York Times, Christian Science Monitor, Los Angeles Times, Washington Post,* and *Wall Street Journal* are indexed in five separate, printed indexes; however, all five are included in *The National Newspaper Index,* a microfilm reader which operates the same way as *The Magazine Index.* Don't forget to write down the title of the article, author (if given), name of the newspaper, date, page, and column (one of six or eight vertical sections of print on a page) so that the clerk at the *Newspaper Service Desk* can easily find the material you request.

Remember that because shelf space is so limited, most libraries store old issues of periodicals and newspapers on microfilm or *microfiche* (small sheets or cards of film on which reduced photographic images of pages are arranged in rows or columns which are magnified when they are viewed with a microfiche reader). Microfilm and microfiche functions are combined in some units, and most readers have built-in copiers so that you can have printed pages of text for reference.

Another valuable source of materials is the *Pamphlet* or *Vertical File.* Pamphlets are publications that are too small or brief or of too temporary interest to be treated as books in the library; however, they are always a good source for current events and issues, such as "gun control." Articles clipped from newspapers or magazines, photographs, charts, graphs, and maps are also kept in this file although maps are often kept in special *Map Rooms* in larger libraries. These materials have their own index since they are not listed in the public catalog.

One of the last stops on your tour is the *Government Publications* (or *Documents) Room.* As their title indicates, Government Documents are published by the U.S. Government, the governments of the 50 states, and by foreign governments. In larger libraries, these documents do not appear in the public catalog; you must locate them through special indexes in the Government Documents Room. There is much valuable material on "gun control" in these publications.

The final stop on your tour is the *Media Services Room.* Here you can find and sometimes check out films, filmstrips, slides, cassettes, videotapes, phonograph records, and art prints. There may be useful media material on "gun control" that could add greatly to your understanding of the subject. This room also stores and maintains the equipment you need to use the media, such as projectors and record players.

Conclusion

The rich variety of materials and help available from library personnel should ensure your success in locating and using materials in the modern American college library. But you can't study all the time, and you should not think of the college library as only a place to do research or prepare for the next test. It's also a place to sit down and enjoy a good novel or browse through a current newspaper or magazine. Some libraries offer special programs, such as book discussion groups, film showings, book and art exhibits, concerts, or lectures. All of these events can greatly enrich your college experience.

WORKING BIBLIOGRAPHY

The minute you begin research, start compiling bibliography cards showing possible helpful references. Use a separate three-by-five or four-by-six inch card for each source. Why use cards instead of notebook paper? Cards save time and promote efficiency in organizing information. They are made of heavy paper, are not damaged by frequent rearrangement, and are easy to handle (unlike flimsy notebook paper that wrinkles and tears easily). You can arrange them numerically, alphabetically, by subject, by author, by title of publication, in the order of your outline, in the order of their usefulness, etc. simply by physically moving them. You can throw away cards citing sources that you don't intend to use. But if you use notebook paper, you have to write numbers, letters, and so on in the margin beside each entry, erasing or scratching out mistakes, changes from the previous order, or discarded sources as you go along. If you cut up the paper and paste or tape individual entries in the right order on another piece of paper, you may accidentally cut up notes on the back of the page or, at the very least, have to recopy notes to avoid losing them in the transfer. After a while, your notes will be hopelessly confused. So, trust your instructor's good judgment when he or she insists that you use cards. You'll be glad you did.

Always record all publication information about each possible reference, whether it is a book, a periodical, reference book, lecture, film, etc. Follow *exactly* the samples of Modern Language Association (MLA) documentation style used for preparing the list of works cited. (Several other approved styles vary the order, punctuation, or capitalization of the facts of publication, omit selected facts, or specify the use of certain abbreviations, but the MLA style is complete enough for you to convert information later. Be sure to ask instructors of courses other than English which documentation styles they prefer. If style sheets, handbooks, or documentation guides are available, follow the rules exactly. Your grade may be lowered if you cite references incorrectly.) In addition, write the call number of each book in the upper right corner of the bibliography card; then you can easily find it in the stacks. If the library does not own the book, list the publication information for the bibliography in which you found it (at the bottom of the card). Your librarian may be able to arrange an interlibrary loan.

If you use correct, complete documentation on each of your bibliography cards, as shown in Figure 9–3, preparation of the alphabetized list of *Works Cited* (the final page of your paper) will be easy. If you do a sloppy job, though, you'll be furious when you are typing your final draft at midnight, the library is closed, and you notice that you need some page numbers or publication dates for citations that are crucial to support your ideas.

MLA DOCUMENTATION STYLE

As you do your research, you will see many examples of the former MLA format that required numbered footnotes or endnotes and a separate alphabetized bibliography to document sources. Now, brief in-text parenthetical citations, giving the author and page number, are used instead of documentation footnotes or endnotes, and a simplified alphabetized list of *Works Cited* replaces the bibliography. In-text citations usually give the author's last name (or the title of the work if no author is given or if more than one work by the same author is cited) and the page number of the quote and look like this:

> Arguments exist in support of both sides of the emotional issue of gun control. Proponents believe that prohibition of private ownership of handguns would save many lives and prevent crime and violence. Opponents point out that "legislating against the freedoms of law-abiding citizens and expecting criminals to willingly oblige" (Constantino 16) is unrealistic.

Full documentation of the source is given in the list of works cited. Begin the list at the top of a new page immediately following the last page of text and number it consecutively with the rest. (If the paper ends with page 8, the list starts on page 9.) Center the title, *Works Cited,* one inch from the top of the page. Begin the first line of each entry at the left margin; indent all other lines of each entry five spaces. Double space the entire list. Alphabetize entries by the last name of the author or the first word of the title (other than definite or indefinite articles) if no author is given. (Titles shown in the text in italics are underlined when handwritten or typed, as illustrated in the list of works cited

Bibliography Cards

Bruce-Briggs, B. "The   344.73
Great American Gun   186
War." *The Issue of*
Gun Control. Ed. Thomas
Draper. The Reference
Shelf 53. New York:
Wilson, 1981: 8-38.

Kates, Don B., Jr. "Gun Control:
The Real Facts." *Field and*
Stream July 1979: 34+.

Figure 9-3a

Bibliography Cards

Meacham, Craig L. "Prop. 15:
Should We Restrict
Handguns? No: It Won't
Cut Crime or Deter
Criminals." Los Angeles
Times 24 Oct. 1982, sec. 4: 1+.

Sherrill, Robert. The Saturday
Night Special. New York:
Penguin, 1975.

Draper. Bibliography 188.

Figure 9-3b

following the student research paper at the end of this chapter.) The list looks like this:

Works Cited

Constantino, Jerry R. "For Your Information." *Shooting Times* Jan. 1981: 16+.

"Interview with Senator Edward M. Kennedy (Massachusetts), with commentary by firearms-law authority Don B. Kates, Jr." *Field and Stream* Aug. 1980: 10+.

Kates, Don B., Jr. "Gun Control: The Real Facts." *Field and Stream* July 1979: 34+.

Rains, John. "Your Right to Live Without Fear!" *Guns & Ammo* Dec. 1980: 28+.

Numbered notes are seldom used with parenthetical documentation. Use them only for (1) content notes that supply supplementary (definition, explanation, or identification) or evaluative information that really doesn't belong in the body of your paper, or (2) bibliographic notes that give alternate sources or make comments about the sources you use in the paper. Try to include the necessary information in the text; otherwise, keep notes short. In the text, notes are indicated by raised (superscript) consecutive numbers throughout the paper and are listed numerically on a separate page, entitled *Notes,* immediately following the text (before the list of works cited). Notes may also be typed at the bottoms of the pages on which they occur. The documentation format differs from that of the list of works cited. Show notes in the text this way:

Senator Edward Kennedy's interest in and legislative response to the issue of gun control[1] is certainly understandable because two of his brothers were assassinated: President John F. Kennedy, in 1963, and Senator Robert Kennedy, in 1968. However, skeptical liberals such as law professor Don Kates[2] doubt that handgun restrictions will reduce crime.

Notes

[1]Kennedy comments extensively on gun control legislation he has introduced in an interview with *Field and Stream,* Aug. 1980. (Bibliographic note; complete documentation appears in the list of works cited.)

[2]Don B. Kates, Jr., ed. *Handgun Restrictions: The Liberal Skeptics Take a Look* (New York: North River Press, 1979), excerpted in *Field and Stream,* July 1979. (Content note explains origin of excerpted material in secondary source which appears in list of works cited.)

Here are samples of the most common MLA citation forms showing the correct order of the facts of publication. For examples of less common forms, consult the *MLA Handbook for Writers of Research Papers,* 2nd ed.

BOOKS

List all available and applicable information. If information is missing, go on to the next item. Punctuate as directed. (Although quotation marks are used to explain abbreviations in the following directions, you should use them *only* to indicate the title of a part of a book as described in 2 of the following instructions.) After each period, leave two spaces before beginning the next segment with a capital letter. Use the following order:

1. Give the author's or authors' names. For one author, list the last name; follow with a comma; leave one space. List the first name; leave one space. Give the middle initial or name; follow with a period and two spaces. For books with two or more authors or for editors of anthologies, see examples).

2. Show the title of a part of a book (a single chapter, an essay, a short story, an article, or a poem in an anthology), follow with a period, and enclose all in quotation marks. Leave two spaces.

3. List the title of book (followed by a colon, two spaces, and the subtitle if there is one), all underlined. Follow with a period and two spaces.

4. Include the editor or translator (abbreviated "Ed." or "Trans."). Follow with a period and one space. Then give the name in correct order, and punctuate with a period. Leave two spaces.

5. Indicate the edition (abbreviated "ed."), except for the first edition, preceded by an ordinal number (2nd ed.) or by name (Rev. ed or Alt. ed, for "revised" and "alternate" editions) followed by a period and two spaces.

6. List the number of volumes when a work is divided into two or more (abbreviated "2 vols."). Follow with a period and two spaces.

7. Give the series title (do not underline or use quotation marks); follow with one space. Show the series number in Arabic numerals, and follow with a period and two spaces.

8. Show the city of publication (printed on the front or back of the title page) followed by a colon and a space; if more than one city is listed, use the

first; if the city is not well known, follow it with a comma, a space, and the accepted abbreviation for the state or the country; use "n.p." if no place of publication is given).

9. List the publisher (use "n.p." if no publisher is shown; if neither place nor publisher is shown, use one "n.p." for both), abbreviated for well known U.S. publishers; for example, Prentice (Prentice-Hall), Scribner's (Charles Scribner's Sons), Dell (Dell Publishing Company), Norton (W. W. Norton & Co. Inc.), Harvard UP (Harvard University Press), U of Chicago P (University of Chicago Press), or GPO (Government Printing Office). Follow with a comma and one space.

10. Include the year of publication or latest copyright date (use "n.d." if no date is shown); follow with a period and two spaces.

11. Give page numbers (for citing a part of a book) for the entire essay, story, poem, etc. (not just the page or pages you cite parenthetically in the text; use "n. pag." if pages are not numbered). Conclude the entry with a period.

Book by one author

Munitz, Milton K. *The Mystery of Existence: An Essay in Philosophical Cosmology*. New York: New York UP, 1974.

Book by two or three authors

Invert the first author's name as for a single author, follow with a comma, and list the second and third authors' names in the correct order (use the conjunction "and" as in a series).

Miller, Casey, and Kate Swift. *Words and Women*. Garden City, NY: Anchor, 1977.

Leggett, Glenn, C. David Mead, and William Charvat. *Prentice-Hall Handbook for Writers*. 8th ed. Englewood Cliffs, NJ: Prentice, 1982.

Book by more than three authors

List the first name as for a single author, follow the period after the middle initial with a comma, and include the Latin words "et al." ("and others.")

Danielson, Dorothy F., et al. *Reading in English for Students of English as a Second Language*. 2nd ed. Englewood Cliffs, NJ: Prentice, 1980.

More than one work by the same author (or authors)

Use the author's name in the first entry. For subsequent entries, instead of the name, use three hyphens (note that the printed version uses a solid line apoproximating the length of three hyphens) and a period starting at the left margin. Punctuate with a period and leave two spaces before beginning the title.

Bellow, Saul. *Mr. Sammler's Planet*. New York: Penguin, 1977.

———. *Seize the Day*. New York: Avon, 1977.

Use the same format for a translator or an editor, but follow the three hyphens with a comma, skip one space, write the proper abbreviation ("ed." or "trans."), punctuate with a period, leave two spaces, and follow with the title.

Barnet, Sylvan, Morton Berman, and William Burto, eds. *Eight Great Comedies*. New York: NAL, 1958.

———, eds. *Eight Great Tragedies*. New York: NAL, 1957.

Book in edition other than the first

The edition number is usually indicated only on the second and following editions.

Barnet, Sylvan, Morton Berman, and William Burto, eds. *An Introduction to Literature: Fiction/Poetry/Drama*. 7th ed. Boston: Little, 1981.

Sandars, N. K., trans. *The Epic of Gilgamesh*. Rev. ed. New York: Penguin, 1972.

Edited book

This citation form is used when a work by one author has been "edited" by another, or when another author may have added a foreword or an afterword, written explanatory notes, or included other clarifications.

To refer to the original author's work and ideas, use this form:

Eliot, George. *The Mill on the Floss*. Ed. Gordon S. Haight. Boston: Houghton, 1961.

Cite the editor's contributions as follows:

Barrett, Michele, ed. *Women and Writing*. By Virginia Woolf. New York: Harcourt, 1979.

Book with an introduction, preface, foreword, or afterword

Cite an introduction, preface, etc. written by an author different from the author of the book, as follows:

Eble, Kenneth. Introduction. *The Awakening*. By Kate Chopin. New York: Putnam's, 1964. v–xiv.

If the author of the book is also the author of the introduction or foreword, use this form:

Shelley, Mary. Preface. *Frankenstein: Or, The Modern Prometheus*. By Shelley. New York: NAL, 1965, xiii–xiv.

Book translated into English

To refer to the work itself, use this form:

Colette. *The Cat*. Trans. Antonia White. New York: Popular Library, 1955.

To cite the work or interpretation of the translator (rather than the original work of the author), use this form:

Ciardi, John, trans. *The Inferno*. By Dante Alighieri. New York: NAL, 1954.

Book in a language other than English

Consult the *MLA Handbook* for specific rules governing capitalization in foreign languages. Each language has slightly different rules. For a French title, capitalize only the first letter of the first word and of proper nouns; otherwise, use the same citation format:

Mauriac, Francois. *Le desert de l'amour*. Paris: Livre de Poche, 1961.

Anthology or collection

Show editors of a work that contains a collection of short pieces (articles, stories, poems, essays) as follows:

Abell, George O., and Barry Singer, eds. *Science and the Paranormal: Probing the Existence of the Supernatural*. New York: Scribner's, 1981. (See **cross-references**)

Cite an individual selection in a collection or an anthology this way:

Browning, Robert. "My Last Duchess." *Browning Poetical Works, 1833–1864*. Ed. Ian Jack. London: Oxford UP, 1970. 367–369.

Cross-references

Cite more than one work from the same collection by cross-referencing, which avoids repetition of publication data. The major reference is to the larger work; cross references are to smaller works included in the anthology or collection.

Hyman, Ray. "Scientists and Psychics." Abell and Singer 119–141.

(See complete reference under **anthology or collection.**)

Book in a series

Do not underline or enclose in quotation marks the name of the series. Include the series number before the publication information.

Chapman, Jane Roberts, and Margaret Gates, eds. *Women Into Wives: The Legal and Economic Impact of Marriage*. Sage Yearbooks in Women's Policy Studies 2. Beverly Hills, CA: Sage, 1977.

Work in two or more volumes

Always indicate the total number of volumes after the title even though you may use only one volume. The parenthetical citation in the text should include the volume and the page numbers used; for example, 2: 1089 (see the sample entry for Tolstoy).

Mann, Thomas. *Joseph and His Brothers*. 4 vols. Trans. H. T. Lowe-Porter. London: Sphere, 1968.

To refer to a specific selection in a work with more than one volume:

Tolstoy, Leo. "The Death of Ivan Ilyich." *The Continental Edition of World Masterpieces*. 4th ed. 2 vols. Eds. Maynard Mack, et al. New York: Norton, 1966. 2: 1084–1131.

Reprinted book

Show the original publication date immediately after the title:

Gilman, Charlotte Perkins. *The Yellow Wallpaper.* 1899. Old Westbury, NY: Feminist, 1973.

Book by anonymous author

Since the author is unknown, begin with the title:

Aucassin and Nicolette and Other Medieval Romances and Legends. Trans. Eugene Mason. New York: Dutton, 1958.

Book with corporate author

A corporate author may be a group of employees who prepare a book about the work or a product of their company, a committee, a charitable organization—even a publisher. The book need not be commercially published.

This book, produced by the staff of a large corporation, explains the characteristics of transistors:

The Engineering Staff of Texas Instruments Incorporated Semiconductor Group. *The TTL Data Book for Design Engineers.* 2nd ed. N.p.: Texas Instruments Incorporated, 1976.

Alphabetize the group author under "E" (for Engineering) in the list of works cited.

Pamphlet

Follow the book documentation format. Pamphlets are often of corporate authorship and are issued by both government agencies (both agency and department are shown as the "author," as illustrated in the following example) and private institutions. Frequently, pamphlets have incomplete publication information.

United States Dept. of Transportation. Federal Aviation Administration. Flight Standards Service. *Flight Test Guide [Part 61 Rev.]: Commercial Pilot, Airplane.* Washington: GPO, 1973.

Some pamphlets are written by individuals:

Belding, Warren D. *TM010 DTSS Library Programs*. Dartmouth College, July 1976.

Government agencies also produce information pamphlets:

California Dept. of Justice. *Women's Rights Handbook*. Information Pamphlet 9. 1983.

Articles in reference books

For entries from well known encyclopedias and dictionaries, you may omit the name of the editor, the volume and page numbers (when articles are arranged alphabetically), and the place of publication. Do include the author's name if the article is signed. If only initials are used, check the list of initials (usually located in the front of the volume) for the author's name.
For a signed article, use this form:

Billingsley, John D. "Small Arms." *The Encyclopedia Americana: International Edition*. 1984 ed.

Cite an unsigned article this way:

"Gun Control." *Academic American Encyclopedia*. 1983 ed.

Citations for less common reference books, many of which have only one edition, should be shown this way:

Blodgett, Geoffrey. "Woodhull, Victoria Claflin." *Notable American Women: 1607–1950: A Biographical Dictionary*. 3 vols. Ed. Edward T. James. Cambridge: Belknap, 1971.

Cite an unsigned article in the first edition as follows:

"30 March 1972: The Women's Rights Movement." *The Almanac of American History*. Ed. Arthur M. Schlessinger, Jr. New York: Putnam, 1983.

Government publications

List the author, if known; otherwise, begin with the name of the government. Then give the name of the agency or body and of the subsidiary. Standard abbreviations are acceptable if their meaning is clear. List the title of the document (underlined), identifying numbers, the place of publication, the publisher, and the date. For Congressional publications (other than the *Congressional Record,* which publishes all the proceedings of the Senate and the House) distinguish between the Senate and the House of Representatives, and include the number of the Congress and the session number. Most federal documents are printed by the Government Printing Office (GPO). Use three hyphens and a period when the name of a government or an agency is repeated.

California. Dept. of Alcohol and Drug Programs. *A Directory of Community Services for Alcohol Abuse and Alcoholism in California.* Sacramento: The Department of Alcohol and Drug Programs, 1980.

———. Dept. of Consumer Affairs. *Got a Consumer Gripe?* Rev. ed. Sacramento: The Department of Consumer Affairs, 1981.

Carter, Jimmy. *State of the Union Message: Message from the President of the United States Transmitting a Report of the State of the Union.* Washington: GPO, 1981.

Cong. Rec. 17 May 1984: 130–65.

United States. Cong. House. *Our American Government: What Is It? How Does It Function? 150 Questions and Answers.* 96th Cong. 2nd sess. Washington: GPO, 1981.

———. ———. Senate. *Hearings Before the Subcommittee on Executive Reorganization of the Committee on Government Operations.* 89th Cong., 2nd sess. Washington: GPO, 1966.

———. Dept. of Justice. Bureau of Justice Statistics. *Intimate Victims: A Study of Violence Among Friends and Relatives.* Washington: GPO, 1980.

———. Dept. of Transportation. *Instrument Flying Handbook,* rev. ed. Washington: GPO, 1971.

PERIODICALS

Magazines (*Time, Life, Newsweek, Popular Mechanics, Business Week,* etc.) and newspapers (*Washington Post, Los Angeles Times, New York Times,* etc.) contain articles written for the general public. Journals (*College English, Technology Review, Scientific American, American Journal of Psychiatry,* etc.) publish scholarship or research and are intended for a limited academic or technical audience. Document periodicals as follows, using the format and punctuation shown in the examples. If information is missing, go on to the next item.

1. List the author's or authors' names as for a book (if no author is given under the title or at the end of the article, begin with 2); follow with a period; leave two spaces.
2. Give the title of the article, *exactly as it appears on the first page;* follow with a period; enclose the title and the period in quotation marks—do not underline it; leave two spaces.
3. Underline the name of the periodical; leave one space.

4. Include the series number, if there is one; leave one space.

5. List the volume number (use the number only; don't include the abbreviation "vol."), followed by a space. (Include the issue number for a journal that does not use continuous pagination throughout the volume year.)

6. Show the year of publication enclosed in parentheses; follow with a colon and one space. Omit the volume and issue number for daily, weekly, or monthly periodicals; instead give the day, followed by a space. List the month (abbreviate all except May, June, and July), and leave a space; follow with the year, a colon, and one space.

7. List the page numbers for the complete article (cite the pages actually used parenthetically in the text); follow with a period. If the pages are not consecutive (for example, if an article begins on page 1, continues on page 2, and is continued on page 48), show the number of the first page followed immediately by a plus sign and a period (for example, 1+.).

Article from journal with continuous pagination

If page numbers begin with 1 in the first issue and run consecutively through each issue, a journal issued four times each year could be numbered as follows: Winter 1–236; Spring 237–498; Summer 499–702; Fall 703–998.

Webb, A. Dinsmoor. "The Science of Making Wine." *American Scientist* 71 (1984): 360–367.

Article from journal that uses independent pagination for each issue

If each issue begins with page one, place a period after the volume number (63), and immediately follow it with the issue number (4), as shown in this entry:

Bianchi, Eugene C. "Christianity and Violence." *National Forum* 63.4 (1983): 16–17.

Article from weekly or biweekly periodical

Omit volume and issue numbers. Give the full date as shown:

"Alive and Well: The Red Brigades Are Back." *Time* 27 Feb. 1984: 46.

Use a plus sign (+) to show discontinuous pages; for example, this article begins on page 41 and is continued on other pages scattered throughout the periodical:

Randolph, Anne. "JPL Set to Integrate Galileo Jupiter Probe with Orbiter." *Aviation Week & Space Technology* 27 Feb. 1984: 41+.

Article from monthly or bimonthly periodical

Omit the volume and issue numbers; give the month(s) and year as shown. Use a hyphen between page numbers that run continuously.

Diehl, Digby. "We'll Take Romance!" *Los Angeles* Feb. 1984: 132+.

McWilliams, Peter A. "Computers: Where the Joys Are." *Playboy* Nov. 1983: 107+.

Vaughn, Lewis. "Folk Remedies That Can Hurt You." *Prevention* Mar. 1984: 70–75.

Article from daily newspaper

If the author's name is not listed, begin with the title of the article. Include the city or state in square brackets, not underlined, following the name if the location is not obvious; for example, *Star-News* [Pasadena, CA]. Do not add a definite article that is not part of the title printed in large letters at the top of the first page (*Los Angeles Times,* not *The Los Angeles Times*). Omit volume and issue numbers, but list the full date as shown in the example. Include the edition if it is specified at the top of the first page; for example, home edition ("home ed."), final edition ("final ed."), western edition ("western ed."). Usually, the pages of each section are numbered separately. List them by letter or by number (with the abbreviation "sec."):

Section A, page 12. Cite as A-12.

Section I, pages 4, 8, and 9. Cite as sec. 1:4+.

Section II, page 1. Cite as sec. 2:1.

"Perfect Under Pressure: Mary Lou Retton Vaults into History." *Star-News* [Pasadena, CA] 4 Aug. 1984: A1+.

Roark, Anne C. "Anthropologists: Scientists Seek the 'Why' of the Olympics." *Los Angeles Times* 5 Aug. 1984, Sunday final ed.: sec. 1: 1+.

"Vatican Seen Retaining Galileo Heresy Finding." *Los Angeles Times* 3 Mar. 1984: sec. 1: 2.

Editorial

If the editorial is signed, begin with the author's last name; if unsigned, begin with the title of the editorial. Follow with the word "Editorial," as shown in the example. Continue with the periodical citation format.

Lemmons, Phil. "Another World: The 68000." Editorial. *Byte* Mar. 1985: 6.

"The President's Cancer." Editorial. *Los Angeles Times* 16 July 1985: sec. 2: 4.

OTHER SOURCES

Speeches, lectures, and public addresses

Show the speaker's names in inverted order as for the author of a book. Place quotation marks around the title of the address; if untitled, indicate the type of speech (Opening Remarks, Welcoming Address, etc.). List the occasion for the speech (such as a meeting, graduation, or convention), if applicable. Follow with the location and the date. Use the order and punctuation shown in the example:

Durant, Will and Ariel Durant. "Can Democracy Survive?" Commencement Address. Occidental College. Los Angeles, 8 June 1974.

Kennedy, Edward M. "Tolerance and Truth in America." Liberty Baptist College. Lynchburg, VA, 3 Oct. 1983.

Television programs

Place the title of the episode (if applicable) enclosed in quotation marks before the underlined program title. Next list the names of the writer, narrator, director, producer, or conductor, as appropriate. If you are referring to the work of one of them, rather than the program as a whole, list that person first. Give the series title (do not underline or place in quotation marks); identify the network, the name of the local station, the city where it is located, and the date of the broadcast.

"In Praise of Pip." Writ. Rod Serling. *The Twilight Zone.* Created by Rod Serling. Dir. Joseph Newman. Prod. Gert Granet. The Twilight Zone Marathon. KTLA, Los Angeles. 4 July 1985.

Herriot, James. "Alarms and Excursions." *All Creatures Great and Small.* Adapt. Brian Finch. Dir. Richard Bramall. Prod. Bill Sellars. With Robert Hardy and Christopher Timothy. PBS. KCET, Los Angeles. 21 July 1985.

Films and videotapes

Show the title (underlined), the director, the distributor, and the year. Optional supplementary information, such as writer, producer, or performers, follows the title. Film characteristics (millimeter, running time, and color or black and white) follow the year. Videotapes should be indicated by name directly following the title. Credit the special work of a writer, director, or actor by beginning the citation with his or her name.

A Little Romance. Dir. George Roy Hill. Warner Bros., 1979.

One-Eyed Men Are Kings. Dir. Edmond Sechan. Prod. C.A.P.A.C. Productions. CRM McGraw-Hill Films, 1974. 16 mm., 15 min., color.

Clavell, James, Dir., Writ., Narr. *The Children's Story . . . but not just for children*. Videocassette. Twyman Films, Inc., 1982.

Computer software

List the author of the program (if known). Underline the name of the program, follow with a period and the words "Computer software" (do not underline or place in quotation marks). Next, show the distributor and the publication year. Punctuate all items as shown in the example. Other information, such as the operating system, name of computer for which it is intended, and the format of the program may follow the entry.

Norton, Peter. *The Norton Utilities*. Computer software. 1984. MS-DOS, disk.

Turbo Pascal. Computer software. Borland International, 1983. Otrona Attache, CP/M 80, disk.

The Word Plus. Computer software. Oasis Systems, 1981. CP/M, disk.

Services that provide electronic data transfer

Cite as printed material. At the end of the entry, cite the name of the service and give identifying numbers for location of the material.

Levinson, W. A. "I'm Building My Tax Shelter with ROCS." *Medical Economics* 13 June 1983: 193+. The Source.

Danielson, Dorothy, and Rebecca Hayden. *Using English: Your Second Language*. Prentice, 1973. DIALOG file 3, item 0472922 0465275XX.

EFFECTIVE NOTE TAKING

First, examine the most promising sources listed on your bibliography cards. Be sure to save all the cards until you have finished the project in case your first choices are poor references. Quickly scan articles, pamphlets, books, and other materials to see if they cover your argument or position. If not, look for new sources right away.

Next, prepare note cards. Use a separate three-by-five or four-by-six inch note card for each piece of information, and write in ink on only one side. Write the author's name at the top of the card. Include additional information as needed (for example, if you are using two works by the same author, give the title of each). After you have written the note or quotation on the card, write the page number. If the source material begins on one page and concludes on another page, mark the break point with a slash (/) and show both page numbers in case you use only part of the quotation. If the note is very long, continue it on another card (indicating on the first card that you have done so; for instance, "continued," "1 of 3," or "more"), and list the source, page number, and note card number on each succeeding card. Examples of note cards are shown in Figure 9–4.

A note card may quote, summarize, paraphrase, or interpret the author's ideas. All quoted material should be enclosed in quotation marks and copied *exactly* as it is shown in the original version. Quotes should be selected so that they (1) provide factual evidence to support a point; (2) explain or define a difficult concept; (3) illustrate the author's expressiveness, vocabulary, tone, or style; or (4) supplement a discussion written in your own words.

To avoid plagiarism, you *must* give the author credit for his or her ideas whether you have summarized, copied, or recreated them from memory. The author "owns" those words. He or she worked hard to create them. If you use them without acknowledging their origin, you are stealing them. Many ESL students are so skilled at memorization techniques that they forget where the author's work ends and their own begins—everything blends together. This form of plagiarism can be accidental, but it is still very serious. Readers can immediately notice differences in the styles of writing and recognize familiar phrases or ideas. Readers expect sources to be identified and borrowed material to be quoted *exactly;* in fact, most papers are improved by openly referring to the works of authorities and experts on the subject. Such references show that the writer is intelligent enough to know where to find information to broaden his or her knowledge of the topic. Unfortunately, some students deliberately copy another person's writing without giving credit and submit it as their own. This kind of plagiarism is not accidental at all; it is extremely dishonest, and it usually brings unpleasant results—an "F" on the paper, a probable "F" in the course, and possible dismissal from college. College instructors are *extremely* sensitive to plagiarism. If you think you might accidentally be plagiarizing something, ask your instructor for help.

Examples of quoting, summarizing, paraphrasing, and interpreting begin on page 333. The passage is from "Noncombatant's Guide to the Gun Control Fight," an article first published in the August 1979 issue of *Changing Times* and included in *The Issue of Gun Control,* edited by Thomas Draper (the complete citation for Draper's book is in the list of works cited on page 353):

Note Cards

Bruce-Briggs

attributes lack of violence
in Britain to "generally
deferential and docile
character of the populace"
(30).

(This probably applies to Japan,
as well. Cultural similarities.)

Kates

Includes personal information about author's experiences
as a civil rights worker
in the South. Quotes
interesting letter from Prof.
John Salter (Navajo University)
stating reasons for citizens
to own firearms. (98)

Figure 9–4a

Note Cards

Meacham   1 of 2

"In a comprehensive 2-1/2 year study funded by the U. S. Department of Justice, James Wright and Peter Rossi concluded that there is little or no con-clusive, or even suggestive, evidence to show that

(more)

Meacham   2 of 2

gun ownership among the population as a whole is, per se, an important cause of criminal violence." (1)

Figure 9–4b

The passage:

> To tell the truth, firearms have been as American as apple pie ever since the first settlers arrived. It's said there were as many guns as colonists in Jamestown. Certainly guns were standard household items, both as implements of the hunt and instruments of self-defense, as long as there was a frontier. It is only in the past century, a period of high immigration, rapid urbanization and resulting chronic social tensions, that unrestricted possession of personal arms, particularly handguns, has come into serious question (*Changing Times* 40).

No author is given; thus, the title of the periodical is used. Since the version of the article used is included in an anthology edited by Thomas Draper, the page number is from Draper's book.

Quoting

If you want to quote only a phrase or a sentence, simply place the quoted material in quotation marks. The best way to use quoted material is to work it into your own writing. Either begin or end a sentence containing a quote by saying something, in your own words, about the subject that the quote illustrates; for example:

> *Changing Times* analyzes the gun control issue quite reasonably when it reminds readers that although "there were as many guns as colonists in Jamestown" (40), living conditions in the United States are not the same as they were then. It is true that today most people don't use rifles to shoot game animals for food, but many inner city residents feel they need to keep handguns for self defense.

Readers generally understand that you have used part of a sentence or paragraph by the structure, capitalization, or punctuation of quoted material. But sometimes you must show that some of the author's original material (a clause, a sentence, a paragraph) has been left out to fit the context of your writing. (Of course, you must be careful not to use an author's words dishonestly; that is, in such a way as to change the original meaning. For example, it would be dishonest to leave out the word "not" in the following sentence to make a phrase fit your point of view: He did not commit the murder.) Such an omission is called an *ellipsis* (ellipses, pl.) and is indicated by a certain number of spaced periods. Within a sentence, use three spaced periods preceded and followed by a space:

> "It is only in the past century . . . that unrestricted possession of personal arms, particularly handguns, has come into serious question" (*Changing Times* 40).

At the end of a sentence, use four spaced periods (including the sentence period):

"Certainly guns were standard household items, both as implements of the hunt and instruments of self defense. . . ." (*Changing Times* 40).

At the beginning of a sentence, use three spaced periods. Leave a space before the first letter of the first word used:

". . . firearms have been as American as apple pie ever since the first settlers arrived" (*Changing Times* 40).

When an entire sentence is omitted from a passage, use four spaced periods followed by a space:

"To tell the truth, firearms have been as American as apple pie ever since the first settlers arrived. . . . Certainly guns were standard household items, both as implements of the hunt and instruments of self-defense, as long as there was a frontier" (*Changing Times* 40).

If you add one or more words to explain a quotation or to make it fit into the grammatical structure of your writing, place your addition (interpolation) in square brackets:

"It's [been] said there were as many guns as colonists in Jamestown [Virginia]" (*Changing Times* 40).

Summarizing

Include only the essential information in your own words:

Unrestricted individual ownership of guns in this country began with the colonists and continued with the frontiersmen, who used them for hunting and self-defense. During the past century, the social problems resulting from immigration and urbanization have caused citizens to question the wisdom of continuing this practice, according to *Changing Times* (40).

Paraphrasing

Use your own words to express the author's ideas, but *be sure to give the author credit for them;* otherwise, you will be plagiarizing. Try to retain the author's tone and any special words that add to the meaning. Place quotation marks around these words. Paraphrasing allows you to use and cite the author's ideas without overusing quotes:

Changing Times remarks that gun ownership is "as American as apple pie" since the practice began with the early colonists, continued with the frontiersmen, and survives today. In early times, guns were needed for hunting and self-defense, but today food and police protection are readily available. During the past hundred years, increasing social problems resulting from massive immigration and almost immediate urbanization have caused many to question the wisdom of allowing unrestricted private ownership of firearms to continue (40).

Interpreting

To explain the meaning or to show your own understanding of an author's ideas, quote the material as needed in your discussion:

> When *Changing Times* says that gun ownership has always been "as American as apple pie" (40), it suggests that many people believe the imposition of gun control would challenge an American institution or remove a basic freedom. But the editors do not seem to agree that because guns were "standard household items" (40) for the early colonists and the pioneers, they should remain so for members of contemporary American society. Citizens no longer have to protect themselves against wild animals or shoot them for food. But many people think they need guns to defend themselves against crime and violence caused by "chronic social tensions," which are attributed to a hundred years of "high immigration" and "rapid urbanization" (40). The passage explains the historical significance of private ownership of firearms and raises the issue of handgun control.

THE INFORMAL RESEARCH PROJECT

Instead of a formal, typed research paper, your instructor may assign an informal research project that requires you to write a short argument in which you discuss your findings about a timely issue. Since the purpose of such an assignment is to help you become comfortable with research techniques, the learning process is as important as the written product.

Work with a partner (preferably someone who is not from your country so that you have to speak to each other in English), researching opposing sides of some current issue that you have read or heard about or that you both feel very strongly about; for example, capital punishment (execution), parental interference in the lives of adult children, the Equal Rights Amendment, the importance of salary in attaining job satisfaction, the need for a college education, a constitutional amendment to allow prayer in public schools, or election of a woman as President of the United States.

After you and your partner choose a topic, search together through periodical and newspaper indexes and the card catalog as you prepare your working bibliography cards. Consult at least three *different* references each, such as periodicals, books, newspapers, and pamphlets, so that you have information from a minimum of six sources to share between you. As you and your partner briefly examine possible references to determine their usefulness, discuss strengths and weaknesses of each. Is the material up to date? Except for historical background, data should be recent. Is the author an authority on the subject? Beware of opinion that is not substantiated by evidence. Can you find only one author that takes your (or your partner's) position? If so, consider changing to an issue that has been more thoroughly discussed in print.

Next, carefully prepare accurate note cards. You and your partner should regularly share information and discuss its validity. When you think you have done enough research, write your opposing thesis statements and prepare your sentence outlines. Then sit down together and talk through your arguments. Are they as strong as you both thought they would be? Should your outlines be revised or rearranged? Are you both presenting your positions in orderly, effective ways? Is the language clear? Are there words or terms you should define? Should you find more facts, double check the accuracy of any quotations, or paraphrase instead of quoting? Have you been careful to identify sources? Have you remembered to include a counter argument?

At last you are ready to begin your first draft of the essay. At this point each of you should be prepared to work alone.

Here are several stages of an informal research project dealing with the issue of gun control. The student author worked with her partner through all the preliminary research processes. Her list of "Works Cited" was submitted along with her sentence outline. Then she wrote the essay in a classroom writing workshop without referring to her notecards in order to practice using her own words, to demonstrate her knowledge of the subject, and to gain experience in revision. The first and final drafts of the essay were completed in three class periods.

(Sentence Outline)

Should Ownership of Guns Be Controlled?

Thesis: Americans should be allowed to own and keep guns for personal use.

I. Personal freedom is a basic right in the United States.

   A. People have the right to own guns for self-defense.

   B. Citizens sometimes need guns to protect their property.

II. Those who oppose gun control say it affects only good citizens.

   A. Criminals do not follow the law and do not register their guns.

   B. The government can not control forged permits or disregard of the permit law.

III. Gun control does not decrease accidental deaths.

    A. Carelessness, not lack of regulation, causes accidents and deaths.

    B. In some countries, guns are kept in every household and used safely.

IV. Registration of guns increases governmental authority over citizens.

    A. The government can more easily abuse its power.

    B. Personal freedom can be threatened.

V. Gun control can only bring disadvantages to good citizens.

Works Cited

Reese, Michael, and Lea Donosky. "A New Push for Gun Control.: <u>Newsweek</u> 15 March 1982: 22.

Shields, Pete and John Greenya. <u>Guns Don't Die—People Do.</u> New York: Arbor House, 1981.

Tonso, William R. "The Press Takes a Second Look At Gun Control." <u>Outdoor Life</u> Oct. 1983: 39.

(First Draft)

Should ownership of guns be controlled?

My Trang Tonnu

For a long time, Americans had a constitutional right to keep and use guns as a self-defense weapon. Nowadays, since our society has become more and more complex, the use of firearms has caused a lot of problems for the government. This complex issue was debated in newspapers and in society. Many people thought a "Gun Control" law had to be enacted, but some opposed this opinion. Why should people be allowed to own guns. Anti-gun control groups have given some reasons.

The United States is a nation where personal freedom is a basic right. But American society is very complex. Several cases of robbery, murder, and kidnapping happen everyday. Thus some people have to keep guns for self-defense. Because of the recent increase in crimes, they want to buy guns to protect their homes from being robbed. They carry guns with them whenever they go outside for personal protection.

Some argue that "Gun Control" did not decrease the number of victims killed by weapons because this law only affected good citizens. Criminals do not register their guns, they also buy any type of gun they can get, so that they do not need the government's permit. They can also have a forged permit. Therefore, the government can not check guns by means of a "Gun Control" law.

In addition, it is not the absence of a "Gun Control" law that causes accidental deaths. They were caused by the people who used it carelessly and inappropriately. For example, in Switzerland, all homes have guns but the crime rate in this country is the lowest rate in the world. For this reason, accidents happen because people are not responsible when using guns.

If the ownership of gun is registered who may or may not have one? Surely, the number of people who have the legal authority will be decreased. The government can eradicate persons who seek to overthrow the government by force. Personal freedom can be threatened. Controlling the guns would affect the firearm industries and hunting.

Some proponents believe controlling the guns will lessen and prevent accident deaths, family tragedies as well as the number of crimes.

In my opinion, ownership of guns should not be controlled because this action only brings disadvantages to good citizens. Crimes and accidents still happen with or without controlling guns. It is a social disease that a "Gun Control" law can not make slow down.

Here is the final draft, written after discussing the essay with the instructor. The student corrected errors, reordered some material, and checked the content of each paragraph against the outline. Watch for changes shown in italics.

(Final Draft)

Should Ownership of Guns Be Controlled?

My Trang Tonnu

For a long time, Americans *have* had a constitutional right to keep and use guns *for self-defense*. Nowadays, since our society has become more and more complex, the use of firearms has caused a lot of problems for the government. Many people thought a *gun control* law had to be enacted, but some opposed this opinion. *This complex issue was debated in newspapers and in society. People should be allowed to own guns, and* anti-gun control groups have given *good* reasons *to support this idea*.

The United States is a nation where personal freedom is a basic right. But American society is very complex. Several cases of robbery, murder, and kidnapping happen *every day*. Thus, some people have to keep guns for self-defense. Because of the recent increase in crimes, they want to buy guns to protect their homes from being robbed. They carry guns with them *for personal protection whenever they go outside*.

Some argue that *gun control* does not decrease the number of victims killed by weapons because this law only *affects* good citizens. Criminals do not register their *guns. They* buy any type of guns they can get, so they do not need *government permits.* They can also *obtain forged permits.* Therefore, the government can not check guns by means of a *gun control* law.

In addition, it is not the absence of a *gun control* law that causes accidental deaths. They *are* caused by the people who use *firearms* carelessly and inappropriately. For example, in *Switzerland,* all homes have guns, but the crime rate in this country is the lowest in the world. *Switzerland's example proves* that accidents happen because people are not responsible when using guns.

If ownership of *a* gun is registered, who may or may not have one? Surely, the number of people who have the legal authority to own guns will be decreased. *Personal freedom can be threatened. The government can forcibly eradicate any persons who are suspected of opposing government policies.* Controlling guns will also affect *employment because firearms industries will have less business. Sportsmen will be unhappy because they will not be able to go hunting.*

Although some proponents believe controlling guns will lessen and prevent accidental deaths, family tragedies, and crimes, in my opinion, ownership of guns should not be controlled because this action only brings disadvantages to good citizens. Crimes and accidents still happen, with or without *gun control. Crime, especially,* is a social disease that *cannot be stopped by a gun control law.*

THE FORMAL RESEARCH PAPER

The informal research project is meant to serve as an introduction to techniques of library research, documentation of sources, compilation of references, and proving arguments. Working with a partner is stimulating and can make the project fun. Writing and revising an essay is something that students do frequently. The nonthreatening nature of the informal project places it in the perspective of a learning experience. Conversely, the formal research or term paper is assigned (in courses other than English) based on the assumption that students know how to do it and will complete it independently. Sometimes instructors assign a specific topic for all students; sometimes students choose from a list of topics prepared by the instructor; sometimes students must generate their own topics and submit them to the instructor for approval. Formal research papers are expected to be substantial in content and scholarship and to show evidence of original thought. They are much more comprehensive than the informal essay shown earlier.

If your instructor requires a formal research paper, he or she will give you some special instructions unique to that assignment; for example, a minimum length, a particular number of citations that must be included, or specific kinds of sources that should be consulted. You may be required to submit a sentence outline along with the final version of the paper. However, the following directions, extracted from the *MLA Handbook,* are quite standard for preparing any research paper:

1. Typed papers make a better impression. Use a new black ribbon and a type style that is easily read. A handwritten paper must be legible and written with black or blue ink. Type or write on only one side of the paper.

2. Use 8½ × 11-inch, twenty pound weight, white bond. Do not use erasable bond, because the print smudges and transfers to fingers and clothing. Use lightweight tissue or copy paper only for a carbon copy, never for a paper you submit to an instructor.

3. Double space the paper, including the heading, title, text, list of works cited, notes, and indented block quotations.

4. Make sure margins are a uniform one inch at the top, bottom, and both sides of each page, except for page numbers that are typed in the upper right corner, one-half inch down from the top of the sheet. Indent five spaces from the left margin to begin each new paragraph. Indent ten spaces from the left margin for the first line of a quotation more than four lines long; indent subsequent lines five spaces. Do not use quotation marks on indented quotes unless they are part of the text you are copying. Shorter quotations should be placed in quotation marks and included in your text.

5. A title page is not required. Instead, place a four-line heading at the top of the first page. Begin each line at the left margin. Include the following information: your name, your instructor's name, the course name and number, and the date. Double space, and center the title. The title should not be underlined, placed in quotation marks, or typed in all capital letters. Capitalize the first letter of all words except articles, prepositions, and coordinating conjunctions (unless one of them is the first word in the title). Underline only words that would normally be underlined (for example, foreign words or the titles of movies or books). No punctuation follows the title unless a subtitle follows it. In that case, use a colon and a space before the subtitle.

6. Double space twice (four spaces) between the title and the text.

7. Number pages (except page 1, which is never numbered) consecutively beginning with page 2.

8. Use a paper clip to hold the pages of your finished paper together. Do not use staples or pins, and do not fold down the corners. Do not use plastic or other kinds of folders or covers.

9. Always keep a copy of your paper until the original is returned to you.

Here is a sample sentence outline submitted for approval by the student before she wrote the final version of her formal research paper on the subject of gun control.

Gun Control Laws Penalize Law Abiding Citizens

Thesis: The government should not be given the power to limit and control citizens' rights to own handguns.

I. Private ownership of handguns by law-abiding citizens presents no real danger to society.

A. Those who legally own handguns rarely misuse them.

1. Most registered handguns are used by police and private citizens for self-defense in life threatening situations.

2. Although handguns are the cause of some deaths, people can be killed both accidentally and deliberately in many ways.

3. According to sportsmen, hunters are not responsible for the majority of deaths of wild animals.

B. Illegal possession and use of guns by criminals cause the major problems.

1. Criminals use guns to commit crimes against unprotected, law-abiding citizens.

2. Guns purchased illegally are not only difficult to trace, but they may also have features that are not allowed in legal weapons.

C. Although many government officials publicly support gun control, they privately acknowledge the need to carry firearms to protect themselves.

II. Civilian ownership of registered firearms has many advantages.

A. In the United States, the crime rate is lowered in areas where small business owners are trained to use firearms.

1. Robberies of all kinds decrease.

2. Rape occurs less frequently.

B. Other countries that allow private ownership of handguns have low crime rates.

1. Citizens of Israel must keep guns on hand for security purposes, but the crime rate is comparable to that of countries that prohibit private gun ownership.

2. Switzerland, too, has an armed civilian militia, but the availability of guns has not increased the murder rates.

III. Gun control laws could have serious effects on society.

A. Law-abiding citizens would suffer.

1. Their constitutional right to protect themselves would be seriously abridged.

    2. Those who live or work in high-crime areas would have to exist in fear.

  B. Criminals would benefit.

    1. Their ability to get weapons would not diminish.

    2. With no opposition except overworked law enforcement agencies, the crime rate would probably increase dramatically.

  C. The laws would be nearly impossible to enforce.

IV. Proponents of handgun restriction believe that responsible citizens should not only be willing to license and/or register their guns, but also to give them up for public good.

  A. They say that the Second Amendment guarantee is no longer applicable because the situation has changed; unfortunately, that change has not been for the better.

  B. They believe that fewer handguns among the general public will reduce crime, but evidence does not support that idea.

V. Anti-gun groups are working against the best interests of average citizens by trying to disarm them and take away their means of self-defense. Gun ownership should be allowed for the protection of society and the individual and for sport.

Eilene Galleher

Professor Scull

Eng. 101

January 11, 1986

Gun Control Laws Penalize Law Abiding Citizens

In November 1982, an initiative that would have imposed strict hand-gun regulations on all citizens was brought before the voters of the state of California. The piece of legislation failed, illustrating that the majority of the people of this state didn't want controls placed on their rights to purchase handguns. However, opinions about this controversial issue are still polarized. Proponents of gun control believe that private citizens have no business own-ing and using firearms because of the availability of police protection and the danger of accidents. Opponents point out that the crime rate is steadily rising, police protection is dwindling, and the dangers of citizens being harmed by criminals are far greater than injuries caused by accidents. The government should not be empowered to limit or control the basic right of its citizens "to keep and bear Arms," which is guaranteed by the Second Amendment to the United States Constitution.

Private ownership of handguns by law-abiding citizens presents no real danger to society. The key words here are "law-abiding," and most Americans fall into this category. For the few who do not, Congress passed The Gun Control Act in 1968 after the murders of Robert Kennedy and Martin Luther

King. This law placed heavy restrictions on the sale and use of guns but had virtually no effect on the crime rate. Critics note that "while the '68 law has done nothing to alter behavior patterns among the criminal element, it has done a great deal to infringe the liberties of the law-abiding" (Evans 1434).

Most registered handguns are used by police and private citizens for self-defense in life threatening situations. Although law enforcement officers would retain their weapons if a gun control law were passed, many honest civilian citizens would be deprived of theirs. Conversely, illegal firearms would not be removed from the hands of those outside the law. With all the violence that is occurring in the United States today, people are frightened and many believe having guns is necessary to protect themselves. People should not have to live in fear. If their privacy is violated and their lives and property are endangered, they should have some means of deterring an invader and should not have to worry about the morality of hurting him. "When a criminal uses force to violate your rights, he has waived your obligation to avoid using force against him" (Rains 28).

Although some accidental deaths and deliberate murders can be attributed to handguns, people can be killed in many ways. Accidental deaths can be caused by a host of freak accidents. People are killed when they are struck by lightning, slip on the wet tile in the bathroom, smoke in bed, drive while drunk, choke on a piece of food, or fail to observe basic rules for human safety. Almost any large object can be used to kill a person; for example, people are bludgeoned to death with baseball bats, golf clubs, sticks of wood, lamps, and telephone receivers. They are stabbed with knives, scissors, ice picks, garden shears, pieces of broken glass, and steel knitting needles. They are strangled, smothered, gassed, starved, run over with automobiles, thrown from bridges and buildings, drowned, and poisoned. A small percentage is shot with handguns; however, "it is infinitely more acceptable to scapegoat the easily identifiable handgun than to admit we don't understand the cultural and institutional factors that produce violence-inclined people" (Kates 96).

Hunters, too, are accused of killing certain species of animal life to the point of near extinction, an especially serious allegation because most hunters kill for sport rather than need. Gun control proponents never mention the huge numbers of animals that die of starvation during harsh winters or periods of draught and, similarly, ignore species that experience massive die-offs because of overpopulation. Wildlife observers say that fewer animals die each year from gunshot wounds than from natural causes or brushes with civilization, such as being stuck by cars. Furthermore, most hunters enjoy the sport so much that they scrupulously abide by limits set by state Fish and Game Commissions. In other cases, according to Grits Gresham, they "insist on good management of the game species they are interested in, and willingly pay for it" (87) through excise taxes on hunting guns and equipment, license fees, or voluntary contributions to preserve habitats, so "it's quite possible the efforts of hunters have saved several [species] from passing into oblivion" (87). The sportsman's credo of voluntary conservation is also reflected in literature. In Hemingway's short story, "A Day's Wait," the narrator, after spending an hour quail shooting, comments that he "killed two, missed five, and started back pleased to have found a covey close to the house and happy there were so many left to find on another day" (438).

The major problems with guns are caused by criminals that possess firearms illegally and use them indiscriminately. Advocates of gun control complain that in the last twenty years the murder rate has risen drastically because of the huge increase in private ownership of handguns. However,

> the causal connection here is not that more handguns have resulted in more violence, but that more violence by the kind of disturbed, aberrant people who commit murders (and by the equally aberrant, but much less disturbed, people who commit robbery, burglary, etc.) has caused law-abiding citizens to buy handguns in self-defense. Homicide results not from the "proliferation of handguns" among the law-abiding, but from the relatively tiny number of disturbed, sociopathic individuals among us. And it cannot be reduced by handgun bans because these people—who won't obey a law against murder—aren't going to obey a law against owning handguns. (Kates 90)

Criminals use guns to commit crimes against unprotected, law-abiding citizens. Short of closing down munitions manufacturers and confiscating all firearms in the country, there is probably no way to stop the criminal element from obtaining weapons illegally. A criminal with a gun has an overwhelming advantage over an unarmed victim. In fact, many law enforcement agencies advise people not to resist, but to cooperate fully when held at gunpoint. Although there is grave danger in "shootout" situations between the perpetrator and the victim, there is even greater peril for the victim if the criminal can count on his being unarmed. This gives the criminal <u>carte blanche</u> to enter homes, hold up stores or gas stations, or mug or rape passersby because he knows most victims will not be stupid enough to resist physically while looking down the barrel of a gun. According to a "comprehensive 2½-year study funded by the U.S. Department of Justice, . . . 'there is little or no conclusive, or even suggestive, evidence to show that gun ownership among the population as a whole is, per se, an important cause of criminal violence'" (Meacham 1). Obviously, honest citizens shouldn't have to resort to handguns to protect themselves, but they shouldn't be left totally defenseless, either.

The characteristics and uses of legal handguns are carefully regulated. Certain types of firearms, such as machine guns, may not be owned by the civilian population. Firearms may not be altered; for instance, sawing off the barrel of a shotgun. Ammunition must be standard issue. Guns must be carried openly (for example, in a holster) or the owner must have a permit to carry a concealed weapon. Registered guns can easily be traced because the serial numbers are on file with the police department. On the other hand, unregistered guns that are purchased cheaply or illegally are not only difficult or impossible to trace, but also may have features that are not allowed in legal weapons. According to Pete Shields, "the real enemy in the American Handgun War remains the small, cheap, easily concealable handgun—like the one used to shoot President Reagan" (46), which can be purchased for as little as $10.00. Further, criminals have no compunctions about altering their weapons in any way to make them more deadly or to avoid detection. They add silencers to revolvers, devise machine pistols, and saw off the barrels of shotguns or rifles. They aren't above using soft-nosed "dum-dum" bullets, outlawed because they expand when they hit and cause large, jagged wounds. They don't hesitate to use teflon coated bullets made of steel or heavy metals (such as tungsten) to penetrate bullet-proof vests. But "gun control proponents, by and large, are reluctant to hold individual offenders accountable for their behavior—preferring to assign the blame for aberrant conduct to external factors, in this case the availability of firearms, and the society which permits them" (Evans 1434).

Although government officials publicly support gun control, they privately acknowledge the need to carry firearms to protect themselves.

While the *New York Times* unceasingly advises ordinary citizens that no one needs a handgun for self-defense, its publisher, Arthur Ochs Sulzberger, has a permit to carry a concealed handgun at all times. So, reportedly, have former Congressmen and ex-New York City Mayor John Lindsay (author of innumerable bills to disarm everyone else) and

Galleher 7

the husband of Dr. Joyce Brothers, the renowned pop-psychologist; her public position is that no one needs a handgun for self-defense and that men who have them may be suspected of sexual disfunction. The U.S. Conference of Mayors lobbies ceaselessly for handgun prohibition, yet virtually every one of the big city mayors responsible for this position feels it necessary to carry a handgun himself and/or has armed bodyguards. (Kates 94)

Civilian ownership of registered firearms has many advantages besides providing citizens with a sense of security and personal safety. The psychological climate changes from one of impotence and fear to one of confidence and competence. Criminals can sense these emotions in potential victims. The criminal instinct is to get something for nothing, preferably from someone who is too weak or frightened to resist.

In the United States, the crime rate is lowered in areas where small business owners are trained to use firearms. Kates reports some dramatic statistics: Rape decreased 90% in Orlando, Florida, in 1968, the year after 6,000 women were trained in handgun combat; in addition, aggravated assault and burglary declined 25%. A well publicized, police-sponsored firearms training program for merchants in Highland Park, Michigan, resulted in armed robberies plummeting from eighty to zero over a four-month period. After a similar merchant-sponsored program in Detroit, and seven robbers being shot by grocers, grocery robberies decreased by 90%. In 1974, during the police strike in Albuquerque, New Mexico, armed merchants and residents protected their businesses and neighborhoods, and the crime rate was the lowest in years (93).

Other countries that allow private ownership of handguns have little crime. Gun control advocates are fond of citing the great successes of Japan and Great Britain in maintaining extremely low crime rates because private handgun ownership is prohibited or tightly controlled in these countries. But Bruce-Briggs points out that the "generally deferential and docile character of the populace" (30), not the gun control laws, is probably the cause of Britain's lack of violence. Perhaps this observation is accurate for Japan, as well. But how can gun control advocates explain the successes of Israel and Switzerland in deterring crime? Israelis are armed for security purposes; most citizens serve an obligatory period in the armed forces or are members of the civil guard. In spite of government restrictions on shotguns and rifles that might have military applications, "the Israelis have accumulated huge numbers of privately owned military weapons, including automatics, in various wars and raids" (Bruce-Briggs 32); however, the crime rate remains very low. The Swiss militia system requires that citizens keep their weapons in their homes. Thus, "600,000 assault rifles with two magazines of ammo each are sitting at this moment in Swiss homes. Yet Switzerland's murder rate is 6 percent of ours" (Bruce-Briggs 31). Both the Israelis and the Swiss are ambitious, hard-working people whose culture does not include the "getting something for nothing" syndrome.

Gun control laws could have serious effects on society. Unfortunately, only the law-abiding citizens would suffer. They would relinquish their handguns (or not be permitted to purchase them in the first place) and give up one of their civil liberties at the same time. Their constitutional right to protect themselves would be seriously abridged. Those who live or work in high-crime areas would have to exist in fear. Furthermore, other provisions in the Bill of Rights might next come under attack. On the other hand, the criminals would benefit. Since they operate outside the law, their ability to get weapons would not diminish. With no opposition except overworked and understaffed law enforcement agencies, crime would be rampant. The crime rate would probably increase dramatically.

Gun control laws would be nearly impossible to enforce and would "divert already scarce law-enforcement resources away from fighting crime into needlessly regulating law-abiding citizens" (Meacham 3). Clearly, the best way to fight crime is to apprehend and punish the criminals; the worst way is to persecute honest citizens who are doing nothing wrong.

Proponents of handgun restriction believe that responsible citizens should be willing to license and/or register their guns and even be willing to give them up for the public good. Opponents are willing to license their ons, but have no intention of allowing them to be confiscated. Gun control advocates say that the Second Amendment guarantee is not applicable because the situation has changed. They say there is no longer a need for citizens to soldier in "a well regulated Militia, being necessary to the security of a free State." Opponents agree that the situation has changed, but not for the better. The enemy is not the invading army of another nation, but our own countrymen who have decided to live outside the laws and moral precepts of our society. They maintain that the right to bear arms "is an unqualified right, like the freedom of the press, not to be compromised on any grounds" (Bruce-Briggs 33).

Gun control advocates believe that fewer handguns among the general public will reduce crime, but evidence does not support that idea. "The December 1980 slaying of rock star John Lennon occurred in New York, a state that passed a stiff gun control law" (Draper 5). In fact, "New York City has had a virtual ban on the private ownership of handguns since 1911 and no one but a Rip van Winkle would claim that New York is crime-free" (Meacham 3). On the other hand, the examples of Orlando, Highland Park, and Detroit show that criminals are strongly deterred from committing a crime if they think they will encounter resistance or get hurt themselves. Further, the Israeli and Swiss populations not only possess handguns, but assault and machine weapons; yet, the crime rates in these countries are comparable with those of Japan and Britain where handguns are either prohibited or severely regulated. Finally, fewer handguns among the honest citizens will simply make crime easier for the dishonest ones.

Anti-gun groups are working against the best interests of average citizens by trying to disarm them and take away their means of self defense. These factions are trying to impose their beliefs on others so that the entire population will conform to their ideas of "right." Because they disapprove of handgun ownership for themselves, they intend to deny everyone the security or pleasure of such ownership. This kind of narrow thinking is often used to force others to accept the standards, morality or behavior of special interest groups. These factions would do better to dedicate their time and effort to strengthening the judicial system so that criminals can't "get off" on technicalities and so that they will be severely punished for acts of violence. In other words, the target should be the relatively small population of hard-core criminals, not the broad spectrum of honest citizens. Gun ownership should continue to be allowed for the protection of individuals and society and for sport.

Galleher 12

Works Cited

Bruce-Briggs, B. "The Great American Gun War." Draper 8–38.

Draper, Thomas, ed. The Issue of Gun Control. The Reference Shelf 53. New York: Wilson, 1981.

Draper, Thomas. Preface. Draper 5–6.

Evans, M. Stanton. "Crime and Gun Control." National Review May 1979: 1434.

Gresham, Grits. "Guns and Hunting: Fact vs. Fantasy." Draper 85–88.

Hemingway, Ernest. "A Day's Wait." The Short Stories of Ernest Hemingway. New York: Scribner's, 1953. 436–439.

Kates, Don B., Jr. "Gun Control: The Real Facts." Field and Stream July 1979: 34+.

Meacham, Craig L. "Prop. 15: Should We Restrict Handguns? No: It Won't Cut Crime or Deter Criminals." Los Angeles Times 24 Oct. 1982, sec. 4: 1+.

Rains, John. "Your Right to Live Without Fear!" Guns and Ammo Dec. 1980: 28+.

Shields, Pete and John Greenya. Guns Don't Die—People Do. New York: Arbor, 1981.

Topics for Research

1. Should public employees have the right to strike?
2. Should the prison system be reformed?
3. Should unwanted pets be used to make pet food?
4. Should religious cults be prohibited by law?
5. Is the separation of church and state really necessary in the United States?
6. Is there a practical and humane way to discourage illegal aliens from entering and staying in this country?
7. Is the United States right to be worried about the spread of communism in Central America?
8. Does advertising have much influence over a person's life?
9. Does television harm children?
10. Should young adults be required to spend two years following high school doing compulsory national or public service of some kind?
11. Should the United States have national health insurance for all the people?
12. Should the government be responsible for cleaning up chemical spills and waste dumps if the problems were caused by private industry?
13. Do our legal and judicial systems favor the accused?
14. Should the United States sell advanced technological equipment to other countries?
15. Should welfare recipients have to work for the public good to earn their money?
16. Are children of working mothers neglected?
17. Should the government intervene in family decisions to let hopelessly ill, tragically deformed, or severely retarded family members die natural deaths (rather than keeping them alive by machines, powerful drugs, and sophisticated surgical techniques)?
19. Should automobile insurance rates be restructured to reflect accident and claim records of the individual rather than risk based on age group or address?
20. Should the United States expand its space program?

10

The Process of Revision:
A Workshop

Native speakers, after silently reading a passage, often say, "That doesn't *sound* right." Even though no words have been spoken, the connections between reading and listening are so natural to them that they imagine they hear the passage. Similarly, an instructor may advise you, as you are writing a sentence or a phrase, "You can't *say* it that way in English," illustrating the equally close relationship between writing and speaking. All of this means that formal written language must *seem* as natural as its less formal spoken counterpart. Most ESL students say that they make the same kinds of errors repeatedly because they don't "hear" the mistakes when they proofread their essays. They only see the words on the paper.

Good writing results when you read, speak, listen, and think fluently enough in English to master the natural flow of the language. This text asks you to practice these skills in every chapter. Class discussion helps speaking, listening, and understanding; analysis of readings and synthesis of ideas in writing promote critical thinking. Throughout, this text gives detailed instructions for getting started on writing projects—choosing a subject, brainstorming with classmates, classifying to separate information, focusing on a limited part of the topic, settling on a thesis, preparing a brief topic outline, writing a more detailed sentence outline, discussing the validity of your ideas with partners, selecting examples that support your thesis, writing in your own words, and planning ahead so that your conclusion relates to the thesis.

Good writing also requires revision, which is much more than simply correcting the obvious errors and neatly recopying the essay. Effective revision means rethinking: improving the vocabulary, idiomatic usage, and style;

changing the content by adding, deleting, or reordering information; and *then* neatly recopying the final draft.

"So," you ask, "what are the best ways to revise?"

1. *Be imaginative.* Before you make any corrections or changes in grammar or punctuation, review the content. Begin by reading the essay aloud softly. Have you written the information as clearly as you could tell it? Delete repetitive material or sections that don't make sense. If you were reading your work to another person, would you have to explain the meanings of any words, sentences, or concepts? Insert more information where it is needed. Would the listener recognize key words and phrases, or even whole paragraphs, taken directly from the work you are discussing? Paraphrase in your own words or quote exactly and give credit. Do any of the phrases or sentences sound mixed up or confused? Change the order of words to improve syntax. Do the ideas fail to flow logically from one to the next? Rearrange sentences within paragraphs or reorder paragraphs within the essay to improve the sequence of thoughts.

Do you *like* what you hear? Do you feel pleased with this product? No? Then go back to the beginning. Is it inviting? Try a bold statement or make an unusual comparison as an opening line. Rework the vocabulary. Get out your dictionary or thesaurus and search for synonyms. Be sure that this introduction is different from every other one you have ever written. If you are bored with it, imagine how the reader will be affected! Cast a critical eye on the thesis, as well. Is it a "stock" restatement of the topic? Does it take a stand or is it weak and insipid? Rework the thesis until it is firm and strong and represents a position worth proving. Is the conclusion a dreary restatement of the thesis or an uninteresting summary of the facts? Rewrite this crucial finale to your work. Give it some style. Close with a striking statement (one that makes the reader say, "Yes! Great ending!"). Make a prediction. Be clever. Be witty, ironic, sarcastic—in short, leave the reader with the impression that you really care about this essay.

2. *Be methodical and thorough.* Scan the entire essay once for each kind of error you are likely to make. To check content, context, syntax, and grammar, read from beginning to end. To test spelling and punctuation, read each sentence out of context from the end to the beginning. The latter technique is especially helpful in identifying fragments, comma splices, and run-on sentences. Each time look *only* for one type of error; for example, if you are checking for verb tense consistency, pay no attention to subject-verb agreement. After you have caught all the tense shifts, go through the essay again and correct the agreement errors. Use this same controlled, step-by-step process over and over again until you are satisfied that you have done your best work. Write changes and corrections neatly above the line on the paper (when you write any essay, skip every other line so that you have room to edit and revise).

3. *Be careful and sensible.* Don't make changes unless you are sure you have made an error. If you think something is wrong, but you don't know what it is, ask your instructor for help or exchange papers with another student (with your instructor's permission). If you are writing an essay examination, view the problem area in its overall context; for instance, if you think you are using an incorrect verb tense, see what tense you used in the rest of the paragraph. Unless the verb you are worried about is in the subjective (non-fact) or the conditional (contrary-to-fact), is included in reported speech, or is part of a time clause, stay in one tense.

4. *Don't waste time.* Discuss questions with the instructor, but try to identify and solve as many problems as you can before you ask for help. This teaches you to revise independently, shows the instructor that you are comfortable with and capable of using the revision process, and allows him or her to advise many students during a single writing period.

Here are the most common writing errors that instructors will identify on your essays and that you will have to correct when you revise your work:

1. *Fragment* (**frag.**)
A fragment is an incomplete sentence.
One type of fragment consists only of a dependent clause; for example:

Because I always become violently ill. (**frag.**)

Since dependent clauses generally precede or follow related sentences, one way to avoid the problem is to connect the clause to the sentence before or after it:

I love all kinds of fruit; however, I never eat peaches *because I always become violently ill.*

Because I always become violently ill, I never eat peaches.

Another way to correct the error is to omit the subordinator and add an interrupter:

I always become violently ill; therefore, I never eat peaches.

A second type of fragment lacks a subject or main verb or incorrectly uses a verbal as the main verb:

Incorrect: Carmen from Colombia. (no verb)
  Correct: Carmen *is* from Colombia.

Incorrect: And lived there five years. (no subject)
  Correct: *She* lived there five years.

Incorrect: Going back to her country after only two months. (no subject; verbal used incorrectly)
  Correct: *She is* going back to her country after only two months.

2. *Comma splice* (**C.S.**)

A comma splice occurs when two sentences or independent clauses are incorrectly joined by a comma. Many students make this error because they use native language intonation patterns when they speak English; therefore, they don't "hear" the end of a sentence when they are writing:

Marie doesn't like most French food, she adores French pastries. (**C.S.**)

Comma splices can be corrected in several ways. Add a coordinating conjunction after the comma:

Marie doesn't like most French food, but she adores French pastries.

Punctuate with a semicolon:

Marie doesn't like most French food; she adores French pastries.

Make separate sentences of the two independent clauses; add an interrupter to show an exception:

Marie doesn't like most French food. She adores French pastries, however.

Subordinate one clause to the other:

Although Marie doesn't like most French food, she adores French pastries.

Although Marie adores French pastries, she doesn't like most French food.

No internal punctuation is used when the subordinate clause follows the dependent clause.

Marie adores French pastries although she doesn't like most French food.

3. *Run-on sentence* (**R.O.**)

The proper punctuation at the end of a sentence is a period or an exclamation or question mark. If no punctuation is used, one sentence is run on to the next:

Marie adores French pastries she eats them for lunch every day she is gaining weight rapidly. (**R.O.**)

Correct run-on sentences as you would comma splices. Place a period after each independent clause:

Marie adores French pastries. She eats them for lunch every day. She is gaining weight rapidly.

Punctuate two or three related independent clauses with semicolons (be careful not to overuse this form of punctuation):

Marie adores French pastries; she eats them for lunch every day; she is gaining weight rapidly.

Punctuate with commas and add a coordinating conjunction:

Marie adores French pastries, she eats them for lunch every day, and she is gaining weight rapidly.

Coordinate the first two clauses, punctuate with a semicolon, and add a result clause:

Marie adores French pastries, and she eats them for lunch every day; consequently, she is gaining weight rapidly.

4. *Punctuation* (**p.**)

Without proper punctuation, writing loses much of its meaning. The standard "signals" on which native speakers rely to make sense of any writing are closely related to speech functions. Periods are used for full stops, commas for pauses, exclamation marks for emotional outbursts, and question marks for both inquiry and confirmation. Because English requires such definite stress patterns and broad intonation ranges, the spoken language sometimes seems too dramatic to nonnative students. However, without punctuation, people would sound as measured and mechanical as computer voice synthesizers. Native speakers read and think with the same imaginary range of expression as they use when speaking. Thus, improper punctuation "sounds" strange when they see it in an essay.

a. An *apostrophe* is used to form a possessive, a contraction, or the plural of a letter or symbol. Apostrophes are also used to replace prepositional phrases and in special expressions.

Singular possessive: The woman's purse was stolen.

Plural possessive: The boys' gym is on the second floor.

Singular possessive (apostrophe follows the *s* when noun ends with *s* or *z* sound): Have you seen Howard Hughes' airplane, the Spruce Goose?

Singular possessive of impersonal pronoun: Everyone's money was stolen.

Singular possessive of hyphenated noun: My mother-in-law's cooking is better than mine.

Special expression in which apostrophe replaces prepositional phrase *of a year:* Louisa thought she would marry Joe after only a year's wait.

Contraction followed by idiom: She didn't know that Lily was his heart's desire. (He loved Lily, not Louisa.)

Plural forms of numbers and letters: Some people confuse l's and i's because they look so much alike.

b. A *colon* is placed between a main title and a subtitle (see documentation format in chapter 9) and at the end of a complete sentence to show that more information will follow:

According to Alfred H. Holt, in *Phrase and Word Origins: A Study of Familiar Expressions,* the heart was originally thought to be "the seat of affection, . . . intelligence and memory." (122)

You should spend your vacation in one of three countries: Greece, Italy, or Spain. (list)

Marilyn spent her junior year of college in Brazil: she learned many things about the customs and culture of that country. (explanation)

c. A *comma* is intended for internal punctuation only. Never end sentence with a comma.

In a series, the last comma is followed by *and* or *or:*

Alex wore a sweater, a jacket, and an overcoat to try to keep warm.

You will be warm enough if you wear a sweater, a jacket, or a raincoat.

A comma, followed by a coordinating conjunction (*and, but, for, so,* etc.) joins two independent clauses:

Jasmine earns a large salary, and she spends every penny she makes.

Jasmine has to earn a high salary, for she spends huge sums on clothes.

Jasmine doesn't earn much money, but she spends every cent on luxuries.

Jasmine's salary is very low, so she can't afford to buy luxury items.

An introductory dependent clause introduced by *after, although, because, if, since,* or *when* is followed by a comma; a dependent clause that follows an independent clause is never preceded by a comma.

Because Henry was a good swimmer, he tried out for the Olympic team.

Henry tried out for the Olympic team because he was a good swimmer.

Participial, infinitive, and prepositional phrases that occur at the beginning of a sentence are followed by a comma:

Blocked in his efforts to find a nice house at a rent he could afford, Bill decided to buy a home of his own. (past participle)

Working hard at day and night jobs for five years, Bill managed to save enough money for a down payment on a home. (present participle)

To reach his goal in such a short time, Bill gave up all activities but working, eating, and sleeping. (infinitive)

Until he is able to buy some furniture and paint the inside of his house, Bill doesn't plan to invite guests to visit him. (preposition)

Paired commas set off an *appositive* (a noun, pronoun, or noun clause that directly follows the noun) or a *nonrestrictive* or *unnecessary clause* (begins with a relative pronoun), both of which provide additional information about or further identification of the noun in a sentence.

My boss, a mechanical engineer, is in charge of the entire production effort. (appositive)

Dr. Rogers, who has delivered hundreds of babies, has no children of his own. (nonrestrictive clause)

Do not set off a *restrictive* or *necessary* clause (needed to identify the noun) with commas:

The waiter who took your order just left for the night.

The dog that bit my sister chased Billy home.

A comma separates an interrupter (*as a result, however, of course, nevertheless, consequently, therefore, on the other hand,* etc.) from the rest of an independent clause or sentence:

Nevertheless, foreign travel is the best way to learn about other cultures.

Foreign travel is the best way to learn about other cultures, *however.*

When the interrupter occurs in the middle of a sentence, use a pair of commas:

Foreign travel, *of course,* is the best way to learn about other cultures.

A comma precedes a tag question or contrasting phrase:

You're really hungry today, aren't you?

I hope we're having steak, not chicken.

You don't like chicken, do you?

Direct dialog is preceded or followed by a comma if other information is included in the sentence:

"I really wish I could afford a new car," Tom sighed.

The salesperson replied, "You can. Monthly payments on this convertible are very low and can be spread over a four-year period."

A comma is used to separate coordinate adjectives:

Elizabeth's long, silky hair was beautifully combed.

Do not use a comma between coordinate adjectives that function as complements:

Elizabeth's hair was long and silky.

d. A *semicolon* is used to join two related independent clauses as shown in the sections on *comma splice* and *run-on sentence.* Use semicolons to separate a series of ideas punctuated with many commas:

Max was hungry, thirsty, and sleepy; he was tired of the cold, driving rain; and he felt that he was going to be very, very sick.

e. A *period, question mark,* or *exclamation mark* must conclude every sentence.

Periods are also used in abbreviations (*et al., Dr., etc.*) and also decimal points (5.7, $79.95).

Question marks are used in direct quotations (questions only) instead of commas before identifying the speaker or the speaker's behavior:

"How much does that handbag cost?" she asked rudely.

Indirect quotations are never followed by question marks:

She asked how much that handbag costs.

Exclamation marks are used only at the ends of sentences to express strong emotion or surprise:

"What! You have no money!"

"Shame on you!"

The last act of the play was outrageous!

f. Double *quotation marks* are used at the beginning and end of direct speech; quoted written material; and titles of short stories, poems, articles, and book chapters (see documentation format in Chapter 9). Single quotation marks are used for a direct quotation within a quotation:

At the end of his relationship with the fox, the little prince begins to understand the secret of relationships with others. "'What is essential is invisible to the eye,' the little prince repeated, (87)" after the fox had explained the concept to him.

g. An *ellipsis* is used to show omission of part of a direct quotation. See Chapter 9 for a complete explanation.

h. The *dash* is sometimes used in place of parentheses or commas to set off non-restrictive clauses and sometimes to replace a colon. Don't use the dash to punctuate sentences in formal writing. Save this usage for informal, personal writing.

When students punctuate many sentences in an essay with dashes—overused substitutes for pairs of commas or parentheses—these dramatic marks immediately attract the eye and distract the reader from the content. An essay punctuated with numerous dashes is similar to a necktie covered with gravy stains—they both attract attention to the wrong things.

i. *Underlining* should be used sparingly. Chapter 9 explains how to underline book, newspaper, and periodical titles. Don't underline the title of your essay. Try to make the language work for you by changing wording to avoid overuse of underlining for emphasis. If you include special expressions, words, or phrases from a language other than English, underline (*and translate*) them.

5. *Faulty paragraphing* (¶ or No ¶)

Indent paragraphs five spaces from the margin, not from the edge of the paper. A paragraph is a unit of your essay that covers one main idea, has a topic sentence, is well-developed, is clearly organized, and sticks to the subject. Don't indent the first word of every sentence as if it were a new paragraph, and don't indent only the first word of the first sentence of the essay. Do include several clearly indented paragraphs in an essay.

6. *Point of view* (**POV**)

Shifts in point of view result from shifts in person. Be consistent throughout the essay in your choices of personal pronouns and nouns relating to them. Don't change abruptly from the first person (I/we) to the second person (you/you) or the third person (he, she, it/they):

People should be careful when driving *their* cars. *You* could easily have an accident. (**POV**; third person shifts to second person)

People should be careful when driving *their* cars. *They* could easily have accidents. (third person; note plural nouns)

You should be careful when driving *your* car. *You* could easily have an accident. (second person)

Similarly, avoid blending objective and subjective tones in writing:

The fire started at eight o'clock last night. Flames lighted the sky for about two square miles. Firemen were called from stations all over the city to try to stop the fire from spreading to nearby homes. Several men were hurt when two large propane tanks exploded. *You could see places on their faces and arms where the skin was burned black.* The fire was so intense that the paramedics were burned trying to rescue the injured. *You could hear the terrible screams.* Because propane is widely used in cooking and heating, it must be accessible to users. *However, we have to have better safety measures for storing propane in heavily populated areas.*

The three italicized sentences should be rewritten so that the entire passage conforms to the objective tone:

The skin was burned black in places on their faces and arms.

Their screams were terrible.

However, better safety measures are needed for storing propane in heavily populated areas.

7. *Verb tense* (**t.**)

Verb tenses must be consistent throughout the essay. Avoid switching back and forth from one tense to another within sentences or even in separate paragraphs.

George and his mother live in the same house. They do not get along well. Often they *would* fight every day. (**t.**; inappropriate shift from present tense)

The present tense is frequently used for expository critical writing. To analyze, discuss, or quote events that occurred or were reported in an essay, an article, or a story, use the present tense:

In *The Little Prince,* Saint Exupéry *stresses* the importance of affection, for humans and animals, when the fox *asks* the little prince to tame him.

However, you can't always write in a single tense. Use the proper sequence of tenses depending on:
Time (past, present, or future)

The little prince *loves* to tell about all the places he *visited* before he *met* the fox. (action takes place in the present; past events are recounted)

After the little prince *leaves,* the fox *will remember* the boy's blond hair every time he *looks* at the golden wheat fields. (future time is indicated)

Aspect (the form a verb takes to show duration or completion of action)

Until he *found* the little prince, the only other humans the fox *had seen* were hunters. (*perfect aspect;* the action in the past tense was completed after that in the past perfect tense)

The fox *is crying* when the little prince *comes* to say goodbye. (*progressive/continuous aspect;* the action in the progressive tense is in process and continues while that in the present is occurring)

Mood (the speaker's attitude toward the action or state expressed)

The fox wants to love the little prince. (indicative/statement)

That is why he says, *"Tame me."* (imperative/command)

The little prince asks, *"What does that mean—tame?"* (interrogative/question)

The fox says, *"If* you *tame* me, then we *shall need* each other." (conditional)

The fox speaks *as if* he *were* human. (contrary to fact)

If the little prince *were* to tame the fox, they *would* need each other. (subjunctive; most common spoken and written form)

The fox *suggested that* the boy *tame* him. (subjunctive; base form of verb follows verbs that suggest or request)

Finally, remember that reported speech requires tense changes (see an example in the section on dialog in chapter 3)

8. *Subject-verb agreement* (**agr.**)

Lack of subject-verb agreement is a serious grammatical error. A singular subject requires a singular verb; a plural subject demands a plural verb.

Non-count nouns take singular verbs: The rice is not cooked properly.

Count nouns take plural verbs: Several grains of rice are not cooked at all.

The verb agrees with the subject after *nor* or *or:* Neither Alice nor her parents sing in the church choir.

Indefinite pronouns are singular: Everyone is absent today.

The names of countries that end in *s* are singular: The United States is full of patriotic citizens.

The verb agrees with the object of the preposition following a determiner or a predeterminer; when no prepositional phrase is included, the verb agrees with the noun:

Some of the food was spoiled, but none of the guests have food poisoning. All books are on sale; all paper is at regular price.

9. *Pronoun reference* (**ref.**)

Pronouns refer to their antecedents (nouns or noun substitutes) and must agree with them in number and gender.

George and Bob drove *his* car to the beach. (ref.; pronoun could refer to either antecedent.)

Mary, a devoted daughter, telephones *his* mother every Sunday. (ref.; pronoun should be feminine)

A singular pronoun is required to refer to indefinite pronouns: (*anyone, everyone, either, neither, each,* etc.):

Did anyone bring her bathing suit?

To avoid sexism (using *his* or *her*) in language, omit the pronoun referring to the indefinite pronoun and replace it with an article:

Did anyone bring a bathing suit?

Another option is to make the sentence plural and omit the pronoun:

Did the guests bring bathing suits?

Relative pronouns have specific uses: *who, whose,* and *whom* refer only to people; *that* may refer to people, animals, actions, and things; *which* refers to everything but people:

All of the people *who* attended the Smith's barbecue were looking forward to a steak dinner.

However, the meat *which* was cooking on the grill was stolen by a hungry dog.

The Smiths, *whose* party was ruined by the dog's bad behavior, complained to its owner that it had eaten their steaks. (use *it* or *its* for an animal unless the gender is known or the masculine or feminine pronoun is appropriate, as for a beloved pet; use *it* or *its* for things)

"There is the dog *that* stole fourteen pounds of New York steak off our grill!" she cried, pointing at the bloated animal.

The owner apologized, "The people from *whom* we bought this dog warned us that he was a steak thief. I'll pay for the damage."

A clear antecedent must exist for each reference.

Incorrect: *They* cook the worst food at this restaurant and expect *you* to like *it*. (*they* and *you* have no antecedents; *it* refers to restaurant)

Reworded: This restaurant serves terrible food but expects the patrons to like it.

Incorrect: The cat sat there eating the mouse *which* was disgusting.

Reworded: The cat's eating the mouse was disgusting. (or) Watching the cat eat the mouse was disgusting.

Incorrect: Jack's friends drove him out to the country, took away his clothes and shoes, blindfolded him, tied his hands behind his back, turned him around and around until he was dizzy, and went off and left him there. *That* was a terrible thing to do!

Reworded: Those were terrible things to do! (or) . . . and went off and left him there, all of which were terrible things to do!

Incorrect: When Bill slipped in the shower, he broke his arm, cut his forehead, and knocked out a tooth. *This* upset him.

Reworded: Bill was upset when he slipped in the shower and broke his arm, cut his forehead, and knocked out a tooth.

Incorrect: All the food is on the plate *that* can be eaten.

Reworded: All the food on the plate can be eaten.

Incorrect: The car *that* Lila bought *it* was expensive.

Reworded: The car that Lila bought was expensive.

10. *Misplaced modifier* (**mod.**)

If modifiers are not placed next to or very close to the words they modify, the results can be funny. Reword or reorder sentences to eliminate this syntactical problem:

Incorrect: Marilyn washed the car *with her grandmother* Saturday. (Couldn't Marilyn have used a cloth or sponge instead?)

Correct: Marilyn and her grandmother washed the car Saturday.

Incorrect: We were shocked to see an old woman going into the restaurant with a young man *in a miniskirt*. (Shouldn't the woman have been wearing the miniskirt?)

Correct: We were shocked to see an old woman, who was wearing a miniskirt, going into the restaurant with a young man.

Incorrect: The baby continued crying although her mother was holding her *loudly*. (What could the mother have done to make that much noise?)

Correct: The baby continued crying loudly although her mother was holding her.

11. *Dangling sentence element* (**dangl.**)

This error is closely related to the misplaced modifier in that a word or phrase does not have a clear reference within the sentence. A dangling element commonly begins with a participle, gerund, or infinitive phrase or a subordinating conjunction followed by one of these phrases and often occurs at the beginning of a sentence:

Incorrect participial phrase: Beaten in the tennis match, the Wimbledon officials disqualified the player from competing further because of poor sportsmanship. (Were the officials beaten?)

Correct: Beaten in the tennis match, the player was disqualified by the officials from competing further because of poor sportsmanship.

Incorrect gerund phrase: By listening to the music, the compact disc player showed the perfection of laser digital recording techniques. (Was the disc player listening?)

Correct: By listening to the music, we recognized that the compact disc player showed the perfection of laser digital recording techniques.

Incorrect infinitive phrase: To learn proper table manners, an etiquette book is helpful. (Is the book learning the manners?)

Correct: To learn proper table manners, young people find an etiquette book helpful.

Incorrect use of subordinating conjunction: Though married, the draft board refused to grant him an exemption. (Was the draft board married?)

Correct: Though married, he was refused an exemption by the draft board.

12. *Parallelism* (**//.**)

Parallel structures, which are necessary for balanced writing, repeat a particular grammar pattern throughout a sentence, a paragraph, or a long passage:

Incorrect: All Bob enjoys is *eating, to drink,* and *going to sleep.*

Correct: All Bob enjoys is *eating, drinking,* and *sleeping.* (-ing form)

Correct: All Bob wants to do is *eat, drink,* and *sleep.* (base form)

Correct: Bob only wants *to eat, to drink,* and *to sleep.* (infinitive form)

Incorrect: Marcia would rather spend her time *working in her garden* than *to read in the library.*

Correct: Marcia would rather spend her time *working in the garden* than *reading in the library.* (both clauses use the -ing form)

Incorrect: *Not only did* the cat *run* out into the street, *but* it *was chased* all the way across by the dog. (*not only* requires *but also;* active changes to passive voice)

Correct: *Not only did* the cat *run* out into the street, *but also* the dog *chased* it all the way across. (correlative conjunctions are balanced; both phrases use the active voice)

Incorrect: *Neither* a *visit* to the doctor *nor going to see* the dentist is a pleasant experience. (noun in one clause; verb in the following clause)

Correct: *Neither* a *visit* to the doctor *nor* an *appointment* with the dentist is a pleasant experience. (noun in both clauses)

13. *Transition* (**trans.**)

Transitions provide continuity within and between sentences and between paragraphs. These "bridges" show relationships between ideas and include:

Coordinating conjunctions: and, but, or, nor, for connect words, phrases, and clauses within a single sentence.

Transitional words and phrases, such as *similarly, in the same way* (comparison); *in addition* (continuation); *conversely, on the other hand* (contrast); *as a result, therefore* (result or consequence); *certainly* (emphasis); *of course, although* (concession); *for instance* (illustration); *however* (qualification); *thus* (explanation); and *in conclusion, finally, in the final analysis* (conclusion).

Pronouns: this, these, that, those (demonstrative); *I, you, he, she, it, they, them* (personal); and *one* (indefinite).

Sophisticated use of transitional devices is discussed in chapter 3.

14. *Wrong word* (**WW**)

Use of a wrong word in writing can change or confuse meaning. At the very least, it is distracting. Some common errors follow:

Confusion of adjective and adverb: At high noon, Gary Cooper walked *slow* and *deliberate* toward the outlaw. (use adverbs; *slowly; deliberately*)

Confusion of comparative and superlative: My fever was *worst* Tuesday than it was Wednesday, but Monday it was the *worse* of all. (use the comparative, *worse,* in the first clause and the superlative, *worst,* in the second)

Confusion of noun and verb because of spelling: The actors who frequent the Hollywood *seen* want to get favorable publicity. (use *scene*)

Confusion of definite and indefinite articles: Eager for its evening walk, the dog ran to *a* front door to wait for its owner. (use the definite article, *the,* since this isn't just any door)

Confusion of the two indefinite articles: I can't find *a* honest person anywhere. (use *an* before a word that begins with a vowel or a vowel sound)

Confusion of prepositions in two-word verbs: Larry went to the telephone to *call on* his mother. (use *call* or *call up; call on* means visit)

Confusion of prepositions in idiomatic phrases: The thief *broke in* the house. (use *broke into; broke in* requires no object) The eldest daughter couldn't finish high school because she had to *care of* the younger children. (use *care for* or *take care of*)

Confusion of plural and singular: She combs her *hairs* every morning. (use the singular, *hair,* for a non-count noun)

Confusion between native language word and similarly spelled English word: There are still a *feu* students left in the classroom. (use *few; feu* is French for fire) I don't *fiel* well. (use *feel; fiel* is Spanish for faithful or honest)

Inclusion of unnecessary articles and prepositions: She asked *to the* mother to fix her *the* breakfast. (She asked *her* mother to fix her breakfast.) James went to *the* Europe for six weeks last summer. (omit *the* since it is not part of the geographical name of the continent)

15. *Better word* (**BW**)

The word is technically correct, but it may be obsolete, old fashioned, or inappropriate:

Many *wenches* come in from the country to work as waitresses in big-city restaurants. (archaic; inappropriate; use *women*)

There is *knavery* in his eyes. (obsolete; use *mischievousness* or *roguishness*)

We saw Mary and Sam *bathing* in the lake last night. (old-fashioned; use *swimming*)

16. *Repetition* (**rep.**)
Sometimes a single word is used repeatedly:

Marlene and Bill liked to spend time *together*. They went shopping *together*, often went out dancing *together*, and went *together* on sightseeing trips as often as they could. (**rep.**)

Reworded: Marlene and Bill liked to spend time together shopping, dancing, and sightseeing.

Sometimes an idea is repeated:

The honor system is an important tradition in this country. The thing that is so important about the honor system is that it is part of the college tradition that is so important to every young person. Young people learn a lot from going to a college or university that upholds this tradition.

Reworded: Young people benefit from attending a college or university that upholds the traditional honor system.

17. *Own words* (**OW**)
The material is copied from the reading or another source. Use your own words.

18. *Omission.* (**∧**)
The most common omissions are single words or short phrases that you "hear" as you are proofreading even though you don't see them on paper:

Give the baby drink of water. (missing article; *a* drink of water)

I asked instructor to help me with the last paragraph. (missing article; *the* instructor)

We went the beach last Sunday. (missing preposition; went *to* the beach)

They often listen music. (missing preposition; listen *to* music)

He was supposed to wait me here. (missing preposition; wait *for* me)

When we go shopping buy many fruits and vegetables. (missing phrase after *shopping;* insert a comma, and follow with a phrase; e.g., *we always* or *we try to* buy)

19. *Spelling* (**sp.**)
Spelling errors vary widely depending on a student's native language spelling rules, but certain problems occur regularly:

Failure to double the final consonant when adding one of the following endings: *-ed, -er, -ing, -ish* (the final consonant must be the last letter of the word and it must be preceded by a vowel; the word must be accented on the final syllable or it must be a one-syllable word; the word has a short vowel sound):

The bus *stoped* at the corner to pick up the little girl. (*stopped*)

Jim's horse is much *biger* than I expected. (*bigger*)

They are *begining* to get on my nerves. (*beginning*)

Don't you think it's a little *pigish* to take so much food? (*piggish*)

Failure to drop the final *-e* before endings beginning with vowels (the final syllable of the word has a long vowel sound):

Lettie had to spend many evenings *wineing* and *dineing* clients while John stayed home with the children. (*wining; dining*)

Addition of an extra consonant on words that drop the final *-e* before endings beginning with vowels:

John was *hopping* to have a little vacation, but he soon learned that child care was a full-time job. (*hoping*)

Addition of a final *-e* on words that end in a consonant:

He wrote his *finale exame* Monday *afternoone*. (*final; exam; afternoon*)

Addition of *-s* or *'s* (instead of the correct *-es*) to make plurals of words that end in *-ch, -s, -sh, -tch,* and *-x:*

Paris is a city of many *churchs*. (*churches*)

Yellow school *bus's* can be found on every corner. (*buses*)

If *wishs* were horses, all beggars would ride. (*wishes*)

Witch's fly through the Halloween sky. (*witches*)

Hoaxs are cruel tricks that are played on people. (*hoaxes*)

Confusion of the many, many words that sound alike but are spelled differently (homonyms); a few examples follow:

I couldn't help spilling the milk; Johnny *maid* me do it! (*made*)

He doesn't *no* what to do. (*know*)

The instructor will not *except* late papers. (*accept*)

She *side* when she saw her grade. (*sighed*)

We never know *whose* going to attend these meetings. (*who's*)

Confusion of the order of *i* and *e* (native speakers use a little rhyme to remember all but the exceptions, which many people have to look up in the dictionary):

I before *e*
Except after *c*
Or when sounded as *a*
As in neighbor and weigh.)

I hope to *recieve* a check in the mail tomorrow. (*receive*)

The word *science* is an exception to the rhyming rule above.

20. *Syllabication* (**syl.**)

Words of one syllable may not be divided. If you run out of space to write all the letters of a one-syllable word, write the entire word on the following line. Place a hyphen (-) after the syllable of the word you are continuing; do not place another hyphen before the rest of the word on the following line. Never divide proper nouns. Divide words between syllables; however, if a word has a one-letter syllable, don't detach it from the rest of the word (*a- bout* should remain *about*). Divide compound words between the two parts (*heart- break; drug- store*). Divide words that contain pairs or clusters of consonants between two consonants (*fel- low; rub- bish; tech- nique*); however, don't divide between consonants that form roots or have specific meanings on their own (*poly- graph; west- ern*). Check syllabication in the dictionary if you are unsure.

Writing Workshop

Begin the workshop by proofreading the following essay for comma splices, sentence fragments, and run-on sentences. There are six of each. The essay contains no other errors. Read the text both forward and backward sentence-by-sentence to locate these mistakes.

The Loss

The old man in Edmond Sechan's film, *One Eyed Men Are Kings,* learns an important lesson from his experiences in the park: lying and deceiving people can not bring happiness. Throughout the film, the son is sneaky, in the end he has to pay for it.

The son is treated like a dog at home. Bobby, the dog, is like a son to the old mother. Who loves him jealously. The old woman hand feeds Bobby at the table, the dog is seated in a chair and has a napkin tied around his neck. The mother wipes Bobby's mouth when he has finished eating. Just as if he were a small child. However, the son isn't allowed to eat his meals at the table instead, he hurriedly gulps down his food while sitting on the sofa. So that he can be ready at a moment's notice to take Bobby for his walk.

At first, the dog and the son hate each other when the son tries to attach the leash to Bobby's collar, the dog snarls, growls, and bares his teeth. When they are outside, the dog does terrible things that embarrass the son each walk brings new humiliations. Later, when the son pretends to be blind. The dog begins to enjoy the walks. In one scene, Bobby strains to escape from the mother's arms, the two "sons" eagerly set off together. At this point, the mother begins to notice their changed relationship, she doesn't like it she wants to have all the dog's affection. The dog cares for her, but he loves the excitement in the park more. Because he gets a lot of attention from the crowd of friends that flock around the "blind" man everyone feeds him cookies, too.

Unfortunately, the dog is not very dependable he runs away one day when the son is at the height of his popularity, he is explaining how he lost his eyesight in the war. The son is escorted home by two of his new friends, and the landlady thinks he is drunk. When he sneaks into his mother's apartment, he is relieved that the dog is there in her lap. He thinks he can go on with his deception. However, the mean, spiteful landlady bursts the bubble of the son's happiness when she informs on him. The mother is delighted to take away her son's dog-walking privileges. In the last scene, the son's face is a tragic picture of loneliness.

In the final analysis, the son learns that there is no way to undo a lie, he can't explain to his new friends that he isn't really blind because they will know that he is a fraud. He can't explain to his mother. Because she will know that he is a liar and a sneak. He isn't creative enough to pretend to be blind without his "guide" dog. By his actions, the old man has condemned himself to a solitary, friendless, joyless life.

The essays that follow are the first drafts of papers that were later successfully revised, rewritten, and corrected in the final drafts. After conferring with the instructor, some students rewrote their papers three or more times before they were satisfied with them. Only then did they submit the essays for grading. These students have graciously allowed their first drafts to be reproduced here so that you may benefit from their initial errors.

PROCESS FOR REVISION

1. Find the thesis. Decide whether the topic is suitably introduced.
2. Read the complete essay. Check for content, support of thesis, and discussion of examples. Be sure quoted material is properly identified and ties in with original ideas.
3. Evaluate the conclusion. Does it relate to the thesis? Would you say the essay has a satisfying ending?
4. Be sure there is a clear relationship between the title and the essay.
5. Make content changes. Revise, replace, relocate, delete, or add material. Rewrite completely, if necessary. (Don't be afraid to "throw out" a draft and begin again on a new topic. When you can't handle a particular topic well, you are better off to start fresh than to waste more time on it.)
6. Run a quick check for grammar, spelling, and punctuation errors. Make needed corrections.
7. Confer with the instructor, and make suggested content changes.

8. Begin the thorough, step-by-step check for grammar, spelling, and punctuation errors. Scan for a single type of error each time you read through the paper. Make corrections above the line as you go along.

9. Recopy the essay, if needed.

10. Submit the essay to the instructor for your grading.

Drafts of Student Essays

(Note: All drafts include errors.)

Essay 1 (Sample revision)

Topic: Should smoking be permitted in the workplace?

Smoking: A Hot Issue

In a society where individual rights, freedom, and privileges are concerned, viewpoints and opinions of pros and cons about smoking should be considered. Certainly, smoking should not be permitted in a workplace or in an enclosed place. A designated place, area, or lounge should be provided for smokers to enjoy consuming nicotine and smoke while they burn their pockets, lungs, and throat. The enclosed places; i.e., offices, factories, shops, stores, dormitories, libraries, schools and building hallways and eating places should be protected from contamination and pollution.

Although smoking is a bad and dirty habit and very hazardous to health, nicotine addicts or smokers should not be deprived of their rights to smoke. They know it is dangerous to health, but smoking has become an addiction or a disease as far as they are concerned. A smoking addict said once, "give me nicotine or give me death." It has been attributed that cigar and cigarette smokers had caused companies and employers big losses, because of absences, gross inefficiencies and less productivity. Specifically, many fires are caused by untended and lighted cigarettes which result to loss of lives and property damages. Brush fires in parks, hills, and mountainous areas are often caused by lighted cigarettes butts. Not only smokers are the ones who caused fires; arsonists had done a great deal of damage in society. The smokers find it helpful for them to inhale nicotine while working, it increases their efficiencies and work production. It does not mean that smokers should enjoy their habit at the expense of the non-smokers. The public's health is at stake if a place for smokers is not designated. Short breaks in work should be allowed the smokers to fill their cravings. At present there is only one warning sign of the surgeon general in cigarette's pack, very soon they are going to print three warning signals in the box concerning death.

That all men are created equal is the basic law of humanity. It is deemed that every individual should not be deprived of the rights due him. I must admit that I am a smoker, but I consider the rights of the non-smokers. It is mandatory therefore, that a place to smoke should be designated and provided for smokers.

Draft by George F. Dianzen

Conference with the instructor

(Note: All student-instructor dialogs are recreated from actual conferences.)

(The student reads each paragraph aloud)

Student: Am I repeating myself in the first paragraph? Something isn't quite right.

Instructor: Let's see. You *do* repeat the word "place" or "places" several times. You can easily fix that problem by using synonyms. But the difficulty you sense isn't repetition; it's wordiness. You need to "tighten" that first paragraph by cutting out extra words and making sure that meanings of phrases are correct. For example, are rights, freedom, and privileges "concerned" or are they "concerns"?

Student: All right. I'm going to go through this first paragraph right now to see what I can change. I'll read it to you as I go along:

> In a society where individual rights, freedom, and privileges
> are ~~concerned, viewpoints and opinions of~~ [concerns,] the pros and cons ~~about~~ [of]
> smoking should be considered. Certainly, smoking should not be
> permitted ~~in a workplace or~~ in ~~an~~ [any] enclosed place. A designated
> ~~place,~~ area, or lounge should be provided for smokers to enjoy
> consuming nicotine and smoke while they burn their pockets,
> lungs, and ~~throat.~~ [throats] ~~The enclosed places, i.e., offices~~, [Offices] factories,
> shops, stores, dormitories, libraries, schools[,] ~~and~~ building hall-
> ways[,] and eating places should be protected from contamination
> and pollution.

Instructor: Yes, that's the idea! Nice use of sarcasm. Go on.

(The student reads the second paragraph.)

Instructor: Can you logically divide some of this information? What are the main ideas included in this paragraph?

Student:	One is the characteristics of smoking and smokers. Oh, and here I begin to explain losses to the companies, but I guess I don't give very many facts about that. Then I mention fires and their causes. At the end of the paragraph, I bring up the Surgeon General's warning.
Instructor:	What is the connection between arson and smoking?
Student:	Maybe I should leave arson out.
Instructor:	Probably a good idea. What is important about the Surgeon General's warning?
Student:	Health dangers.
Instructor:	To whom?
Student:	Smokers.
Instructor:	Are there dangers to non-smokers?
Student:	Weis says so.
Instructor:	Why don't you quote him? Why not include some facts and figures from his article? Why not make health one of your major points?
Student:	Yes. I can do that.
Instructor:	How many major ideas does that leave?
Student:	Characteristics, cost to employers, and damage to public property. Should I have a separate paragraph for each one?
Instructor:	Could any of the three ideas be part of the counterargument? Where *is* the counterargument, by the way?
Student:	I didn't put it in a separate paragraph. Well, I guess the first part of the second paragraph explains the smoker's needs. And later in the paragraph I talk about smoking increasing their efficiency. I could make that the counterargument, couldn't I?
Instructor:	Yes, you could. How could you organize the rest of the material?
Student:	I could put the characteristics in the opening or with the counterargument. Then I could have two sections of argument: employer and public costs and health dangers. The counterargument and concluding paragraph could follow.
Instructor:	Sounds fine. Check now for grammar, syntax, spelling, and punctuation problems you might have missed. Then I want you to explain the reasons you made the corrections.

(The student scans the essay forward and backward and makes some, but not all, the needed changes.)

Instructor:	Good. You found the two incorrect verb tenses.
Student:	I changed "had caused" and "had done" to the present perfect.
Instructor:	Here is a phrase that is used incorrectly: "It has been attributed that. . . ." Begin with a noun and follow with "has been attributed to . . ."; for example, "Cancer has been attributed to cig-

> arette smoking." Otherwise, omit the phrase and just discuss cause and effect.

Student: All right. Going on, I removed the comma preceding "because". Also, in several places I punctuated two coordinating adjectives with a comma and deleted "and". The preposition after "result" should be "from". In several sentences I corrected adjectives and nouns that I had accidentally made plurals. And here is a group of mixed up words that I reordered. I corrected a comma splice in the last sentence of paragraph three. In the last paragraph, I placed a comma before "therefore".

Instructor: Excellent. You caught almost everything. There are two changes you still need to make in that last paragraph. One of them is to reword that negative passage; the other is to avoid sexism in language.

Student: I'll make that "him or her." But I don't know what to do with the negative.

Instructor: After "that," the first word should be "no".

Student: Oh, yes, "that no individual should be deprived."

Instructor: That does it. You're ready to rewrite the rest of the paper.

(The student continues the revision process with paragraph two. Although the final revision omits some material, the essay is expanded from three to five paragraphs. The counterargument is clearly shown.)

C

~~Cigar and~~ cigarette smokers have caused companies and employers big losses, according to William L. Weis, who wrote "Curbs Give a Boost to Productivity, Morale." Smoking causes absences, gross inefficiencies, and ~~less~~ lower productivity, and "is a prime source of impaired morale among workers." Weis quotes a telephone company survey that shows 80% of all employees (even smokers) disapprove of smoking at work except in designated areas. Employers save money in ∧ health, fire, and life insurance premiums ~~(health, less property damage life, and fire)~~ ∧ and have when employees don't smoke. ~~Moreover, employers have damage to their property when employees smoke.~~ The Surgeon General's warning on cigarette packages is directed only to smokers. ~~At present there is only one warning sign of the surgeon general in cigarette's pack, very soon they are going to print three~~ "Reasonable men and women now recognize that involuntary smoking . . . is a serious health hazard," ~~warning signals in the box concerning death.~~ All workers have

Weis states.

certain employee rights and clean air to breathe is one of the most basic. Similarly, all employees have some obligations to their fellow workers. Courtesy and consideration are two of them.

~~The public's~~ _{All employees'} health is at stake if a place for smokers is not designated or if smokers do not use that area. Smoky air makes non-smokers (and even smokers themselves) sick. Absenteeism increases. Non-smokers have to use their precious sick leave because of smokers' selfishness. Then, when non-smokers catch the flu or a cold, they have no sick leave, so they spread the disease around the workplace and everyone loses time.

Although smoking is a bad ' ~~and~~ dirty habit and very hazardous to health, nicotine addicts ~~or smokers~~ should not be deprived of their rights to smoke. They know ~~it~~ _{smoking is a "disease" that} is dangerous to health. ~~, but smoking has become an addiction or a disease as far as they are concerned. A smoking addict said once, "give me nicotine or give me death." The~~ _{Thus,} smokers find it ~~helpful for them~~ _{necessary} to inhale nicotine while working~~,~~ ~~it increases~~ _{to maintain} their efficienc~~ies~~ _y and ~~work production. It does not mean that~~ _{productivity, but} smokers should _{not} ∧ enjoy their habit at the expense of the non-smokers. ~~Short breaks~~ _{Smokers should be able to} ~~in work should be allowed the smokers to fill in~~ _{satisfy} their cravings, during regular rest periods.

~~That all men are created equal~~ _{Equality} is the basic law of humanity. ~~It is deemed that every~~ individual should ~~not~~ _{No} be deprived of ~~the~~ _{his or her} rights ~~due him~~. I must admit that I am a smoker, but I consider the rights of the non-smokers. It is mandatory ~~therefore,~~ that ~~a~~ ~~place to smoke should~~ _{smoking areas} be designated ~~and provided by employers for smokers.~~ by employers and used by smokers. This action will improve health and working conditions for all employees, will save employers money, and will uphold individual rights.

ESSAYS FOR REVISION

Read the following essays and the recreated instructor-student conferences. Then revise the essays. Add, delete, or rewrite material. Correct grammar, syntax, spelling, and punctuation after you are satisfied with the content. Remember to read your work aloud.

Essay 2

Topic: Should prisons be used to punish or to rehabilitate prisoners?

Punishment

People do things that are proper sometimes and improper other times. When improper actions are done, they should be opposed by some kind of reaction so as to stop them, and this kind of reaction is what we know as punishment. So prisons should be used for punishment for those who deserve it.

Criminals who do illegal things should be punished. They should know by some way or another that life cannot go on with their criminal actions hurting the innocent, the harmless and the naive. A person who tries to get what he wants without his/her personal efforts is a failure and does not deserve to live like other people do. Those crimes are stopped by law, giving each person what he deserves in life with justice. But the law should consider the kinds of criminals, and punish them according to the kinds of crimes they have committed. For instance, some criminals are worth execution and should be subject to capital punishment. Others should have solitary confinement, which is one of the worst kinds of punishment. Some criminals should be subject to some kinds of heavy labour, like working on the grounds around the jail, digging and moving heavy rocks from place to place.

I do agree with the conservatives who think that criminals are worthy of punishment and isolation. I think that prisons should be in reasonable standards fit for humans. Adequate food and good medical services should be available. On the other hand, those prisons should not be provided with some of the facilities in life like T.V.s, radios, games and libraries which are provided for their mental satisfaction.

Finally, prison conditions should be improved to a level that criminals get what they deserve, which is being treated humanely but also be deprived decisively from the most important element in life which is freedom.

Draft by Lucy Mekhjian

Conference with the instructor

(The student reads the essay aloud.)

Student: This essay seemed so easy to write and so complete until I read it aloud. Did you notice that I kept adding information and explaining ideas to you as I went along?

Instructor: Yes, I did. But thinking aloud is part of the revision process. Many times you can tell someone something much more easily than you can write the same information. You seem to have strong feelings about the purpose of prisons.

Student: I have. Oh, I know. Feelings aren't proof.

Instructor: So how *can* you prove your point?

Student: I'm not sure. I know I'll have to use more specific examples, for one thing.

Instructor: Yes. Examples, facts, details, statistics—all are useful as evidence. You do explain various punishments, but not the crimes from which they result. In fact, the essay as a whole is much too general.

Student: So, I should add all the things I told you as I was reading?

Instructor: Many of those additions would be good. But let's look carefully at that first paragraph. Your entire essay is going to be governed by the opening. You need a clearer focus. It seems to me you need to mention rehabilitation so that you can explain why punishment is better, more practical, necessary, or whatever position you decide to take.

Student: Suppose I say that prisoners deserve to pay for their crimes by being punished rather than by getting training at honest citizens' expense.

Instructor: That statement would certainly clarify your position, but it wouldn't satisfy critics who believe that rehabilitation helps convicted criminals get honest jobs when they are released from prison, and that punishment makes criminals bitter, angry, and revengeful.

Student: I don't know how to answer those criticisms. I just know that criminals deserve punishment. They shouldn't get lots of privileges.

Instructor: Maybe you should differentiate between serious crime that endangers society and minor offenses.

Student: You mean I should say that not all criminals should be punished?

Instructor: It's up to you. Perhaps you could strengthen your position by qualifying it.

Student: Okay. Maybe I'll say that only the really bad, deliberate criminals should be punished with no chance for rehabilitation. I guess the accidental criminals could reform. These ideas go along with my statement about punishment for those who deserve it.

Instructor: Yes, they do. You have narrowed your focus well.

Student: Okay. Look at the second paragraph. I made a note while I was reading it aloud that a criminal *is* someone who does illegal things, so I should change "criminals" to "people".

Instructor: Good. What about examples here? Shouldn't you include a few? What kinds of criminals do you think deserve imprisonment?

Student: Oh, murderers, rapists, kidnappers, bank robbers, burglars, check forgers, drunk drivers, people who don't pay their income taxes—

Instructor: Should their punishments be the same? Does an income tax evader deserve the same sentence as a murderer or a rapist?

Student: Oh, I see. I should classify all these crimes from least to most serious. Or maybe I should just choose the most and least extreme. That would show more contrast.

Instructor: It would. Be sure to say which kind of criminal should move rocks and which kind should be placed in solitary confinement. Let's move on to the third paragraph. I'm a little confused by some of your word choices here; for example, "to be worthy" has a positive connotation. What other word or words can you substitute?

Student: How about changing that whole phrase to "criminals deserve punishment and isolation"? I guess I could also say "criminals should be punished and isolated."

Instructor: Either one is fine. Look at the next sentence in which you mention prison standards for the first time. Your opening gives no hint that you will discuss this issue. Perhaps you should go back to the opening and insert something about the need for prisons to have—not "be in"—reasonable, humane living conditions.

Student: l don't know how I missed that.

Instructor: Let's go on to the conclusion. I like what you have said. Could you break up the information into separate sentences and add your evaluation of the new ideas you plan to include?

Student: Yes. I see that I've changed the focus from prisons having reasonable standards to improving prison conditions. I guess I should stay with punishment or else develop both prison conditions and punishment equally.

Instructor: Yes, but be sure that the conclusion relates to the thesis.

Student: I'll work on the content. Is everything else okay?

Instructor: Your writing flows nicely, but some of your sentences are too long. You have a dangling sentence element in the second paragraph and a punctuation error and a faulty pronoun reference in the third.

Student: I don't see the dangling—oh, is this "with justice" it?

Instructor: Yes.

Student: How should I fix that? Could I make it an adverb—"what he justly deserves"?

Instructor: Good.

Student: —and a comma should follow that introductory clause. But I don't see what's wrong with "their". It refers to prisoners.

Instructor: Where is the word "prisoners" earlier in the sentence or even earlier in the paragraph? The antecedent should be close, preferably in the same sentence.

Student: Yes, I remember that now. All right, I'll get started on the revision. Thanks.

Instructor: Come back for help if you need it.

Essay 3

Topic: Compare and/or contrast John's and Lettie's attitudes and behavior after they exchanged responsibilities, as discussed in Jim Sanderson's article, "Confessions of a Househusband." What lessons were learned?

Job's Exchange

In Jim Sanderson's story, "The confession of a househusband," although there were some similarities between John and Lettie, there were more differences. However, both John and Lettie learned a lot about the other's work.

John resigned his job for he thought that he would be happier if he stayed home and look after the children and the house. He also thought that there were too much pressure and competition in his job. John liked his new job because it was more relax. He loved making up games and going out with the children. But six months later, John recognized that the job was no fun at all. He felt isolated and bored of this job. And that there was no regular hour for him. He had to wake up earlier in the morning and work until the time he went to bed. He seemed to need his wife more than she needed him. Every time he asked her to go out with him, he was refused with such reasons as: Having homework to do or being exausted after a hard working day. He finally ended up with jealousy. He thought that while his wife ate at a famous restaurant with many people, he had to stay home and ate spaghetti with the kids.

On the other hand, Lettie was eager to return to her work. She thought that she would have freedom and have the chance to deal with people outside the home. She then replace John in taking care of the family's finances. Then things happened since she took John's position. She started to need him less than ever. She enjoyed having fun by herself and refuse to go out with John. Their sex life, therefore, was not as attractive as it was before they exchanged job. She finally ended up as a selfish and uncaring person.

As we know, later John and Lettie agreed to share "fifty-fifty" of their children and the house. We did learn from this story that the fact that women can't handle men's jobs was false. It is true in many cases, but not all. On the contrary, men also can not always do what woman can.

Draft by Tho Ton-That

Conference with the instructor

(The student begins reading the essay aloud.)

Student: Is the thesis all right?

Instructor: Does it respond to the topic? Does it mention John's and Lettie's attitudes about responsibilities?

Student: No. I'll revise it.

Instructor: Should you give a little more background about Jim's and Lettie's situation?

Student: In the next paragraph, I say that Jim resigned his job.

Instructor: Did he resign only because he thought he would be happier staying at home with the children?

Student: No, he was transferred to another part of the country.

Instructor: If you omit that information, John is not shown fairly. Remember, he had some unselfish motives for resigning, too.

Student: Not wanting his family to have to move away from their home and friends?

Instructor: Yes. Did he ever intend to stay home permanently?

Student: I don't think so. Just until he got a different job. Maybe he would have a little vacation first.

Instructor: Did it turn out to be a vacation?

Student: No. I talk about that in the second paragraph. I'll read that now. (*Reads aloud.*)

Instructor: I think that first sentence will have to be reworded to comply with what we've already discussed about John's motives. Maybe you could begin with a time clause and then go on to say that John thought he would like his new duties.

Student: "After John resigned his job, he thought that he would enjoy ~~to~~ ~~stay~~ staying home and ~~look~~ looking after the children and the house."

Instructor: Good.

Student: Should I put the second sentence in the opening paragraph as background?

Instructor: That would work. You could also make it clear that John didn't realize that the pressure and competition in his job were so stressful until he started staying home. In the next sentence, you say that John liked his new job. When was that?

Student: "At first." I'll add that.

Instructor: Fine. It balances "six months later" to show before and after. You repeat the word "job" several times. What synonyms could you use?

Student: "Work," "duties," "tasks"—

Instructor: Good. What rewards did John gain from his new work?

Student: There weren't any rewards. He never got any praise, and he didn't earn any money.

Instructor: Should you mention these problems?

Student: Yes. They will contrast with Lettie's feelings about working outside. I'll read that now. (*Reads aloud.*)

Instructor: Did Lettie have other reasons for wanting to work? Didn't John mention them somewhere in the article?

Student: Oh, yes. She felt just like he did—frustrated and unrewarded. Maybe I should add something about her feelings following the first sentence and then go on with what she expected from an outside job.

Instructor: What happened to Lettie emotionally when she "replaced John in taking care of the family's finances"?

Student: She probably felt worried.

Instructor: Why?

Student: Because she had all the responsibility.

Instructor: So would that have affected her behavior?

Student: Yes.

Instructor: Do you think she wouldn't go out with John because she really "enjoyed having fun by herself"—taking clients to dinner?

Student: Didn't she like to be with other people more than with John?

Instructor: Most people who have to do a great deal of business entertaining don't enjoy it much because they have to try to sell products or ideas at the same time. They can choose the food but not the company.

Student: So would she have preferred to stay home and eat spaghetti with John and the children?

Instructor: Probably.

Student: Then why did the author say that their sex life "dwindled down"?

Instructor: Well, if Lettie had to work very hard to prove her ability in her new job, don't you think she might have felt tired and nervous?

Student: Yes. And John felt the same way because he hated staying at home. Maybe the problem wasn't all Lettie's fault.

Instructor: So what actually happened to these two individuals when they exchanged jobs?

Student: They exchanged attitudes and behavior, too. And they began to see what the other person hated and to act the way the other person had.

Instructor: All of which ties in with your conclusion, don't you think?

Student: Yes. Should I mention Lettie and John in the final paragraph?

Instructor: Definitely. Do you have other questions about the content?

Student: No. My worries now are about grammar and punctuation. I read through the essay many times and corrected several errors, but I know I missed some.

Instructor: All right. Punctuation first. Let's read from the end to the beginning. No problems in the final paragraph. None in the third, either. Here is a sentence fragment about halfway through paragraph two. In the first sentence of that paragraph, a comma should precede the coordinating conjunction. In the first paragraph, you should have copied the title exactly as it appeared in the article. Look at your own title. ls it really possessive? You found most of the errors without my help.

Student: I had some trouble with the grammar. I didn't know what verb to use with "pressure and competition."

Instructor: Let's see. "Much" is used with a non-count noun and takes a singular verb. You can't use a singular verb with two nouns, so that second noun needs its own structure. Also, "pressure" can be either a count- or a non-count noun. I would reword the sentence.

Student: Could I say "there were too many pressures and there was also a lot of competition"? Or how about "the pressure and competition in his job were too large"?

Instructor: Use "too great." Either structure is fine. In the next sentence, the base form of the verb should be changed to a participle because the word follows the verb "to be" and the modifier "more".

Student: "Relaxed" or "relaxing"?

Instructor: Are you stressing the working atmosphere or the effect of the job on John?

Student: The effect. "Relaxing".

Instructor: All right, but you still have an incomplete comparative. His new job was more relaxing than what?

Student: Than the old one.

Instructor: The next error is idiomatic. Use a different preposition with "bored".

Student: "Bored by"? "Bored with"? "Bored in"?

Instructor: Either of the first two is preferable. In the sentence fragment that follows, you will have to use the plural of "hour". People work regular hours; stores are open certain hours. Then the verb will have to agree.

Student: I know the next two sentences aren't quite right.

Instructor: Use the verb "feel" with "jealous". What form?

Student: "-ing".

Instructor: Could you rephrase that sentence to tighten it? Use "became".

Student: "He finally became jealous" . . . Oh, should I combine the last two sentences of this paragraph?

Instructor: Try using cause/effect. Give the latter first. Also, how do you know the restaurant was famous? Who were the "many people"? Were Lettie and these people there only to enjoy a good dinner?

Student: Okay. "He finally became jealous because ~~while his wife ate at a~~

~~famous restaurant~~ ~~with~~ ~~many~~ ~~people~~, he had to stay home and ~~ate~~ eat spaghetti with the kids while his wife went to nice restaurants for business reasons."

Instructor: Good. You could also say "while his wife went to business dinners in nice restaurants". You also corrected the verb in that last clause. There are two more incorrect verb tenses in the third paragraph. Do you see them?

Student: Yes, "replace" and "refuse" should be in the past tense.

Instructor: In the second sentence, you need an article between "have" and "chance". In the third sentence, "finance" should be plural. I would omit "then" at the beginning of the next sentence because you have a time word in the next clause (but "since" is a wrong word). You need a preposition after "took" (you need to show that she *assumed* his position rather than that she took it by force). "Job" should be plural in the next to last sentence.

Student: I'm glad I made some notes.

Instructor: Well, if you have questions, I'll be glad to answer them.

The last student paper is a final essay examination that was written in the classroom. The time allowed was two and one-half hours. Students were not allowed to use books or notes but were permitted to use dictionaries. Students were instructed to write on every other line in their blue books and to make needed corrections. Students worked independently; the instructor gave no assistance or advice of any kind.

Evaluate the essay. Identify its strengths and weaknesses. What, if anything, would you do to change it?

Essay 4

Topic: Compare and/or contrast the main characters in "The Story of an Hour," by Kate Chopin and "Miss Brill," by Katherine Mansfield. What makes these women behave as they do?

Final Examination

Kate Chopin, in "The Story of an Hour," tells us about a widow who imagined a new life for herself after she heard about her husband's death. Katherine Mansfield's story, "Miss Brill," is about an old woman who lived most of her life in illusion. Both characters behaved in certain ways which showed their reaction to the society.

In the first story, Mrs. Mallard had been the wife of a wealthy man.

Since she had ~~a~~ heart trouble, ~~a~~ great care was taken of her. She had to do exactly as her husband told her. However, she wanted to be alone and have more independence; therefore, she stayed most of her time in her room thinking about herself and her life. She loved her husband, in a way, but she was not romantically in love with him. After she heard about her husband's death, although she felt sorry for him, she thought that she could have a better life without him. Her imagination wouldn't let her realize the truth, which was that her heart disease could ruin all her ~~fantasies~~ fantasy of a long and new life. She was enjoying and celebrating the freedom when suddenly Mr. Mallard, who wasn't really killed, came home. She was ~~extremely~~ shocked and surprised to see her husband, ~~whom~~ who she thought was a victim of the railroad crash. Mrs. Mallard's happiness and freedom didn't last long because she died of ^ a heart ~~disease~~ attack caused by the shock.

The second story is about an old maid named Miss Brill, who was an English teacher. She also read newspaper to an old invalid gentleman to get the money to manage her life. Miss Brill used to go to the park on Sundays to listen to ~~the~~ other people's conversations. She was a lonely woman who wanted company. Her fur was like a real pet to her and she talked to it ~~like a real pet~~ as if it were ~~a real pet~~ alive. She considered herself an actress ~~in~~ on the great stage of the world on which all people were actors and actresses. Her imagination was between her and the truth; however, she enjoyed her life ~~the way it was~~ very much. One day in the park, the conversation between a young couple and their criticism about her and the fur made her see that she was just a lonely old woman whose life was no better than the lonely people she pitied. Unfortunately, the young boy's remark that Miss Brill's fur looked like a fried whiting spoiled her imaginary relationship with her "pet". Later, when she ~~crawled~~ crept back to her closet-like room, she passed right by the bakery without stopping to buy a piece of almond cake, her only treat each week. When she closed her fur in its box and thought she heard it crying, her fantasy life was dead, for Miss Brill knew then that it was the sound of her own weeping that she heard.

Both women wanted happiness, but neither one found it. Mrs. Mallard realistically accepted her life as an invalid until the event that led her to hope that she could exist in an imaginary world. On the contrary, Miss Brill realized the truth after she had been imagining a long time. These examples show us that either reality or illusion may cause disappointment. Sometimes people need dreams and illusions because their lives are so empty or unhappy, but in the end they cannot escape reality. Mrs. Mallard was the exception; she escaped because of her sudden death. Miss Brill had a long time to think about the truth.

Written by Sevak Gevorkian

Index